Developing Teaching Skills in Physical Education

Developing Teaching Skills in Physical Education

THIRD EDITION

Daryl Siedentop

OHIO STATE UNIVERSITY

 MAYFIELD PUBLISHING COMPANY
Mountain View, California
London   Toronto

Library of Congress Cataloging-in-Publication Data

Siedentop, Daryl.
    Developing teaching skills in physical education / Daryl Siedentop. --3rd ed.
      p.   cm.
    Includes bibliographical references (p.) and index.
    ISBN 0-87484-899-7
    1. Physical education teachers—Training of—United States.
    I. Title.
    GV363.S5 1991
    613.7'07—dc20   90-25194
                                                                          CIP

Manufactured in the United States of America
10 9 8 7 6 5 4 3

Mayfield Publishing Company
1240 Villa Street
Mountain View, CA 94041

Sponsoring editor: *James Bull*
Production service: *Fog Press*
Manuscript editor: *Kay Yarborough Nelson*
Text designer: *Al Burkhardt*
Cover designer: *In-House Graphic Design Group*

The text was set in 10/12 ITC Garamond by Fog Press and
printed on 50# Finch Opaque by Fairfield Graphics.

For Bobbie...

Contents

Part Two

Creating the Conditions for Effective Teaching in Physical Education 65

Preface

When teachers fail, is their failure due primarily to lack of subject matter knowledge or lack of teaching skills? If you address this question to school principals and district superintendents, the ones charged with evaluation of teachers and with hiring and firing decisions, they will almost always say that lack of teaching skills is the more acute problem.

We have learned more about effective teaching in the past 20 years than we learned in the previous 100 years. Not only do we know more about effective teaching practices, but we know that people can acquire effective teaching skills through teacher education and in-service education programs.

Effective teaching occurs when students learn thoroughly and efficiently, when they develop positive attitudes about what they have learned, and when their own self-esteem has been enhanced throughout the process of learning. The skills necessary to develop and maintain an effective learning environment are multifaceted and often made exceedingly complex by the difficulties encountered in many current school settings. We do not know all we need to know about these skills or how they can be applied sensitively to different educational contexts. We do, however, know a great deal about the basic skills of teaching and how they can be applied. These skills and applications are the subject of this book.

Key Features

The skills and practices advocated in this text have been identified through research; they do not represent one person's view of how teachers should teach, nor do they represent an idealized set of skills that can be developed only by a few special people. The research which revealed these teaching practices was conducted in schools of all types, with regular teachers and the full range of students that one finds in schools today.

Although many teaching practices will be advocated in this text, I have not attempted to formulate or defend a particular theory or style of teaching that I believe is superior to others. My position has always been that the critical characteristics of effective teaching can be found in many different styles. However, the adoption of a particular teaching method without the assimilation of these characteristics will surely cause serious problems in the classroom.

Teaching skills develop through practice. Simply *knowing about* effective teaching isn't enough; one must practice the appropriate skills in applied settings with careful supervision and feedback. Suggestions to help the reader practice these skills are provided throughout the text.

Whether the reader's goal is to develop his or her own teaching skills or simply to learn more about the effects of certain teaching practices, the reader will need to produce data regularly to achieve the goal. Practice and evaluation based on extensive data are key features of this text, and a full chapter at the end of the text is devoted to observation protocols for producing useful data.

Teachers need to be reflective and thoughtful about their practices and the effects these practices have on students. As indicated above, observational data help to make that reflection more meaningful. An overall model for organizing and understanding the teaching process is also helpful. Such a model is provided in Chapter 5 and is referred to consistently throughout the rest of the text. This task-system model is grounded theoretically in actual teaching and has the value of being helpful and practical on a daily basis.

Finally, I use many examples and vignettes to help illustrate the teaching practices advocated in this text.

Organization

This edition is divided into four parts. Part One (Chapters 1–4) focuses on the systematic improvement of teaching skills and provides a review of the literature on effective teaching in both general education and physical education. It also provides an assessment model for understanding, practicing, and refining teaching skills.

Part Two (Chapters 5–8) introduces the task-system model in Chapter 5, then focuses on management and discipline. Most experts on teaching now agree that effective management and discipline provide the foundation from which effective instruction is built and sustained. Many teachers fail to provide good instruction simply because they cannot manage student behavior. The emphasis in Part Two is on preventive management, those practices which reduce the potential for disruption and misbehavior. Part Two also focuses on the important interpersonal skills teachers need to achieve their goals.

Part Three (Chapters 9–13) focuses on effective teaching. This section begins with a chapter on building a humane physical education setting; teachers need to think about the overall humanistic purposes of their teaching before they begin to plan units and lessons. Chapters 10 and 11 provide strategies for developing content effectively and for building excellent units of instruction. Chapter 12 focuses on the generic features that characterize effective instruction. Chapter 13 describes the various instructional formats teachers might utilize to accomplish their different goals.

Part Four (Chapters 14–16) focuses on issues and concepts that teachers need to be aware of in order to make a smooth transition from student life to professional life as a teacher. Chapter 14 focuses on school issues ranging from liability to teacher organizations, and Chapter 15 describes strategies for maintaining and improving one's effectiveness. The final chapter of the text describes how to conduct systematic observation and offers a number of observation protocols, some general and some specific, which teachers can use to help improve their effectiveness.

Acknowledgments

Systematic, field-based research in schools is not done in isolation—it requires a team effort. In the Sport Pedagogy Research Program at The Ohio State University, I have had the opportunity to work with faculty colleagues, graduate students, undergraduate physical education majors, and local, school-based physical educators in a series of research studies designed to enhance the understanding of the complexities of teaching and coaching. To all of you I extend my appreciation—much of your effort is in this text.

My own Ph.D. students continue to be a major source of professional satisfaction. Their contributions to the development of the ideas and methods in this text are considerable. Through their own work at Ohio State and later at their own institutions, they continue to extend the frontiers of our work and improve the quality of our research products.

I am grateful to my faculty colleagues in the School of Health, Physical Education and Recreation for both their support and the intellectual challenge they continue to provide. I am particularly in debt to my immediate Sport Pedagogy Program colleagues who share Pomerene Hall 309 with me: Shan Bumgarner, Jackie Herkowitz, Mary O'Sullivan, Sandra Stroot, Jim Sweeney, and Deborah Tannehill. I also want to thank my colleagues who reviewed the manuscript: Roy Clumpner, Western Washington University; Hubert Hoffman, University of South Florida; Larry Locke, University of Massachusetts, Amherst; Melissa Parker, University of North Dakota; and Deborah Tannehill, The Ohio State University.

My wife, Bobbie, is the elementary school physical education specialist at the Maryland Avenue School in Bexley, Ohio. When I came to Ohio State in 1970, I got to know her because I was interested in effective teaching and she was reputed to be the best elementary specialist in the Columbus area. Those who gave me that information were right! Bobbie's work and her continuous efforts to teach well have both informed and inspired my own work. In a fundamental sense, she and I have the same goals. I do not pursue teaching research as an end in itself and she does not try to improve her performance and her program as ends in themselves. We are both interested in helping students in the schools in our society have a better physical education experience—one that is more positive, more successful, and that equips them with more skills and the desire to utilize those skills. Indeed, these are goals to which we all might dedicate ourselves.

D.S.
Columbus, Ohio

PART One

Understanding and Improving Teaching Effectiveness

Teachers are effective when students reach important learning goals and do so in a way that enhances their development as productive human beings. Few national resources are more important to our collective future than a highly effective teaching force. The chapters in Part One provide background information for you to understand what teaching effectiveness is, what research has shown about effective teachers and their classes, and what strategies and techniques can be used to help teachers and persons preparing to teach to become more effective.

When you master the content of these chapters, you should be able to discuss the concept of teaching effectiveness, cite and utilize in your discussions the results of research on teaching effectiveness, and understand what strategies should be used to improve your own teaching.

CHAPTER **1**

The Systematic Improvement of Teaching Skills

Teacher education, both at the preservice and the inservice level, should adopt as primary goals the development of the competencies needed to create and maintain the learning environment, to engage pupils in learning-related activities, and to implement the kind of instruction that research indicates is provided by effective teachers. There is an abundance of practical knowledge available about how to do these things; what has been missing in the past is a clear conviction on the part of teacher educators that these things are what teachers ought to be doing.

Donald Medley, *The Effectiveness of Teachers* (1979)

CHAPTER OBJECTIVES

To value the role of motivation and practice in learning to teach effectively

To distinguish between a skillful and artistic approach to teaching

To distinguish among teaching, learning, and pedagogy

To understand the role of appropriate practice with feedback in teaching skill development

To explain the data-based approach to teaching skill development

To distinguish among stages of skill development

To understand how your own beliefs affect your view of teaching

To explain the difference between effectiveness and expertise

Motivation, Feedback, and Knowledge

My three goals in writing this text are to help you to better understand the dimensions of effective teaching in physical activity settings, to help you to improve your teaching skills, and to make you want to teach better, both now and in the future. Of those three goals, wanting to teach better—the motivational component—is the foundation on which all else is built. It isn't *bad* teaching that plagues physical education so much as it is *non*teaching (Locke, 1975). Teachers who have not yet developed effective teaching skills may not teach very well, even though they try hard; however, if they continue to try hard and get some help, they will improve quickly. A more difficult and troubling situation is presented by those teachers who know how to teach well, but are not motivated to do so.

If you are properly motivated, teaching skills can be developed with some good practice. Basic skills, once understood, can be practiced and refined. Higher-level skills can then gradually be achieved. With further experience, you can become an effective teacher. When you have the opportunity to practice teaching skills in varied contexts, the skills become stronger and your effectiveness becomes more general. An *effective teacher* is one who manages students well to decrease disruptions and increase time for learning. An effective teacher then organizes that learning time with activities matched to student abilities so that an optimal amount of learning takes place. An assertion is embedded within this description of the effective teacher: Teaching effectiveness is judged by student learning! It starts with the *intention* of having students be different because they have come in contact with your educational environment; that is, with the intention of having them *learn*.

If there is no intention to have students learn, then the teacher is reduced to an activity director at best and a high-priced "baby-sitter" at worst, trying to arrange for students to have fun and not be too disruptive in doing so. Make no mistake! There are physical education teachers who are satisfied when their students are well behaved and having fun in some activity. These teachers have little intention for them to really learn skills, utilize strategies more effectively, be more fit, or know more about sport and fitness. The goals of this kind of teacher are merely to keep students busy, happy, and good (Placek, 1983).

The professional physical educator intends for students to learn and then teaches effectively to achieve that goal. This text is written on the assumption that you want to be that kind of teacher. If you have the motivation to become an effective teacher and persevere in that quest during your first several years of teaching, you can achieve a level of effectiveness that will mark you as a competent, professional educator. The skilled, experienced teacher orchestrates a repertoire of finely tuned skills to meet the ever-changing demands of the learning situation. Few things are more enjoyable to watch than a motivated, skilled teacher totally in control of a learning setting in which students are not only learning but are also obviously enjoying the learning.

This book is about effective teaching in physical education, about *doing* it, not just knowing about it! To learn to teach effectively, you have to practice teaching and get good feedback about your own performance and that of your students. Many effective, experienced teachers in today's schools got that way by (a) being motivated, (b) intending that their students learn, and (c) paying attention to the feedback they could get about themselves and their students. They truly learned through experience, because they had little knowledge about effective teaching and no opportunity to get accurate feedback from a knowledgeable observer. As Chapters 2 and 3 will show, however, we have learned a great deal about effective teaching in the past 20 years. The skills and strategies necessary for achieving effectiveness are described in some detail throughout this text. Knowing about these effective teaching strategies is important, but it isn't enough. You have to practice those strategies under conditions in which you will be able to get accurate, specific feedback about your performance and that of your students.

Having the opportunity to practice relevant skills with the provision for systematic feedback is the quickest way to develop skill in teaching. For a long time we have known that to be true for developing sport skills. It also appears to be true for teaching skills. A major feature of this text is that it provides a systematic approach to the development of teaching skills. In this text, the skills themselves and the situations they can be used in are explained clearly. It also presents methods for evaluating your use of the skills and the effects they are having on students. In addition, ways of using these data to improve your own performance are clearly outlined. In this sense at least, there can be no failures as you learn to be an effective teacher, only experiences in which you try to do the best you can and from which you receive specific feedback that can be used to make changes as you continue to improve.

The major purpose of Chapter 1 is to alert you to the basic assumptions that underlie a systematic approach to teaching skill development, the kinds of data that can be generated, and how those data can be used to improve your skills.

Basic Assumptions Underlying a Systematic Approach

Every approach to teaching is based on some underlying assumptions. Stating those assumptions explicitly can provoke discussion and provide an understanding of the use of certain strategies. An examination of these assumptions also reveals ways to judge consistency between them and how a teacher actually teaches. A systematic approach to teaching must entail some regular data collection to be truly "systematic." In addition, an experiential approach to learning must provide for a substantial amount of actual teaching practice.

You may not agree with all the assumptions stated in this chapter. There is room for disagreement in teacher preparation, even when the major objectives are agreed on. What teaching skills are important? How can they best be learned and perfected? I hope that the following sections provoke discussion among you, your fellow students, and your instructors. One of the best ways to focus your views on teaching is to have to explain and defend your assumptions about physical education teaching skills and how they can be developed.

Science and the Art of Teaching

The development of teaching skills is approached in this text as if it were a science—that is, amenable to systematic evaluation and capable of being broken down into a series of tasks that can be mastered. This does not suggest that teaching can or should be viewed as a mechanistic enterprise. Nor does it suggest that there is no room in effective teaching for personal style, inventiveness, or intuition. Effective teachers artistically orchestrate a set of highly developed skills to meet the specific demands of a learning setting.

Some people, however, view teaching solely as an art. They believe teaching skills can't be learned—that good teachers are born, not made. This view implies that we can discover nothing about teaching that can be passed on to those preparing to teach. Clearly, if teachers are born, not made, then enormous sums of money are being wasted each year on so-called teacher education.

1.1 The Reality and the Hope!

Do things *always* get better naturally? Or do we need to *act* to improve things? John Goodlad, a noted American educator, suggested more than 10 years ago that our society may not be up to making the necessary improvements that would lift education out of its near-quarter-century demise (Goodlad, 1979). Indeed, he said, it is possible that schools may deteriorate further and the public's dissatisfaction and disaffection may increase.

Fact: National polls have shown that over the past 25 years parents have increasingly indicated that they don't want their children to become teachers.

Fact: Too many teachers haven't done well in basic tests of literacy or in general knowledge tests.

Fact: Assaults on teachers by students increase each year. Teachers increasingly ask for guidance related to "stress management" and burnout.

Fact: The illiteracy rate of the United States is three times higher than that of the Soviet Union.

Fact: It appears that national averages on academic tests have gone up mainly because drop out rates have increased.

Fact: Although education reform has been front-page news for 10 years, schools and teaching seem to have changed little.

Fact: With each new major social problem, schools are asked to do more and more (drug education, AIDS education, etc.) yet still improve on what people typically refer to as the "basics."

What is the best, quickest way to improve the picture in schools? The effect of schooling on the individual pupil depends to a considerable extent on who his teacher is. Personnel costs themselves represent so large a share of the day-to-day cost of education that the best hope for improvement in cost-effectiveness lies in improving the effectiveness of the teacher. (Donald Medley, Professor of Education, University of Virginia, 1979)

Another view of teaching seems to be based on the assumption that both a strong motivation to help students and a knowledge of the subject to be taught are required. Many laypersons seem to hold this view, assuming that they too could teach a subject they knew well. I have already supported the notion that motivation is crucial to effective teaching, but is that, coupled with a firm grasp of the subject matter, all that is necessary to teach effectively in today's schools?

No, there is little support for this view, even though it is widely held. The correlation between a teacher's knowledge of subject matter and student achievement is typically quite low (Berlinner, 1985). The conclusion supported by the evidence on this topic is quite straightforward: "Knowing your subject well is no guarantee that you will be an effective teacher of that subject" (Evertson, Hawley, & Zlotnik, 1984, p. 30). What's missing, of course, in these points of view is recognizing the crucial importance of teaching skills. Subject knowledge is important, but it's of little use if you can't translate that knowledge through effective teaching in ways that relate to the specific needs of learners in a particular context.

People who seriously argue the artistic versus the scientific approaches to teaching are raising a pseudo-issue. All artists—musicians, painters, dancers—understand that there are basic skills to be mastered and that much can be learned about these skills through scientific approaches. Practice with systematic feedback is vital for becoming a better artist. When basic skills are mastered through repeated practice, newer, more complex skills are added to the artist's repertoire.

Viewing an artistic performance from this perspective does not render it less artistic, nor does it dehumanize the performer. Artists differ in their performances even though they have had similar training. Teachers differ in their teaching even though they have mastered similar sets of teaching skills.

Much of the information in this text has been developed by systematically studying effective teachers over the past 25 years. Much more can be learned from a continuation, extension, and refinement of this systematic research effort. The teaching skills described in this text can be thought of as basic to effective teaching. However, I will not try to account for all the individual styles of effective teachers. No attempt will be made to fit all teachers into a single mold or to deny individual styles, except when such styles clearly don't contribute to students' achievement and growth.

Think about it in the context of basketball. I can't explain the individual styles of a Michael Jordan, a Larry Bird, or a Magic Johnson, nor would I try to impose any of those styles on a young player. I can teach young players fundamental skills (dribbling, passing, shooting, and defending) and I can teach them basic strategies (zone defense, fast break, and so forth). I can also arrange good practice conditions in which these skills and strategies can be developed and refined. The players will eventually develop their own styles even though they practiced the same fundamentals and learned the same strategies. What is true for learning to play basketball is also true for learning to teach.

The materials in this text will not fit you into some preconceived mold of how all teachers ought to operate. Rather, the text aims to help you to want to improve your teaching skills, to understand what effective teaching means, and to develop the skills and strategies of better teaching by practicing under appropriate conditions. Eventually, your own style will emerge, and you will have your own unique impact on the students you teach and coach.

Teaching, Learning, and Pedagogy

The basic task of teaching is to help students learn and grow; to design educational experiences through which students will grow in skill, understanding, and attitude; and to do so in a way that enables students to enjoy both the learning experience and the activity or subject being studied. The most meaningful way to understand teaching is by looking at what happens to the students being taught. It is increasingly difficult to assert that a teacher taught but the students did not learn. We must begin to evaluate teaching in terms of its effect on students. Without such evaluation, the activities of teaching become abstract and meaningless.

Teaching can be defined generally as the professional behaviors exhibited by teachers as they engage in their work. Teachers do things such as plan, explain, lecture, question, manage, and provide feedback. Hopefully, these are all done with the purpose of helping students to learn and grow. These are skills and strategies that can be practiced and improved. It also needs to be noted that many persons other than certified teachers use these behaviors—such as mothers, fathers, employers, friends.

Learning is a change in behavior that is the result of experience rather than genetic development. Clearly, not all learning is the result of teaching. People can learn from mistakes. Even in situations in which people are troubled or hurt, they can learn valuable lessons. Yet nobody would suggest setting up potentially harmful situations so that they can learn those lessons. For our purposes, we need to link the things teachers do with the positive, growth-oriented things that students learn. The concept that seems to do this best is that of pedagogy.

Pedagogy can be defined as the skillful arrangement of an environment in such a way that students acquire specifically intended learnings. Pedagogy links teachers' actions with students' outcomes. For pedagogy to have occurred, certain student outcomes must be attained. No outcomes, no pedagogy!

If pedagogy is defined primarily in terms of its effect on students, then it is necessary to observe what is happening to students so that we can describe and evaluate what kind of pedagogy has occurred. Part of that assessment is to describe what the teacher is doing, and part of it is to describe what is happening to students. A complete assessment, however, must link the activities of the teacher to the additivities of the students. A consistent strategy of this text is to link teaching activities to their effect on students.

Eventually, you will find the most useful method of evaluating your own teaching is to examine what your students are doing. When you are in schools observing other persons teaching, you will want to spend most of your time watching what the students are doing. You will have learned that to watch the teacher is to risk being fooled! What teachers do and how they do it is important, but the real importance of pedagogy can be found in how teachers affect students. For example, an elegant demonstration and explanation of the volleyball forearm pass may seem to be good teaching—but not if students don't pay attention to it and immediately follow it by trying to take each other's heads off in an impromptu, unauthorized game of bombardment!

1.2 National Board Defines Core Propositions about Teaching

In 1987 a National Board for Professional Teaching Standards was established. It has proposed a system of national teacher certification to be operational as early as 1993. This system aims to identify and honor teachers who effectively enhance student learning. Individual teachers will be able to apply to the National Board, and some districts and even states have indicate a desire to reward teachers who meet National Board standards with higher salaries. While the exact nature of the certification process has not yet been fully established, the nature of the evaluation program can be seen clearly in the following five core propositions that the Board feels exemplify effective teaching.

1. Teachers are committed to students and their learning.
2. Teachers know the subjects they teach and how to teach those subjects to students.
3. Teachers are responsible for managing and monitoring student learning.
4. Teachers think systematically about their practice and learn from experience.
5. Teachers are members of learning communities.

The picture painted by these core propositions is a long way from the stereotype of a physical educator "throwing out the ball" while working on strategies for an afternoon athletic practice. Will this approach to raising standards for teachers and elevating the teaching profession work?

Improving Teaching Skills Through Appropriate Practice

The best way to improve your teaching skills is to teach under appropriate conditions. "Appropriate conditions" means having specific goals for you and your students. It also means receiving information on the degree to which those goals have been met. While this doesn't sound like a revolutionary notion, it is still not achieved in many teacher education programs. Sometimes very little practice is provided for teacher education students. Occasionally, no practice is provided before they reach the student teaching experience. In other cases, practice opportunities are provided in campus-based clinical settings or in schools. However, objectives for those experiences are unclear, and little feedback is provided for the practicing teachers.

Gaining knowledge about teaching through lectures, books, films, and videotapes is important—but it is not a substitute for practice. Learning *about* teaching is similar to learning *about* tennis. You can learn about tennis through books, instructional films, televised matches, or by watching people play on local courts. Much of this can be enlightening and fun. Eventually, if you learn enough about tennis, you might even become an expert about tennis. But none of this will help you hit your backhand better or get more spin on your second serve.

The only way to improve your tennis skills is to play tennis. Not only do you have to play, but you also have to play against someone who is better than you or receive instruction from someone who can help you improve your skill as you play. Books, films, and all the rest are important, but they should be seen in proper perspective—as support sources for skill development, not as substitutes for direct experience in the skill itself.

Teaching skills can be defined in ways that are similar to those in tennis, even though teaching effectively is more complex than playing tennis well. Just as situations can be set up for you to practice your backhand or volley shots, teaching situations can also be set up to practice management or instructional skills. And, just as in tennis, there should be specific purposes for practice and frequent feedback about performance.

Goals and Feedback

Feedback can be defined as information about a response that is used to modify the next response. Feedback is necessary for learning. Think, for example, of how you might learn to draw a line that is precisely 17 inches long. You attempt to draw the line, but you get no feedback. You then make a second attempt that is slightly longer. Again, no feedback. Was the second attempt closer or farther away? If someone could tell you "too long" or "too short," after each attempt, you would soon be able to draw the line correctly. If someone would tell you "1.5 inches too long" or "three-quarters of an inch too short," you would be able to draw the correct line even more quickly. Feedback is necessary for learning. Precise feedback helps you learn more quickly than does general feedback.

The example described above would be equally difficult if someone had provided you a goal that said "draw a short line." How short? Goals must be specific if they are to lead to meaningful learning experiences.

Teaching skills can be stated as specific goals. Teaching performance relative to these goals can be monitored and used for specific feedback to help teachers improve. For example, it is known that teachers do not always distribute their attention equitably among students of various skill levels. Distributing your attention (in skill feedback or personal comments) more equitably can easily be stated as a goal and monitored by an observer. The resulting information can help you understand where you stand relative to the goal and what you have to do to achieve the goal more fully.

Too often teachers are told to "be firmer with students," "relate to them more at their level," or "give your directions more clearly." These not-so-clear goals are often followed by less than precise feedback, such as "much better," or "okay," or "that's not quite it yet." The method usually employed to monitor teacher and student performance in such cases is what I call *eyeballing*. The supervisor sits and watches the class for a session and then provides a summary comment or two. Under these conditions, it's just as likely that the teacher's skills will deteriorate rather than get better.

The total of all the precise goals will not necessarily yield an effective teacher, just as establishing of a series of precise tennis goals will not lead simply to a highly successful competitive tennis player. Goals and feedback will improve your teaching, just as they would improve your tennis game. There is much we still do not know about effective teaching. Some higher-order teaching skills cannot yet be stated in terms of precise goals and feedback. Yet this should not deter us from doing what we can to improve teaching.

Data-Based Approach to Developing Teaching Skills

Most of the suggestions for improving teaching skills that are presented in this text require collecting some data so that people can work toward the skill development goal. For the most part, the data collected will be either in time units or in response units. For example, you might learn than in one lesson you taught there were nine transitions (episodes where some change is made within a lesson) with a total time devoted to transitions of 12:40 minutes, an average of 1:24 minutes per transition. You and your supervisor might deem this to be too much time in transition and discuss ways of organizing transitions more efficiently. You might also learn that in one lesson you provided 36 instances of skill-related feedback, but that only 16 of those instances were specific rather than general. With the same data, you might learn that you provided 26 of those feedbacks to boys but only 10 to girls. These data might suggest two areas that need attention—more specific feedback and a more equitable distribution among boys and girls.

The techniques of observation and feedback are fairly easy to master. Once you learn to be a reliable observer yourself, you observe your peer students and help them improve, and you can also begin to set your own goals and monitor your own performance.

The fact that this text is based primarily on a data collection format doesn't mean that you can't or shouldn't take every opportunity to learn through informal conversations with peers, supervisors, and cooperating teachers. The data collection format provides a base for developing teaching skills. It is not a substitute for the many subtleties and nuances of skill that an experienced teacher can pass on to you. Every opportunity to discuss teaching openly and frankly with peers, supervisors, and cooperating teachers should be vigorously pursued. The right piece of information about a student's home life, the right tip about voice articulation, or a good bit of advice about organizing for a particular activity can help you tremendously. This text makes no claim to cover all the factors that contribute to good teaching. It does provide a format through which a solid foundation of good teaching skills can be built. The degree to which this foundation provides the base for further professional development rests largely with the professionals and peers with whom you are working.

1.3 Practicing Teaching Skills Informally

Do you need a specific assignment to practice important teaching skills? Do you need a microteaching setting or a trip to a local school? No! Teaching skills can be practiced in many places—indeed, in almost any place where you interact with other people.

For example, becoming a more effective praiser can be practiced with brothers, sisters, or roommates. Asking clearer, better questions can be practiced in other classes, in an informal discussion with classmates, as a church school teacher, or as a volunteer at a youth agency. Providing direct, informative feedback can be practiced at a summer camp, as a YMCA volunteer, or simply helping a neighbor child jump rope in the backyard on a weekend afternoon.

The point is that many important teaching skills can be practiced on a daily basis in the settings you now frequent as part of your daily routine. You simply need to pick out one skill at a time, consciously try to improve your use of it, and be sensitive to how you are doing. Some of the techniques for self-assessment presented later in the text may also be very helpful in such informal practice.

If you want to improve, try practicing on your own.

Stages of Skill Development in Teaching

For two decades our research program has experimented with ways of helping both teachers in training as well as inservice teachers to improve their teaching skills (Siedentop, 1981; Taggart, 1989). Even though teachers have learned and practiced different teaching skills in different settings with different age groups, most have gone through predictable stages. It is important for you to understand these stages because you are likely to experience them also, especially when you are involved in interactive teaching skills such as providing specific skill feedback, praising, questioning, and similar skills. What is important is that you recognize them as stages. Progress through the stages can occur rapidly if you want to improve and are provided opportunities to practice the skills.

Stage 1: The Initial Discomfort Stage

It may be hard for you to learn to interact in new ways. You may have a limited repertoire of words to use to convey your messages. You may even feel embarrassed in saying phrases in ways that are new. This is particularly true for learning how to praise students effectively—and this is an important skill. For some reason, people have very limited practice in being nice to one another. Teaching alone or small-group peer teaching is especially useful to help you to get beyond this stage. Please do not feel that you are unusual if you feel awkward, discomforted, or even embarrassed at learning to behave differently as a teacher. It seems to be a first stage, and most students grow through it quite quickly.

Stage 2: Learning a Variety of Techniques

When you first learn to praise, or to give specific feedback, or to be more enthusiastic, you will have a limited repertoire of ways to do so. And you will tend to repeat the same phrases and do the same thing over and over again. In giving positive feedback and praise, you will be giving what one research team once labeled as the "global good"; that is, you will interact more frequently with your students (you will have increased your rate of interacting), but you will have a limited number of ways of interacting (for example, saying, "Good job" over and over). This, too, appears to be a stage most people experience. Don't worry! If you persist, and if you get help through systematic feedback, you will learn a greater variety of ways to give feedback, to be enthusiastic, to praise students, to use your nonverbal behavior.

Stage 3: Learning How to Do More Than One Thing at a Time

The next stage seems to be learning to focus on improving one skill or strategy while still being able to do other things at the same time. This is an important stage, because it indicates that you have progressed far enough so that the skill is becoming more habitual. This lets you focus on other important aspects of teaching. Now, for example, you can continue to improve your feedback skills while also focusing on the improvement of some managerial techniques. When you have reached this stage, you're on your way to becoming a skilled teacher!

Stage 4: Learning How to Use Your Skills More Appropriately

It is one thing to learn how to give feedback, say the words, to increase the variety of things you say. It is another thing to give the right feedback at the right time. The early stages of development of this kind of skill are like hitting a baseball off a batting tee. Batting tees are a nice way to learn a smooth swing, the transfer of weight, and a good follow-through. But eventually you must hit a pitched ball! You can also learn many good techniques for praising students, both verbal and nonverbal. Now you must learn to praise the right student at the right time for the right behavior. In other words, you must learn to *apply* your skills appropriately and accurately. Here, too, it helps immensely to have specific goals and regular feedback as you try to master this stage of development.

Stage 5: Confidence and Anticipation

The final stage occurs when you have practiced the skill, used it in real settings, and can begin to see the benefits of it in the reactions of your students. Skills eventually become habits—good habits, in this case. As your skillfulness as a teacher increases, and your confidence with it, you will gradually acquire the ability to anticipate events that are about to occur in your classes. Anticipating allows you to direct events most appropriately and to be ready to apply the right teaching skill at exactly the right moment. You can get to this stage! But you have to work through the other stages.

Sources of Help

It is worth repeating that experience alone does not guarantee improvement in teaching. This is true for real experience, and it is also true for simulated experiences. Each teaching experience you have will no doubt change you a bit for the better. Bad habits are learned, just as good habits are. A systematic approach to the development of teaching skills helps maximize the chances that you will learn good habits and helps minimize the chances of your acquiring bad habits. You can no doubt learn a lot on your own, just as you might learn how to be a decent tennis player without any instruction or coaching. But it is also true that you can be even better if you get the right instruction and coaching along the way. Now, who or what can help you?

First, a systematic approach can help you. You may not always like to have specific goals for a teaching episode. You may not always like to have your teaching observed. You may not always like to have to deal with feedback about what you did. Very few of us like to be held accountable for achieving goals. But these constraints help you improve. Having a goal gives an experience the necessary specificity to make it useful. Learn to ask for clear, specific goals. Similarly, observation is the only way to develop good feedback. The observation process is a main aid in helping you to improve. You should want to know how well you did. Just as a player likes to know his or her statistics, teachers should want to know how well they did relative to the important skills of their "game." In other words, the systematic approach is your friend, not your enemy.

Second, you can help yourself. Mirrors, audiotape recordings, and videotapes can all be used in order to help yourself improve. Third, your instructor can help you improve. Your instructor is not just your evaluator but should also be your helper. If you have specific goals to achieve, then your instructor can provide practice and feedback to help you improve. You are partners in teacher education. You are on the same team. That doesn't mean that you will always get along in every situation. It simply means that you ought to keep in mind that you both have the same goals—becoming a better teacher.

Your peers can also help you improve. This can be done specifically through techniques such as peer teaching and reflective teaching. It can also be done by having the peers observe you as you teach and provide feedback to you afterward. Most importantly, improvement can be enhanced through the development of a professional attitude within your peer group—an attitude that takes teaching seriously and motivates discussion, questioning, and a desire to improve. If you and your undergraduate peers do not care much about learning how to teach now, there is no reason to expect that you will care much about improving once you get on the job.

Finally, practicing physical education teachers in schools can help you to improve. They can do so in the first instance simply by allowing you to watch them—*if you watch specifically with a goal in mind*. Learning through observation is more than sight-seeing. Teachers in schools can also help you by discussing specifically what they do in certain situations or how they organize or manage. A skilled teacher makes certain tasks look effortless. Don't be fooled. When you talk seriously to such teachers, you find out very quickly that they have worked very, very hard to achieve that "effortless" look.

Confronting Your Own Beliefs about Teaching Physical Education

In recent years, research has shown that what teachers *believe* about teaching and learning affects how they think about their teaching, how they conduct themselves in their educational settings, and how they learn through experience in those settings (Grossman, Wilson, & Shulman, 1989). Researchers typically distinguish between *beliefs* about teaching and *knowledge* about teaching, even though they recognize that in any one person belief and knowledge are probably inseparable.

Beliefs about teaching are more subjective than knowledge about teaching. They are also likely to engender more emotion. Beliefs are also more arguable than is knowledge and provoke more debate. For any one of us, however, it is difficult to distinguish between our own beliefs about teaching physical education and our knowledge about it.

Three types of beliefs are particularly relevant to teaching. One relates to what you believe about the content you are teaching, the subject matter called physical education. What do you believe physical education to be? Is it fitness? Is it sport? Is it social development? Is it knowledge development? Is it all of these? How important is it in the school curriculum? Is physical education as important as art and music? As reading and mathematics?

The second type of belief important to teaching is your orientation to that subject matter—what you believe is important to be learned and how you believe students learn it. If you believe your subject matter to be teaching sport, what is most important for students to learn? How do you think they learn it? Is skill development most important? Or is learning to play the game comfortably more important? How should they learn? Through your telling them? Through repeated practice? Through direct experience?

What you believe about teaching and learning represents the third important set of beliefs that will affect your teaching. Should teachers be direct or indirect? Are some students natural learners and others not? Can all your students learn most of what you have to teach them? Do boys and girls learn in the same way?

Beliefs are important because you will interpret what you are learning about teaching in your teacher education program within the framework of your belief system. If you don't examine that system—test it—then your tendency will be to simply incorporate new knowledge about teaching into that well-developed belief system. You will be likely to put aside knowledge about effective teaching that runs contrary to your belief system, without really allowing that new knowledge to modify your belief system. Worse still, you may demonstrate new knowledge on tests and even new teaching skills in practice teaching to "play the grade game." But that knowledge and skills are what your instructors and supervisors believe to be important in teaching physical education, not what you believe.

Having said all this, it also needs to be made clear that you have a right to your own belief system about teaching physical education. It will guide you throughout your career as a teacher/coach. But you should not be afraid to test that belief system and to modify it to accommodate knowledge and skills that can help you to be better. You can't do that unless and until you're willing to examine your belief system carefully and compare it to those of your classmates and to those of your instructors and supervisors.

1.4 Teaching in Urban Schools: A Test for Beliefs

For most men and women who haven't grown up in urban schools, a teaching experience in an urban school can provide the context for an important encounter with their belief systems about physical education, teaching, and learning. A large percentage of the nation's students attend urban schools. Here are some salient demographic characteristics of what those schools will be like in the year 2000.

- One-third of the students will be Black or Hispanic.
- One-sixth of the students will be children of a teenage mother, and more than three-quarters of those mothers will be unwed.
- One-quarter of the students will be from families whose income falls below the federal poverty line.
- Drop out rates are likely to reach 45%.
- We will continue to spend progressively less on urban schools and more on their suburban counterparts. This has been a consistent trend for 20 years.
- Nearly a third of all classes will be taught by a teacher not certified for the subject being taught.

Do you want to teach in urban schools? What do you believe about students whose background is similar to the characteristics described above? Is physical education important for these students?

Toward the Expert Physical Education Teacher

Physical education will prosper as a subject matter to the degree that those who teach it are effective and even expert. The more effective and expert teachers become, the more likely they will be to engender the respect of parents and the community. This will make the teaching profession more esteemed—and better paid, too!

The study of teacher expertise is a relatively new research enterprise (Berliner, 1986). Once it was discovered that effective teaching has discoverable characteristics, it was natural that researchers would try to distinguish between effectiveness and expertise. If effective teachers promote student learning and growth, expert teachers do so to a greater degree; that is, the difference is one of degree rather than kind. Expert teachers are able to design content, deliver it, and motivate learners in ways that go beyond effectiveness. And, although it's possible that experts might know more about their students and the context for learning, it's absolutely clear that experts know their subject matter more completely than do effective teachers.

Siedentop and Eldar (1989) used the expertise research literature to examine seven effective elementary physical education specialists. Their conclusions about expertise were:

1. *Expertise is highly specific to context and subject matter.* It is useful to talk about an expert volleyball teacher at the middle school level or an expert gymnastics teacher with young children. However, the expertise shown in one subject and at one level may not generalize to other subjects and levels.

2. *Expertise is performance-oriented.* Expert teachers often may not be able to explain their own expertise. The expertise is in the *doing* rather than the explaining of it.

3. *Experience is a necessary condition for expertise but not a sufficient condition.* Expertise probably develops over long periods of time in ways that are not clearly understood. Thus it is unlikely that expertise can be taught in the same way as effective teaching skills.

4. *Expertise lies at the nexus of highly skilled teaching and mastery of a particular subject matter* (that is, gymnastics or pole vaulting or basketball). Thorough mastery of a subject is a necessary condition for teaching expertise. You can teach effectively with a limited knowledge of a subject, but to teach expertly, you have to have expertise in the subject.

5. *Teaching effectiveness is within reach of most first-year teachers.* The skills are identifiable and can be improved through practice. Expertise takes longer and the paths toward its achievement are less clear.

Summary

1. If teachers are properly motivated, they can learn to be effective with good practice.

2. Effective teaching is intentional—it is achieved when students achieve the goals set by the teacher.

3. The quickest way to develop skill in teaching is to practice relevant skills with systematic feedback.

4. *Effective teaching* is the artistic orchestration of a repertoire of skills that can be identified and acquired through a scientific approach.

5. *Teaching* refers to the professional behaviors exhibited by teachers in their work, while *learning* is a change in behavior that is the result of experience.

6. *Pedagogy* is the skillful arrangement of a learning environment so that students acquire specifically intended learnings.

7. To learn to teach, you need to have specific goals to achieve and systematic feedback related to those goals.

8. A data-based approach to teaching skill development requires systematic observation with resulting feedback.

9. As students acquire skill in teaching, they go through predictable stages of development. Confidence and anticipation occur in the final stage.

10. There are several sources of help in practicing teaching skills, including the systematic approach, self-help, peer help, and teaching in schools.

11. Your beliefs about the content of what you teach, your orientation to that subject field, and your beliefs about teaching and learning will affect how you interpret information about teaching effectiveness.

12. Expertise is different than effectiveness. It combines highly effective teaching with a mastery of a subject field.

13. Expertise is probably specific to a subject and to the context within which that subject is taught.

CHAPTER 2

The Active Teacher— The Learning Student

The last 15 years have produced an orderly knowledge base linking teacher behavior to achievement. Although just a beginning, this is a major advance over what was available previously. If applied with proper attention to its limits, this knowledge base should help improve teacher education and teaching practice... Elitist critics often undervalue teaching or even suggest that anyone can teach ("Those who can, do; those who can't, teach"). The data reviewed here refute this myth as well.

Jere Brophy & Thomas Good (1986)

CHAPTER OBJECTIVES

To explain why effective teaching is important

To describe the major reasons early research efforts failed

To distinguish among climate, management of behavior, and management of teaching

To describe how effective teachers are identified and studied

To describe major limits to the present research effort

To describe the major findings from teacher effectiveness research

To explain the concept of *Academic Learning Time*

To explain the concept of the *active teacher*

To describe the components of effective class management

To describe the relationship between achievement outcomes and attitude outcomes

To describe contextual variations of active teaching

To describe the concept of the learning student

Why Effective Teaching Is Important

Each of you has no doubt experienced what it means to be in contact over a period of time with a truly outstanding teacher. What teachers and coaches do is extraordinarily important. A skilled, motivated elementary classroom teacher can, in one year's time, give a young girl or boy untold chances for personal and academic growth. A skilled middle or high school teacher can open the riches of a subject matter during a particular term. At the same time, a poorly skilled, uncaring teacher can make a year or even a term seem like an eternity and can be responsible for what John Dewey called "miseducation"—the stunting of personal and academic growth.

Physical educators need to be effective teachers. Students won't develop lifetime habits of fitness and sport participation if they get "turned off" to physical education during their school years. Nor will these habits develop if students fail to learn skills. Having a good time in physical education is not enough. Students have to learn skills, gain knowledge, and grow in their appreciation of the joys of participating in sports and the importance of lifetime personal fitness.

Education is our largest industry. In fact, we spend more on it than we do on national defense. That is no doubt wise, because in the long run a well-educated citizenry is probably our best source of ongoing security, freedom, and prosperity. Over two million full-time teachers are in our nation's schools and they account for the largest part of the expenses of education. The importance of having effective teachers is, therefore, quite clear. Both from a personal, experiential point of view and from a social, economic point of view, more effective teaching in schools should be a national priority.

Do teachers make a difference? Yes! Unequivocally yes! The research evidence about effective teaching has grown considerably in the 1960-1990 period. Those who suggest that "anyone can teach" know little either about teaching research or about the realities of today's schools. A great deal is now known about the teaching strategies that are effective in today's schools. The purpose of this chapter is to present the general strategies that have been shown through research to produce high gains in achievement and self-growth.

False Starts and Inappropriate Techniques

Research on teaching doesn't have a very good reputation. It has suffered through a long history of inconclusive results, inappropriately asked questions, and less than useful techniques. Most of what transpired in teaching research between 1900 and 1960 is gathering dust on the back shelves of university libraries, and deservedly so. Many of the early researchers attempted to sort out the personality profiles of successful teachers. There were two major problems with this approach. First, success was too often judged by the ratings of supervisors, principals, and peer teachers, some of whom may never have seen the teacher teach. These rating and judgment systems were invalid and unreliable. They most certainly were not good indicators of success in teaching. A second problem was to have hypothesized in the first place that "personality" had something to do with effective teaching. Personality is most often judged by responses to questions on paper-and-pencil tests, and there is little reason to suspect that responses to these kinds of tests told anyone much about what kind of teacher a person might be. The results of these efforts were uniformly inadequate. They revealed little other than that teachers had different personalities and this related little to their success as teachers.

Another research strategy was to compare teaching "methods" to see which was best. Often, a favored strategy was compared against what was labeled a "traditional" method; for example, the "part" method versus the "whole" method in teaching motor skills. This kind of research was very value-laden, in the sense that the researchers often set out to "prove" that the innovative method was better. Often the method labeled "traditional" was simply bad teaching. The methods strategy in teaching research was no more successful than the personality strategy. The methods were most often too rigid and too stereotyped to bear much resemblance to what went on in real classroom, where teachers tend to use a variety of "methods" to achieve different goals. Pet methods tend to come and go, while the central task of the teacher remains fairly constant. If we've learned anything from the methods strategy, it should be to be very skeptical about magical methods for achieving teaching success.

All in all, the pre- 1960 research on teaching doesn't constitute a striking series of successes. Instead, the failures were so consistent that many came to believe that teaching research could not possibly describe, analyze, and explain effective teaching. Indeed, during the 1960s many came to believe that a major reason for this continued failure might be that teachers simply don't make an important difference—that they are not sufficiently powerful influences to show up in measures of achievement and student growth. We now know that such pessimism is unwarranted. Teachers do make a difference! And it has been through teaching research that we have come to understand how they can make a positive difference in the educational lives of the students they teach.

The Turning Point: The Study of Teachers Teaching

It is most interesting that the turning point for teaching research—from failure to success—was the development of strategies for observing teachers as they teach in real schools with real students. Systematic observation of teachers, through the lenses of many different kinds of observational systems, finally provided the methodological tool through which teaching research began to understand the nature of teacher effectiveness. These were not special teachers, chosen for special reasons. They were ordinary, certified teachers—the kind one finds in schools throughout this society.

The observation systems developed were of many different kinds. Some of them, such as the systems developed from the Flanders Interaction Analysis tradition, used categories that explicitly valued some teaching styles more than others. In Flanders-type systems, teacher indirectness is valued. So too are student-initiated interactions. Other systems chose categories that were more value-free in the sense that the categories represented ordinary language descriptions of teachers doing their jobs—categories such as "instructs students," "gives directions," "reprimands students," and "asks question" were simple, everyday descriptors of what goes on in classrooms. Some categories such as "reinforces appropriate student behavior," "cues student responses," or "punishes inappropriate behavior," were everyday occurrences familiar to most teachers yet also traceable to theories of human behavior.

The era of 1960–1975 saw a rapid development of observational systems and the techniques of securing good, reliable data through observation of teachers teaching. Some category systems fell by the wayside. Others survived. Much was learned about how to observe, how to be in schools as an observer without changing what went on in those schools, and how to develop and use reliable data about teaching and classroom processes. The result was a growing understanding of how things are, rather than romantic visions of how things should be. And the ability to describe things as they are was prerequisite to being able to analyze teacher effectiveness.

2.1 Classroom Climate and Teaching: Conceptual Confusions

It is common among laypersons, and even sometimes among teachers themselves, to confuse the emotional climate of a class with the way the teacher manages and controls the behavior of the students and the learning tasks they pursue. *Classroom climate* refers to the positive, neutral, or negative affect exhibited by the teacher and the students. Classes can be warm, supportive, and nurturant. They can be basically neutral; that is, without much affect in either direction. Or they can be negative, threatening, and coercive.

The climate of a class should not be confused with how the teacher manages student behavior and controls the presentation and pursuit of learning tasks. *Management of behavior* refers to how the teacher controls the physical movement of students and the ways students socialize. Managerial control can be very firm and tight, or it can be loose and fluid. The management of behavior is also different from the *management of learning tasks,* which can be defined as how learning tasks get selected and carried out. This area of class control can range from a completely teacher-directed format to one in which students choose what they do and when they do it.

The most typical confusion comes from assuming that a teacher who exerts firm control over student behavior also creates a negative class climate. On the contrary, research suggests that the opposite is more nearly true; that is, effective teachers exert firm control over student behavior but typically do so within a warm, nurturant class climate. A second typical source of confusion arises from the assumption that teachers who directly control student behavior must also directly control the presentation and pursuit of learning tasks. Not so! Many successful teachers manage student behavior very directly and firmly, yet allow students different amounts of latitude in selecting and carrying out learning tasks within the class.

Maintaining the class climate, managing student behavior, and controlling learning tasks are *independent* features of an educational setting. Don't assume that a teacher who operates in one way in one of those three dimensions must necessarily operate in a similar way in the others. How do you see yourself at the moment? What combination of the three best represents your approach? Would you be warm, neutral or negative? Would you manage behavior firmly and directly, or would you be loose? What latitude would you allow students in learning tasks?

(*Source:* Soar & Soar (1979); Brophy & Good (1986))

Effective Teachers: How They Are Identified and Studied

In the past decade, rapid strides have been made in teacher effectiveness research, enough so that a beginning picture of effective teaching has begun to emerge. The major strategy through which these findings have developed goes something like this. A large number of classrooms are identified through a sampling strategy that tends to account for variations such as the socioeconomic status of the children attending the schools, geography, and ethnic heritages. The identified classrooms are studied for an extended period of time, typically a school year. Throughout the year, the classrooms are observed systematically with observation systems that focus on teacher behavior, classroom processes, and student behavior. Achievement data are collected at the end of the research period. These achievement measures tend now to be content-valid (rather than standardized tests that might not be sensitive to local goals) and multidimensional. A useful measure of beginning performance also is collected so that the final measures can be adjusted according to entering abilities. Measures of students' personal growth, attitude, creativity, and problem solving are often included in the assessment battery. After the final data on achievement are collected and adjusted according to the entering abilities of the students, the high- and low-achieving classrooms are identified. The researchers then go back to examine the teacher, student, and classroom process data to discover patterns that tend to differentiate between the higher-achieving group of classes and the lower-achieving group of classes. Those patterns of teaching, classroom interactions, and student processes that are associated with the high-achieving classrooms become the elements from which patterns of effective teaching emerge. If similar studies, using slightly different approaches, in different locations, with different students, yield similar results, then one begins to have more confidence in that emerging picture of effective teaching.

Once effective teaching strategies are discovered through the approach described above (most often referred to as the *process-product approach*), the next step in establishing their validity is to test them experimentally. Let's say that one group of teachers is trained at the start of the school year in effective teaching strategies. Another group, matched in most ways to the first group, teaches in the conventional manner. The students in the classes of both groups of teachers are tested both at the start and end of the school year. All the teachers are observed periodically during the year. By observing the teachers, we can tell whether the teachers who received the effectiveness training did indeed teach that way. The student achievement data allows us to know whether students in those teachers' classes learned more and had different attitudes about the subjects than did their counterparts in the conventional classes.

This kind of experimental research has been done several times, and the results have been consistently in favor of the experimental teachers. This indicates that teachers can learn to use effective strategies and, when they do so, the achievement of their students increases (Rosenshine & Stevens, 1986).

The Active Teacher—The Learning Student

The general picture that emerges from 30 years of teacher effectiveness research is that of an actively involved teacher and a consistently engaged, active student. In effective educational settings, students do not work alone without supervision and they do not have long periods of time when they are not working

2.2 Limits on Our Present Understanding

While the status of teacher effectiveness research allows for a cautious optimism and a beginning understanding of effective teaching, the picture is far from complete. As you digest the material in this chapter, you should understand the limits of this research field.

1. A high percentage of research studies have been completed in the elementary school. More studies in the middle and high school are needed, but, the research so far tends to confirm the general results found in the elementary school.

2. Most studies focus on basic achievement in reading and mathematics. These studies should be extended to other subject areas, using a broader range of achievement criteria. To date, however, research done in other subject areas tends to be confirming.

3. Research on teacher effectiveness has adopted a rather standard view of the purpose of schools. The nature of the research seems to accept the notion that school is primarily a place to learn academic skills and knowledge. It is important to keep in mind that any kind of "effectiveness" research must define the criteria by which effectiveness will be judged: and different criteria may produce a different notion of teaching effectiveness.

(Brophy & Good, 1986). Effective teachers frequently use whole-group instruction and well-organized small-group instruction. When students are assigned tasks to work on themselves, the teacher supervises that work carefully. In an effective class, students are seldom passive. They respond often. The pace of the instruction and practice is vigorous, yet within the students' abilities or developmental levels. Eventually, students receive the "message" of this approach to teaching, and they learn to work independently with a sense of purpose. What follows are brief summaries of the major findings from teacher effectiveness research (Smith, 1983; Brophy & Good, 1986; Rosenshine & Stevens, 1986; Evertson, 1989). These findings describe the active teacher and the learning student.

1. *Time, opportunity to learn, and content covered*. Effective teachers intend for students to learn important content. They allocate as much time as possible to that content coverage and provide students with sufficient opportunities to learn. Conversely, they seriously limit time devoted to other than academic objectives.

2. *Expectations and roles*. A teacher's intentions are easily seen in the expectations communicated to students. The effective teacher communicates high, yet realistic expectations for achievement and strong, positive expectations for work involvement. The teacher's and students' roles in this process are carefully defined, and practice time is allowed for students to learn their roles.

3. *Classroom management and student engagement*. Effective teachers are good managers. They establish routines at the start of the school year and generally manage by using these well-developed organizational structures. Rules are established and enforced, often through positive motivational strategies. The effect of such management is to increase time for student engagement in academic activities. Management is predominantly positive. Coercive, negative, or punitive teacher behavior is virtually absent from the effective class.

4. *Meaningful tasks and high success*. Effective teachers arrange for students to be engaged in meaningful activities related to academic objectives. Tasks are suited to the achievement levels of the class and are challenging, yet allow for high success rates.

5. *Pacing and momentum*. Effective teachers create and maintain a strong forward pace to their lessons and prevent events from disrupting that momentum. Tasks are typically broken down into small steps to ensure success, yet teachers pace the class so that students move quickly through these tasks.

6. *Active teaching*. The effective teacher tends to communicate content to students directly instead of depending on curricular materials. Short, effective demonstrations are typically followed by guided student practice in which teachers frequently prompt and check for understanding.

7. *Active supervision*. When guided practice indicates that students understand the tasks and are making few errors, they are shifted to independent practice. This independent practice is actively supervised by the teacher, who monitors progress, maintains an on-task atmosphere, and provides help where needed.

8. *Accountability*. Teachers hold students accountable for completing tasks. A variety of mechanisms, most of them positively oriented, are used for this purpose.

9. *Clarity, enthusiasm, and warmth*. Effective teachers are clear in their presentations, tend to be enthusiastic about the subject matter and their students, and develop and maintain a warm classroom climate in which student attitudes can be positive.

The characteristics of effective educational settings described above are particularly useful and relevant to (a) teaching children, (b) teaching slower or less able students, (c) teaching beginners at any age level, and (d) teaching well-structured subjects in which learning tend to build on learning. It should be noted that much of what physical educators do in their daily work falls into one or more of these categories. What percentage of physical education settings might be characterized by an active teacher and a group of learning students? After comparing the information presented in Chapter 3 with your own experiences, you will have an informed response to that question.

2.3 Active Teaching Results in High Rates of Academic Learning Time

Why is active teaching more successful? Because it results in a group of learning students! In the 1970s and 1980s it became clear that teachers do not directly affect student achievement and attitude. Instead, what they do is directly affect the kinds of activities students engage in. It is the nature of student engagement over time that determines achievement and attitude. One important way of conceptualizing this distinction is the notion of academic learning time (Berlinner, 1979), or *ALT* as it has come to be known. ALT is a unit of time in which students are engaged in tasks related to the class objectives. While they are engaged in this way, they experience consistent success. Students who are consistently and successfully engaged are learning students.

Academic learning time-physical education (ALT-PE) is a unit of time in which a student is engaged in relevant physical education content in such a way that he or she has an appropriate chance to be successful. Appropriate success rate is usually about 80 percent probability of doing the task correctly as it is defined in the lesson. ALT-PE is thought to be a powerful way of evaluating the degree to which teachers perform effectively. In a recent study of teaching physical education, in which over 100 lessons were evaluated, Professor John McLeish (1981, p. 31) concluded that

> It was one of the major impressions received in the use of the ALT-PE system that this supplies the missing element, or indeed, the major component, for evaluating effective teaching in physical education. Time on-task, academic learning time, opportunities to learn—call it what you will, and measure it if you can—this is the vital component of effective teaching in general.

What percentage of total time will your students be engaged in activities in which they have a good chance to be successful?

Active Teaching: A Framework, Not a Method

The characteristics of active teaching presented above do not describe any particular "method" or recipe that requires teachers to adhere specifically to a formula. Rather, they present a framework that has substantial room for individual style and different approaches to teaching content. This framework is described here as *active teaching,* although in other places it is referred to as *direct instruction, systematic teaching, explicit instruction,* or *effective teaching.* Indeed, any method or style that produces high rates of academic learning time and positive student attitudes must be considered as effective. The proof of effectiveness is *not* so much in how the teacher conducts the class, but rather in what the students do in the class.

The framework for effective teaching described above works well in today's schools. Clearly, it is the kind of teaching most often being done in classrooms where students are achieving differentially more and developing good attitudes about their work than students in classrooms where these teaching strategies are not used. This has been a consistent research finding for more than 25 years. On the other hand, the same research field has shown that less formal and less structured approaches tend to produce differentially less achievement among students. Permissiveness, spontaneity, lack of class structure, and student selection of learning goals all tend to be *negatively* correlated with both achievement and attitude. But it must be recognized that this is so because these patterns of teaching *do not usually produce high rates of academic learning time.* The lesson seems clear. It is not that open classroom techniques, informal educational styles, or humanistic education methods are inherently deficient. But it does seem that they must be planned and controlled very carefully to produce high rates of academic learning time.

The techniques of active teaching appear to be easier to master, control, and use on a day-to-day basis in the complex world of today's schools than more complex, exotic teaching methods. There is substantial evidence (Siedentop, 1982; Rosenshine & Stevens, 1986) that both teachers in teacher education as well as teachers on the job can learn and perfect the teaching skills that comprise active teaching. Thus you should feel confident that you can learn to be an active teacher and that you can plan and implement a physical education program in which students learn important content and enjoy their learning.

Effective Management: Necessary but Not Sufficient

It is clear from research that effective teachers are, first of all, effective managers of their classrooms and their students. There are clear indications about what kinds of strategies contribute to the expert management of student behavior. Effective teachers develop clear and unequivocal classroom structures and routines. They take time to carefully teach students all the appropriate ways in which to behave in their educational setting. They typically do this right at the start of the school year. They also provide enough practice for the students to internalize these managerial routines and act accordingly throughout the school year. Questions such as "How do I get the attention of the teacher?", "How and when is it OK to talk with my classmates?", "What do I do if I don't have the right equipment?", and "What do I do if I finish the task early?" are not only answered but also made part of class routines.

Class rules are developed, taught, and practiced—and there is an accountability system tied to them. Teachers prompt rule-related behavior often at the start of the year, and they frequently reinforce students who behave accordingly. Students who break rules are controlled quickly. Effective managers know what is going on in their classes. They have what researcher Jacob Kounin (1970) calls "with-it-ness," a quality that makes students believe that the teacher has "eyes in the back of his/her head."

2.4 Plenty of Perfect Practice

The physical education program at the Adelaide College of Advanced Education in Adelaide, South Australia, uses the phrase "plenty of perfect practice" as a main guideline in its teacher education program. Plenty of perfect practice is realized when practice is

Pertinent: The lessons are appropriate for the abilities, interests, and experiences of students.

Purposeful: Children are kept on task in a climate that is both safe and challenging.

Progressive: Skills are ordered correctly and lead to significant learnings.

Paced: The learning space between one activity and the next in a progression is large enough to be challenging yet small enough for success.

Participatory: As many students are active as much of the time as possible.

It is interesting that the notion of plenty of perfect practice is thoroughly consistent with research on teacher effectiveness; that is, a teacher who provides practice that is pertinent, purposeful, progressive, paced, and participatory will be an effective teacher. The program at Adelaide was not developed from research, but rather from institutions, experience, and just plain common sense of a group of teacher educators in physical education. They certainly have "hit the nail on the head" in a way that many of us would do well to emulate.

Effective teachers tend to develop and maintain these managerial structures positively. The atmosphere of the class is task-oriented, yet warm and happy. Threats, coercion, and strongly punitive actions are almost totally absent from such settings.

However necessary good management is to effective teaching, it is not, in and of itself, sufficient for effective education. Sadly, some physical education teachers manage in precisely the ways described above but then do not really try to teach anything to their students. A well-managed recess or a well-managed recreational period does not constitute an effective physical education.

Effective management has two important purposes. First, it is important for the teacher that the teaching day not be ruined by managerial and behavioral problems. Elementary physical education teachers often teach 7 to 12 classes a day. Middle and secondary school physical educators often teach 5 to 7 classes a day. Stress in teaching is more often associated with managerial and behavioral problems than anything else. Effective management makes life in the gym easier and less stressful for all involved. The second purpose of effective management is to create an optimum amount of time that can be devoted to students' learning. Effective teachers manage well so that they can provide students with more academic learning time. As you gain experience, you will notice that it is possible to achieve the first purpose while neglecting the second purpose.

Achievement and Attitude

What is the relationship between the achievement of students and their attitudes? You might guess that classrooms that are highly task-oriented—ones in which achievement was strong—might produce negative attitudes. However, the evidence doesn't support such a conclusion. In an early review, Medley (1977) found that strategies producing the highest achievement were most often exactly the same ones that produced the best attitudes. Rosenshine (1979) reached the same conclusion in his review of research. He at least hinted at some possible explanations for this phenomenon:

> Classrooms in which students chose their own activities and followed their own interests, were responsible for class planning, and were not dependent on the teacher were also classrooms characterized by rowdiness, shouting, noise, and disorderliness. Permissiveness, spontaneity, and lack of control in classrooms were found to be negatively related not only to gain in achievement but also to positive growth in creativity, skills in inquiry, writing ability, and self-esteem. (Rosenshine 1979, p. 41)

Positive attitudes toward a subject matter and toward oneself are evidently related to educational success. That seems to make sense. We tend to feel better about ourselves in those areas of our life in which we have demonstrated some competence. School is no different. It is difficult for students to grow in self-esteem and improve their self-concepts if they don't learn skills that are valued in the real worlds of the school and the community.

It is also abundantly clear that a strong subject matter focus must be established if achievement gains are to be made. This means quite simply that the teacher must be a skilled manager of time and must devote as much time as possible to the subject matter. Less effective teachers tend to devote too much time to "nonacademic matters," often in the form of informal conversation and discussion in the classroom. The analog for the gymnasium would be time devoted to "free play" or unsupervised, poorly planned kinds of experiences such as certain kinds of skill practice, warm-up time, or games that have no specific educational purpose. Starting late, finishing early, taking too much time for transitions, too much time for management, too much time for non-physical education matters all result in less time to learn the subject matter of physical education. The teacher needs to value achievement, expect students to learn, and try as hard as he or she can to arrange things in the physical education class so that those motivations are translated into high proportions of appropriate learning time for all the students. And this needs to be accomplished without resorting to a negative, punitive atmosphere or managerial style.

Contextual Variations of Active Teaching

The active teaching framework described in this chapter is not a panacea that is to be applied in all cases in exactly the same way. Research has consistently shown that powerful contextual influences modify the main findings about active teaching (Rosenshine & Stevens, 1986). Five contextual factors are sufficiently well documented to merit consideration. They are (1) grade level, (2) the student's socioeconomic status (SES), (3) the student's aptitude or ability level, (4) the teacher's objectives or intentions, and (5) the subject matter being taught.

Age-Related Variations

Clearly, the nature of effective teaching changes as students grow older. Developing explicit classroom management routines typically occupies more time with younger children than with older students. Younger children have not yet learned task persistence, how to delay gratification, or how to be self-controlled in a setting with other learners. Much of their curriculum focuses on basic skills that require careful structuring, repeated practice, and a substantial amount of support and feedback. In higher grades, teachers can attack more complex kinds of learnings and use more divergent kinds of teaching strategies. With older students, clear expectations tied to consistent accountability become more important.

The Educationally Disadvantaged Student

A second contextual factor is the SES of the learner—the so-called educationally disadvantaged student. It should be recognized that "educational disadvantage" does in no way imply "cultural disadvantage." Low SES students often come from rich ethnic and racial backgrounds with strong cultural emphasis. But in terms of the kinds of skills and behaviors necessary to achieve and grow in schools, they often are at a disadvantage. They tend to be less far along in terms of basic school skills such as paying attention, persisting at a task, and delaying gratification. They also may be less far along in terms of the language skills of the predominant mode of culture within society. Along with this they often bring poor attitudes toward school and low self-esteem as learners (this does not mean that they do not have high self-esteem in other aspects of their lives). The combination of poorer, less well-developed academic skills, and less useful attitudes and self-esteem create the need for highly structured educational settings that are considerably more nurturant and supportive than for children who are a bit further along. Thus the positive emotional climate of effective teaching seems to help to bring educationally disadvantaged students along most quickly, along with highly structured settings that require much academic responding and result in consistent, recognizable academic successes.

Student Ability Levels

A third contextual factor is the aptitude or ability level of the student. Low-aptitude learners tend to learn best when the setting is highly structured, requiring many academic responses, with useful academic feedback, all within a highly nurturant climate. High-aptitude learners can benefit better and more quickly from educational strategies that allow for individual work. Aptitude, of course, is often specific to the subject matter being studied. Therefore, a student who has low aptitude in reading might benefit most from a very controlled direct instruction format. In mathematics or physical education, the same student may have high aptitude and thus may be able to profit from strategies that more nearly allow for his or her aptitude to advance as quickly as possible.

Teaching Objectives

The fourth contextual factor is represented in the objectives the teacher is trying to achieve. Obviously, what constitutes effective teaching varies with the teacher's objectives. Achieving specific objectives, such as sport skills, requires exactly the kind of approach described here as active teaching—clear explanations and demonstrations, guided practice, and many opportunities to achieve accuracy and speed in the skill. However, if the teacher doesn't really intend skill development as an objective, but simply wants to create an awareness of what a skill looks like and how it is used in a sport, then a different teaching approach is appropriate. Likewise, if the teacher wants to take time to have students explore the possible ethical and moral dimensions of sport performance, a less structured, less practice-oriented teaching strategy is more appropriate.

The Subject Matter

The fifth contextual factor is the subject matter being taught. As mentioned previously, active teaching is most appropriate for subjects that are structured and hierarchical; that is, subjects where learnings systematically build upon learnings. For example, much of what we know about active teaching has been discovered in the field of mathematics, which is a highly structured subject. But similar results have been found for subjects such as reading and history. As you will see in the next chapter, a great deal of the teacher effectiveness research completed in physical education also supports the general findings for active teaching.

The Learning Student: Providing Opportunities to Respond

It seems abundantly clear that the effectiveness of active teaching stems from the fact that within this strategy students are provided many opportunities to make relevant, successful responses. In the neat phrase coined by our Australian friends (see Box 2.4) students get "plenty of perfect practice." In the classroom, particularly with young children, this is seen in the type and frequency of the questions teachers ask. Effective teachers ask lower-order, factual-type questions that have definite answers, and they ask them frequently. Students, therefore, get to answer many questions, most of them successfully. Stallings and Kaskowitz (1974) called this the *factual question-student response-teacher feedback* cycle. They judged it to be the most important component of effective teaching.

There is no doubt that this strategy has a correlation in physical education. Rink (1985) has called it the *movement task-student response cycle* and describes it as the fundamental unit of analysis for understanding teaching in physical education. Providing students with plenty of perfect practice in a beginning, modified-volleyball unit presents different, and in many cases, more difficult problems for the physical education teacher than a unit in fractions does for the classroom teacher of mathematics. Nonetheless, the research is quite clear that if achieving skills is the goal, then high quantities of repetitive, successful, and relevant practice is the best way to achieve that goal.

Repeated practice is necessary for achieving the kind of mastery students require to actually use the skill in applied settings. This is true for learning fractions in mathematics, and it is true for learning the forearm pass in volleyball. Repeated, successful, relevant practice leads to accuracy and speed, the two necessary components of skilled performance. To be used in applied settings—like games—skills need to reach the level of "automaticity" (Bloom, 1986), where they can be used quickly and accurately according to the changing demands of the setting. It seems to me that this is exactly the level of skill that physical educators need to achieve with their students if they want those students to build lifelong habits of participation. For this purpose, it appears that active teaching is the appropriate strategy.

However, active teaching doesn't necessarily require the teacher to always be in "center stage" and in direct control of student practice. If students are to become lifelong learners and participants, they need to learn how to practice independently. This can be accomplished within the framework of active teaching, but it needs to be addressed carefully and systematically. The general framework of active teaching is teacher demonstration and explanation with students actively responding, followed by teacher-guided practice with prompts and feedback, and, only then, followed by independent student practice with active teacher supervision. The next step in this process is to teach students to practice and learn independently. It is in independent practice that active students begin to assume a role that can contribute to lifelong learning.

Although many educators have goals for the development of independent learners, there are few proven strategies for achieving those goals. Nonetheless, the goal is worthy and widely shared.

> One of the prominent, recurring themes in the history of school reform is that "effective" schooling enables every student to become an *active* learner; one who assumes responsibility for acquiring knowledge and skills and sustains a pattern of self-directed, lifelong learning. (Wang & Palincsar, 1989, p. 71)

There have been many suggested strategies for developing self-directed learner, but little research to establish their validity. Perhaps the most successful among them is student cooperative practice (Slavin, 1980), where students are taught to help each other during independent work and sometimes are even judged on a common product they can produce. Cooperative practice seems to develop the kinds of skills and predispositions that are common among self-directed learners.

Summary

1. Effective teaching in physical education is important not only for fitness and participating in sports, but also because, without it, we are wasting our education dollars.

2. Early research on teaching failed because it focused on teachers' personalities and was unwilling to systematically observe teachers and students.

3. Class climate, management of student behavior, and management of student learning are independent features of educational settings.

4. The turning point for understanding effective teaching was the systematic study, over time, of teachers and students in regular classes.

5. Limits to the present research findings are (1) too little emphasis on middle and secondary schools, (2) too little emphasis on subjects other than reading and mathematics, and (3) a standard view of the purposes of schools.

6. The effective teacher provides maximum time in content; communicates expectations and roles; manages to produce student engagement; designs meaningful, high success tasks; provides a brisk pace to the lesson; actively supervises independent student work; provides consistent accountability; and is clear, warm, and enthusiastic.

7. Active teaching is a framework rather than a specific prescription.

8. Academic learning time occurs when students are engaged in task-related activities at a high success rate.

9. Effective teachers manage by developing class routines and rules that are taught at the start of the school year.

10. Effective management reduces the chances for disruptive behavior and increases time that can be used for academic purposes.

11. Achievement and attitude gains are typically attained together by using effective teaching strategies.

12. Contextual variations include grade level, SES status of learners, aptitude of learners, objectives of the teacher, and the subject being taught.

13. The student is provided sufficient opportunities to respond until learning becomes automatic.

14. While most effective teachers maintain a direct role in the class, it is clear that students can learn to practice independently.

CHAPTER 3

Teaching Effectiveness in Physical Education

Everybody knows something about teaching. For too long, however, expertise has been self-styled, dogma has gone unchallenged, and individual style has been the excuse for a plethora of dull, ineffective, and inadequate teaching behaviors. . . . Certainly, many different words have been used to identify teaching (*teaching, counseling, supervising, helping, intervening, change assisting*), which accounts for the great variety of approaches used in the (observation) instruments developed. Whatever the variables, however, systematic observation provided a formula whereby the teaching act could be placed under microscopic scrutiny for analysis, critique, and refinement.

John Cheffers, *Observing Teaching Systematically (1978)*

CHAPTER OBJECTIVES

To describe the historical development of research on teaching physical education

To describe the main benefits derived from this research field

To explain what research says about how teachers manage students

To explain what research says about how teachers instruct and interact

To explain what research says about how teachers use time

To explain how students spend time in physical education

To explain research results related to ALT-PE

To explain research results related to student responding

To explain research related to teacher improvement in physical education.

To describe the composite picture of teaching effectiveness in physical education

Chapter 2 described and explained what research has shown to be the characteristics of effective classroom teaching in the context of today's schools. The research the information Chapter 2 was developed from was done in real schools with real students—and with all of the problems that beset schools today. Chapter 3 presents a similar description and explanation based on research on teaching physical education (RTPE).

The Background

The RTPE reviewed in this chapter includes only those studies in which the data were obtained through direct or indirect observation of actual instructional episodes (Locke, 1977). This definition excludes some interesting areas, such as research on the backgrounds or beliefs of physical education teachers, so that we can maintain our focus on what is happening in real teaching in real schools.

RTPE based on actual observations of teachers and students is a young field, slightly more than 20 years old. It began with observational studies describing the activities of teachers and students in physical education classes. The prototype for these early studies was the group of research projects undertaken at Teachers College under the direction of Dr. William Anderson. This was later published as a monograph under the now famous title "What's going on in the gym" (Anderson & Barrette, 1978). These studies provided the models and the enthusiasm for many that followed—and for the development of a large number of observation instruments. (An *observation* instrument is a category system for recording the number of events, the amount of time, or both, that teachers and students spend in the behaviors defined by the categories.)

Among the most widely used of the early instruments was the Cheffers Adaptation of the Flanders Interaction Analysis System (CAFIAS). CAFIAS was used in a number of studies done under the direction of Dr. John Cheffers at Boston University. It was followed by a further series of studies using CAFIAS under the direction of Dr. Vic Mancini at Ithaca College.

Most of these early studies were descriptive, using different observation systems as different lenses to provide research pictures of what teachers and students were doing in physical education and what their interactions were like. However, not all the early studies were descriptive only. A series of experimental studies was completed at Ohio State University, mostly aimed at improving the teaching skills of student teachers with various kinds of supervisory interventions (Siedentop, 1981).

In the 1980s research utilizing the Academic Learning Time-Physical Education instrument (ALT-PE) (Siedentop, Tousignant, & Parker, 1982) was widespread. Both descriptive and intervention research was completed using the ALT-PE instrument as the main data collection strategy. So much ALT-PE research was completed during the 1980s that two major reviews could be presented, the first by Dodds and Rife (1983) in the initial monograph published by the *Journal of Teaching in Physical Education* (JTPE) and the second by Metzler (1989).

Early descriptive and experimental research had relied almost exclusively on quantitative methods, but in the 1980s qualitative methods began to be used. By the end of the decade they have become established as an alternative method for coming to know about teaching physical education. A series of qualitative studies has been done at the University of Massachusetts under the direction of Dr. Larry Locke and Dr. Pat Griffin. Quantitative methods depend on numbers, statistics, and graphic pictures of what teachers and students do—rates of feedback, percentages of comments to low-skilled students, amount of time in management, and the like. Qualitative methods depend on thorough, long-term narrative descriptions of what teachers and students do, especially trying to capture the perspectives of those involved in the teaching-learning setting. Qualitative researchers present their results and interpretations with words rather than numbers. Many have suggested that the two approaches, when used carefully together, can add to our growing understanding of teaching and learning in physical education.

Benefits from Research on Teaching Physical Education

Even though the field is still young, benefits have clearly been derived from its youthful productivity (Locke, 1982; Siedentop, 1983; Graham, 1985). A technical language has developed that aids both researchers and practitioners as they try to understand and work with each other. Terms such as *transitions, ALT-PE, desisting, interval recording,* and the *"competent bystander"* have specific meanings that are understood by researchers and, increasingly, by practitioners. A number of valid, reliable observation instruments have been developed, some quite general and others quite specific. These instruments have been cataloged in a text (Zakrajsek, Darst, & Mancini, 1989) and are being used increasingly with students preparing to become teachers (see Chapter 16 for examples).

After more than 20 years a substantial literature exists, both within the United States and internationally. A research journal devoted exclusively to research on teaching in physical education—JTPE—is in its tenth year of publication in 1990. International organizations focusing partially on teaching research meet regularly and publish research and comment (Pieron & Cheffers, 1982). The research literature has gradually become more methodologically sophisticated, focusing on more complex issues.

A main focus of research on teaching in physical education has been classroom management and discipline (Luke, 1989). The results of this research alone—and the management techniques that have been shown to be successful—have begun to change how physical education is taught in schools. Techniques such as time out, behavior games, and contingency contracting are used regularly, both for regular and mainstreamed students (Jansma, French, and Horvak, 1984; McKenzie & Wurzer, 1988).

Materials have been developed that have immediate application in the preparation of new teachers and the inservice education of experienced teachers. Among these are research-based textbooks (Anderson, 1980; Siedentop, 1983; Rink, 1985) and methods texts in which research-based teaching and classroom mangement strategies are featured (Graham, et al., 1987; Siedentop, Herkowitz, & Rink, 1984; Siedentop, Mand, & Taggart, 1987; Gallahue, 1987). Useful training materials have also been produced, notable among them the equity materials developed under the leadership of Dr. Pat Griffin at the University of Massachusetts.

All of this research activity has had an impact on teacher education, too. A new type of teacher educator has been prepared in the last two decades—one who knows the research literature and ways of putting it into use in teacher education programs. Newly certified teachers today are much more likely to know about and have skills in classroom management, discipline, supervision of practice, and other teaching skills than they were 20 years ago. They are also more likely to have been observed systematically as they practiced teaching in schools and had those observations used as feedback to improve their performance.

If there is as much progress in the next 20 years as the last 20, we can look forward enthusiastically and optimistically, expecting that our understanding of the complexities of teaching physical education will expand and grow. We can also look forward to new generations of physical education teachers who not only know more about effective teaching but who also have effective teaching skills when they enter the teaching profession as first-year teachers.

3.1 The Teacher as Ringmaster

The instructional act itself has one pervasive quality—complexity. In full swing, a class of 35 fourth-graders doing a gymnastics lesson is a seething mass of human interactions. Events happen at high speed, with high frequency, in multiple and simultaneous patterns, and take subtle forms. In one recent clip from two minutes of that reality, the following was observed:

Teacher is working one-on-one with a student who has an obvious neurological deficit. She wants him to sit on a beam and lift his feet from the floor. Her verbal behaviors fall into categories of reinforcement, instruction, feedback and encouragement. She gives hands-on manual assistance. Nearby two boys perched on the uneven bars are keeping a group of girls off. Teacher visually monitors the situation but continues work on the beam. At the far end of the gym a large mat, propped up so that students can roll down it from a table top, is slowly slipping nearer to the edge. Teacher visually monitors this but continues work on the beam. Teacher answers three individual inquiries addressed by passing students but continues as before. She glances at a group now playing follow-the-leader over the horse (this is off-task behavior but as she does a student enters and indicates he left his milk money the previous period. Teacher nods him to the nearby office to retrieve the money and leaves the beam to stand near the uneven bars. The boys climb down at once. Teacher calls to a student to secure the slipping mat. Notes that the intruder, milk money now in hand, has paused to interact with two girls in the class and, monitoring him, moves quickly to the horse to begin a series of provocative questions designed to reestablish task focus.

That was only 120 seconds out of the 17,000 the teacher spent that day in active instruction. No description fits this picture of complexity so well as Smith's concept of the teacher as ringmaster (Smith & Geoffrey, 1969). Surrounded by a flow of activity, the ringmaster monitors, controls, and orchestrates, accelerating some acts, terminating others, altering and adjusting progress through the program, always with an eye for the total result.

Source: Locke, L. The ecology of the gymnasium: What the tourists never see. *Proceedings of SAPECW,* Spring 1975. (ERIC Document Reproduction Service No. ED 104 823)

What Teachers Do in Physical Education

How much time do teachers spend in various activities? What behaviors do they exhibit? To what do they devote their attention? Results from a large number of descriptive studies tend to produce a fairly uniform picture of the typical physical education teacher. Three major functions occupy most of the attention of physical educators as they teach: managing students, directing and instructing students, and monitoring/supervising students.

Managing refers to verbal or nonverbal teacher behavior that is emitted for purposes of organizing, changing activities, directions about equipment and/or formations, and taking care of class routines, as well as all nonacademic activities, such as collecting permission slips, taking roll, and the like. *Transitions* are management episodes that deal with the movement of students among the various activities within a lesson. Research shows that 15–35 percent of class time is typically devoted to management (Luke, 1989; McLeish, 1985), with the average being 25 percent for elementary classes and 22 percent for secondary classes. These are startlingly high figures! Teachers manage the start and end of class, the transitions within a lesson, the moving of equipment, and such things. These managerial episodes are typically devoid of learning time for students.

Management is typically high in some activity units, such as team games and gymnastics, and typically lower for others, such as aerobics. Elementary classes often have slightly higher management times, probably because there are more activities requiring more transitions. When counting teacher behavior rather than tracking time, research indicates that about 60 percent of managerial behaviors are substantive, related to the lesson activity, while 40 percent are nonsubstantive, related to social or procedural issues.

Most studies indicate that disruptive behavior is infrequent in physical education classes, although minor kinds of off-task behavior are far more frequent. Physical education teachers seem to control off-task behavior primarily by responding to it with reprimands (Stewart, 1980). Reprimands are of two types. *Nags* are low-intensity reprimands such as "keep that line straight," "listen-up over there," "John, be quiet," or "Sh'h." *Nasties* are harsher, more punitive reprimands in which the teacher shows some anger and temper. Nags tend to outnumber nasties by about a 20:1 ratio (Quarterman, 1977). There is no evidence that nagging students reduces their off-task behavior more than momentarily.

A second large chunk of class time is devoted to teachers instructing students. This would include demonstrations, explanations, group feedback, and closure episodes. Pieron (1980) has suggested that teachers spend about one-third of their time managing and about one-third instructing. It should be noted that, if this is true, then two-thirds of class time has no practice opportunities for students. Research clearly shows that most physical education teachers use direct styles of teaching, keeping control of the instructional and managerial functions themselves. Instruction can account for anywhere from 10–50 percent of class time. The great variation in instruction is due to two factors. First, instruction in classes like aerobics is minimal: the activity being done affects the amount of instruction necessary. Second, and more important, the amount of instruction varies across the duration of a unit (Metzler, 1980). Instructional time is typically high at the start of a unit and low toward the end of a unit, when students are more likely to be engaged in culminating activities.

Table 3.1 Teacher Behavior as Described by Two Systems

Flanders System		McLeish System	
Accepts feelings	1.5%	Positive affect	1.7%
Praises	4.2	Negative affect	2.0
Accepts ideas	1.5		
Criticizes	.6		
		Compared To	
Lectures	25.0%	Commands	30.0%
Directs	25.0	Controls	22.0

The third large chunk of teacher time in physical education is spent in monitoring and supervising students as they practice. *Monitoring* refers to passively observing students. *Supervising* refers to behaviors that attempt to keep students on-task, such as moving about the perimeter of a class and scanning the whole class frequently. During student practice time, teachers also provide feedback to students, both in terms of their organizational/social behavior and their performance.

It appears that monitoring and supervising account for 20–45 percent of teacher time in physical education. Of all aspects of teaching physical education, less is known about what actually happens and what functions teacher behavior serves during this time. Teacher effectiveness research has shown that actively supervising students' independent practice is crucial to strong academic outcomes. Clearly, when students know that a teacher is supervising practice closely, they tend to keep on task. Monitoring no doubt can serve to fulfill this important function, especially if it is done in appropriate ways. But there is no evidence in physical education research concerning how much of this large chunk of time is spent in productive supervision rather than simply standing in one place and occasionally glancing at students.

Teachers do interact with students during monitoring/supervision time. *Behavioral interactions* refer to those directed at the organizational or social behavior of students. *Skill interactions* refer to those directed at the academic performance of students. Teacher interactions that serve to guide and direct student behavior but that are not directly in response to previous student behavior are usually called *directions* or *prompts*. Teacher behavior that is in response to student actions is usually called *feedback*. All feedback interactions can be divided into those that are *general* and those that have *specific* information content. Feedback can be further subdivided among those that are *positive*, *corrective*, and *negative*. Descriptive research has provided the following general picture of the feedback patterns of physical education teachers.

1. Feedback tends to occur with reasonable frequency, often at the rate of 30–60 events per 30 minutes of teaching (Quarterman, 1977; Fink & Siedentop, 1989).

2. Feedback is more frequently general than specific.

3. Feedback is most frequently corrective, rather than positive or negative.
4. Behavior feedback is typically in the form of nags, while positive behavior feedback is rare.
5. Skill feedback occurs more frequently during skill practice than during game or scrimmage conditions (Ormand, 1988). Interventions during game/scrimmage activities are more likely to be short duration prompts.
6. Feedback is typically directed toward an individual rather than a group or the class as a whole (Fishman & Tobey, 1978).
7. Very little teacher feedback follows patterns of effective praise as detailed by Brophy (1981).

For skill feedback to be effective, it has to be accurate; that is, when a teacher tells a student what he or she did correctly or incorrectly, the teacher must have accurately diagnosed the student's performance (Hoffman, 1977). There is little descriptive evidence concerning the degree to which physical education teachers provide accurate or inaccurate feedback to their students. However, it can be assumed that to provide accurate feedback, the teacher would have to know the skill well enough to accurately discriminate the presence or absence of critical skill elements in the student's performance. All of the related evidence suggests that most teachers do not have this kind of discriminatory capability (Biscan & Hoffman, 1976; Kniffen, 1986; Wilkinson, 1987; Halverson, 1988). This finding suggests that all research about skill feedback needs to be interpreted carefully, because the feedback may not always be accurate.

The research evidence focusing on teacher accountability for student performance is limited, but what there is suggests that students are typically held accountable for minimal levels of "trying," rather than for performance in sport and fitness (Tousignant & Siedentop, 1983). Physical education teachers consistently hold students accountable for attendance, for dressing in the right uniform, and for non-disruptive behavior, but not always for learning to do the subject matter better. It appears that when there is accountability for skill performance, students respond more often and more accurately (Alexander, 1982; Lund, 1990).

It is not always easy to know whether it is the teacher or the students who set the "tone" or climate of a class—no doubt both contribute. However, it is fair to suggest that the teacher is the professional responsible for establishing a productive educational climate. Classroom research (Soar & Soar, 1979) has indicated that both positive and neutral class climates can be educationally productive but that negative emotional climates are unproductive. While there is little research evidence to support a contention that physical education classes are strongly negative, there is equally little evidence that class climates are typically positive. In fact, several researchers have commented on the clear lack of positive affect in the classes they studied.

By comparison with the total recorded teacher behaviors, virtually no acceptance of student feelings and ideas, praise or questioning behaviors were recorded...the use of sympathetic-empathetic behavior was almost nonexistent. (Cheffers & Mancini, 1978, pp. 46-47)

Taking the 104 lessons as a group, the broad impression conveyed to this observer is that there is very little concern with the most basic principle of learning theory—that positive reinforcement (by successful performance in the first place and by encouragement, praise, and constructive guidance by the teacher) provides a guarantee that the desired behavior will be elicited in future performance. There is a noticeable absence of positive affect in these lessons. (McLeish, 1981, p. 30)

McLeish's research employed two quite different observation systems. The percentages of teacher behavior from each of the two systems are presented in Table 3.1 to show the contrast he found between teacher behaviors that might produce a positive climate and those that might, at best, result in a neutral climate. While it is no doubt true that most physical education teachers see themselves as warm, caring persons, there is little evidence that those feelings are apparent in their daily teaching behavior.

In summary, the typical physical education teacher spends a great deal of time and behavior organizing and managing students, presenting information to students, and then monitoring and supervising them during practice. Interactions are typically of short duration and corrective, both for social/organizational behavior and for student performance. There is no evidence for a positive emotional climate in the gym, but there is no strong evidence that the gym is a punitive, coercive place, either. The evidence suggests that the climate is predominately neutral and that teacher-initiated interactions are typically corrective.

What Students Do in Physical Education

Research evidence about student behavior in physical education is of two varieties: time based and response based. Perhaps the most startling aspect of RTPE is the low percentage of time students are actually engaged in motor activity within a physical education class. Naturally, students cannot be in motor activity 100 percent of the time. There are managerial chores to accomplish, equipment to change, transitions from place to place, and instructions to be received. But one would expect that, in a physical education class, students would be engaged in motor activities a fairly high percentage of the available time. In fact, they are seldom engaged in motor activities more than 30 percent of the time. Their functionally effective time involvement is even less than that. What are they doing, if they aren't engaged in some sport or fitness activity? They are most likely waiting for something to happen!

The term *waiting* refers to time prior to, between, and after instructional, managerial, and practice activities—time when students are not involved as they wait for the next event to occur. When students are in "wait time," they are doing nothing that contributes to the goals of a lesson—and, far too often, they may be tempted to engage in off-task or disruptive behavior. Waiting typically accounts for 20–30 percent of student time in physical education. This amount of waiting represents the teacher's inability to organize and manage to keep students productively involved in the lesson. This problem in physical education teaching was recognized early and has been a consistent finding.

> The organizational ability of the teachers probably also contributed to the large percentage of time that students waited. For example, during the coding of student behavior for almost 300 clock hours, it was evident that some teachers had trouble organizing groups for an activity, making maximum use of available equipment, and moving groups from one area to another. (Costello & Laubach, 1978, p. 18)

Students also spend a large chunk of time doing managerial tasks—from roll taking, to organization for practice, to choosing teams, to transitioning from place to place—and changing activities and equipment within a lesson. Management typically accounts for 15–20 percent of student time in a lesson. Managing effectively in physical education is not easy because large spaces, large classes, and a subject matter in which students move around a lot. But the managerial chores are not insurmountable, and the evidence suggests that physical education teachers often do not utilize effective managerial skills.

Students also spend a large chunk of class time receiving information—directions, organizational information, descriptions of skills, plans for a drill, lectures about safety or good behavior, or descriptions of a game. The research data suggest that 15–30 percent of student time is spent listening to the teacher in a whole-class or group format. While some amount of time must be spent conveying accurate information to students, it is clear that teachers often spend too much time talking to their classes, losing valuable opportunities to engage them more actively in the subject matter.

The fourth chunk of student time is spent in motor engagement in the subject matter—practicing skills, playing in games, doing fitness activities. Time when students are involved in motor behavior has been described in several related ways—*engaged time, motor engaged time, active learning time, functional time* and *ALT-PE*. What we have here are two kinds of student motor involvement, and the difference between the two kinds of involvement is crucial for learning. One kind of time involvement is implied by the terms *engaged time, motor engaged time,* or *active learning time*. This kind of time would be counted whenever a student was physically involved with lesson activities, no matter what the nature of that involvement. The second kind of time—designated as ALT-PE or functional time (Metzler, 1989)—occurs when a student is engaged in lesson activities in such a way that success is likely to occur. It is this second kind of time— high-success, engaged time most widely known as ALT—that is strongly related to achievement.

Research has shown that there are large ranges of student engaged time, as low as 10–15 percent to as high as 70–80 percent of class time. The average amount of engaged time is 25–30 percent (Anderson, 1978; Pieron, 1980; Metzler, 1979; Rate, 1980). But the amount of engaged time that is actually *functional* for learning is always lower, sometimes a great deal lower. When only ALT-PE time is reported, an average class of students gets no more than 10–20 percent of class time in functional engagement in activity (Metzler,

3.2 The Funnel Effect in Student Engaged Time

Teachers often plan a certain amount of time for students to be engaged in lesson activities. They also no doubt expect that most of that engaged time will be functional for their learning. But time planned by the teacher does not always translate well into functional learning time for the student. This can be seen in the three kinds of time described below and how time is lost in what Metzler (1980) called the "funneling effect."

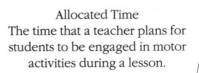

Allocated Time
The time that a teacher plans for students to be engaged in motor activities during a lesson.

Engaged Time
The time a student is actually physically engaged in the activities.

ALT–PE

What is important for student learning is the amount of time at the bottom of this funnel. When engaged time is far less than allocated time, the teacher usually has a problem managing and organizing students. When ALT-PE is far less than engaged time, the teacher has problems with designing activities in which students can experience success.

(Source: Adapted from Metzler 1979)

1989). Research has shown the following to be true for this important kind of learning time.

1. Teachers tend to produce widely varied amounts of ALT-PE based on activity, with fitness and dance highest, individual sports next, and team sports and gymnastics lowest.
2. Elementary students get more ALT-PE than do middle or senior high students.

3. Girls and boys get about the same amount of ALT-PE.
4. Low-skilled students get substantially less ALT-PE than do middle- or high-skilled students.
5. Students with disabilities that are mainstreamed get less ALT-PE than do regular students (Aufderheide, 1983).
6. Students get more ALT-PE toward the end of a unit than in the beginning.
7. ALT-PE can be substantially increased through improving managerial effectiveness (Birdwell, 1980).

The second major method for focusing on what students do in physical education is to observe each response they make, producing a response-based record rather than a time-based record. There has not been nearly as much response-based research as time-based research; however, that which has been completed shows a picture much like that of the time-based research. Response-based research has focused primarily on the nature of the learning responses that students make in physical education and how those responses relate to learning outcomes. The research allows for the following statements.

1. Generally, low-skilled students make fewer responses per unit of time than do medium-or high-skilled students and have a much lower percentage of successful responses.
2. In game settings, low-skilled students very seldom make responses that are either appropriate in form or successful in the context of the game (Parker, 1984; Brown, 1986).
3. Student response rates are substantially higher when accountability measures for performance are applied (Alexander, 1982; Lund, 1990).
4. Students often modify the tasks teachers ask them to do in order to make the tasks easier to do or more challenging (Tousignant & Siedentop, 1983).
5. Students learn best when they get more opportunity to practice the kinds of tasks they will be tested on (Pieron, 1983; Silverman, 1985).
6. Even when student responding is successful in the context of an assigned activity task, the physical form of that response is most likely to be inappropriate (Son, 1989), especially for low-skilled students.

In summary, students in physical education classes spend most of their time waiting for the next portion of class to begin, performing management activities, and receiving information from their teacher. The amount of time spent engaged in task-related motor activities is low, and the amount of that engaged time that is successful is even lower. Student motor responses are often inappropriate in form, even though they are sometimes successful in the context of the assigned task. Low-skilled students seldom make motor responses that are both appropriate in form and successful, especially in game situations. If appropriate and successful motor responding is the "right stuff" for a successful physical education—and there is every reason to believe that it is—then RTPE suggests that the "right stuff" is far too often missing in physical education classes.

3.3 The "Right Stuff" for Learning in Physical Education!

Research evidence suggests that student motor responses that are appropriate in form and successful are the ones that contribute to learning. "Appropriate in form" does not mean that responses are technically perfect, but only that the major critical elements of a performance are seen and no major errors are made—what we call a "working form" (one that if continued will lead eventually to skillfulness). Success is always judged in the context of the task as assigned by the teacher. A drill always has a goal; if it is achieved, then it is "successful." In a game, if the response allows the game to continue or scores a point, it is a successful response.

Here is a useful and interesting learning exercise for you! Watch a physical education class. Pick out a low-skilled and high-skilled student. Observe each motor response they make and judge it in terms of the appropriateness of the form displayed and the success of the response. Then record each response in one of the four categories: (a) appropriate-successful, (b) appropriate-unsuccessful, (c) inappropriate-successful, or (d) inappropriate-unsuccessful. The total number of responses in the appropriate-successful category will give you a good indication of the value of that class for a particular student and begin to help you to understand whether students in that class are getting the "right stuff."

Evidence about Teacher Improvement and Its Effects

While the evidence from descriptive research on teachers and students in physical education does not present a consistently optimistic picture, the evidence on teacher improvement and its effects is more hopeful. There is substantial evidence that teachers can develop effective teaching skills during their preservice preparation (Siedentop, 1986). There is also evidence that physical education teachers on the job can improve their teaching skills and that when they do, their students get substantially more ALT-PE (Birdwell, 1980). Finally, there is also evidence that student teachers can improve markedly with appropriate supervision and that when they do, their students experience more ALT-PE (Siedentop, 1981; Hutslar, 1977; Cramer, 1977; Randall & Imwold, 1989).

The bulk of this evidence suggests the following conclusions about teacher improvement and its effects.

1. Teachers in training can develop effective teaching skills if they get adequate practice and supervision.
2. Teachers on the job can improve their teaching skills and when they do, their students get more ALT-PE.
3. Student teachers can improve their interactive teaching skills and the behavior of their students (less management time, more ALT-PE, fewer disruptions) if they get adequate supervision.

4. Both preservice and inservice teachers can learn learn positive interaction styles.

5. Both preservice and inservice teachers can learn to provide more specific skill feedback.

6. Preservice teachers can learn to discriminate critical elements and common errors in a variety of sport skills.

7. Both preservice and inservice teachers can reduce management time significantly.

8. Both preservice and inservice teachers can learn to become more enthusiastic in their teaching (Rolider, Siedentop, & Van Houten, 1984).

9. Direct intervention on improving ALT-PE with preservice teachers can result in marked increases in student ALT-PE (Randall & Imwold, 1989).

It seems clear that women and men preparing to become physical education teachers can develop effective teaching skills if they are provided knowledge about those skills, the opportunity to practice them, and systematic feedback about their progress. The evidence about improvement of inservice teachers suggests that developing of effective skills can begin during teacher education and continue throughout a professional career in teaching. Of all the research that has been completed, this certainly has to be the most hopeful.

Effective Physical Education Teaching

One way to assess the general level of effectiveness in physical education teaching is to take the profile of the active teacher and learning student described in Chapter 2 and compare it with the descriptive research reviewed earlier in this chapter. As you will see, those comparisons do not allow us to conclude that physical education teaching, in general, is done effectively.

1. *Time, opportunity, and content covered*. Students in physical education do not get sufficient opportunity to practice skills, especially in a success-oriented fashion.

2. *Expectations and roles*. While the physical education research is thin on this point, the general picture of a class that emerges is not one in which high expectations for learning could be attributed.

3. *Classroom management and student engagement*. Physical education teachers spend far too much time managing, and students spend far too much time waiting. This results in lowered activity-engagement rates.

4. *Meaningful tasks and high success*. Practice tasks and games in physical education tend to be too difficult for many students. Low-skilled students seldom experience success.

5. *Pacing and momentum*. The consistent findings on student-waiting time eliminates the possibility for brisk pacing and consistent momentum.

6. *Active teaching*. Physical education teachers tend to teach directly without a strong reliance on curriculum materials, but guided student practice is less evident, and teacher presentations tend to take too much time.

7. *Active supervision*. The evidence very strongly suggests that student practice is not supervised adequately and that students are shifted to independent practice before they are ready or able to profit from it.

8. *Accountability*. There is little evidence to suggest accountability for subject matter outcomes (sport skills, fitness, and so forth), but there is accountability for attendance, dress, and non-disruptive behavior.

9. *Clarity, enthusiasm, and warmth*. While there is little evidence about the degree to which physical education teachers are clear in their directions, the evidence cited above suggests that in the typical physical education class, there is little enthusiasm or warmth.

This pessimistic review does not mean that *all* physical education teachers teach ineffectively. It should also be recognized that many physical education teachers work under conditions that are less than favorable for effective teaching. However, we cannot ignore what the descriptive evidence implies about the general level of teaching in our subject field. Fortunately, there is also evidence from research specifically intended to evaluate and assess effective teaching in physical education—and that evidence is more optimistic.

The evidence about effective teaching in physical education comes from four sources: the teacher improvement research cited above; descriptive studies aimed at assessing effectiveness as it exists in schools (McLeish, 1981; Phillips & Carlisle, 1985); small-scale studies aimed at assessing effectiveness experimentally (Pieron, 1981; DeKnop, 1983, 1986; Silverman, 1985); and recent studies aimed at examining the work of teachers who had been identified as effective (Siedentop, 1989). While this is not a large body of research, the studies completed tend to show that an effective physical education teacher performs in ways that are remarkably similar to his or her classroom counterpart.

McLeish and his colleagues' analysis (Howe & Jackson, 1981) categorized 104 physical education lessons into best (n = 18), average (n = 48) and poor (n = 38). It indicated that the major determining factors distinguishing the best from the poor were higher rates of appropriate learning time and lower rates of waiting time. Time spent in a knowledge focus did not discriminate among the three groups. McLeish reached the following conclusion:

> The theoretical basis of the ALT-PE system is what is now conventionally referred to as *learning theory*. By this we mean that we accept as established fact certain basic principles: (1) that learning is maximized in direct proportion to the number and type of opportunities to learn; (2) we learn best by concentrating on practicing the motor, cognitive, or psychomotor skill by actually doing; or (3) by observing others performing the skill. There is (4) no advantage to be gained in practicing the skill at a difficulty level which results in a level of failure rate greater than 10 percent. Effective teaching means structuring the lesson to maximize the amount of time in direct practice by each individual at a level which at once ensures a continuing development of the skill compatible with the minimal number of mistakes. (McLeish, 1981, p. 29)

These results and conclusions are very similar to those found in classroom research. Phillips and Carlisle (1983) studied 18 teachers and their students, concluding that learning outcomes were most dramatically related to the specific motor engagement rates of the students. Engaged skill learning time and success time were three times as great in the more effective classes.

Similar results have been found in small-scale studies designed to assess teaching effectiveness experimentally. Pieron (1983) found that students learned best when they had the most chance to practice the tasks they would be tested on. Tasks related to but different from those criterion tasks contributed as much to student learning. Silverman (1985) concluded that the number of practice trials students got and the difficulty level of those trials were most strongly related to learning, more so than the amount of time students were engaged in skill practice.

A group of faculty and students from Ohio State studied seven effective elementary physical education specialists for an entire school year (Siedentop, 1989). They found that the teaching practices of these seven looked remarkably similar to the active teacher-learning student characteristics described in Chapter 2 and above. These seven teachers clearly intended that their students learn and made those intentions clear, particularly through the way they managed students and provided substantial amounts of ALT-PE for them. The average ALT-PE in their classes was more than 45 percent, about three times higher than the average shown from descriptive research (Eldar, Siedentop, & Jones, 1989). These teachers also spent a great deal of time developing gymnasium routines at the start of the school year and then used those routines to keep classes running smoothly and efficiently, another common strategy of effective classroom teachers (Fink & Siedentop, 1989). Student practice was always supervised carefully and students were held accountable, mostly through informal mechanisms, for learning the skills and strategies they were being taught.

In summary, the research on effective physical education teaching confirms that the strategies that produce differentially higher learning outcomes in the classroom are those that do so in the gymnasium, too. It would be very useful to us all if this kind of research were to expand in the future, giving us more detail about how effective physical education teachers cope with the many problems that confront them daily in their work.

Summary

1. Research on teaching physical education is only 20 years old, but has produced a substantial body of knowledge from descriptive, interventionist, and qualitative research.

2. Benefits from this research field include the development of a technical language, a growing literature, a set of managerial techniques, research-based texts and training materials, and different approaches to teacher-education, as well as a new breed of teacher educator.

3. Teachers spend a substantial amount of time managing students, lesser time instructing them, and a major portion of time supervising their practice.

4. The emotional climate of physical education is typically neutral, with a definite lack of positive affect.

5. Teacher feedback is frequent, general rather than specific, corrective rather than positive, and typically directed toward individuals rather than groups.

6. The indirect evidence suggests that much skill feedback may not be completely accurate.

7. Students spend the largest amount of time waiting, with the next largest amount of time in managerial tasks, and the smaller amount engaged in subject-matter activities.

8. Functional student time (ALT-PE) is even less than engaged time and typically lower still for students with disabilities or low-skilled students.

9. Response-based research shows a similar picture, with low-skilled students seldom making technically appropriate and successful responses.

10. Teachers in preparation can improve their teaching skills if they get adequate supervision and practice.

11. Teachers on the job can improve their skills, and when they do, their students tend to get higher amounts of ALT-PE.

12. Both preservice and inservice teachers can improve management, instruction, and interaction skills, as well as become more enthusiastic in their teaching.

13. The research on teaching in physical education provides a profile that is substantially at odds with the characteristics of effective teaching.

14. Research on effective teaching in physical education indicates that it is very similar to results from classroom teaching: effective teachers provide an environment that is focused on learning and managed well.

CHAPTER 4

Learning about, Assessing, and Improving Teaching

Teaching makes only the difference it can make; it is not magic. Teaching is vital because it is the only factor we really can do much about in the short run. It is impossible to change a student's heredity, and socioeconomic conditions change only slowly over generations. The quality of teaching, on the other hand, can make an immediate difference. . . . A small but substantial portion of what any student achieves in the gymnasium is a consequence of what we do as teachers. It is now possible to find out which behaviors are effective and how they work. It is possible to learn from teaching.

Larry Locke, (1979)

CHAPTER OBJECTIVES

To distinguish between assessment and evaluation

To explain reliable, valid assessments

To distinguish among teacher process, student process, and student outcome variables for assessment of teaching

To describe how the basic assessment model is used

To explain how and why assessment must be related to goals

To distinguish among discrete teacher/student behavior, teaching units, and criterion process variables

To distinguish between ALT and OTR as criterion process variables

To respond to common concerns about assessment of teaching To describe and distinguish among steps in the assessment process

Chapter 1 emphasized the distinction between knowing about effective teaching and knowing how to teach effectively. Another important issue was also discussed—that of wanting to teach well, of being motivated to improve your teaching. The information in Chapters 2 and 3 provided an overview of the strategies effective teachers use and the characteristics that define effective classes, along with a review of research on teaching physical education. Research on effective teaching provides a frame of reference you can compare your own efforts against to become an effective teacher. Chapter 4 focuses on concepts and strategies that will allow you to learn about your teaching, to assess your teaching, and to improve it as well.

The more and better information you can get about your own teaching behavior and the behavior of the students you are teaching, the easier it will be for you to improve. In sports, coaches have long known that players need regular assessment to improve. Players, too, come to understand that and seek information about their performance. For example, basketball coaches regularly assess performance in practice and games—shooting percentages, turnovers, rebounds, steals, assists, and the like.

They also might utilize videotape to "grade" the defensive performance of each player or to assess how the team executed the offense. This information helps players to know what aspects of the game they have to work on, and it allows them to have some sense of how their own efforts compare to those of teammates and other players. While teaching is *not* a game in which there are winners and losers, it is clear that information about what goes on during a class can help a teacher understand the class better and improve its performance, which means that students will learn more and enjoy it better.

The Purpose and Nature of Assessment

Part of this chapter is about assessment concepts and strategies. Unfortunately, for most of us, assessment has too often meant comparison against others for the purpose of grading. I intend that *assessment* be taken to mean the collection of reliable, valid information for improving performance. In this sense, I would distinguish between assessment and *evaluation,* which I take to imply making a judgment about the worth of a performance. Good assessment should occur regularly throughout teacher education. Evaluation has to occur also, because grades need to be turned in. Information developed through assessment may eventually become part of an evaluation. The difference, however, is that the immediate purpose of assessment is to help someone improve her or his performance.

In order to assess your teaching skills, you first of all must be in a situation where you actually teach. While this sounds straightforward, there still persist some notions that performance on quizzes or tests *about* effective teaching is an assessment of teaching itself. Knowledge about effective teaching is important, but a written assessment in the form of a quiz or exam doesn't provide any information about how well you can teach any more than a written test about basketball can provide an assessment of your playing skills.

It should be made equally clear that no single assessment of teaching gives a complete picture. Similarly, no individual statistic from a basketball game allows assessment of play, nor does the data from one game give a fair picture of a player's abilities. Several indicators of effectiveness are needed before a complete picture begins to emerge. Likewise, multiple assessments over a period of time are necessary to provide a fair and accurate assessment of the educational effectiveness of a class.

For assessment to be useful, the information generated must be good. What makes information good? First of all, it must be *reliable*—which means there is some assurance that what happened actually did happen! For example, if a classmate or instructor observes your teaching for the number and length of managerial episodes (an individual episode of management that is measured by its duration), you want to be sure when the observation is completed that both the number of episodes and their durations were reliable estimates of what really happened during the class. If an observer misses one or two episodes and codes the length of episodes inaccurately, then the information presented will be unreliable. Chapter 16 provides methods for ensuring that observational data are reliable.

Good information is also *valid*—which means that measure chosen for observation truthfully represents the concept or skill you are trying to assess. For example, what would you choose to observe if you were trying to provide assessment information for a teacher about the degree to which a class climate was positive, neutral, or negative? Would you code instances of behavior praise, nags, and nasties? Would you count the number of times the teacher smiled or joked with students? Would you give the students a short paper-and-pencil assessment on their perceptions of the class? What kind of measure would give you valid information about class climate? In this example, the answer is not obvious; an important debate about what constituted valid measures of class climate could easily occur.

Obviously, the more narrowly and behaviorally a concept can be defined, the higher will be its *face validity*. If you want to assess the frequency of corrective feedback, and do so by counting the number of instances that a teacher watches a student perform a skill and then gives the student specific information about an error made during the performance, you will have achieved a high level of face validity in your assessment of corrective feedback. On the other hand, if you wanted a valid assessment of the quality of corrective feedback, you would have do something more than just count the number of times it occurred. You would have to make judgments about the degree to which the information provided by the teacher was accurate and related to the student's performance.

Effective teaching requires using a repertoire of skills and applying them to the unpredictably changing demands of an educational setting. It is not yet possible to assess completely the full range of skills needed for effective performance. But this is no reason not to assess specific skills when and where you can. The more good information you have about your teaching, the more you will understand it. The more specific the information is, the more you will be able to improve.

An Assessment Model

Three assessment categories are suggested here. The first category consists of *teacher process variables*. These include teaching skills such as giving instructions, questioning, providing feedback, stopping misbehaviors, and praising appropriate behavior. Teacher process variables also include strategies for organizing the class, managing behavior, helping students make transitions, and dealing with intrusions into the flow of an activity. Teacher process variables relate directly to the teacher's performance and are measured by direct observation of the teacher while he or she is teaching.

A second assessment category consists of *student process variables*. These variables begin to shift attention away from the teacher and toward the learner. Student process variables relate to those actions performed by students that potentially contribute to or detract from learning. Examples of such variables include the amount of time it takes for students to move from one place to another, the level of misbehavior in a class period, the amount of appropriate learning time an individual student gets in a 40-minute period, the number of skill attempts a squad gets during a volleyball lesson, the percentage of time a class is

4.1 Observing Teaching: Supervision Is More Than Sight-seeing

Traditionally, the observation of teaching has been little more than an infrequent visit to a school, a short time watching the teaching intern, perhaps some nonspecific summary comments afterward, and a brief and too often meaningless period of chit-chat to conclude the visit. This supervision method—if you can call it a method— is what I refer to as *eyeballing*. This method is inadequate even for those who have enormous experience and a very heightened capacity for intuitive judgments about teaching. Good observation requires some data collection—our intuitive sense of what is going on in the gymnasium is not often sufficiently specific or precise to provide useful feedback for the teacher. The teacher is trying hard—the observer should try hard, too.

Anecdotal records in the form of detailed note taking, rating scales, and checklists can be helpful. The rating scales and checklists are easy to do, but the information they provide is less than precise and not often sufficiently specific for teachers to improve from session to session.

Observations are best done with a system developed for the specific purpose of the teaching episode. These involve counting time, behaviors, and instances of analytic units. Chapter 16 describes many kinds of observation systems. Observation can be done by peers, by an instructor, or by a cooperating teacher (or by you, if the session is videotaped.) Wouldn't you like to know what you are doing—specifically? Without such information, you are much less likely to improve.

on task during a lesson, and the amount of time students spend receiving information. These variables are linked directly to learning. Student process variables are measured through direct observation of students while they are in class. A third assessment category consists of *student outcome variables,* or student *product* variables. Such variables indicate student achievement, changes in learners that are considered to be evidence of learning and growth. Generally speaking, these variables are typically more familiar to physical educators than the preceding two categories because they consist of increased skill, better game-playing ability, higher levels of fitness, increased knowledge about the subject matter, and improved attitudes toward physical education. Such variables are most often assessed by tests or other evaluation instruments, ususally at the end of a teaching unit. But there are also other forms of outcome or product evaluation, such as the achievement of objectives, the completion of designated tasks, the reaching of criterion levels of performance, and direct observation of performance on a regular basis.

It is useful to consider the differences between short-term outcome measures and long-term outcome measures. Long-term outcome measures are much more difficult to assess, but they may provide valuable information relative to the overall goals of a physical education program. Physical education has always been concerned with "carry-over" values such as fitness, participation in leisure

4.2 What Counts for Success in Long-Term Assessment of Student Outcomes?

Educators are usually quite adept at measuring short-term student outcomes. Quizzes, exams, fitness tests, skill tests, estimates of game play, and estimates of social behavior are all used to assess students, most often so that grades can be turned in. Educators also often express a concern for long-term student outcomes but seldom take the time to think about them and what they mean for how classes should be planned and conducted.

Let's assume that you are a middle school physical education teacher and you want to assess long-term outcomes for the three years you have students in your school. How would you do it? What *indicators* would you choose as evidence for success in your physical education program? Which of the following would or would not fit your notion of success?

- Students participate in out-of-school cardiovascular fitness activities. Students sign up for intramural sport competition.
- Students try out for interschool sport teams.
- Students seek opportunities to participate in community youth sport programs.
- Students watch less television.
- Students maintain healthy eating habits.
- Students attend sport contests more frequently.
- Students are more intelligent sport spectators.
- Students exhibit appropriate sports behavior when they compete.

Are there indicators on this list you disagree with? Are there indicators that you want to add? How would *your* list affect your program planning?

activities, and proper sportsmanship habits. Many of these cannot be evaluated fairly in the short term simply because their long-term strength gives evidence of the degree to which a program has achieved its goals.

The basic assessment model is shown in Figure 4.1. The model suggests that teacher and student process variables influence each other in ways that eventually affect outcome variables, both in the short term and in the long term. The model shows two feedback loops. One uses information about student processes to change teacher behavior and teaching strategies. For example, an assessment that showed low rates of on-task time for a gymnastics class—a student process variable—might lead to a different instructional format designed to increase on-task time. The second feedback loop uses information on student outcomes to change teaching strategies. Here, for example, evidence from fitness scores that indicates lack of upper body strength among students—a student outcome variable—might lead to devoting more class time to activities that contribute to upper body development. Or skill test scores in volleyball indicating poor serving skills might lead to more technical instruction on serving or more practice time devoted to serving drills.

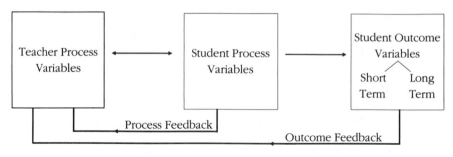

Figure 4.1   The Assessment Model

Notice that the line between the teacher and student process variables shows arrows in both directions. Far too often we assume that teachers exert a one-way influence over students. The fact is that teachers are influenced very directly by the students they teach! In some cases, it is difficult to tell whether the students or the teacher is exerting the stronger influence in terms of the directions a class has taken. Unless this *dual-directional influence* is understood, mistakes can be made in interpreting events in classes. For example, when it is suggested that enthusiasm is related to achievement, we should not automatically assume that teacher enthusiasm *causes* student achievement. Such an assumption represents a one-way view of influence between teachers and students. No doubt an enthusiastic teacher can influence student achievement, but it is equally true that a high- achieving class also influences a teacher to be more enthusiastic! This dual-directional influence will be examined more closely in Chapter 5.

The assessment model shown here is a *mediating process* model. The assumption of the model is that teachers and students interact with each other to influence what students do in the context of the class. It is what students actually *do* that influences short-and long-term outcomes for the class. In other words, teachers do not directly influence the fitness of their students, or their skillfulness, or their self-concepts. What teachers can do is to influence what students do in the context of the class and the nature of that *doing* is what will, eventually, influence their fitness, skillfulness, and sense of themselves. The major focus of this model, then, is the activity of students. Do they listen? How often do they practice? Under what conditions? Are they motivated? Do they like what they are doing? Do they help each other? Answers to these questions and others like them, will provide the most meaningful information related to student outcomes.

Assessment of Teaching Must Be Related to Goals

Assume you are teaching a volleyball unit to seventh graders and you have decided that your main goal is to teach playing strategy. You want the students to move appropriately on the court and respond to offensive and defensive play with appropriate team strategy. You know that their individual technical skills—

serving, bumping, setting, spiking, blocking—might not improve as rapidly as they would if you focused more on skill development, but you made the choice so students could learn how the game of volleyball is actually played. A supervisor comes along and observes your class. The *assessment* feedback indicates that little time has been spent in skill practice, and the *evaluation* suggests that you might consider spending more time teaching skills. The supervisor didn't ask about what your goals were! Was this assessment and evaluation fair? Was it useful to you?

Assessments of teaching must take into account the goals of the teacher. While it is perfectly legitimate to assess and then evaluate goals, it is not fair to disregard goals when assessing and evaluating teaching. Physical educators often have quite different goals when they plan units of instruction. Some orient their teaching toward fitness goals. Others focus more on skill development. Some emphasize strategic game play. Still others are more concerned with achieving goals in the *affective* domain—self-concept, creativity, confidence. Some physical educators focus primarily on *social development* goals, such as responsibility, honesty, sharing, and helping. In trying to reach these very different goals, teachers will plan and teach in ways that sometimes look very different. The activities they choose, the ways they organize students, the frequency and focus of their interactions with students, and the kind of instruction they provide will all change somewhat, based on the goals they are trying to achieve. Valid assessments of teaching must take these goals into account the goals. While this would be obviously true if one were going to test the students to measure outcomes, it is just as true—even if not so obvious—if one were to observe the teachers and learners to provide assessment information about teaching and learning processes.

On-Site Assessment of Teaching

Ultimately, teaching needs to be assessed in terms of the outcomes achieved, both short-term and long-term outcomes. Are the students more fit? Are they more skilled? Can they play games better? Do they voluntarily seek out activity opportunities? The box titled "What Counts for Success in Long-Term Assessment of Student Outcomes?" identifies some of the long-term outcome measures that physical educators might utilize to assess and evaluate the success of their efforts. When you are learning to teach, however, you can't wait for outcome measures, even short-term measures, to provide information to improve your teaching. When you teach a lesson you want to know now—and you need to know now—how you did and how you can get better. Thus, on-site measures of teaching are needed for you to improve on a day-to-day basis.

Three levels of on-site assessment are useful for the improvement of teaching: (1) assessment of discrete teacher or student behavior, (2) assessment of teaching units, and (3) assessment of criterion process variables. These levels provide a useful framework for examining teaching, regardless of whether it occurs in a microteaching lesson on campus, small-group teaching in a local school, or student teaching. Each of these levels can be used to generate information that

4.3 A Universal Objective for Education

Teachers have many different objectives they try to achieve in physical education—fitness, skill, strategy, affective goals, social goals, knowledge goals. There are heated debates about what the most important goals for physical education are, and there is room for legitimate differences within these debates. Regardless, however, of what a teacher's main goals might be, it can be argued that all teachers should try to teach in ways that help students learn to love and value physical activity.

Robert Mager said that the universal objective for all teachers should be to help students like what they are learning and to like the process of learning. Mager showed that students learn to like or dislike a subject matter while they are learning it.

> The object of this paper is to discuss the importance of designing learning experiences in such a way that they do not teach students to hate the very things about which they are learning. It is the object of this paper to suggest that each and every instructional sequence or event, each and every lecture, each and every program, should have as its number one objective the intent to send the student away from the learning experience with approach tendencies toward the subject matter equal to or greater than those with which he arrived. (Mager, 1973, p. 3)

Students who experience a consistently negative and coercive educational environment or who experience consistent failure will learn to dislike the subject taught—and eventually to dislike learning. Positive, successful learning experiences help students like and value the subject matter—and eventually to like and value learning. Teaching for approach tendencies—behaviors of students that indicate that they like and value the subject—should be an underlying goal for all teachers.

is useful immediately both to help teachers improve and to evaluate their teaching. Information at each level is generated by directly observing teachers and students. Each of these levels provides different information, useful for different purposes, and each should be used appropriately relative to the specific goals of any practice teaching episode.

Level 1: Assessing Discrete Teacher and Student Behaviors

It is often useful to define important teacher and student behaviors carefully and measure the degree to which they occur during a teaching episode. This level of assessment is particularly useful for the early stages of skill development where teachers practice skills in fairly controlled settings: small-group teaching, peer teaching, and micro-teaching. A *discrete behavior* is a single behavior with an identifiable beginning and end. Examples would be teacher feedback, student skill responses, teacher questions, or student disruptions.

Discrete teacher or student behaviors can be counted or timed. Counting produces a record of frequency that can be converted to a rate measure by dividing the frequency by the length of the observation. For example, 24 feedback statements in a 6-minute teaching episode would be a rate of 4.0 per minute. Some behaviors are more meaningful when timed rather than counted; for example, it would be important to know how much time students were off-task during a 20-minute teaching episode.

Sometimes the most useful information about a discrete teaching behavior might be its accuracy or appropriateness. Thus, the appropriateness of a feedback statement could be the target for observation. This requires observing all feedback statements and making a judgment about the appropriateness of each one. The resulting information could be expressed as a ratio of appropriate feedback statements to the total number of feedback statements made.

Level 2: Assessment of Teaching Units

Discrete teacher or learner behaviors often do not give information that is sufficiently rich and complex to provide useful assessment information for the improvement of teaching. For example, knowing how many managerial behaviors you *emitted* during a 30-minute teaching episode would provide only limited information about your managerial skills. For a more complete assessment, it is useful to develop ways of combining teacher and learner variables into units that represent important elements of the educational process. *Teaching units* refers to combinations of teacher variables, learner variables, or both, that provide information about important elements of the educational process.

An example of a teaching unit that has proven to be useful in improving managerial skills is the *managerial episode*—a sequence of time that begins when a teacher issues a managerial directive and ends when the students complete that directive and begin the next instructional or practice activity. Consider the situation in which a teacher has four squads playing two volleyball games. The time has come for the two sets of teams to exchange opponents. The teacher initiates this managerial episode by blowing a whistle, which stops play. The teacher then explains that Squad A will now play Squad D on court 2 and Squad C will play Squad B on court 1. The teams then organize for their new games. When the new games begin, the managerial episode comes to an end. The total length of time from when the teacher initiated the episode with the whistle to when the new games began would be the duration of that managerial episode. The number of episodes, their various lengths, and the average length of episodes in a lesson provide useful information for teachers trying to improve their managerial skills.

Another useful teaching unit for assessment purposes is the teacher prompt—student response—teacher feedback cycle, which can be analyzed from several perspectives. The teacher gives a brief prompt about what to do ("keep your shoulders level while swinging"). The student attempts a response. The teacher then evaluates the response and provides feedback ("much better, they were nearly level").

Another useful teaching unit is the sequence of events that occurs when the teacher informs students about a task and students make their initial attempts to do the task, a sequence that occurs regularly during each lesson. A teacher states an instructional task; the class responds; the teacher reacts to their responses. What kind of task was stated? How long did it take for students to respond? Did they modify the task when they responded? How did the teacher react? These are all useful questions to use in analysis of this teaching unit.

Level 3: Assessing Criterion Process Variables

Often teachers—and those supervising them—need to have information that represents the degree to which students are learning. Student achievement data, however, can't be collected until the end of a unit or term. What is needed is a measure that can both be collected at any time and be strongly related to achievement. This kind of measure is called a *criterion process variable,* a student process variable that provides direct evidence of student learning.

I will suggest two criterion process variables for which there is strong evidence of a direct link to student achievement—academic learning time (ALT) (see the box titled "Active Teaching Results in High Rates of Academic Learning Time" in Chapter 2) and appropriate opportunities to respond (OTRs). These variables can be thought of as "proxy" variables for achievement, or they can be considered to be direct measures of student learning. ALT and OTR are simply different ways to measure the same phenomenon, the degree to which students are engaged in learning activities in a way that will lead to achievement. ALT observations provide a measure of the amount of time students are engaged in goal-related learning tasks at a high success rate. OTR observations give you the number of appropriate learning trials a student had during any lesson. Chapter 3 showed that ALT is typically low in physical education and that in many situations students get few OTRs (see pages 42–43).

Both ALT and OTR provide teachers a good measure of the degree of learning that is likely taking place in their classes—and they have the added benefit of providing that estimate of learning immediately without having to wait for outcome data. ALT and OTR also allow for useful diagnosis and assessment of other discrete teaching behaviors and teaching units. For example, it might be determined that fewer and shorter managerial episodes are related to increases in ALT. You might find that when teachers increase their active supervision of student practice that students increase their OTRs. Certainly, decreasing waiting time would seem to provide more time when students could engage in practice, with increases in ALT and OTR. However, it is also possible that students might be engaged for longer periods of time or do more responses, but much of that time could be at too high a level of difficulty, or too many of those extra responses could be inappropriate. The comparisons between engaged time and ALT, or between total number of responses and those that were appropriate, provide extremely valuable information for teachers.

This approach to the assessment of learning—through the measurement of criterion process variables—is consistent with our definition of effective teaching: Effective teaching exists where teachers have arranged things so that

---

4.4 Objections to Measuring Teaching and Learning

Have you heard people say "The really important things can't be measured." Or "I don't measure teaching because it is dehumanizing to do so." These objections need to be dealt with.

Some things are harder to measure than others. Teacher enthusiasm or student cooperation is harder to measure than accurate feedback or opportunity to respond. Here the problem is not really measurement but definition. If cooperation or enthusiasm can be defined adequately, it can be measured reliably. If it can't be defined adequately, then how can we pretend to help teachers become more enthusiastic or students more cooperative?

Measurement is often misunderstood. When a teacher finishes a class and says "We really had fun today," a measurement has been made. The measurement may not be precise, and the teacher may not even understand the basis of the judgment, but the fact that the statement was made implies that a quality or element within the class was measured in some way. We measure things all the time in this imprecise way. The issue is really not whether educationally important phenomena can be measured, but whether they can be defined adequately so they can be measured reliably. The problem with poorly or unspecifically defined notions about teaching and learning is that they are often highly susceptible to the bias of an observer trying to measure them. If teaching or learning phenomena are considered to be important, then every effort should be made to reach agreement about what they specifically mean. Once that agreement has been reached, measurement can proceed reliably.

---

students engage in goal-related activity frequently and successfully. Thus teaching is assessed by reference to what students actually are doing in classes! Surely, improving your ability to give clear directions, increasing the frequency with of accurate feedback, and asking better questions are all important improvements in teaching skills. To improve your effectiveness as a teacher, however, these improvements should translate into increased ALT/OTR.

Steps in the Assessment Process

Regular assessment is crucial to the improvement of teaching. Some assessment can be made by the teacher while teaching, even without the aid of systematic observation. If teachers can watch carefully for certain things that happen (or do not happen) during a teaching episode, they can at least get some information about how they are doing. For teaching to improve dramatically in short periods of time, however, it needs to be more systematically assessed, as you might do during teaching practice in a teacher education program. What follows are important steps in the assessment process.

1. *Discover what learning goals are being sought.* Teaching is a goal-oriented activity. It is not possible to decide whether a student is in ALT or has had an appropriate OTR unless you know what goals the teacher is attempting to reach. The more specifically the teacher has defined the goals, the easier it will be to assess the effectiveness of the teaching.

2. *Recast learning and teaching goals in behavioral terms.* If being a "fair player" is a goal, what student behavior will count as an instance of appropriate or inappropriate behavior relative to the goal? If a teacher wants to improve her or his enthusiasm, what will we observe as related to this phenomenon? If student leadership is an important social goal, how will we know when leadership has been shown? To answer these questions, we would have to recast these goals in behavioral terms. The term *behavioral* refers to things that people do that can be observed directly by someone else. Some important behaviors—how you feel about things, for example—can only be observed by you and reported to someone else. Goals that are defined behaviorally are not only necessary for reliable, valid observation but are also helpful to teachers because they require them to define exactly what they will teach their students.

3. *Achieve specificity for teaching assessment.* The number of teaching goals assessed can be few or many, depending on the purpose of the assessment. Regardless of the number, however, each teaching goal needs to be stated specifically for it to be assessed fairly. Specificity is achieved in two ways. First, the target for the assessment should be specific. It is not enough to suggest, "Let's focus on improving management skills." Instead, it is better to agree to try to "reduce management time," "reduce the average length of managerial episodes," "reduce the number and length of transitional episodes," or "spend less time in equipment changes." The second aspect of specificity is setting a criterion by which goal achievement will be judged; for example, reduce total managerial time to fewer than 10 minutes or reduce average transitional time to less than one minute. The criterion should be realistic, high enough to provide a challenge for improvement, yet low enough that it is achievable.

4. *Use baseline data for setting goals and criteria.* To know how much you have improved, you have to know where you started! In assessing and improving teaching, it is important that thorough information be developed about your current efforts—what we shall call the "baseline" to which future data can be compared. *Baseline data* are descriptions of your teaching efforts used to set goals and establish criteria. Baseline data can also be used to make comparisons about improvement. If possible, it is useful to have more than one teaching session contribute to the establishment of a baseline. Baseline data reveal your strengths and weaknesses as well as what should be priorities for improving your teaching. You may have a low level of management time for beginning

and end-of-class sequences, but a level of transition time that is too high. You may provide good explanations and demonstrations, but the ALT of your students may be too low. Baseline data will also help to set criteria for improvement. If your management time during baseline sessions is 37 percent of total class time, then setting an initial criterion of 25 percent is realistic. Eventually, you might be able to manage well enough to achieve 10 to 15 percent, but that should come gradually.

5. *Achieve goals through specific strategies and regular measurement.* Getting better at teaching is like getting better in sport—you have to have some specific strategies, the opportunity to practice them, and some regular measurement of the degree to which you can execute them. The various chapters in this text contain strategies for class management, discipline, instruction, and supervision of practice. Wanting to improve is important. Having specific strategies to help you improve is important. Executing those strategies will actually bring about the improvement. For example, reducing management time might be achieved by (1) establishing an entry activity (see p. 92), (2) teaching signals for attention and dispersal (see p. 92), and (3) playing a management "game" with the students (see pp. 93–94). Executing these managerial strategies appropriately will reduce management time significantly.

6. *Maintain gains as new skills are attended to. Goal maintenance* means that you maintain an adequate level of performance in areas that have been achieved while you move on to new teaching goals. For example, can you maintain an adequate level of skill feedback interactions while you to try to improve your behavioral interactions? Maintenance is greatly helped when occasional observations are made to assess goals previously worked on. Eventually, adequate levels of a number of teaching skills will become habit—you will have developed into a truly effective professional teacher.

7. *Take control of your own teaching.* A final step in the assessment process occurs when you take responsibility for your own teaching. Full-time teachers do not have the help of a supervisory team. They are periodically evaluated—by principals or supervisors—but these evaluations are often poorly done and not useful for the maintenance or improvement of teaching skills. Teachers can use the process described here to maintain and continue to develop their teaching expertise. You can find ways to observe your teaching: tape recorders, self-recording of events or time, even an occasional videotaping. Specific goal achievement can be assessed through reliable measurement. This is the epitome of good teaching—holding yourself accountable for what goes on in your gymnasium.

Examples of the Assessment Process in Action

Bill is in a teacher education program in physical education. Providing specific skill feedback is an important goal in the program. This is a worthy goal. Specific skill feedback is important, and the evidence from teaching research indicates that physical education teachers often do not provide enough of it. Bill is participating in a 14-day middle school teaching experience as part of a secondary school physical education methods course. A peer student is observing each class he teaches. The first two days of teaching will provide a baseline for several teaching skills, including specific skill feedback. After the baseline period, Bill and his supervisor decide that he will attempt to provide a minimum of three specific skill feedbacks per minute during practice time and that his ratio of specific to general skill feedback statements will be no less than 50 percent. They discuss ways of providing more and better skill feedback related to the unit plan from which Bill is teaching. The peer continues the observation, and each of the next three lessons Bill achieves the criterion for the goal, even surpassing it substantially in the last lesson. At this point a new skill goal is chosen, but Bill decides that he will try to maintain his specific skill feedback at the criterion of three per minute during practice time.

Deborah is an experienced elementary physical education teacher. She has recently read an article in a national journal about the importance of teachers' distributing their attention equitably among boys and girls and among children with differing levels of skill. The article suggested that teachers too often respond more to boys than girls and more to high-skilled children than to either low skilled or average children. The article made Deborah curious about her own distribution of attention as she is teaching. For the next several days Deborah carries a small clipboard with her as she teaches, recording in columns the number of interactions she has with boys and girls, and among children of varying skill levels. These data become her baseline. She is pleased to see that her attention is equitably distributed among skill levels, but surprised and not pleased to see that she interacts more frequently with boys than girls. She decides to change this and sets a 50/50 goal for gender-related interactions. She monitors her performance with her clipboard for several days and achieves the goal. Two weeks later she checks herself again, this time when a student from a nearby university is in the gym to observe her teaching. She asks the student to record instances of interactions with boys and girls. The record continues to show a more equitable distribution of attention.

None of the skills or processes described above are difficult to learn or do. Chapter 16 presents information on how to make reliable observations and discusses a number of different observation systems.

Summary

1. *Assessment* is the collection of reliable, valid information for purposes of improving performance, while evaluation is making a judgment about the worth of a performance.

2. Assessment requires good information—and good information must be reliable and valid.

3. *Teacher process variables* describe teaching behaviors, while *student process variables* describe student behaviors, and outcome variables

describe performance at the end of a unit or behaviors changed as a result of the learning experience.

4. The basic assessment model suggests that teachers and students influence each other in ways that affect what students do, and it is what students do that affects short- and long-term outcomes.

5. Assessment, to be fair, must be related to the goals of a particular learning environment.

6. A universal objective for all teachers is to teach in such a way that students develop approach tendencies toward physical activity.

7. On-site assessment of teaching can focus on discrete teaching/learning behaviors, teaching units, or criterion process variables.

8. Discrete teaching/learning behaviors have identifiable beginning and end points and can be counted or timed.

9. *Teaching units* are combinations of teacher and/or learner variables that provide information about important elements of the educational process.

10. A *criterion process variable* is a measure of student behavior that provides direct evidence of student learning.

11. ALT and OTR are both good criterion process variables. One is based in time and the other is based on frequency counts.

12. Important steps in the assessment process are discovering goals, recasting goals in behavioral terms, achieving specificity in targets and criteria, collecting baseline data, achieving goals through specific strategies and regular measurement, maintaining skills once developed, and assuming control of your own teaching.

Creating the Conditions for Effective Teaching in Physical Education

Many teachers have effective instructional skills and strategies but seldom get to use them because they cannot create the conditions to use them. This happens because teachers and teacher preparation programs have for too long viewed teaching primarily from the perspective of instruction, while neglecting the important managerial and discipline functions. The chapters in Part Two provide a model to help you understand the relationships among class management, discipline, and instruction; the important strategies of managing to prevent discipline problems from occurring; techniques for dealing with disruptive and off-task behavior; and the important interpersonal skills necessary for teachers to have positive effects on their students.

When you have mastered the content of Part Two, you should be able to recognize and explain the relationships that form the ecology of physical education, describe and discuss the management practices that prevent disruptive and off-task behavior, describe and discuss options for dealing with disruptions when they do occur, and recognize the skillfulness needed for successful interpersonal relations among teachers and students.

CHAPTER 5
The Ecology of Physical Education

What, then, is the practical utility of an ecological approach to research on teaching? It would seem that the ecological model can best be viewed as an analytic framework for understanding how classrooms work. Such an understanding would appear to be especially useful to teachers for interpreting problems and generating solutions to meet the practical contingencies of specific classrooms.

Walter Doyle (1979)

CHAPTER OBJECTIVES

To describe the purposes of an ecological framework

To distinguish among managerial, instructional, and student-social tasks

To distinguish among stated, actual, and contingency-developed tasks

To describe how accountability, ambiguity, clarity, and risk relate to task systems

To describe the role of negotiations in establishing task boundaries

To describe how the task systems interact to produce an ecology

To describe how supervision and accountability drive the task system

To explain results from task system research in physical education

To explain the components of a learning-oriented ecology

This text is a primarily focused on the use of teaching skills singly and in combination to produce a reliable, effective education for students in physical education. These skills should never be applied mechanically. Skillful teaching is always in response to the demands of the teaching/learning environment and the needs, interests, and capabilities of the students; that is, it is sensitive to its context. A major premise of this text is that teachers need to develop a level of skillfulness that allows them to achieve their intended educational goals, even though the environments they work in are complex and sometimes very difficult. As mentioned previously, teaching and learning are often misunderstood by those who assume that the sole direction of influence in education is one way: from teachers to students. While it is teachers' professional responsibility to influence students in ways that are educationally valuable, it is clear that they are influenced by their students—and that sometimes the influence of the students is stronger than that of the teacher. Thus teaching can only be properly understood by examining the *dual directional* influences among teachers and their students.

The purpose of this chapter is to provide an overall view of teaching physical education, a total framework in which the skills and strategies of effective teaching can be interpreted and understood. It is sometimes said that people "can't see the forest because of looking only at the trees." This chapter provides a view of the "forest," while the chapters that follow tend to focus on the many different kinds of "trees" that inhabit it.

This chapter is about the ecology of physical education. In its generic sense, *ecology* refers to the study of the habitat of living objects, the relationships between organisms and their environment. An ecology is typically made up of a number of systems that interact with each other so that a change in one system influences what happens in the other systems. Ecologies often exist in a delicate balance that can be upset when one or more of the systems is disrupted or altered. Just as the natural environment we live in can be understood as an ecological system, so too can teaching/learning in physical education.

The ecological framework described in this chapter developed from research on real teachers in real classrooms. The ecological model was originally described by Doyle (1979) and first applied to physical education by Tousignant and Siedentop (1983). Our understanding of the ecology of physical education has since been informed through a series of research studies at Ohio State University (Alexander, 1982; Tinning & Siedentop, 1985; Marks, 1988; Jones, 1989; Son, 1989; Lund, 1990). The information in this chapter derives from the ecological model defined by Doyle and the study of that model in the context of physical education.

The Task Systems That Comprise the Ecology of Physical Education

Teaching/learning in physical education can be viewed as an ecology with three primary systems, each of which is developed around a series of tasks to be accomplished. These systems are the *managerial task system,* the *instructional task system,* and the *student-social system.* The interactive influence among these three systems forms the ecology of physical education.

A *task* is defined by a goal and a set of operations to achieve the goal. Tasks are communicated through "a set of implicit or explicit instructions about what a person is expected to do to cope successfully with a situation" (Doyle, 1981, p. 2). A *managerial task* relates to the organizational and behavioral aspects of physical education—all the non-subject matter functions necessary for students and teachers to exist together over a period of time. For example, a single managerial task occurs when a teacher says "Form into four groups for volleyball teams by counting off in fours!" An *instructional task* relates to the subject-matter activity of physical education, the intended learnings students are to acquire by participating in the instructional activities. For example, a single instructional task occurs when a teacher says "Work in pairs, six feet apart, and keep the volleyball in play by forearm passing to one another." The student-social task system is different in that it is typically arranged and directed by students rather than the teacher.

Nonetheless, it is clear that students have a social agenda when they come to physical education, and that agenda can be interpreted as a task system. A *student-social task* relates to the intentions for social interaction that students seek in physical education. Examples of student-social tasks range from having fun with a friend during the appropriate completion of the instructional volleyball task just described to going completely off-task with fellow students to engage in some behavior that is social in nature but viewed as disruptive by the teacher. Student-social tasks are not "announced" publicly and then pursued, as are the managerial and instructional tasks. These tasks are often communicated among students in clever, subtle, and often surreptitious ways. The pursuit of these tasks often interacts with the other task systems in ways that produce problems for the teacher.

A *task system* is a regularized pattern for accomplishing tasks. It is composed mostly of the tasks that tend to recur frequently within physical education. Thus there is a mangerial task system composed of all the many different managerial tasks that recur frequently, such as entering the gym, taking roll, transitioning, organizing for instruction, regrouping, getting equipment out and away, staying on-task, obeying rules for behavior, and class closure. The instructional task system is composed of all the learning tasks that teachers ask students to engage in, such as taking part in drills, playing in games, doing fitness activities, writing tests, and taking part in activities designed for social or affective outcomes. The student-social system is much more difficult than the others to define because it is less predictable and less easily observed. It is composed of all the individual and group social intentions of the students in a class. In any class of 28 students, there might be a number of different social tasks being pursued by different individuals and groups within the class. One group of students may find ways to socialize within the boundaries of the instructional task system. Another group, however, may find their "fun" in disrupting the instructional task system. This tends to make the student-social task system more variable than either the mangerial or instructional task systems, and thus more difficult to analyze. Make no mistake, however. The student-social task system does operate and does affect what happens in the other two systems.

Tasks and Their Development

To understand the ecology of physical education, you must be able to see how tasks develop—how the actual task systems develop over time and interact with one another. Managerial and instructional tasks begin as *stated tasks* that the teacher usually describes verbally. However, the *actual* managerial and instructional tasks that students develop over time are primarily a result of how teachers respond to student task-efforts, rather than how the tasks were described originally. An "actual" managerial or instructional task tends to develop through the following sequence. The teacher states a task. Students respond to that task. Their responses may or may not be congruent with the task described by the teacher; that is, they may do the task as stated or modify it in some way. The teacher then supervises the students and, on occasion, responds to their task-efforts. It is this cycle of stated task—student response—teacher supervision—teacher response that eventually defines the actual task: what Alexander (1982) described as the *contingency developed task system*. The cycle that determines the actual task is shown graphically in Figure 5.1. Describing this cycle as a "contingency developed system" means that the key operational variable is the reactions of teachers to task-efforts by students. It also seems clear that teacher reaction is the key factor in the level of student socializing that occurs within a physical education class. Thus, although student-social tasks do not begin with a task statement by a teacher, the pattern of task development in this system is no doubt similar to that in the managerial and instructional task systems.

A Contingency-Developed Task

Teacher states task
  Student responds (congruent or modified)
    Teacher supervises
      Teacher responds to student task-efforts
        Actual task develops

Figure 5.1 *Contingency-developed task [Adapted from Alexander (1982)]*

Once you understand the cycle through which the actual tasks in a class get defined, a number of questions immediately arise. How clearly do teachers state tasks? How different are the actual tasks from those stated originally? How often and in what ways do students modify tasks? How often and how well do teachers supervise beginning task responses? How do teachers respond to modified tasks? How do students learn what is acceptable and unacceptable in any of the three task systems? These are exactly the questions we have asked in our research program. The answers to these questions form the basis for the remainder of this chapter.

Important Concepts in the Ecological Framework

Four related concepts help to further our understanding of how tasks develop: accountability, clarity/ambiguity, risk, and task boundaries. *Accountability* refers to the practices teachers use to establish and maintain student responsibility for appropriate conduct, task involvement, and outcomes. In his original formulation of the ecological framework, Doyle recognized that accountability drove the instructional task system. Without accountability, he found, task systems become very loose and sometimes are even suspended.

> Moreover, if accountability is not present; i.e., if answers are not required or if any answer is acceptable, then the task system itself is suspended. (Doyle, 1980, p. 103)

Accountability, of course, comes in many different forms. Among them are tests that students perform for grades, teacher feedback, teacher praise and reprimands, active teacher supervision, challenges and competitions, public recognition of performance, and keeping records of performance. Eventually, task systems are defined by what teachers hold students accountable for, both in the managerial and instructional systems. In the student-social system, teacher accountability is also a key variable. However, the accountability is typically only for keeping socializing within boundaries defined by the managerial and instructional systems. When socializing begins to threaten the stability of those boundaries, then teachers typically intervene to control and redirect it.

Clarity and *ambiguity* are related concepts that refer to the degree of explicitness and consistency in defining tasks. These concepts are relevant both in the original description of a task (the stated task) and in how the task eventually develops (the actual task). A fully explicit task defines the conditions students are to perform under, the performance expected, some standard by which to judge the performance, and the consequences for performance (Alexander, 1982). An example of an explicit managerial task would be "I want Squad 4 to play Squad 1 on court A and Squad 2 to play Squad 3 on court B. I want you to be in your 6-person game formation to begin the game, with the odd-numbered team serving within 15 seconds after I blow my whistle." A task that is less than fully explicit becomes ambiguous; that is, there are gaps in information about performance expectations. Students may not know exactly what to do, or under what conditions to do it, or how well it needs to be done, or what the consequences will be for doing it well or poorly.

Clarity and ambiguity also affect the cycle through which tasks develop. Here, however, the concepts refer to consistency of the teacher's responses to student task-efforts. If one kind of response is accepted by a teacher on one occasion but not on another, then the task becomes ambiguous and student responses are likely to become more varied.

Risk refers to the interaction among the ambiguity of the task, its difficulty, and the degree of accountability applied to it. Ambiguous tasks always produce risk for students until it becomes clear to them that the tasks are either not difficult or are tasks they will not be held accountable for. A difficult task with strong accountability results in a high degree of risk for the student. Easy tasks and loose or weak accountability measures result in less risk for the students. Risk and ambiguity are obviously related, especially when accountability is strong. If a task is ambiguous, then it becomes very risky for the student, who will not know what the performance expectations are for completing the task.

Task boundaries refer to how tightly or loosely accountability is applied to task completion, and how clear and unambiguous are the requirements for task compliance and completion. Task systems can have narrow and consistent boundaries. This typically occurs when tasks are explicit and accountability is strong and consistent. Task systems can also have very loose boundaries, which occurs when tasks are ambiguous and accountability is loose, inconsistent or both. Again, however, it should be made clear that accountability drives the task systems. Weak or inconsistent accountability tends to eliminate risk and makes ambiguity irrelevant; that is, when students know that they will not be held accountable, then trying to cope with an ambiguous task is less of a problem and provides little risk.

5.1 The Competent Bystander

In her analysis of task systems in middle and high school physical education, Tousignant (1981) observed student strategies for "hiding" non-participation in the instructional task system, but doing so in such a clever way that the teacher did not notice. She called students who used these strategies *competent bystanders*.

The competent bystander always behaves well in terms of the managerial task system. This is what teachers would call a well-behaved student. Yet the same student cleverly avoids participation in the instructional task system and does so in such a way that the teacher does not notice. The competent bystander is always in line, moving from fourth to third to second place, but then reinserting himself so that he avoids being first and having to take a turn. In game play, the competent bystander attaches herself to a good player, knowing that the good player will perform the necessary action when the ball comes in their sector. Or, in basketball, for example, the competent bystander cruises up and down the floor but manages to stay away from all the action involving the ball.

Remember, this is a *competent* bystander. The teacher, when asked about this student's skill involvement, typically responds that the student is fairly well skilled and actively involved. By always being within the boundaries of the managerial task system, the student is seen to be "good."

When you next observe a physical education lesson in a school, try to see if there are any competent bystanders in the class.

Needless to say, the student-social system is seldom as well defined as the managerial and instructional task systems, thus making it more ambiguous and often riskier. Still, students often persist in trying to see what the boundaries of the student-social system might be in any given class.

Negotiation within Task Systems

Students learn about the boundaries of task systems in several ways. Some teachers explain the boundaries of a task system very carefully and hold students accountable for compliance within those boundaries quickly and consistently. Other teachers explain the boundaries clearly, but their students gradually learn that the boundaries are different than those originally described; that is, the *actual* boundaries of the system develop contingently through the process described earlier for individual tasks. Still other teachers do not explain the boundaries clearly or completely, and students have to learn through daily experience what they have to do to stay within the boundaries and what behaviors are considered to be outside the system.

Students also bring their own social agendas with them when they come to physical education. Thus they must also learn what kinds of student-social interactions are allowable and under what conditions.

One of Doyle's initial findings was that students attempt to negotiate tasks to fix the "ecological balance" of the task systems at a level they can handle and enjoy. *Negotiation* can be defined as any attempt by students to change tasks, to change the conditions under which tasks are performed, or to change the performance standards task completion is judged by. How teachers respond to student attempts to negotiate the demands of task systems tends to be the primary factor in determining the ecological balance among the three task systems—management, instruction, and student-social—within a class.

In classrooms, negotiation tends to be verbal, particularly within the instructional task system. A teacher assigns an instructional task, and students attempt to reduce its ambiguity and risk by verbally negotiating with the teacher. How long does the theme have to be? Can it be on this topic rather than the one you assigned? Can it be turned in Tuesday instead of Monday? How much will this count toward our grade? Will you take off for spelling errors? Does it have to be typed? All of these questions serve to negotiate the demands of this particular task. How the teacher responds to the questions, and later to the themes that are turned in, will determine the actual task.

In physical education, students negotiate task demands by modifying the task during practice rather than by asking questions. When a teacher describes an instructional task, the students then go about doing the task, but often they modify it so that it is somewhat different than the one the teacher described. They can modify the task upward to make it more challenging than the task described by the teacher, or they can modify it downward to make it easier to do successfully. When the teacher supervises this practice and responds to the modified tasks, the actual nature of the task gets defined by what the teacher accepts. Over time, students learn how much they can modify an assigned task and still stay within the boundaries of the instructional task system.

For example, a teacher asks her students to organize in pairs with partners eight feet apart. The task is to forearm pass the volleyball back and forth between partners so that the ball goes over head height with each pass, but not more than 3–4 feet over the head. Some of the students in class are on the school volleyball team. For them this is an easy task, so they modify it by moving further apart and passing the ball higher. For others, the task is too difficult, so they move a bit closer together and don't pay much attention to the height of the pass. A few other students use sets instead of forearm passes when the ball comes to them at or above shoulder level. The teacher is now supervising this practice. How she responds to each of these modifications will determine the *actual* task in this case, and it will also provide students with knowledge about the degree to which they can modify assigned tasks and still stay within the boundaries of the instructional task system; e.g., they will know how much they can change the assigned task without being considered "off task."

Students often negotiate in their social task system by trying to pair up with friends or get certain students together on a team. These negotiations are often "hidden" as instructional negotiations, but they have a clear social emphasis and purpose.

Negotiation between Task Systems

Negotiations also occur among the three task systems that form the ecology of the gymnasium. There is little doubt that for most teachers the initial and fundamental goal of teaching a class is to gain and maintain student cooperation (Doyle, 1981). Teachers are responsible for many classes each day. Administrators expect them to have control of their classes. For these reasons, it is understandable and should be expected that a teacher's primary concern is to establish and maintain an orderly class in which students cooperate with good behavior rather than disrupt constantly. Research also has revealed that teachers tend to establish the boundaries of the managerial system first, often in the very first few days of the school year (Brophy & Good, 1987).

The issue here is clear. It is understandable that the managerial task system is established quickly, and that students need to cooperate with the demands of that system to produce a "peaceful" class throughout the school year. How do teachers negotiate with students to produce consistent compliance with the demands of the managerial task system? Remember, teachers also have an instructional task system to develop, and students have their own social agendas they want to attend to during class. Clearly, there are several kinds of negotiations that might occur among these three systems that form the ecology of the class. Teachers might reduce the demands of the instructional system to gain cooperation with the managerial system. Teachers might allow for certain kinds of student social interaction to gain the necessary cooperation. In some cases, for some students, teachers might simply suspend the instructional task system and allow those students to engage in nondisruptive socializing rather than instructional tasks, as long as they cooperate with the demands of the managerial task system. Each of these negotiations produces a different ecology. Each has been identified in research studies. The degree to which teachers need to negotiate with their students to produce the necessary cooperation is determined by the difficulty of the context in which the teaching takes place, the intentions and expectations the teacher has for learning and achievement, and the degree to which the teacher possesses effective teaching skills.

The way that the managerial, instructional, and student-social task systems interact and influence one another determines the ecology of the gymnasium. The sensitive, effective teacher will understand how these systems interact and work to develop an ecology that students not only cooperate and behave well within, but one that is also learning-oriented and accommodates student-social needs. To develop and maintain this kind of ecology in a typical class in today's schools is not easy. It requires that teachers have strong intentions to build this kind of educational environment and the managerial and instructional skills to make it happen.

5.2 Hiding Social Engagement within Instructional Tasks

In a recent study of task systems in Korean high school physical education, Son (1989) found a particularly interesting kind of engagement pattern in some highly skilled students. A teacher would describe an instructional task. The highly skilled student would do the task exactly as described and do it very successfully. The student would proceed to do 4–6 repetitions of the task. Then, however, a curious change would occur. The highly skilled student would modify the task to make it easier and then engage in it, but in an unsuccessful manner. What could explain this task modification and unsuccessful engagement with a high-skilled student?

Clearly, the student knew that he could do the task and, indeed, did it successfully several times. Then it was time to do a little socializing, but to do so in a way that was hidden within the instructional task system. This was accomplished by modifying the task to make it easier and then to engage in that task, but with little thought to success. Instead, the student's attention was diverted away from task-success to socializing with a fellow student. If the teacher saw the students, he would see task engagement, albeit it on a slightly modified task and without high success. While this might result in some feedback from the teacher, it would no doubt be related to the instructional task performance rather than to the socializing. Typically, however, because the students are "on-task," the teacher would not intervene, and the students would have successfully hidden their pursuit of their own social goals within the instructional task system.

Supervision and Accountability

Early in his studies of classroom ecologies, Doyle (1979) indicated that accountability drove task systems. Without accountability, the task system was suspended and what happened was attributable solely to student interests and enthusiasms. This was most true for the instructional task system.

All the evidence suggests that accountability is as powerful a force in the ecology of physical education as it is in the classroom. However, the ecologies of the classroom and the gymnasium operate differently. In the classroom, what Doyle (1979) called the "performance-grade exchange system" tends to be the primary accountability mechanism. Students in classrooms often are required to perform for grades—quizzes, homework, themes, and so forth. The classroom is smaller than the gymnasium or playing field, and the placement of students within the classroom makes supervising of their work easier, whether they are working in a whole-group format or independently at their seats. Negotiations in the classroom are often verbal, with students asking teachers questions or making requests that tend to reduce the risk and ambiguity associated with an assignment.

In physical education classes, it is less common to have students perform for grades in specific assignments on a regular basis. Many physical education teachers test for skill and knowledge at the end of units but seldom involve students in performance-grade exchange assignments on a daily basis throughout a unit. Gymnasia and playing fields are often quite large, and students move about them in ways that make supervision difficult. Negotiations in physical education more often occur through students' modifying tasks than asking questions or making requests, which makes negotiations difficult for the teacher to see and respond to. Thus, as regards supervision and accountability, the physical education setting is considerably more complex and difficult than the classroom.

Supervision and accountability may be the two most important teaching skills in the repertoire of the effective physical educator. *Supervision* was defined earlier in this chapter as the practices teachers use to establish and maintain student responsibility for appropriate conduct, task involvement, and outcomes. Teachers use many different forms of accountability—public recognition, verbal interaction, keeping records, challenges, and performance-grade exchanges. They must also actively supervise students to ensure that these accountability mechanisms work. The most important aspect of supervision is monitoring student work. *Monitoring* means to "watch, observe, or check, especially for a special purpose" (Webster's *New Collegiate Dictionary,* 1979, p. 737). The special purpose in this case would be for the teacher to see if student performance was congruent with the tasks described and assigned in the managerial and instructional task systems.

Here is a typical example. Joe is teaching basketball to ninth graders. He is focusing on the two-person "pick and roll" strategy that is fundamental to many different basketball offenses. He has the class together as a whole. He describes and demonstrates the main technical points of the pick and roll with the help of several students. The explanation is clear and to the point. The demonstrations are well set up. Joe has the demonstrators show both the correct technical aspects of the pick and roll and the most common errors. Joe then has the students "walk through" the strategy so that he can be sure they all understand the critical elements—what we later in this text will refer to as "guided practice." He provides feedback and answers student questions.

Joe then describes clearly how he wants the pick and roll practiced at the several basket areas in the gym. He uses four students to demonstrate how the practice drill should be done, what to emphasize, and what to avoid. Again, he provides feedback and answers questions. He then disperses the students to the basket areas and signals the beginning of the drill—what we later shall refer to as "independent practice." Up to now, what has been described appears to be a terrific lesson! But here, at the critical point where students will *practice* the pick and roll, the crucial teaching skills of supervision and accountability are lacking. As students begin practicing independently, Joe makes some notes on a clipboard. He then stays at one end of the gym and watches one of the groups but makes no comments to them. He sits down to chat with a student who has been ill and did not bring gym clothes for today's lesson. Eight minutes have passed since he dispersed the students. One of the groups has been playing a two-versus-two game with no effort to practice the pick and roll in the drill described. Another group is doing the drill incorrectly. A third group is doing the drill appropriately but making critical errors in technique each time they do it. Another group, at the far end of the gym, did the drill for a few minutes but has now started a shooting game.

How would you describe the ecology of this class? Joe knows basketball. He demonstrates and explains well. The drill he designed appeared to be a good drill, appropriate to the skill level of the class. At eight minutes into the practice phase, however, almost nothing is happening that one would consider to be good in terms of the assigned practice task! At this rate, few of the students will learn to be good at the pick and roll maneuver. However, none of the students are being disruptive. All of them are physically involved in something related to basketball, even though a very small percentage are actually doing the assigned practice task, and an even smaller percentage are doing it successfully. In some parts of the gymnasium, the student-social system appears to have taken over completely, even though it is "masked" by active involvement in basketball. Joe obviously does not supervise actively. He does not monitor student performance. There appears to be no accountability for performance except that which comes with his direct physical presence near a practice group.

The instructional task system in Joe's class has been almost completely suspended. It appears from the description that students understand that they will not be supervised carefully. There is little evidence of accountability for performance. Students are not disruptive, so one might assume that there is accountability in the managerial task system. Some students have modified tasks to have "more fun," thus accommodating their social-agenda within a modified instructional task rather than going off-task. All the students are physically active, so one might assume that Joe holds them accountable if they are not physically involved in some task related to the activity. A visitor who walked into this gym would see active students who seemed to be enjoying themselves. Each of the groups at the various baskets are doing something somewhat different, but nonetheless doing some kind of basketball. There would be no signs of disruptive behavior. What would the visitor conclude about this class and this teacher? Looking at the same class from the ecological perspective, what would you conclude?

Some Results from Task System Research in Physical Education

If you look carefully at the quote that introduces this chapter, you will see that the primary usefulness of the ecological model is that it provides a framework within which teachers can interpret what goes on in their classes and generate solutions to problems that arise. It helps teachers to be able to understand the ongoing events in their classes within a framework that takes into account the two-way influence between them and their students. The major purpose of this chapter has been to explain an ecological framework through which physical education teachers can interpret the managerial, instructional, and social dimensions of their classes.

What follows are some results from research in school physical education that has utilized the ecological framework (Alexander, 1982; Tousignant & Siedentop, 1983; Marks, 1988; Fink & Siedentop, 1989, Jones, 1989; Son 1989; Lund, 1990). Remember, the results described below represent a summary of research studies done in schools. While what is described is typical of the results of those studies, there is no doubt variation from teacher to teacher, and there is no intention to suggest that these results are typical of all physical education teachers.

1. The managerial task system tends to be more explicitly described and more carefully supervised than the instructional task system. Accountability for compliance in the managerial system is more quickly and consistently applied, thus its boundaries are more narrow and consistent than are the boundaries of the instructional system.

2. Actual instructional tasks tend to develop contingently and are often different from stated tasks. Students modify tasks to make them more or less difficult or to make them more fun. How teachers react to these modified tasks sets the boundaries of the instructional task system, which is typically less consistent and broader than the managerial system.

3. Teacher supervision is prerequisite to reacting to student task-responses. When teachers do not supervise actively and monitor student task-responses, the instructional task system becomes very loose, allowing students to modify the tasks at will and, on occasion, to cease engaging in them completely.

4. Instructional tasks are seldom described in fully explicit terms. The conditions tasks are to be practiced under are often not described fully, nor are the criteria for judging their completion. Students learn these aspects of the task, if they learn them at all, through the way the teacher reacts to their responses.

5. Some students don't pay much attention to teacher descriptions of instructional tasks. They learn what is required by asking fellow students during the transition from instruction to practice or by watching students begin the practice task. Students learn quickly how much or how little attention they have to pay to task descriptions.

6. Managerial tasks are typically a set of routines. They become established structures and require less teacher attention, especially in the classes of effective teachers. Students are held accountable for compliance with these routines. Rules are typically made clear and enforced. Teachers who need to interact frequently to keep students well behaved are typically less effective managers, because they have failed to establish a routine managerial task system.

7. In a well-supervised instructional task system, students will modify tasks to make them either more challenging (modify them up) or easier to do (modify them down). Teachers tend to set the limits to these modifications through their reactions to student task-responses. Some teachers sanction these modifications in the way they initially describe tasks to students.

8. In a poorly supervised instructional task system, students modify tasks both for the above reasons and also to engage in social interactions with their peers.

9. Cooperation with the demands of the managerial task system appears to be the most important and most immediate goal of the teacher (just as in classrooms). Teachers sometimes appear to accomplish this goal by trading cooperation within the managerial system for demands in the instructional system; for example, if students attend class, wear the appropriate uniform, and behave well, they can earn a high grade in the class. Thus, the first goal of the teacher—and sometimes the only goal—is for the student to be what Tousignant called a "member in good standing" of the class.

10. Other teachers require that students be both members in good standing and make a visible effort to engage in the assigned instuctional tasks. Accountability in this kind of system is directed at "effort," so students who are perceived to be consistently engaged in tasks get high grades, no matter how well or poorly they perform.

11. In fewer instances, we have seen accountability systems that require some skill or knowledge performance to earn high grades, but these occur less frequently than do the systems described in points 9 and 10.

12. On a few occasions, we have seen teachers describe an accountability system that involves performance, but, in fact, students have only to be a member in good standing and make a consistent effort to earn the highest grade. We have called these systems examples of "pseudo-accountability."

13. Some clever students hide within the instructional task system. Those students who appear to take part in the instructional tasks but actually avoid most involvement have been called "competent bystanders" (see Box 5.1 titled "The Competent Bystander"). Some students engage in the instructional system appropriately for a while and then shift their engagement so that it is more social even though it appears to be on-task (see Box 5.2 titled "Hiding Social Engagement within Instructional Tasks").

14. Instructional task systems that seem to be highly on-task and intended to produce skill outcomes are characterized by consistent accountability measures, although few of these can be characterized as performance-grade exchanges. Effective teachers hold students accountable through challenges, public performance, frequent task-related feedback, frequent prompting for on-task behavior, and recording performances. Elementary physical education teachers also use many informal accountability mechanisms, such as point systems, posters, and challenge systems.

15. Most physical education classes appear to be highly social. The differences among them seem to lie in whether the student socialization takes place in ways that disrupt or suspend the instructional task system, or whether teachers find ways for students to socialize while still taking part appropriately in the instructional task system.

Toward a Learning-Oriented Ecology

It is clear that teachers and students need to cooperate to make life in physical education pleasant for all concerned. It is also clear that students come to physical education seeking and expecting a social experience. The managerial and student-social systems are, therefore, crucial to understanding the ecology of physical education. But what of the instructional system? Should teachers accept an ecology that has as its major goal that students behave well and have fun? Can physical education survive as a school subject if good behavior and a good time are its main outcomes? What teaching skills are most important for a teacher who wants to develop an ecology in which students not only behave well and have fun but learn important skills, too? Those teaching skills represent the primary focus of the remainder of this text.

Summary

1. Teaching and learning need to be understood in terms of the two-way influence existing between teachers and students.
2. An *ecology* is a series of interrelated systems in which changes or disruptions in one system affect the other systems.
3. The managerial, instructional, and student-social systems comprise the ecology of physical education.
4. Tasks begin as stated tasks, but the task students actually do is typically developed through a contingency developed process.
5. *Accountability* refers to practices teachers use to establish and maintain student responsibility for appropriate conduct, task involvement, and outcomes.
6. *Clarity* and *ambiguity* refer to the degree of explicitness and consistency in task definition.
7. *Risk* refers to the interaction among the ambiguity and difficulty of a task and the degree of accountability applied to it.
8. Task boundaries can be tight or loose, depending on how clearly tasks are defined as well as how accountable students are.
9. Students typically negotiate task demands by modifying the tasks and seeing how teachers respond to the modifications.
10. Some teachers trade demands in the instructional system for compliance with the boundaries of the managerial system, because the first goal of teaching is to gain and maintain the cooperation of students.
11. Supervision and accountability are the key factors driving task systems.
12. In the absence of accountability, the instructional task system can be suspended and what happens is left to the interests of the students.
13. Research has revealed many features of physical education ecologies, including task explicitness, contingency-developed systems, task routinization, patterns of involvement, patterns of task modification, various accountability formats, and how systems interact to produce an ecology.

CHAPTER 6
Preventive Class Management

Effective classroom management consists of teacher behaviors that produce high levels of student involvement in classroom activities, minimal amounts of student behaviors that interfere with the teacher's or other students' work, and efficient use of instructional time. These criteria have the advantage of being observable.

Edmund Emmer & Carolyn Evertson (1981)

CHAPTER OBJECTIVES

To explain the nature and purpose of preventive management

To explain the importance of an effective managerial task system

To explain erroneous assumptions about teaching

To explain the nature and role of rules and routines

To describe important routines and how they develop

To describe important rules and how they develop

To explain managerial time and describe how it can be reduced

To describe the skills and strategies important to a preventive managerial task system

To describe how a managerial system can be assessed

Effective management in physical education doesn't just happen! Classes that run smoothly, are free from disruptive behavior, and optimize the amount of time available for instruction and practice are the result of a serious effort on the part of a skilled teacher to ensure that a good learning environment is developed and maintained. There is an old adage that "an ounce of prevention is worth a pound of cure." Nowhere is this more true than in the development of a managerial task system that maintains appropriate student behavior and provides an optimal amount of learning time.

Preventive classroom management refers to the proactive (rather than reactive) strategies teachers use to develop and maintain a positive, on-task climate in which minimal time is devoted to managerial issues. Preventive management in physical education requires planning and instruction by the teacher and practice by the students. What is learned are the appropriate ways of behaving within the managerial and instructional task systems of the class. Sensitive and skilled teachers also take into account student-social agendas as they teach the behavioral and organizational skills necessary for making the class run smoothly, efficiently, and

6.1 Exerting Behavioral Control for the Right Reasons!

There is no doubt that effective teachers develop managerial structures for promoting appropriate behavior, minimizing disruptions, and saving time. It is important, however, to avoid a "me-them" mentality in establishing and maintaining the managerial task system. Effective teachers don't control students just for the sake of "flexing their muscles." The purpose of effective management is to develop an appropriate learning climate.

What is an appropriate learning climate for physical education? While we might differ somewhat in the exact details of a definition, most of us would agree that students need to experience the joys and satisfactions of physical involvement in sport, dance, and fitness. Getting better at those activities and learning about the enormous satisfactions derived from making them a regular part of one's life-style are the "goods" we pursue in the name of physical education.

These "goods" are not likely to be achieved in a class climate that is authoritarian, rigid, and lacking in joy and spontaneity. Sport, dance, and fitness activities tend to be very social in nature, which is one reason people willingly pursue them throughout their lives. Effective teachers must develop managerial systems that allow the gymnasium and the playing fields to become places of healthy, even joyous interactions among students as they learn. Effective teachers channel the students' social agendas into the activities so they co-exist *within* the limits of the managerial and instructional task systems.

positively. Of all the lessons learned from research on effective teachers, none is more clear than this: Their effectiveness is based on a sound, preventive managerial task system.

The managerial task system establishes the structures through which the physical education class becomes a predictable and smoothly operating system. The system establishes the limits for behavior and the expectations the teacher has for students. A clearly defined managerial task system is unambiguous for students. They know what to do, how to do it, and when to do it. They also understand the consequences for behaving in ways that stretch the limits of the system or violate its boundaries. The managerial system, when set up well, frees the teacher from the need to attend constantly to managerial details and allows the students to operate responsibly within the boundaries of the system.

Why is a managerial task system important? Why is it important that it be done well? There are two reasons. First, teachers and students need to exist together for long periods of time. The elementary specialist might have six to twelve classes per day. The middle school or secondary teacher might have six classes per day. This is repeated five days per week throughout the school year. It is important that teachers and students exist together peacefully! No teacher can withstand a "state of war" with students on a daily basis throughout the school year. A level of cooperation must be achieved that allows teachers to function effectively. This clearly is the first and most important function of a managerial task system.

An effective managerial task system is also important because it saves time. Time is the most precious commodity that teachers have because time is necessary for learning. If a teacher intends for students to learn, then finding enough time for that to happen becomes a primary goal. Time spent managing students and responding to disruptive behavior can't be used for learning. Thus, strategies that reduce management time and disruptive behavior produce time that can be used for learning.

Don't Make Erroneous Assumptions about Teaching

Teachers often make assumptions about the conduct of a class. Teaching interns are especially prone to making unwarranted assumptions concerning the behavior of students. Interns spend time carefully planning lessons and approach the teaching experience with anticipation. But they spend less time examining the assumptions that underlie any lesson plan.

Common assumptions are that students will enter the gymnasium quickly; that they will be eager to begin the lesson that has been planned; that they will be attentive to instructions and demonstrations and will attempt later to imitate demonstrations; that they will organize and change activities quickly; and that they will make an honest effort to engage in the planned learning activity and will generally behave in a manner that is consistent with accomplishing the goals of the lesson. When only one of these assumptions is violated, it tends to disrupt the flow of a well-planned instructional experience. When several of them are compromised during the same lesson, the well-planned instructional experience fails—not because it was poorly planned or executed, but because the teacher had not paid enough attention to the behavioral assumptions that underlie a positive learning environment. Too often this kind of experience creates tension between teacher and students, and if it happens frequently, it is one of the main ingredients in a teacher's growing dissatisfaction with his or her job. Many teachers feel that they are trained to teach and are paid to teach. If honest and sincere efforts to teach well fail because of student disruption, inattention or lack of effort in organization or practice, then the learning environment can quickly deteriorate into a battleground where teachers go to war with students. Teachers have traditionally relied on parents to raise their children in such a way that the children come to school with certain behaviors already fairly well developed, and other behavioral predispositions solidly entrenched. Traditionally, it is in the home that children have learned to pay attention, to respond to instructions, to respect an adult authority figure, and to approach school with the clear expectation that these ways of behaving will also occur at school. Parents not only helped develop these behaviors at home but also made sure that the child was exhibiting these behaviors when he or she went to school. If the child did behave differently at school, it was usually quite easy to change this by threatening some punishment or by hinting that a note would be sent home or the parents asked to come in to discuss the problem. In many schools, this situation still exists to a large degree, but in many others, it is increasingly dangerous to assume that children come to school equipped with these behavioral tendencies. The result is that classroom management has assumed more importance in teaching.

A common assertion in the educational literature is that discipline is inherent in good teaching; that is, if you teach well you will have no discipline problems. The implication is that the right choice of activity combined with the right teaching method will automatically produce learners who behave well and try hard. No one would disagree with the proposition that discipline is less problematic when activities are chosen and taught well, but this does not ensure that all students will suddenly turn into eager learners. To assert such a relationship between teaching and discipline is at best simplistic. Teachers should strive to improve their programs and teaching methods, but they can also attack the problems of classroom and gymnasium management directly.

Classroom management skills are essential to good teaching. This is true in every classroom and in every subject. It is true in the open classroom. It is true in a classroom where the children sit in neatly arranged rows of desks. It is also true in the gymnasium, on the playground, and the playing field. The result of the positive application of management skills is that students learn self-management. Once students have learned self-management, it becomes easier for the teacher to proceed with good teaching. It is a mistake to ignore the management function or to assume that students will exhibit the behaviors necessary for a positive and effective learning environment. The goal of this chapter is to provide you with the skills necessary to manage your class effectively and positively.

Routines and Rules:
The Foundation of the Managerial Task System

An effective managerial task system begins with the development of routines and the establishment of class rules for appropriate behavior. A *routine* is a procedure for performing specific behaviors within a class, behaviors that tend to recur frequently and, unless structured, can potentially disrupt or delay the pace of a lesson. *Rules* identify general expectations for behavior that cover a variety of situations. Rules can be developed by defining acceptable behavior ("be quiet and pay attention when the teacher is talking") or by defining unacceptable behavior ("don't talk while the teacher is talking"). Rules tend to imply both acceptable and unacceptable behavior, no matter which way they are written.

Evidence from the study of effective teachers indicates that their major teaching focus during the first few days of school year is the establishment of class routines and rules (Brophy & Good, 1986; Fink & Siedentop, 1989). For younger children, the routines are taught just as if they were content. For example,

6.2 Getting Started on the Right Foot

Research has indicated clearly that teachers who spend time in the early part of the school year—the first several weeks—teaching specific classroom and gymnasium routines not only have an easier time of managing and disciplining throughout the school year but also have students who learn more. Teachers who take time to specifically teach routines such as how to contact the teacher, use equipment, and move around the available space have fewer problems. Gymnasium routines become part of the content that is taught, which has a high payoff.

Hayman and Moskowitz (1975) found that what junior high school teachers did on the very first day went a long way toward determining their overall effectiveness for the year. Before patterns of inappropriate behavior can develop, the teachers taught specific patterns of appropriate behavior—laid down the ground rules for getting along together in the class. According to Emmer and Evertson (1981), "All classroom management systems, good, poor, or in-between, have a beginning. The way in which teachers structure the first part of the year has consequences for their classroom management throughout the year."

most elementary physical education specialists use what we call an "attention/quiet" routine. This routine involves a specific teacher signal for gaining the attention of students (a whistle blow, a hand clap, the word "freeze") and the students quieting quickly and facing the teacher. In our study of seven effective elementary specialists (Fink & Siedentop, 1989), the seven teachers used this routine 346 times in the first several days of teaching first and fifth grade classes. Activities were chosen that included frequent stops and starts by the teacher just so this routine could be practiced. Students were told exactly what was expected and were then given ample opportunity to practice. The behavioral expectations for the routine were described, prompted often, and reinforced frequently. After several classes, most students were behaving appropriately when the attention signal was given. Those few students that were not compliant were then given quiet, yet effective reprimands. This attention/quiet routine was used in each unit throughout the school year. To have students quiet down quickly (typically in less than three seconds) and to have no disruptive behavior related to gaining the attention of students not only makes teaching easier and more pleasant but also saves valuable time that can be used for learning.

Routines and Their Development

Routines should be taught for all aspects of student behavior that tend to recur frequently and have the potential of disrupting or delaying the pacing of the lesson. Remember, routines are specific ways to accomplish certain tasks within a lesson. Some routines that are used effectively in physical education are shown in Table 6.1.

Table 6.1 *Examples of routines typically used in physical education*

Routine	Purpose
Entry	What to do when entering the gymnasium. Most often includes an initial practice activity or warm-up and a specific space to go to.
Warm-up	A specific warm-up to engage in without teacher prompting or supervision.
Attention/quiet	A teacher signal for attention and the expected student response to the signal.
Home base	A specific place (spot, number) on the gym floor that the student goes to when instructed.
Gain attention	An appropriate way for the students to gain the attention of the teacher.
Gather	An appropriate way to gather in a central location when directed by the teacher and the formation to gather into.
Disperse	An appropriate way to disperse from a central location to a more scattered practice formation.
Equipment	Appropriate ways to obtain or put away equipment.
Retrieve	An appropriate way to retrieve a ball when it has invaded the space of classmates during a game or drill.
Start	A procedure for initiating activity quickly on a signal.
Boundaries	Specific procedures for staying within defined boundaries, whether inside a gym or outside on a playing field.
Finish	A specific procedure for ending a lesson that typically includes both a cool-down and a closure to the lesson.
Leave	A procedure for leaving the space and returning to the classroom or locker room.
Housekeeping	All procedures for dealing with things like dressing, using the bathroom, getting a drink, or leaving the space.

In addition to the routines described in Table 6.1, teachers might develop routines that are specific to their own curriculum or students. For example, elementary specialists often teach concepts of self and general space to young children as routines, because these concepts are used throughout the movement development curriculum. Other teachers like to add certain elements to routines to make them more complete. For example, some teachers add directions about equipment to the attention/quiet routine when students are in an activity where they are using balls. The addition might be that when the signal occurs, students not only stop their activity, become quiet, and face the teacher, but also, if they have a ball, put it down near their feet and don't touch it. Teachers who start classes inside a gymnasium and then move their class to an outside space should develop a routine to get that transition done quickly and without disruption.

Routines need to be taught just as specifically as one might teach how to dribble or how to pass. The behavioral expectations of the routines should be explained and demonstrated, and students should be provided the opportunity to practice. Teachers need to prompt the behaviors, provide specific feedback, praise students for compliance, and reprimand them for noncompliance. Prompts, feedback, and praise should be very frequent when first teaching the routine and then gradually lessened as the students learn to do the routine quickly and well. Reprimands should be avoided at the outset, while the routine is being learned, but then used quickly and firmly for students who are still noncompliant when most of the class has learned the routine.

Rules and Their Development

Rules define general expectations for behavior in many situations. They are described as "rules" to students and often posted as rules on the wall of the gymnasium. Rules also often have consequences. Sometimes the consequences are explained to students, and on fewer occasions, the consequences for rule violations are also posted on the gymnasium wall. Rules are less specific than routines; they relate to behaviors that occur in a variety of situations. Still, students need to have the rules explained and be given examples of following and violating rules. When rules are broken, the behavior should be desisted immediately and the appropriate consequence provided. Students should also be reinforced for following rules and prompted about them at times other than when rules are violated. Rules, to be effective, need to be made clear and then enforced consistently.

Rules differ from routines in that they specify general kinds of behavior that occur in many different situations. A rule such as "respect your classmates and their equipment" refers to a group of behaviors that may differ from situation to situation but tend to have the same effect. There are important guidelines to follow when developing class rules.

1. Rules should be short and directly to the point.
2. Rules should be communicated in language or symbols appropriate to the age level of the students.
3. No more than five to eight rules can both communicate important categories of behavior and be remembered by students.
4. When possible, state rules positively, but make sure that both positive and negative examples are provided.
5. Make sure class rules are consistent with school rules.
6. Relate consistent consequences to rules.
7. Don't create rules you cannot or are not willing to enforce.

Rules need to be taught differently than routines. The group of behaviors that fulfill a class rule such as "be polite and helpful" will differ somewhat from situation to situation. Therefore, the range of behaviors that comply with the rule—and those that violate it—need to be considered. Teachers should prompt compliance with rules often by pointing out positive instances of following rules, as well as instances of breaking them. Students need to be reminded about rules at times other than when a rule violation occurs. Asking students about behavior related to rules is a good way to judge the degree to which they understand the rule.

It is also important that students understand *why* rules are chosen. Reasons for rules do not have to be conveyed in long lectures—indeed, that would be ineffective. However, students need to understand why safety is important and why cooperation among learners is essential for their own development as students as well as for the good of the class as a whole. This is best accomplished through concrete examples given when specific prompts or feedback is provided to students after a rule-following or rule-breaking incident. For example, when students misuse equipment, it can be explained that the equipment may not last very long and students will have less good equipment to use.

Almost all teachers develop class rules. Not all, however, teach them effectively. Nor do all enforce them consistently. Teachers need to consider seriously the degree to which they will specify consequences for rule violations. Some teachers like to specify consequences and post them along with the rules. In such cases, there are typically a hierarchy of consequences, such as a time-out penalty for the first violation, a more extreme penalty for the second violation, and perhaps a visit to the principal's office for the third violation. Other teachers leave consequences unspecified but try to use them consistently. Still other teachers use a point or marking system of some kind, which allows them to use both rewards and punishments for following and violating rules. These systems will be reviewed in Chapter 7.

6.3 Should You Use General Rules or Behavior-Specific Rules?

Teachers should decide how specific they want to be with their rules. A general rule such as "always be considerate of others" will have to be taught in many different situations before students begin to understand clearly what you mean by "considerate." A more specific rule such as "raise your hand before asking a question" can be taught much more quickly and enforced much more easily.

It is difficult, however, to develop a specific rule for all the important situations that occur in physical education. In general, you should avoid long lists of rules. You need to consider carefully if there are crucial forms of student behavior that would warrant a behavior-specific rule. If there are, from your point of view, then develop a specific rule, teach it, and enforce it consistently. An example might be: "Always have permission before using any equipment." On the other hand, it is important that students learn what general concepts such as respect and cooperation mean in the many different activities and situations encountered in physical education. This will result in more teaching and will require real consistency in dealing with students, but in the long run, the payoff for both the students and the teacher is worth it.

However rules are specified, taught, and handled, teachers typically develop them so that they cover a variety of behaviors important to an effective physical education. Physical education rules tend to cover behavior in the following categories.

1. *Safety.* This involves behavior appropriate to certain kinds of equipment as well as behavior relative to classmates—using gymnastics equipment only with permission, walking a safe distance behind a student swinging a golf club, always wearing protective glasses when playing floor hockey.
2. *Respect others.* This involves behavior related to the teacher and classmates—encourage others, don't insult, don't talk back.
3. *Respect the learning environment.* This involves behavior related to equipment and the physical space—don't sit on balls, keep the gym clean, put away all the equipment you used.
4. *Support the learning of others.* This involves behavior related to sharing, supporting, and helping the group—share equipment and space, don't tease, encourage classmates.
5. *Try hard.* This involves behavior such as using time well, staying on-task, and making an effort to learn—be on-time, be on-task, always try hard.

Rules need to be enforced fairly. This means that they must be dealt with consistently from day to day and from student to student. Consistency is particularly important in the application of consequences. From a student point of view, "fairness" is very much bound up with how consequences are applied by persons in authority. The managerial task system—particularly the routines and rules that define its foundation—is crucial to the success of the class and to the "sanity" of the teacher. As suggested in Chapter 5, actively supervising student responses is necessary to make sure that student behavior is consistent with the guidelines suggested by the routines and rules. The boundaries of the system will be tested by students, sometimes inadvertently and sometimes purposely. How teachers respond to these "tests" will, more than anything else, determine the success of the managerial task system.

Managerial Time: What It Is and Why to Reduce It

Managerial time refers to the cumulative amount of time students spend in organizational, transitional, and non-subject-matter tasks. It is time when no instruction is given, no demonstrations are made, no practice is done, and no observation of student performance is made. It contains no opportunities for students to learn the subject matter. Roll taking, getting equipment out, waiting for an activity to begin, organizing teams, moving from one place to another, and discussing an upcoming school event all contribute to total managerial time. In Chapter 3, it was noted that management time accounts for a substantial part of the typical physical education lesson—too much, in the opinion of most observers. Teaching research also supports the common sense notion that disruptive student behavior is more likely to occur during managerial time than during instruction or activity time. Reducing the amount of managerial time, therefore, not only provides more time for learning but also reduces the likelihood of disruptive behavior.

An important concept in understanding and reducing managerial time is the *managerial episode,* which is a single unit of management time. A managerial episode begins with a managerial behavior emitted by a teacher (or a predetermined signal) and continues until the next instructional event or activity begins. The total of all the managerial episodes plus the total amount of time students spend waiting in a lesson equals the total managerial time for that lesson. Focusing on managerial episodes allows for a more specific analysis of where in a lesson and for what purposes managerial time is being accumulated. The following are examples of managerial episodes.

- Students come from the locker room and await the first signal from the teacher to begin the class (time from the official beginning of the period to the moment when the first instruction is given).

- A teacher blows her whistle and tells the class to assemble on one side of the gym (time from the whistle until the class is assembled and another instruction is given).

- A teacher, having explained a drill, signals the class to go to their proper places to begin the drill (time from the dispersion signal to the moment the activity actually begins).

- Inside a gym, a teacher finishes instructions for an activity and sends the class outside to begin the activity (time from signal to leave until the outside activity begins).

- A teacher takes roll (time from the signal for beginning roll taking until the next instruction or activity begins).

Often it is not any one managerial episode that wastes a major portion of time but rather the accumulation of individual episodes that are each too long. Many teachers are surprised at the number of managerial episodes that occur within a class and the total time devoted to them, but are pleased to learn that managerial time can be reduced substantially—and often easily. The data in Table 6.2 are from an experiment to reduce managerial time with three physical education student teachers. The length of the teaching period was 35 minutes.

Table 6.2 Reducing managerial time. (Adapted from Siedentop, Rife, and Boehm, 1974.)

		Baseline	Intervention
ST-1	Total managerial time per class	10:37	1:46
	Average time per managerial episode	1:49	0:23
ST-2	Total managerial time per class	11:36	2:03
	Average time per managerial episode	1:37	0:25
ST-3	Total managerial time per class	13:33	1:23
	Average time per managerial episode	1:38	0:13

Each of the student teachers in the experiment saved approximately 10 minutes per class when they focused on reducing managerial time. They used a simple managerial game (see page 94) to accomplish the reductions. A substantial amount of evidence suggests that physical education teachers spend too much time in management and that managerial time can be reduced substantially by using the techniques described in this chapter.

In most physical education lessons, there are many instructional tasks. Teachers need to change from one task to another or from one variation of a task to another. A *transition* is a managerial episode in which teachers change the task focus, when students move from one task to another, when teams need to change courts, when substitutions are made in games, or similar situations. In lessons with young children, whose attention span is not great, teachers may provide as many as 15–20 different tasks per lesson, each of which requires a transition. In middle and secondary school, there are often fewer transitions, but the spaces are larger and the number of students being transitioned is typically greater. While any one transition might not take much time, the accumulated time in transitions represents a major portion of managerial time in a lesson. Effective teachers establish routines for all recurring aspects of managerial time, from roll taking to transitions. The "gather," "disperse," and "start" routines described earlier in this chapter are crucial for effective transitions.

When a managerial task system is well established, it not only reduces managerial time and the opportunities for disruptive behavior but also quickens the pace of a lesson and maintains the momentum of that pace throughout the lesson. A quick pace that is maintained throughout the lesson is important to convey to students that they are in a learning environment. A quickly paced, upbeat lesson in which the pace is maintained through a well-established managerial task system probably does more than any other factor to impress upon learners the teacher's intent that they learn and improve. On the other hand, research (Kounin, 1970) has shown that slowing the pace of the lesson or breaking its momentum with interruptions or other "slow-down" events tends to increase disruptive behavior and lessen the learning time students acquire.

A *managerial interaction* or *managerial behavior* refers to the verbal and nonverbal teacher behavior needed to develop and maintain the managerial task system. Managerial behavior includes such actions as a hand clap signal for attention, blowing a whistle, giving instructions for organization, or reprimanding students who were misbehaving. When a teacher has established an effective managerial task system, only a minimal amount of managerial behavior is needed to maintain it. Indeed, if you visit a physical education class and see a teacher who emits a large amount of managerial behavior (especially prompts and reprimands), you are probably observing a less than effective manager. That is the purpose of a system! Students learn to manage themselves within the system and do not need constant prompting from the teacher. They behave well and efficiently within the system and therefore are not the targets of frequent reprimands for moving too slowly or behaving inappropriately.

6.4 Are Your Students too Dependent on You?

Situation. The teacher is doing a movement education lesson with second-graders. The lesson involves solving movement problems that are structured around a rope lying on the floor. Each child has a rope in his or her own space. The teacher has the students sit down in a line. The teacher then walks about placing the ropes on the floor. The children are instructed to disperse to find their own spaces. There are at least six instances of two children on one rope. The teacher takes one child from each pair and directs him or her to a vacant rope. The lesson proceeds. After the lesson, the teacher has the children sit down while he or she puts the ropes away.

Results. Far too much time is spent in management, and a very high rate of managerial behavior is emitted by the teacher.

Analysis. The students have everything done for them. They are not learning to manage themselves within the context of the gymnasium and the movement education curriculum. Second-graders are perfectly capable of learning how to put away equipment and how to find their own spaces quickly without further prompting from a teacher. If this situation continues, the students will not learn self-management. All evidence indicates that "sitting in lines" is an opportunity to misbehave. After all, why shouldn't a student misbehave when there is nothing to do but but watch a teacher walk around placing ropes on the floor!

Prescription. This lesson offers a perfect opportunity to teach self-management skills. Students can be taught how to place the equipment. Students can be taught how to find their own places. They need to practice these skills, and they need feedback and positive interactions when they perform them well. The major point is that it is perfectly legitimate to teach these as separate, identifiable skills and not merely as ancillary aspects of the movement education lesson.

The Skills and Strategies Most Important to Preventive Class Management

Developing and maintaining an efficient managerial task system is accomplished by using key strategies and some important teaching skills. The purpose of this section is to describe those skills and strategies. Remember, the major goal is to develop a *system* that requires students to do a great deal of self-management, that makes them responsible members of the class, and that allows the teacher to attend to learning-related issues rather than managerial issues.

1. *Control the initial activity.* When students enter the gym, they should have something to do that contributes to lesson outcomes, whether it be a warm-up or some initial practice activity. Initial activities can be posted on a bulletin board or chalk board. Information should include where to be and what to do. The activity should be a familiar one that can be done successfully with no instruction. With young children, diagrams of formations and location work can be used along with pictures. If students enter the gym early, they can engage in productive practice or warm-up rather than do nothing or, worse still, engage in off-task behavior. Controlling the initial activity by developing a routine also eliminates the need for the teacher to gather students to organize them for an initial activity.

2. *Start the class promptly on time.* Each class should begin at an appointed time and the teacher should be consistent in initiating instruction or activity at that time. Promptness at the beginning establishes the pace and momentum of a class and reinforces the importance of what is done in physical education.

3. *Use a time-saving method for roll call.* If you are required to take attendance daily, as many teachers are, then you need to establish a routine that allows you to fulfill that obligation but does not create student waiting time. Students can sign in as they enter the gym. There is evidence that public signing-in reduces tardiness (McKenzie & Rushall, 1973). Roll can be taken during the initial activity if it has been controlled so that students are in assigned places. If you use a "home base" routine (see page 85), then attendance can easily be taken by noticing the vacant spots.

4. *Teach signals and routines for attention, gathering, and dispersing.* Situations in which these routines are necessary occur frequently. The routines need to be prompted frequently at the outset and practiced. Students also need to be held accountable for compliance with the behavioral expectations of the routine. Accountability is better done positively than negatively. Frequent, sincere praise for appropriate behavior is useful. Feedback on time saved helps. With younger children, saving time can be made a game.

5. *Utilize proactive teaching through prompts, hustles, and enthusiasm.* When you first develop managerial routines, these proactive teacher behaviors need to be used frequently. Specific prompts relative to the routines are helpful. A hustle is a prompt that focuses on energizing the students to respond quickly—"let's go," "hustle," "quickly, now." A teacher shows enthusiasm through many facets of behavior: a strong voice, an upbeat pace to instructions, smiling, tone of voice. It is not possible to be a "cheerleader" for eight classes a day, but an appropriate level of enthusiasm sends important messages to students.

6. *Communicate high, yet realistic expectations.* An *expectation* is a teacher statement describing a future process or outcome that is hoped for and expected. Expectations typically describe process ("I expect you to move quickly when you change stations") or outcomes ("I think you will all get

a lot stronger if we save time to do more fitness work"). It is important that students understand your expectations for them. It is even more important that your performance as a teacher follows through on those expectations. Students will learn very quickly that you do or do not follow through on expectations. If you say "I expect you to hustle between activities" and then allow students to loaf between activities, they will quickly learn that you don't mean what you say.

7. *Use high rates of specific feedback and positive interactions.* When first teaching routines, student practice of the routines should result in frequent specific feedback and positive interactions. *Specific feedback* contains information relevant to the behavior—"Squad 1 changed stations and got busy in only nine seconds!" *General feedback* supports behavior but contains no information relative to it—"way to go," "good job." At the outset, teachers should concentrate on praising students who do well in routines. Noncompliant students often get the "message" that way. Praise is important, even with older students, although the way the praise is conveyed needs to be adjusted for different age groups (see Chapter 8). As the managerial task system develops, feedback and praise should become less frequent, but should never be completely neglected.

8. *Avoid slow-downs and breaks.* A quick pace to a lesson is important. Therefore, events that tend to slow down the pace should be avoided. Breaks that completely stop the pace should also be avoided. To avoid breaks and slow downs, teachers need to be able to handle "intrusion events." An *intrusion* event is any unpredictable event that requires the attention of a teacher to be diverted from the class—a message from the central office, a student who gets slightly injured, a youngster who begins to cry. Teachers need to deal with these events, but they also need to keep the momentum of the lesson going. Slowdowns also occur when teachers dwell on irrelevant events, lecture too long, or give too many details. Momentum can also be jeopardized by having one student do something when the entire class could be doing it.

9. *Post records of the managerial performance of students.* A more formal approach to feedback and motivation for management is to keep records of management time and to post the results somewhere in the gymnasium. The chronographs that are widely available allow teachers to easily measure managerial episode lengths. Notes can be jotted down on clipboards. Classes can set have target goals and then be assessed to see if they meet them. One class can compare their performance to other classes.

10. *For quick results, use a management game.* In certain situations, it may be useful to improve managerial performance quickly by motivating students through a management game. A *management game* is a behavior-change technique in which students are rewarded for achieving managerial goals within a game format. Management games are typically used at the elementary and middle school levels to get managerial control to establish routines and rules. To use a management game, the class should be divided into teams of five to eight students. A set of specific managerial goals should

be established (such as, start time, target transition times, attention within five seconds, and so forth.). Management games are easiest to administer if a *group contingency* is utilized, in which every member of a team must be behaving appropriately for the team to earn points. Points are awarded each time a target managerial goal is achieved. All teams can win. Teams compete against the point standard for rewards, not against each other. Free time is the easiest form of no-cost reward to use. Teams meeting a daily standard can accumulate free time. Eventually the game can be played on a weekly or even on a unit basis. Box 6.5 titled "Group Contingency Management Game," shows a managerial game used successfully at the middle school level in the experiment described in Table 6.2.

Assessing the Managerial Task System

There are obvious ways to monitor the effectiveness of a managerial task system. This should be done periodically to make sure that the system is running as smoothly and efficiently as possible. Monitoring important information about to managerial efficiency is not a difficult task and should not be too time consuming for the teacher. Time is a major determinant of success. You can

---

6.5 Group Contingency Management Game

Three student teachers were having a difficult time dealing with class management. Too much time was wasted; disruptive behavior was too high. A simple management game was instituted, and played with the entire class. The reward for the class was to accumulate free time minutes that could be used to do activities of their choice in physical education. For the class to accumulate free time minutes, all students had to meet each criterion. There were three managerial goals.

1. Students read the posted opening activity when entering the gym and had to be at assigned stations and practicing by eight minutes after the hour (two minutes of free time for each successful class beginning).
2. Whenever the teacher blew the whistle for attention, the class had to be attentive and quiet within five seconds (one minute of free time for each successful instance).
3. When transitioning from one activity to another in class, the next class segment had to begin within 15 seconds of a start signal (one minute of free time for each successful instance).

Teachers kept records of free time minutes accumulated. These minutes were "spent" during each Friday's lesson. During free time, students had the choice of engaging in several different activities (gymnastics, basketball, or sitting in the bleachers and talking). The use of this management game produced the changes shown in Table 6.2.

monitor managerial episode lengths with a wrist chronograph. You can also tally the number of prompts and interactions you have relative to managerial issues. You can observe specific routines for efficiency. You can also occasionally observe selected students to see how often they have to wait for the next lesson segment to begin. Instances of off-task behavior can be tallied on a clipboard. Not all of these observations should be made in the same lesson—you still have to teach! Over the period of a week, however, you can collect data for each of these managerial issues. This will provide the most important kind of information about the degree of success you are achieving in your managerial task system.

More specific information about observation and managerial observation systems can be found in Chapter 16.

Summary

1. *Preventive management* refers to the proactive strategies used by teachers to develop and maintain a positive on-task climate.

2. An effective managerial task system produces cooperation among teachers and students and also saves time that can be used for learning.

3. Rules identify general expectations for behavior that cover a variety of situations.

4. *Routines* are procedures for performing specific behaviors within a class, particularly those behaviors that recur regularly.

5. Routines need to be taught early in the school year and taught well, so that they become habitual.

6. Rules need to be taught throughout the year, mostly by pointing out behavioral examples of following and violating rules, as well as why the rule is important.

7. Rules need to be enforced fairly and consistently.

8. *Managerial time* is the cumulative amount of time students spend in organizational, transitional, and non-subject-matter tasks.

9. *Managerial episodes* are single units of management time.

10. *Transitions* are managerial episodes between one class focus (instruction, practice, and so forth) and the next class focus.

11. *Managerial interactions* are verbal and nonverbal behaviors needed to develop and maintain the managerial task system.

12. A number of teaching skills and strategies have been identified for developing and maintaining an effective managerial task system, including initial activity control, start time, roll call, routines, enthusiastic teaching, expectations, specific feedback, posting managerial records, and management games.

13. Monitoring how time is spent and checking how often students are on and off-task are ways to assess the managerial task system.

CHAPTER 7

Discipline Techniques and Strategies

The mastery of classroom management skills should not be regarded as an end in itself. These techniques are, however, necessary tools. Techniques are enabling. The mastery of techniques enables one to do many different things. It makes choices possible. The possession of group management skills allows the teacher to accomplish her goals—the absence of managerial skills acts as a barrier.

Jacob Kounin (1970)

CHAPTER OBJECTIVES

To describe different ways discipline can be defined

To explain why discipline is important

To define appropriate and inappropriate behavior

To explain and apply strategies for changing behavior

To explain and apply strategies for increasing appropriate behavior

To describe effective praise and interaction strategies

To explain and apply strategies for decreasing inappropriate behavior

To describe constructive alternatives to punishment

To describe formal behavior-change strategies

To explain the ultimate goal of a discipline strategy

This chapter is about discipline. The material in it needs to be considered in the context of the managerial task system described in Chapters 5 and 6. The foundation for good discipline in any educational setting is the preventive managerial task system that the teacher develops and maintains. Discipline is much less likely to be a problem when an effective managerial task system is in place. This is true, as you will see, because the most important definition of discipline is that of developing and maintaining appropriate behavior.

In this text, *appropriate behavior* is defined as student behavior that is consistent with the educational goals of a specific educational setting. Different settings often require differing definitions of appropriate behavior, yet each setting requires a high percentage of appropriate behavior in order to achieve whatever educational goals have been set. Therefore, I will say very little here about what kinds of student behavior ought to be defined as appropriate. Eventually, that will be up to you. Is always being quiet appropriate? Is wearing the prescribed physical education uniform appropriate? Is keeping in a straight line appropriate? Ultimately, schools, departments, and teachers decide these things based on their own convictions and their interpretations of the concerns of local parents and administrators. However, a basic assumption is made here that high rates of appropriate student behavior are universally sought after by teachers. I have some opinions about what should be considered appropriate, but when I cite or discuss them they will be clearly delineated as opinions rather than as universal "do's" and "don'ts."

Teachers make decisions every day about what is or is not appropriate for the classroom and gymnasium. Whenever a teacher reprimands a student, he or she is helping to delineate the boundaries of acceptable behavior. Every educational environment has rules of behavior. Sometimes they are made public, but most often they learn by violating one and being the target of a negative interaction. Most unwritten class rules are negative; they come across as "don'ts" rather than "do's."

The term *discipline* has always been important in a teacher's vocabulary. In today's schools, many teachers are judged primarily by their ability to maintain good discipline. Discipline is an important component in education, but discipline can be approached from a positive as well as a negative viewpoint. Many people, if asked to define the characteristics of a well-disciplined class, would probably respond with a definition close to the one used here for appropriate behavior; that is, "behavior consistent with the educational goals of the specific situation." That constitutes a positive approach to discipline.

But many people define discipline by the absence of inappropriate behavior; to them, *discipline* means "keeping the troops in line," and the military analogy is not used without reason. For many teachers, maintaining discipline amounts to developing and maintaining a rigid, military atmosphere in the gymnasium. If you value that kind of atmosphere, you will have great difficulty with the positive approach to discipline advocated here.

The crux of the matter can be seen by examining the following two definitions of discipline: (1) training to behave in accordance with rules, and (2) punishment carried out by way of correction. The first definition allows for a positive approach, for teaching students to "behave in accordance with rules" can be done through a positive or a negative approach. But the second definition allows no room for anything positive. Indeed, when used as a verb (*to discipline*) the term implies an act of punishment.

It is important that you understand my perspective on discipline from the outset. Punishment is a behavior management technique. Several punishment techniques are discussed later in this chapter. Punishment is used in schools and is sometimes an extremely valuable technique in a teacher's overall repertoire of management skills. But, the sole purpose of punishment should be to redirect disruptive or otherwise inappropriate behavior into more useful and productive forms of behavior. Punishment techniques should be used skillfully and without emotional overtones, such as angry outbursts at students. Punishment should not be used in retribution or merely to "flex your muscles."

Punishment is a much overused discipline strategy that is usually of short-term benefit only and is fraught with potential problems. There is too much punishment in schools! The main reason for this is quite simply that too few teachers have and use the skills necessary to maintain discipline through positive strategies. Appropriate behavior is important, but it is also more than the absence of inappropriate behavior! The basic task of discipline is not only to reduce forms of disruptive and inappropriate behavior but also to develop the kinds of appropriate behavior through which students can learn and grow.

Why is Discipline Important?

Discipline is important for many reasons. First, parents and administrators *expect* classes to be well managed and students to behave well. While they understand that disruptions occur and that occasionally some students can present difficult discipline problems, they still *expect* that a certified teacher can handle these disruptions and problems. For every one teacher that gets a bad evaluation based on teaching ability, there are probably 25 who get bad evaluations based on their inability to maintain effective discipline! Teachers are also concerned with discipline. For many years, they have ranked it as the most important topic for inservice education. Why? Discipline problems are common in many schools today, and teachers often have had inadequate preparation for dealing with them. Nothing produces teacher fatigue and strain more than having to deal constantly with discipline problems. For your own sanity and well-being, therefore, it is important that you learn as much as you can about both preventive class management and discipline strategies.

It is also commonly suggested that discipline is important because a well-disciplined class learns more. There is no doubt that an effective managerial task system and good discipline strategies create the time and atmosphere in which more learning *can* take place. Teacher effectiveness research has shown that classrooms where more learning takes place are the better-managed classrooms (see Chapter 2)—and less learning is often associated with more poorly managed classes. I believe that effective management is a necessary prerequisite for learning to occur. On the other hand, it is *possible* for classes to be well managed but for little learning to occur. In other words, you should consider it important to develop and maintain an effective managerial task system in your classes, but you cannot assume that by doing so you have guaranteed a high rate of learning. There are many gymnasiums across this country where there is very adequate discipline, but few skill, strategy, or fitness goals are achieved by learners. Good management results in the opportunity for learning to take place, but teachers must seize that opportunity and fill it with good instruction and practice if the learning goals are to be realized.

Defining Appropriate Behavior: Avoiding Discipline by Default

Effective discipline is a positive, proactive strategy, the heart of which is the development and maintenance of appropriate student behavior. To achieve effective discipline, you need to come to grips with what you believe to be appropriate behavior for the students you teach. The general definitions of appropriate behavior suggested below are just that and nothing more—they are general! I have chosen

99

Defining
Appropriate
Behavior:
Avoiding
Discipline by
Default

7.1 Tardiness

Situation. Tardiness is a problem in a junior high school physical education class. The teacher decides to make each student who comes in after the tardy bell run two laps of the gym.

Result. No change. Tardiness does not decrease.

Analysis. The imposed punishment is not effective; it does not decrease the rate of tardiness, because the students do not consider it a punishment at all. Moreover, it is unwise to use an activity (running) as a punishment and then in another situation to try to sell the students on it as a good activity. The problem can be viewed as one of attempting to eliminate tardiness or one of attempting to strengthen the habit of coming to class on time. The results would be the same, but the methods would be drastically different.

Prescription. Are there positive reasons why students should attempt to get to class on time? Is the first activity promptly started and fun to do? Do students who come on time ever get complimented? The best strategy would be to ignore those who are tardy and provide some positive interactions for those who come on time. It would be especially important to target the students who are often tardy and compliment them when they come on time. Having a prompt and pleasurable first activity would also help. Severe or chronic tardiness may need a punishment that would indeed serve as a punishment.

to do this purposely so that you are forced to define the behaviors of your students that would give specific meaning to these general categories. If you don't think about and consciously strive to achieve certain kinds of appropriate behavior among your students, then you will have left the definition of discipline to default. If students are not *taught* what is appropriate and inappropriate—taught it directly and specifically—then they will be left to learn it by default. The most likely way they will learn the boundaries of what you are willing to tolerate is when they step across those boundaries. That is not pleasant for them, and it will not be pleasant for you.

Appropriate behavior is *not* the absence of inappropriate behavior. Teachers must deal with inappropriate behavior quickly and effectively, but you will not be successful in developing good discipline if you concentrate only on eliminating the inappropriate behavior. Every time an inappropriate behavior is stopped or eliminated, a more appropriate, alternative behavior should be developed. That is why defining appropriate behavior for your classes is important. In "discipline by default," teachers typically rely on punishment to reduce and eliminate inappropriate behavior. The class atmosphere becomes defined by punishment and the threat of punishment. When this approach is carried to an extreme, students often withdraw from active participation, are less willing to respond, suffer humiliation in front of their peers, and even utilize punishment more among themselves. It is worth repeating one of the major results from teacher effectiveness research: Classrooms that are characterized by negative interactions, shaming, ridicule, and punishment are classrooms where academic achievement is low and affective development is stifled.

Effective discipline requires a dual approach—both inappropriate and appropriate behavior must be defined. Inappropriate behaviors are those that are detrimental to achieving class goals. Appropriate behaviors are those that are necessary for class goals to be achieved. The dual approach is necessary because the mere absence of inappropriate behavior does not result in the behavioral climate necessary for learning goals to be achieved. Williams and Anandam (1973) suggested a simple, four-category system for defining appropriate and inappropriate student behavior.

1. *Task-relevant behavior* refers to all the behaviors students need to accomplish for successful participation in a lesson.
2. *Appropriate social interaction* refers to student-student interaction as well as teacher-student interaction.
3. *Off-task behavior* refers to any form of inappropriate participation or nonparticipation in assigned class activities.
4. *Disruptive behavior* refers to any form of inappropriate behavior that is immediately harmful to students or disrupts the class lesson.

What do you believe are good, specific definitions within each category? What is "OK" for your students to do and what is "not OK"? What do you need them to do reliably for your lessons to go well? What level of disturbance do you consider to be disruptive? What kinds of behavior are you willing to tolerate—at least until students can learn to improve? Are some behaviors appropriate in certain situations but not in others? The answers to these important questions reflect your own personal views. While these important definitions will be left to you, I would be remiss if I did not state my view that a gymnasium full of silent students is not consistent with the goals of physical education as I see them. I do not believe in "discipline for discipline's sake" (see Box 6.1 titled "Exerting behavioral control for the right reasons"). When I am giving instruction, I want students *absolutely quiet and attentive*. However, when they are engaged in practice and game play, I want them exuberant and excited. The techniques and strategies outlined in this chapter should allow you to achieve both goals with your students.

Basic Strategies for Developing and Changing Behavior

Behavior is changed and developed through the careful, consistent application of contingencies. A *contingency* is the relationship between a behavior and a consequence. The contingencies are the "reasons" for behaving that students need so that they can learn new and more appropriate forms of behavior. Students may eventually behave well because it is "expected" or because "others do it" or because "it's the right thing to do" or because of "self-pride." In the beginning, however, they need more immediate, more concrete reasons for changing their behavior. Strong consequences, related to specific behavioral goals, provide those reasons.

Certain basic strategies apply to all behavior change situations. These principles, if followed carefully, form the basis for a teacher's repertoire of discipline skills.

1. *Be specific.* Make sure that you and the student(s) understand what behavior is to be changed. Don't expect that saying "Stop fooling around" will work often if students aren't told specifically what it means. Also, defining the target of behavior change specifically and carefully prevents the possibility that you will change more behavior than you want or less than you want. For example, you might want to use a punishment technique to stop inappropriate behavior but you don't want the student to think that you don't like him or her. Likewise, you might want to increase the likelihood that a student will ask a question, but you don't want to create a situation of nonstop questioning on the part of students.

2. *Define the change contingency carefully.* A contingency is the statement of relationship between a behavior and a consequence. It should be defined carefully; for example, "If you do X, then Y will happen." "If you are late to class again, you will be sent to the office." "If you stay on task for 25 minutes, you can pick an activity to end the class for the final 5 minutes."

3. *Think small.* Don't try to change the world in a day or the entire personality of a student in one week. Start with a small, but significant behavior problem, define it specifically, provide consequences for it carefully, and then observe it as it changes. Then move on.

4. *Move gradually.* Be satisfied with small, consistent improvement, especially if you are working with small rewards and punishments. If you can generate some large consequences, then you can move ahead more quickly. But don't expect enormous amounts of change for trivial consequences.

5. *Be consistent.* Stick to your contingency and apply it in the same manner all the time. Nothing confuses students more, or makes them more distrusting, than to have contingencies change from day to day without being told. If you want consistent behavior, then establish clear contingencies and stick to them. You will get only what you arrange.

6. *Start where the student is.* Don't expect miracles of good citizenship from a student who has been in constant trouble for years. Define an immediate problem. Change it. Then, build on success gradually. Continued success should allow for larger and larger chunks of behavior change as you go along. You have to get students to school before you can teach them. You have to get them on time and on task before they can learn.

7.2 The Show-Off

Situation. A student tends to be a show-off. The student acts up just enough to get some snickers and glances from the rest of the class. The teacher tries to stop the behavior with some reprimands.

Result. The misbehavior continues.

Analysis. The behavior pattern is probably controlled by the attention provided by the peer group. If this is the case, a teacher reaction that might be effective in another situation will not work here. In order for a teacher reaction to change this behavior pattern, it must be stronger than the attention provided by the peer group.

Prescription. The choice here is rather clear. A very strong reprimand will usually desist this kind of behavior; however, it will not replace the positive strokes that the student received from the peer attention. If a negative interaction is used, then the teacher must find a way for the student to receive peer attention for some more appropriate behavior pattern. Because the cooperation of the peers will be beneficial anyway, it might as well be used from the outset. When the student is away from the group, the teacher can ask the rest of the class not to provide attention for the kinds of behavior he or she wishes to eliminate. The teacher may also ask them to try to interact with the student more often when he or she does other things.

The basic strategies described above apply to decreasing inappropriate behavior, to replacing it with more appropriate behavior, and to developing entirely new forms of behavior with students who haven't yet learned to behave in appropriate ways. Small, specific improvements in behavior are achieved by applying contingencies consistently, by using effective consequences, and by gradually moving to larger, more expanded, and more appropriate behaviors. As the behavior becomes "habit," the immediate contingencies that supported its development gradually fade.

When a student misbehaves, the immediate tendency is to eliminate the inappropriate behavior as quickly as possible. That is OK—all teachers share that tendency. Yet we should also remember that the student was behaving for some reason—peer approval, recognition by the teacher. Thus the inappropriate behavior not only needs to be eliminated quickly, but a more appropriate form of behavior through which the student can receive some approval and recognition also needs to be developed. When that happens, the longer-term goals of discipline have begun to be achieved.

Strategies for Increasing Appropriate Behavior

A teacher can't build good behavior without focusing on it in a specific and systematic way. Teachers tend to be far too stingy about focusing on good behavior. That observation is not only a fact of my own experience in schools but is also well documented in classroom and gymnasium research. Typically, teachers tend to react negatively or correctively to students when they misbehave. The gymnasium is far too full of "Be quiet," "Pay attention," "Listen," "Straighten up that line," "Sh-h," and "That's enough, over there." There is far too little "Thank you," "Jack, you have been very good today," "That's the way to get that drill started quickly," or "I appreciate the way the class really worked hard today."

Don't expect to build good behavior and have a warm, nurturant gymnasium climate without focusing on good behavior and finding ways to recognize it and reinforce it. Enough is known about the nature of effective teaching in today's school to be absolutely sure that high levels of achievement and on-task behavior, and warm, nurturant gymnasium climates are not only compatible, but indeed may actually depend on one another.

Let's be very clear about what the research says and what this text advocates. The "hard-liner" and "stern taskmaster" will find no comfort in these pages—not, at least, if those descriptions include a harsh and punitive gymnasium climate developed mostly through an overreliance on punishment and the threat of punishment. You don't have to be an unlikable, hard-nosed punisher to develop and maintain good discipline. However, the teacher who believes that all that is needed for good discipline is to teach the subject matter well is also in for a rude shock. It is my contention that the former view tends to be self-serving and often downright cruel, while the latter view is naive and romantic.

7.3 Shouldn't Students Behave Well Without Having to Be Rewarded?

There is no good answer to this question. When teachers use behavior change techniques, they are often criticized by people who assume that students should always behave well just because that is "expected" and the "right thing." That may be good enough for mature adults who behave properly because they have been taught to do so and value the acceptance that society provides for these ways of behaving. It is seldom enough for students who are not very far along to adulthood. No teacher should feel that using specific behavior change techniques is inappropriate. However, teachers need to use the techniques skillfully and wisely. Far too often, tachers use large consequences (rewards or punishments) where small ones would do nicely. An important principle of behavior change programs is referred to as the "principle of least intervention." What it means, quite simply, is that you do as little as possible to get the job done! If you can teach young children to behave appropriately by using social praise and positive feedback, then special privileges or material rewards would be unnecessary. But in some situations, privileges and rewards are much more useful because systematic social praise is ineffective or not powerful enough. Eventually students should behave well without always being rewarded.

And neither stands much of a chance to achieve any important educational goals. The techniques described in this chapter (along with those for preventive management, described in Chapter 6) can be learned, perfected, and used to produce good discipline, high proportions of learning time, and a supportive gymnasium climate.

The effective teacher has a large number of positive techniques for developing and maintaining appropriate behavior. Each technique can be practiced and improved. The skillfulness that comes from experience in using them is not only in refining the techniques themselves, but also knowing when to use the right technique in terms of the situation; such as, the kind of student or students, the setting, the type of behavior, and so forth. Techniques for positively influencing appropriate behavior follow.

1. *Clear, specific prompts and rules.* Teachers not only need to state rules clearly but also to remind students frequently of the appropriate behaviors expected of them. A *prompt* is a teacher behavior or environmental stimulus that reminds students of what is expected of them. At the outset, students should be prompted often. Some teachers tend to prompt students only after a misbehavior has occurred. This is an error in technique. If your rules are specific, then prompts will tend to be specific too. If, however, you have chosen general rules (see page 87), then your prompts should provide students with the necessary specific guidelines to provide real examples of the behaviors specified by the general rule.

2. *High, yet realistic expectations.* Teachers should let students know what they expect of them. Most discipline-expectation statements will be directed toward process behaviors—behaving safely, courteously, helpfully, and staying on-task, for example. These should be realistic for the setting and students, yet should be optimistic about what they can accomplish.

3. *Frequent and appropriate reinforcement.* Students can be reinforced as a group or individually. Providing reinforcement for students is a *skill*. It can be done ineffectively, or it can be done well. Research shows that it is often done ineffectively. The largest single technique error seems to be what Hughley (1973) called "the global good"—high rates of simple, repetitive statements such as "good job," or "way to go." Effectively delivered praise is reinforcing for students. Ineffectively delivered praise is not reinforcement; that is, it does not improve behavior. Box 7.4 shows guidelines for delivering effective praise. Box 7.5 "Motivating Appropriate Behavior Through Positive Interaction" provides examples of the various types of positive interactions teachers can utilize with students in order to motivate appropriate behavior.

4. *Effective, positive nonverbal interaction.* Many authorities have suggested that nonverbal interaction is as or more powerful than what you say to students.

Pupils assume that nonverbal cues are more consonant with the actual feelings and thoughts of a teacher; therefore, those detecting a

7.4 Guidelines for Delivering Effective Praise

Effective praise:

- Is delivered immediately and contingently, yet does not intrude on task-related behavior
- Identifies specific aspects of behavior that were done well
- Provides information about why the behavior is important
- Is matched well to the behavior being reinforced
- Is related to standard criteria or previous performance rather than compared to other students
- Properly attributes success to effort and ability
- Includes expectations for continued success and improvement
- Shows variety, sincerity, and enthusiasm

Major technique errors in delivering praise are:

- Providing only nonspecific, global reactions
- Not providing specific information about the performance
- Comparing too often against peers
- Over- or under-exaggerating relative to the performance
- Intruding on task-related behavior
- Being insincere, unenthusiastic, bland

Source: Adapted from Brophy (1981)

contradiction between a teacher's verbal and nonverbal behavior will accept the nonverbal as being more valid. (Galloway, 1971, p. 70)

You are no doubt familiar with the commonly used negative nonverbal interactions: the finger to the lips, the teacher standing with hands on hips staring down a class to get them quiet, the menacing look that tells a student that something inappropriate has been done, and the even more subtle cues that indicate displeasure of disapproval. Positive nonverbal interactions can be just as powerful—thumbs up, the thumb and forefinger in a circle, the fist punched in the air, high fives, and a sincere smile are all potentially strong sources of approval (see Box 7.5 "Motivating Appropriate Behavior Through Positive Interactions.")

5. *Public and private communications.* There are endless ways teachers can communicate their approval to students publicly and privately. Simple, inexpensive thank-you or praise notes can be made up so that only a student's name needs to be written before delivery. Students who behave well can write their names on a good behavior poster. Stick-on stars can

be used on class rosters to indicate good behavior. Hard-work certificates can be handed out. Class performance related to gym rules can be charted on a bulletin board. A note praising student behavior can be sent to parents. While it is important that these communications be done in a way that is appropriate for the students' ages, it is also important to avoid the assumption that such communications work only with young children. If you received a nice, sincere note from a teacher expressing appreciation for your contributions, how would it make you feel?

Strategies for Decreasing Inappropriate Behavior

When disruptive behavior occurs, it must be stopped quickly before it spreads and interferes with your lesson. Disruptive behavior will occur, even when a sound managerial task system is in place. When it does, teachers should have alternatives for dealing with it effectively—and then clear and effective strategies for redirecting the student or students into more productive patterns of behavior. Remember, it isn't enough just to eliminate the disruptive behavior. Instead, strategies for eliminating dis-

---

7.5 Motivating Appropriate Behavior Through Positive Interactions

General positive interactions (no specific information content):

Yes	Good	Nice job	Excellent
Beautiful	Terrific	Way to go	Nice going
Thanks	That's the way	You're doing better	Everybody did well
Great	Outstanding	Nicely done	Fantastic

Nonverbal positive interactions:

Smiling	Nodding	Clapping hands	Thumbs up
O.K. sign	High fives	Winking	Applauding

Specific positive interactions (can be combined with nonverbals):
  Squad 2 did a great job of organizing quickly that time!
  Thanks for paying attention, Jack!
  Did you all see the way William helped Deborah?
  The entire class worked hard at that drill!
  This group (pointing) was quiet right at the signal!
  Great job of getting ready—you took only 12 seconds!
  I appreciate your cooperation with the equipment, Mary!

Positive interactions with value content (value content describes why the behavior is important):
  That's the way to get quiet. Now we can begin the game more quickly!
  Thanks, Bill, when you make an effort the other guys seem to also!
  Ann, you did a great job this week and I'm sure you had more fun!
  Squad 3 did a great job with the equipment. Now we can start earlier!
  Nice going! When you work that hard in drills, you play the game better!

ruptive behavior need to be combined with strategies for building appropriate behavior. The following strategies have been shown to be effective in a wide variety of educational settings.

1. *Use effective desists.* The most common strategy for dealing with disruptive behavior is the verbal reprimand—what I will refer to as a *desist*. Verbally desisting a misbehavior is a useful strategy when it is done effectively and when it is combined with a positive, preventive management system so that it doesn't have to be the primary discipline strategy. Research (Kounin, 1970) has shown that some methods of desisting are better than others.

   A desist should be clear. A clear deisist is one that contains specific information telling the student exactly what was wrong. Instead of merely saying "Stop that," a clear desist would be "Stop sitting on the basketball; that ruins its shape."

   A desist should also be delivered with firmness. The word *firmness* refers to the degree to which the teacher follows through on the desist, in order to let the offender know that what was said is indeed meant. Eye contact for a moment is a good way to follow through. So too is moving a bit closer to the offender. Desists that lack follow-through simply occur in a moment and then are gone, and their effectiveness is limited.

   An effective desist is well timed; that is, a misbehavior is desisted immediately when it is recognized and not allowed to spread before the desist is delivered. Bad timing occurs when a misbehavior occurs and spreads before it is desisted by a teacher. Similarly, effective desists are properly targeted; that is, the desist is directed toward the original offender and not toward some second or third party to the misbehavior. Targeting errors also occur when a serious misbehavior is not desisted and a less serious misbehavior is desisted. When students learn that your timing and targeting is accurate, they then know that you know what is going on in the class—that you are "with it," seemingly having eyes in the back of your head.

   A desist does not have to be punitive to be effective. In fact, research shows that roughness is counterproductive and does not help reduce misbehavior. A harsh or rough desist seems to have one typical outcome: It makes all the students uncomfortable. In Kounin's research program, he found that "rough desists did not make for better behavior in the watching children—they simply upset them" (Kounin, 1970). Desists should be clear, firm, well timed, and well targeted, but they should not be rough or harsh.

2. *Extinguish attention seeking behavior.* Attention from a teacher is often reinforcing to students. Sometimes students—especially young ones—will try to get the attention they seek by behaving in ways that are inappropriate or disruptive. If you pay attention to them in these situations, the inappropriate behavior might be strengthened. *Extinction* is a behavior-reduction strategy in which inappropriate behavior is reduced by

removing the source of reinforcement—in this case the attention of the teacher (see Box 7.6 titled "The Pest").

The teacher reinforcement that maintains this kind of attention-seeking behavior is social in nature—looking at the student, smiling, talking with the student, even mildly reprimanding the student. To eliminate it, you must eliminate the social interaction. The simplest way to do this is to turn and move away from a student whom you believe is engaged in attention-seeking behavior. This extinction technique should be combined with reinforcement for more appropriate ways of behaving. Thus, when the student is behaving well, you should go out of your way to pay attention to him or her. In this way

---

7.6 The Pest

Situation. A second-grade boy always seems to be causing minor disturbances. In a parachute activity, he is often doing the opposite of the directions. The teacher calls numbers to run under the lifted parachute and the boy goes on someone else's number. The teacher says, "Run under," and the boy crawls. The teacher says, "Lift and pull out," and the boy lifts and ducks under. After each of these occurrences, the teacher gives the boy a "Come on, get with it" look, provides a mild verbal reprimand, puts the boy back in the right place while going on with further instruction or gives some combination of these reactions.

Result. The boy continues to misbehave mildly.

Analysis. This behavior is typical of a child that most teachers would consider a "pest" type. He is not a real problem; in fact, he is well liked by his teacher and peers. He wants attention and is getting all he desires. The teacher assumed that the verbal and nonverbal negative reactions would reduce the "pesty" behavior when, in fact, they actually encourage it. This is a dangerous strategy, not only because the teacher is unwittingly encouraging inappropriate behavior but also because other children may imitate that behavior in order to get similar attention. What the teacher assumes to be a punishment is actually a reward to a child who badly wants some attention.

Prescription. Such behavior should be ignored if it is of no harm to other children. The boy should receive attention when he behaves in a manner that is more consistent with educational goals. Attention must be given to this kind of child because he or she needs it, but the key is *when* to give attention, verbal and/or nonverbal. Ignoring the misbehavior without giving the child attention for more appropriate behavior is likely to produce outbursts of temper. This kind of child is accustomed to getting attention and won't like it if it is taken away. If pestiness is going to be ignored, the child must receive attention when he or she is behaving well.

the student will get the needed attention, but it will be contingent on appropriate rather than inappropriate behavior.

3. *Be consistent in ignoring tolerable behavior.* Behavior you believe to be disruptive or inappropriate should be desisted immediately. As indicated earlier, however, each teacher has a different view of where the line falls between behavior that is inappropriate and behavior that is "tolerable." *Tolerable* behaviors are those minor infractions that do not interfere with instructional goals or the teacher's attention to those goals (Wurzer & McKenzie, 1987). Each teacher has a different ability to tolerate certain levels of disturbance. You must decide the level of noise or the kinds of student interactions that you can tolerate and still perform your instructional functions effectively and happily. The important point here is not where that line is drawn, but rather that it be drawn consistently. If what you tolerate changes from day to day, then students have difficulty knowing what is expected on any given day. If, over a period of days, they seem to be behaving inconsistently, then one of the first things you should check is to determine whether the inconsistency is truly among the students or whether it is in your reactions to them.

Tolerable infractions do not warrant verbal desists or punishments. Instead, teachers should deal with tolerable infractions by gradually reinforcing more appropriate behavior. Strategies for dealing positively with tolerable infractions are described in point 5 of this section.

4. *Use specific and effective punishment strategies.* By definition, punishment means achieving a decrease in a particular behavior by applying a consequence to it. Punishment should be used carefully and skillfully, as should any other professional teaching skill. The following behavior change strategies have been shown to be effective in school settings for reducing misbehavior.

- Omission training: With this strategy, the teacher rewards the student for *not* engaging in a particular behavior. Thanking a student for not talking out during an explanation is an example. Another is a child earning one point for each gym period in which he or she does not argue with peers. After five points are accumulated, the student earns some privilege or access to a favored activity.

- *Positive practice:*   With this strategy, a student is required to engage in an appropriate behavior a specified number of times each time he or she engages in an inappropriate behavior. The two kinds of behavior are usually opposites. For example, a student does not put equipment away properly. As a result, that student must get out the equipment and put it away properly five consecutive times. The result is that improper treatment of the equipment decreases in frequency.

- *Time out:*   With this strategy, a student loses a specified amount of time from physical education activity for an infraction. For this strategy to work, obviously, participation in physical education must be rewarding to the student. A time-out strategy is analogous to a penalty box in ice hockey. The time-out, typically no more than 2 minutes, is of short duration and tied specifically to rule violations. The time-out space should be such that the student is fairly well cut off from social contact with peers for the brief period of the penalty. Time-outs should be timed. Egg timers or clocks in the time-out space should be available.

- Reward cost: With this strategy, a student loses something as a result of misbehaving. For example, a student loses time in the time-out strategy. Students could also lose accumulated points, privileges, or access to other activities such as intramural events. Reward costs are the most common form of punishment in society; violations of many rules in society (such as traffic rules) result in loss of money.

Punishments should always fit the nature of the misbehavior in a fair, balanced manner. Just as the use of very strong rewards should be avoided, so too should the use of overly harsh punishments. Simple rules violations should result in simple punishments. This reflects the tradition in our society, and it also reflects the principle that the least intervention necessary is the most effective.

5. *Use constructive alternatives to punishment.* There are three specific ways teachers can reduce inappropriate behavior and develop more appropriate behavior without resorting to punishment strategies (Wurzer & McKenzie, 1978). These strategies are particularly relevant to refocusing tolerable infractions (see point 3 in this section). *Reinforcing alternative behavior* is a strategy in which the teacher specifically and frequently reinforces behavior that is incompatible with the inappropriate behavior; for example, being quiet while the teacher is giving directions is incompatible with talking while the teacher is giving directions. *Reinforcing fewer infractions* occurs when teachers praise students for doing less of what they were doing inappropriately. In the technical behavior-change literature, this is referred to as DRL (differential reinforcement of lower rates of behavior). *Reinforcing the absence or nonoccurrence* of inappropriate behavior is also referred to as omission training (see point 4 in this section).

Examples of these three strategies can be found in Table 7.1. When using these strategies, teachers should pay particular attention to the guidelines suggested earlier in this chapter. You should start where the student is, more gradually in small steps, and consistently use specific interactions.

Formalizing the Behavior-Change Strategy

Teachers can do much to build and maintain good behavior simply by using their own teaching behavior skillfully and systematically. Establishing class rules, prompting students frequently, using hustles, using higher rates of positive interactions for good behavior, ignoring pesty behavior that is not disruptive to the class, and desisting skillfully can improve and maintain good behavior

Table 7.1 Constructive Alternatives to Punishment.

Examples of Inappropriate Behavior	Reinforcing Alternate Behavior	Reinforcing Fewer Infractions	Reinforcing Absence or Nonoccurrence
Being Out of Squad	Reinforce in-squad behavior: *"Thanks, Dana, for staying in line!"*	Reinforce reduced occurrences of out-of-squad behavior: "Dana, I appreciate that you've stayed with your group more."	Reinforce the non-occurrence: "You weren't out of squad once today, Dana. You earn two points."
Blurting For Attention	Reinforce hand raising: *"Yes, Chris, you had your hand up?"*	Reinforce reduced rates of blurting out: *"Well done, Chris, you reached your target today."*	Reinforce not blurting out for increasingly longer time periods: *"You didn't blurt out once, Chris, during that discussion. Well done!"*
Tardiness To Class	Reinforce promptness: *"I'm glad to see you before the bell, Pat."*	Reinforce reduced tardiness: "You were only late once this week, Pat. That's much better."	Reinforce lack of tardiness for extended periods: *"You've been on time every day for a week, Pat! I'm really pleased."*
Skill Errors	Reinforce proper execution of skill/play: *"That's the right way to follow through, Robin."*	Reinforce reduced skill/play errors: *"You're getting better, Robin, you followed through on all but two of your shots."*	Reinforce the absence of errors over a time period: *"Great, Robin, you didn't forget to follow through on any of your shots during the game."*
Incomplete Tasks	Reinforce task completion: *"Thanks, Jamie, for putting all those racquets away."*	Reinforce reduced numbers of incompleted tasks: "You did better putting away racquets today than yesterday, Jamie."	Reinforce the nonoccurrence of incompleted tasks: "You haven't failed to put racquets away once all week, Jamie. That's great."

(Wurzer & McKenzie, 1987. This article is reprinted with permission from *Strategies*, 1987, 1(1), 7–9. *Strategies* is a publication of the American Alliance for Health, Physical Education, Recreation and Dance, 1900 Association Drive, Reston, VA, 22091)

and a warm, nurturant gymnasium climate. More drastic stategies are called for when things are so seriously out of control that they need special and immediate attention. In such cases, it is useful to consider making the basic behavior change strategy more formal in order to give it even greater power and specificity with one offending student, a small group of students, or even an entire class. What follows are some ways in which behavior change strategies have been formalized in school settings and resulted in important behavior changes among students.

Behavior Proclamations

A *behavior proclamation* is a formal statement of contingencies that might apply to an individual student, a group of students, or even to an entire class. The proclamation states the behavior to be achieved (and perhaps the behavior to be avoided) and the rewards that can be earned for fulfilling the contingency. The teacher decides both the level of behavior necessary and the amount of reward to be earned. The behavior is monitored frequently, and the reward is earned when the specified amount or length of behavior has been achieved. An example of a behavior proclamation is found in Figure 7.1. Naturally, the behavior must specify, clearly and understandably, what the students are to do or not to do. Also, the reward specified must be sufficiently strong so as to motivate the good behavior.

Figure 7.1. Example of a Behavior Proclamation

```
                G O O D    B E H A V I O R

 Betsy Smith              will (1) take part in all games

                               (2) not argue with

                               classmates for four (4)

                               weeks in Phys. Ed.


 For this good behavior    Betsy          will get to

 help Mrs. Jones after school 15 minutes a day

 for two (2) weeks


                               Mrs. Jones
                               Physical Education Teacher
```

Behavior Contracts

A *behavior contract* differs from a behavior proclamation in that the student (or students) has a role in defining the behaviors, deciding on a reward, and establishing the precise contingencies (how much, for how long, and so forth). Teachers should not use behavior contracts unless they are willing to negotiate with students on these matters. From a learning and development point of view, the behavior contract is an important step forward from the behavior proclamation and starts students on the road to self-control.

The elements of the contract are the same as for the proclamation. It is important that all parties sign the contract. Many teachers who use contracts successfully also have a third party sign the contract, thus underlining the importance and seriousness of having each party fulfill his or her side of the bargain. An example of a behavior contract for an individual student is shown in Figure 7.2. It should be emphasized that contracts can also be written for groups of students.

Good Behavior Games

One of the quickest ways to "turn around" a group of students who are misbehaving too frequently is to use a *good-behavior game*. Behavior games have been used successfully in many different kinds of elementary physical education settings (Young, 1973; Huber, 1973; Siedentop, Rife, & Boehm, 1974; McKenzie, 1976). Many different kinds of behavior games can be developed. What follows is a description of the most common game formats used to reduce inappropriate behavior quickly.

1. The class is divided into four groups. Groups are allowed to choose a name for their team.
2. It is emphasized that each team can win and that teams are competing against a behavior criterion rather than against each other.
3. Four to six behavior rules are explained thoroughly (see the section on rules in this chapter).
4. Rewards are discussed and decided on by the group.
5. The game is explained. Points will be awarded each time a signal goes off (the students won't know when the signal will occur). The teacher will check each group when the signal occurs. If all team members are behaving according to the rules, the team gets one point. If any team member is breaking any of the rules, the team gets no point.
6. A cassette audiotape is preprogrammed with a loud noise to occur periodically (a bell or a buzzer works well). Eight signals are programmed. The intervals between the signals vary. Several tapes are preprogrammed. When class begins, the teacher simply turns on the tape recorder with the volume up (often he or she doesn't know when the signals will occur).
7. When the signal occurs, the teacher quickly glances at each team and makes a judgment on their behavior. Teams that win a point are praised and told about their point. Teams that do not win a point are told why. (After doing this for a few days, the teacher can usually manage this kind of behavior game easily, not taking more than 15 or 30 seconds at each signal to record and announce points.)
8. At the end of the period, the teacher totals the points and posts the scores for the day.
9. At the end of a specified period (ranging from one day to as long as eight weeks), the rewards are earned by each team that has met the criterion.

```
                B E H A V I O R   C O N T R A C T


        Sarah Caldwell and Mr. Roman agree that the following
        plan will be in effect for the next four weeks.

        Starting date  January 6      Ending date  February 3


        Sarah will

        1.  Remember to bring her gym clothes for each PE day

        2.  Not disturb the class by talking or fooling around
            with Melanie

        3.  Participate in all activities and try hard to
            improve skill


        Mr. Roman will

        1.  Give Sarah individual help on the balance beam

        2.  Count one point for each day Sarah meets the three
            points stated above

        3.  Let Sarah help with the 4th-grade class for two
            weeks if Sarah earns seven (7) points during this
            contract


                    Signed  Sarah Caldwell

                            Mr. Roman

                            Mrs. Sylvia, Principal
```

Figure 7.2 *Example of a Behavior Contract*

10. If one player on a team loses more than two points for his or her team two days in a row, the team meets and decides whether this player should sit out from gym class for a day (this "doomsday" contingency very seldom needs to be used).

11. With each consecutive game played, it is possible to reduce the number of signals per class and increase the length of the game. As good behavior becomes the norm for the class, the game can gradually be phased out.

With eight checks per day and a three-week game for a class that meets twice weekly, a team might have to accumulate 42 out of 48 points to earn a reward. The extra gymnasium time is combined with access to favored activities and is usually sufficiently powerful to motivate good behavior. With a particularly unruly class, the contingency might have to begin as a daily game where the reward is five minutes of free gym time at the end of the period (if they don't win, they return to their classroom five minutes early). Once good behavior has been achieved, the game contingencies can be stretched out.

The criterion for winning the game can also be made progressively more stringent, thus allowing the teacher to get continually better behavior for the same amount of reward. The number of behavior checks programmed on the cassettes can be reduced gradually so that less time is taken to manage the game.

Behavior games can also be played as "management games," with the outcomes defined in terms of managerial and organizational behavior. An example of a management game was presented in Chapter 5.

Token Systems

The most fully developed, formalized system of behavior change is known widely as the token economy. A *token system* is a formal program including academic, organizational, and managerial outcomes with a clear and specific exchange system in which students earn and accumulate "tokens" that can be exchanged for a number of different kinds of rewards. Our society operates on a massive token economy system where the tokens are different denominations of money. People earn "tokens" (money) and can exchange them for the goods and services the society offers. A small version of this system could be developed for a physical education program or even for a single physical education class.

To develop a token system, teachers must define very carefully all the behaviors they would like included in the system (or work this out with students). Then rewards are developed. The best way to do this is to ask students to rank the available kinds of rewards in terms of their attractiveness. The most attractive (highest ranked) is the most powerful reward. The least attractive probably won't motivate much behavior.

Typical rewards used in physical education have been public recognition (start a name board, list a player of the week, post a photo on a bulletin board in the hall), choice of activities (develop a reward time when students who have accumulated a sufficient number of points get to choose from among attractive activities), extra physical education time, field trips (to a local university or professional game), or privileges (such as being gym aide or a tutor for a younger class). Once the behaviors and the rewards are defined, then the most important phase of the development occurs—deciding how much behavior is necessary to earn "tokens" and how many tokens are necessary to earn the different rewards.

In physical education, it is best to use points as tokens rather than physical objects such as chips or paper money. The "point system" then defines the "rate of exchange" for behavior and consequences within the token system. Lambdin (1981) outlined a token system that rewards good behavior and punishes inappropriate behavior. Each class has a behavior sheet that lasts for at least five class sessions (weekly in this case). The students' names are listed down the left-hand side of the sheet. A simple coding system is used to designate important class behaviors: "L" for listening, "P" for practicing, "F" for following instructions, "Sp" for sportsmanship, "Eq" for care of equipment, and "Sh" for proper footwear. When a student is disruptive or violates a class rule, the student is given a minus by the teacher. For example, the teacher might say, "Jane, that is a minus for talking while I'm explaining the rules." An "L-" would be recorded next to Jane's name, either immediately or at the end of class. Conversely, students are awarded pluses when they do a particularly good job. For example, a teacher might say "Bonnie, you get a plus for practicing so hard." The public awarding of the pluses and minuses tends to motivate and educate other students. At the end of the week (or whatever period of time is chosen), a "choice day" is provided students so they can participate in favored activities. During choice day, students with minuses must "pay back" five minutes of sitting quietly on the sidelines for each minus they received. Pluses and minuses are also reported on periodic grade reports to parents.

The Ultimate Goal of a Discipline Strategy

Discipline strategies have both short-term and long-term goals. Clearly, the major short-term goals have to do with reducing inappropriate behavior, preventing disruption, and building good behavior to achieve the immediate goals of a daily lesson or a unit. Longer-term goals are more likely to include (or should) some notions about self development, self-control, and self-direction. In the longer term, physical education should contribute to a student's growing ability to make decisions wisely, to behave responsibly toward his or her peers, to accept responsibility for his or her own actions, and to be able to do all this and persevere in it without constant supervision or the need for frequent reinforcement.

In summary, the longer-term goals should be to bring students into a responsible, mature relationship with their peers, the subject matter they are studying, and the small society of the school. This will not happen overnight. It takes time, patience, and careful instruction, just as does the acquisition of any important behavior habit. There is also the danger that it may not happen at all. Too often students are brought into a pattern of conformance and then left there, never to grow beyond it into a more mature, self-directed status. To take students beyond the stage of conformance, teachers must give them progressively more responsibility and more freedom to exhibit responsible behavior. To become truly self-directed, students must be weaned gradually and carefully from the normal kinds of behavioral supports that the school provides for them as they are learning how to become responsible people. Teachers must take some risks to do this, but it is necessary if the longer-term goals are to be achieved. The same principles of specificity, consistency, and gradual change apply to achieving these goals as they do to reducing off-task behavior and to increasing cooperative behavior. Also goals won't be achieved unless they are striven for directly and systematically.

7.7 Fooling Around

Situation. Two high school students tend to disrupt class with their fooling around and do not take part in activities in a manner conducive to learning and the smooth functioning of the group. The two students are always together and create the disturbances as a pair. A series of reprimands seems only to discourage them temporarily, and no permanent change is seen.

Result. No long-run change occurs, and the two students tend to become enemies of the teacher.

Analysis. It is virtually impossible to know exactly why this kind of behavior pattern occurs. The two students provide attention for one another, regardless of what is going on in the class. To break them up would take away their source of enjoyment but would not by itself be a solution. Indeed, it would probably produce further hostility and perhaps more serious misbehavior.

Prescription. The students are asked to come in for a conference where the situation is discussed. The students are asked, as a pair to desist from certain behavior patterns and are encouraged to behave in some specifically different ways. In class, the teacher has frequent, private positive interactions with the pair when they are engaged properly. If any improvement occurs, they are privately thanked outside of class. The bond between the pair is respected, and their standard of behavior is turned toward more positive outcomes.

Summary

1. A positive view of discipline, is training to behave in accordance with rules, resulting in the soundest educational approach.
2. Discipline is important because administrators and parents expect well-disciplined classes and because life in schools is much more pleasant when discipline problems are minimal.
3. Well-disciplined classes create the conditions in which learning may take place, but for learning to occur, good instruction and practice must follow.
4. Unless students are specifically taught what behaviors are inappropriate and appropriate, they will be left to learn them by default, which typically results in high frequencies of punishment.
5. Basic strategies for changing behavior include being specific, defining the contingency carefully, starting with small, significant chunks of behavior, making gradual changes, being consistent, and starting where the student is.

6. Strategies for increasing appropriate behavior include clear, specific prompts and rules, high yet realistic expectations, frequent reinforcement, effective nonverbal interaction, and public and private communications.

7. Effectively praising requires adhering to guidelines and avoidance of technique errors—as well as using a variety of techniques.

8. Strategies for decreasing inappropriate behavior include effective desists, extinguishing attention-seeking behavior, consistently ignoring tolerable behavior, specific and effective punishment, and constructive alternatives to punishment.

9. Formal behavior-change strategies include behavior proclamations, behavior contracts, good-behavior games, and token systems.

10. The ultimate goal of a discipline strategy is to bring students into responsible, mature relationships with their peers, the subject matter, and the society within the school.

CHAPTER 8

Interpersonal Skills in Physical Education Teaching

What makes us human is the way we interact with other people. In *humanizing* relationships individuals are sympathetic and responsive to human needs. It is positive involvement with other people that we label *humane*. There is nothing more important in our lives than our interpersonal relationships. The quality of our relationships, as well as the number, depends on our interpersonal skills. It takes skills to build and maintain fulfilling and productive relationships.

David W. Johnson (1981)

CHAPTER OBJECTIVES

To explain why good interpersonal relations with students are important

To explain the dangers inherent in focusing solely on interpersonal relations

To describe the evidence from research about interpersonal interaction patterns in physical education

To explain the kinds of messages that are conveyed to students

To explain why interaction skills need to be perfected

To explain the technical features of good interactions

To explain how good rapport can be developed and sustained

To examine how you come across to students

To describe ways in which your teaching space can better communicate information, motivation and recognition

To describe effective communication skills

To explain why and how the student-social system can be accommodated

Your life as a teacher will be more pleasant and fulfilling if you establish and maintain good relationships with your students. Good relationships with students also help to establish a positive context within which students can achieve important educational goals. Most persons who prepare to become teachers sincerely want to build good relationships with their students. What they lack—and often seriously underestimate—are the interpersonal skills necessary to do so. It is important to want to have growth-promoting relationships with your students. It is my experience that most women and men preparing to teach have that desire. What they lack are the skills needed to translate their motivation into productive relationships. The purpose of this chapter is to identify important interpersonal skills and show how they can be used in physical education.

A note of caution is important at the outset. Some teachers confuse good interpersonal relationships with the achievement of educational outcomes (see Box 8.1 titled "Tension Between Good Teaching and Good Interpersonal Relations"). It *is* important that teachers and students cooperate to make life in school peaceful and even pleasant. Teachers, however, sometimes fool themselves when they believe that having established good relationships with their students means they have met their responsibilities for educating those students. Teacher effectiveness research has shown that effective teachers not only promote academic growth, but tend to do so with warm, nurturant educational climates, within which good teacher-student relationships exist. The warm, nurturant climates, however, do not themselves constitute an effective education—instead, they provide the context where educational goals can be achieved.

The Evidence from Physical Education

Positive teaching styles in physical education are hard to find in the descriptive research that has been done. That sad fact needs to be restated here. Cheffers and Mancini (1978) used an interaction analysis system to examine the junior high and high school teaching episodes in the Columbia videotape data bank (Anderson, 1978). They concluded that "by comparison with the total recorded teacher behaviors, virtually no acceptance of student feelings and ideas, praise, or questioning behaviors were recorded . . . the use of sympathetic-empathetic behavior was almost nonexistent" (pp. 46–47). Were these data simply a fluke? Unfortunately, it appears that they were quite similar to what every other investigator has found no matter where the data have been collected.

Quarterman (1977) described the teaching behavior of 24 physical educators teaching kindergarten through eighth grade. Eighty-five percent of all their feed-back interactions with students were negative or corrective (a behavioral interaction is a teacher response to student behavior other than academic behavior). Physical educators in a different part of the country were studied by Stewart (1980), who concluded, "If we are to accept the notion that high rates of positive behavior and low rates of negative, monitoring, and managing behavior are desirable, one is led to conclude that teachers in this study were not performing very well" (p. 81).

McLeish (1981) reported results of a large study in which 104 teaching episodes were examined from various perspectives, one of which dealt with interpersonal interactions by teachers. He felt compelled to conclude that "there was a noticeable absence of positive affect in these lessons."

Thus, the evidence from research in physical education is consistent, but not very encouraging. This evidence makes the content of this chapter and that of Chapter 9 quite important—at least if we are to someday change the picture that is described by teaching researchers. The notion of change allows us to end this brief review on a hopeful note. A series of experimental research studies at the Ohio State University (Siedentop, 1981) shows that physical education teachers and student teachers *can* change their interpersonal interaction-skills and *can* create positive educational settings. They can also improve related teaching characteristics such as their enthusiasm (Rolider, 1979) and can also help their students to relate better to each other (Westcott, 1977). The established fact that teachers can change, and often very quickly, is a very positive finding, one that lends a hopeful note to this chapter and the next.

8.1 Tension Between Good Teaching and Good Interpersonal Relationships

A survey asked students and teachers to place in rank order what they felt to be important in their educational experience (Cohen 1970). The teachers were asked to rank the list in terms of what they thought their students wanted out of the educational experience, and the students were asked to rank the list in terms of what they did in fact want. The teachers picked items such as commitment to students, ability to communicate, and closeness of teacher-student relations as the most important factors, and ranked specific learning objectives last. The students ranked specific learning objectives first and tended to rank interpersonal relations items last. The message was clear. Students were most interested in what they were learning, while teachers thought students were most interested in good student-teacher relations. Cohen (1970) labeled this discrepancy the "cult of personality in teaching," and he suggested that too many teachers view their own personality as the most important variable in the educational environment.

As a teacher you are responsible for student learning. Administrators, parents, and taxpayers expect more from you than just being on good terms with your students. It *is* important that students respect you! It can be very helpful when students also like you! The issue is: How do you achieve respect and popularity among your students?

For some teachers "being well liked" becomes a major objective. They tend to rely on their personalities to establish relationships with students. Sometimes they lower expectations for educational outcomes to gain that popularity. Sometimes they seem to buy into the student social system at the expense of educational goals. This doesn't happen in one day. It happens gradually over several years. Can it happen to you?

Have you had a teacher who was well liked but taught very little? How did that kind of teacher differ from teachers who were respected and liked, but also taught their subject matters well?

The Message of the Gymnasium

Whether you are teaching in a multipurpose room, a cramped half gym, a playground, or in the best physical education facility imaginable, you must come to view it as a total learning environment. This is not an easy task, but those who claim that teaching is an easy profession are not aware of the complexities involved. Your students will learn what you teach them, but they will also pick up subtle messages from you and the environment. They will learn movement skills, dribbling, headstands, bump passes, and lowered heart rates; they will also learn some things that you may be much less aware of. A few of the many possible messages that your students will gather from the learning environment are the following:

1. Learning physical education is primarily an active or a passive experience.
2. Risk taking is good, or one should follow all directions and not rock the boat.
3. Physical education is fun, or it is a drag.
4. Physical education teachers are open, consistent, caring people, or they are rigid, uncaring authoritarians.
5. School can be fun, or it can be boring.
6. Physical activity is enjoyable, or it is too much of a hassle.

You could easily double the list of subtle messages that will be conveyed to students by your teaching manner. This is why you must look at what you do in terms of its total impact on your students. Two teachers could teach from identical lesson plans for a volleyball unit and even use similar teaching methods, but the results would be different because the hidden messages conveyed would be entirely different. The impact on one group of students could be negative, while another group could get excited about learning physical education skills.

Conveying a message to students through your teaching manner underlies many of the techniques suggested in this text. The messages meant to be conveyed through the techniques advocated in this text are that physical education is fun, learning is enjoyable and challenging, physical educators are good people, and school is a good place to be. Whether you are involved in planning for instruction or managing your class, you should be thoroughly aware of the hidden messages emanating from everything you do.

This chapter attempts to deal with some of the more important hidden messages conveyed to students, including the messages that you value them as people, that they can accomplish things in physical education, and that you care about their lives beyond the classroom. The skills to be developed here should be integrated with management and instructional skills so that one message conveyed to all who observe you is that effective teaching, good discipline, and strong interpersonal relations are not distinct but can be skillfully interwoven into what would be described as good teaching.

Teacher-Student Interaction Skills

It might seem odd that this text approaches interpersonal interactions with students in a way similar to other teaching skills, such as providing feedback or establishing managerial routines. Some have suggested that interpersonal relationships are best established when you follow the advice—"just be yourself." The assumption underlying this advice seems to be that when people are "themselves," everything possible has been done to improve interpersonal relations.

I question this assumption and the advice based on it. Our "selves" are not static; we are changing as we have new experiences. Certainly our teaching "selves" are most fully developed in the first several years of teaching. Thus, if you have not yet begun to teach full time, the teacher you will eventually become has yet to develop. All the evidence suggests that the kind of school you first teach in will exert a strong influence on that development. Thus, "just be yourself" advice to new teachers needs to be interpreted in terms of the strong likelihood that they will change substantially in their first several years of teaching.

A second problem is that our perceptions of ourselves and our actual behavior may differ. For example, the evidence suggests that while student teachers in physical education see themselves as caring, supportive persons, their interaction patterns with students are predominantly neutral and more often negative than positive.

A third issue is that a person may be perfectly well integrated in his or her own personality and still not possess the *skills* to help students grow in a positive way. *Wanting* to care or *intending* to care are important, but these motivations cannot be realized without having the *skills* for effective caring with a particular set of students. You need to have interpersonal skills that are effective with different age groups, with both boys and girls, with students who differ from you racially or ethnically, and with students with disabilities.

Fortunately, there is ample evidence that teachers can change, and can adjust their own teaching behavior so that it is more congruent with their images of themselves as caring, humane teachers (Siedentop, 1986). Teachers can learn to be more positive, more specific, and more enthusiastic. You have to want to develop these skills. You need to be observed while teaching and get specific and regular feedback about your changes and growth. It does work!

Interpersonal interactions are approached in this text with the assumption that there are skills and techniques that can be learned and that will help to make a teacher a more effective, caring person. I do not claim that the skills outlined in this chapter represent all there is to know about interpersonal relations, nor do I suggest that the sum of the skills presented here equals a totally effective teacher. Much is not understood about the specifics of human interactions. For example, we are just learning to be more sensitive to the differences in effective interaction patterns among different ethnic and racial groups. What are presented here are some "tools of the trade" for improving basic abilities in the interpersonal relations area. The goal here is to behave in ways that are perceived by your students to be sincere and caring—and to avoid behaving in ways that are perceived as phony and uncaring.

Be Consistent in Your Interactions

Suppose, for example, that a student attempts a comic stunt in a gymnastics lesson or a trick shot in a basketball lesson and you show some approval in the form of a smile and a chuckle. The next day, the same thing occurs and you reprimand the student. What message did the student receive? Will that student perceive you to be sincere? Nothing is potentially more devastating to your relations with students than inconsistency. Students are very sensitive to inconsistency—which they perceive to be strongly related to fairness—and in their developing value systems, inconsistent treatment from adults ranks among the worst of all sins.

8.2 "Teacher, What's My Name?"

"Hey, you over there—get back in line!" Have you ever been called "Hey, you?" Do you remember what it feels like to think that a teacher with whom you interact on a daily basis doesn't even know your name? The *personal* in interpersonal must at least mean that you know the name of the student with whom you are interacting.

Try to use students' first names in interactions. There is no evidence indicating that using first names results in a more effective interaction, but experience and logic support the contention that nothing is more devastating for a student than doubting that the teacher even knows who he or she is. The use of first names should add a personal touch to the interaction. The extent to which first names are used in interactions can easily be measured via event recording.

It might be assumed that as time goes by, the teaching intern would naturally learn the names of students and come to use them more and more frequently. Unfortunately, this is yet another invalid assumption. Research indicated that student teachers in physical education hardly ever used first names, whether they were in the first or the fourth week of a ten-week student teaching experience (Darst, 1974; Boehm, 1974; Hamilton, 1974). When, in the same studies, a terminal objective was set that 50 percent of interactions include first-name use and when regular feedback was provided, all student teachers began to use first names regularly. This is one of those "little" interaction skills that may not develop unless a specific goal is set and sufficient feedback is provided to gauge progress toward the achievement of that goal.

Some interns learn names by using name tags for the first week. Others ask students to help them by providing feedback on how they are doing; that is, they try to remember the student's name and have the student say immediately whether the correct name was used. If an intern teaches four classes and each class has 30 students, he or she has 120 students and learning their names is no easy task. This is why some systematic effort to learn names is helpful and why feedback about using those names helps development of this skill.

To be consistent, you must first of all be very much aware of those behaviors you want to approve, those you want to ignore, and those you want to desist immediately (see page 109). Then, you need to observe your own performance relative to these behaviors. This can be done by having someone else observe you or by tape-recording your lessons.

Consistency also requires that you treat students similarly. You can't play favorites! Boys and girls need to be treated similarly. High- and low-skilled students need to be treated similarly. This does not mean that all students will be treated identically—they all have somewhat different needs. However, if those needs become so different that substantially differential treatment is required, it is best to inform the class of this requirement. If students are provided with a reasonable explanation for differential treatment, they are usually willing to tolerate it, but if they think you just don't act consistently, you can't expect your interactions to be effective.

You will like some students better than others. You have some students that you simply do not like well. That happens! Your responsibility as a professional teacher, however, is to make sure that your own liking or disliking for a student does not interfere with the educational opportunities provided that student—and, an observer in your class should not be able to pick out the most and least liked among your students, based on your interactions with them.

Direct Interactions Toward Significant Student Behavior

A warm, sincere interaction based on a trivial aspect of student behavior may be perceived as phony. In terms of developing interpersonal relations, an interaction will be most effective when it is based on a significant aspect of the student's behavior. How do you determine what are significant student behaviors? One way is to examine what behaviors are considered valuable in the educational context. You might decide that following instructions, making an effort, completing a difficult task, and other such matters are of significance. The problem with this approach is that it reflects your view and that of the educational establishment. Although it is important that you attempt to have the student view these behaviors as significant, that is more a task of instruction than of developing interpersonal relations. For purposes of interpersonal relations, the significance of student behavior should be viewed more from the student's point of view. If you want to relate better on a personal basis, the way to do it is to interact with students on matters that are important to them. The development of this aspect of sincerity requires a keen and sensitive eye. There is no need to guess at what students consider important. Most often you can learn what students value by watching them. What do they do on the playground or at lunchtime? What do they read on their own? What do they like to talk about? What group of students does a student relate most to, and what characterizes this group? This approach means meeting students on their own turf and interacting with them about whatever interests them most.

If you interact with students on the basis of their interests, you will begin to develop good personal relationships with them. Having done this, you can begin to extend the interaction into areas that you consider significant, and you can do so assured that your efforts will be perceived as sincere. I am not suggesting that you "con" students. Interaction is a matter of give and take. It is important that you interact with students in terms of what they value, but it is also important that you attempt to help them appreciate what you consider significant. It is a matter of timing and trust. You must start on their terms and develop the relationship so that eventually you can help them come to know what you consider significant in the educational environment. Without making any effort to interact with students to find out what they consider important at their particular stage of development, teachers expect students to adopt the values of the adult education establishment. The teacher who is considered sincere and caring is often the one who takes the time to learn what a student values and to interact with the student about the activity or interest.

Match the Interaction to the Task

Matching interactions to the task is another aspect of interaction skill that contributes to the degree to which the interaction is perceived as sincere. An extravagant, flowery interaction based on a relatively minor student behavior or task will be considered phony, especially if the excessive manner is applied to several students. A student who is told, "That's the best headstand I've ever seen," will probably be suspicious. The student will be even more suspicious if he or she hears you react similarly to a headstand performed by another student.

Likewise, there are times when understated interactions can adversely affect the degree to which students perceive you to be sincere. If a student struggles with a difficult, risky stunt (such as a front hand spring) for some time, and when he or she finally achieves it, your reaction is merely "Way to go," the student may wonder how much you really care about his or her development.

This chapter makes it seem that developing effective interaction skills that are considered sincere and caring by students is a difficult and touchy business. It appears that way because that's the way it is! Being perceived as a sincere and therefore effective interactor with students is no easy task. There are indeed some teachers who do not have to develop this skill, for they have it well developed when they start teaching. They are fortunate. They have had experiences that have helped them become positive people and sensitive to the interests and values of those with whom they work. But many of us have not had sufficient opportunity to develop this skill to its fullest potential.

A single thread runs through these first three suggestions for implementing interpersonal relations: all three depend on a sensitivity to students. Just as directing interactions toward significant student behavior depends on what students feel as significant, interacting in a manner commensurate with the task depends on what students feel is the importance of the task. This is yet another area where the imposition of adult value systems sometimes works against effective interpersonal relations. What seems a small task to you might be an enormously significant accomplishment for a student. Some things you consider to be important might be shrugged off by students.

A good guideline is to have interactions relate precisely to the task. This can be accomplished by having the interaction contain specific information. If you say, "That's a fine headstand, your feet are very straight," you run little danger of being too flamboyant or not concerned enough. The specific information tells the student not only that you appreciate the skill demonstrated but also that you cared enough about the performance to watch it carefully, as shown by the fact that you can respond to some detail of the performance. This kind of interaction combined with a nonverbal component such as a smile or a pat on the back can be potent without being effusive.

8.3 The Elitist Teacher, or "Don't Bother Me with Any Average Kids"

Situation. A teacher interacts well with the highly skilled students in class, but interacts with poorly skilled students only to correct errors. Observations show that the teacher interacts in terms of feelings and nonschool factors only with the 7 most highly skilled students (there are 26 in the class). Interactions directed at these 7 students account for 63 percent of all interactions in the class.

Result. Seven students perceive the teacher to be a sincere, caring teacher. Nineteen students have no feeling about the teacher or else doubt his or her sincerity. They feel no sense of personal relationship with the teacher.

Analysis. The concentration of interactions with so few students shows a real imbalance. The teacher will be viewed as one who has no time for anybody but the best students, or as one who plays favorites. The students who are not highly skilled will not react favorably to the teacher and will learn that physical education is a good activity only for highly skilled people.

Prescription. Goals should be set to disperse interactions over a more representative group of students. Interactions with low-skilled students should be more positive, and there should be interactions based on nonschool factors and on feelings.

Interact with Students on the Basis of Nonschool Factors

The term *interpersonal* includes the word *personal,* and thus suggests that good interpersonal relations must be based on personal factors. Teachers need to know students as persons as well as student—thus, they must interact with them on personal as well as academic matters. For example, sincere comments about dress, classroom school work, parents, or community events can often act as "openers." Once a relationship begins to develop, the topics for interactions naturally become more personal as you get to know students better and they are willing to be more open with you. This takes time. It shouldn't be rushed.

It should be noted, however, that the bulk of these interactions should take place outside of the main academic time of the class. High rates of academic learning time and a strong academic focus are primary indicators of effective teaching. There are times—before class, during breaks, after class—when these more personal interactions are appropriate.

Sustain Enthusiasm to Improve Instruction and Interpersonal Relations

Few would argue with the assertion that enthusiasm in teaching is important. A teacher's enthusiasm about the subject matter, the students, and the act of learning provides an important vehicle for communicating many of the messages listed earlier in this chapter. A teacher can teach volleyball in a manner that communicates to students that this activity is OK, a drag, a really enjoyable recreational activity, or an enjoyable, highly skilled competitive sport. Part of the message is communicated directly through talk about the activity and through the instruction itself, but much of it is communicated through the teacher's enthusiasm or lack thereof.

Research indicates that enthusiasm is an important quality in teaching (Rosenshine, 1970). Studies that have manipulated enthusiasm as an independent variable or correlated it as it occurred naturally have shown that it is often strongly related to student performance. Gage (1972) feels that the evidence is sufficiently strong to discuss enthusiasm as one of the very few characteristics of teaching that can be identified as important in helping students achieve.

There are three fairly distinct areas toward which your enthusiasm can and should be directed. First, you should be enthusiastic about the content of what you are teaching, be it basketball, gymnastics, or movement education. Second, you should be enthusiastic about learning or improving in the skills that comprise the activity. Third, you should be enthusiastic about your students, be they highly skilled or awkward.

You might reasonably interject at this point that it is easy to discuss enthusiasm and suggest its importance, but it is difficult to describe it precisely. You're right. A major problem with the research just cited is that there was no consistent definition of the components of "enthusiastic teaching." Enthusiasm is one of those qualities that each of us has some ideas about, but that none of us can define completely and adequately. Several approaches to enthusiasm are suggested here.

One aspect of enthusiasm is a positive teaching style. Focusing on appropriate behavior, praising student efforts, providing positive, specific feedback, and communicating optimistic expectations about what students can achieve, all combine to project enthusiasm. How many times have you heard a student or an athlete suggest that a large part of his or her success came from a teacher or coach who "believed in me"? When you ask students what they mean by that, they most often reply with the characteristics described above.

In all you do as a teacher, you send "messages" to your students. Are you fit? Do they see you doing fitness activities? Do you enjoy playing? Do they see you play? How do you approach your daily teaching responsibilities? Are you reasonably upbeat when the students arrive at the gym? Do you talk positively about sport and fitness? Do you know "what's going on" in the school in terms of sport and fitness? Your students' perceptions of you as enthusiastic or unenthusiastic derive from these many "messages."

Effective teaching is quickly paced and upbeat (see page 24). The way a lesson is conducted conveys enthusiasm. Do students have to wait a lot? Are transitions slow? Do you prompt hustling and give a quick pace to the lesson? Are you on time? All these behaviors suggest to students that you are enthusiastic about your teaching and enthusiastic about them.

One of the most direct kinds of evidence about enthusiasm is the degree to which you voice positive, optimistic expectations for your students. Do you tell them that you expect them to learn, to enjoy it, to get better? Are these expectations communicated to all students, not just the more skilled athletes? Do your students know that you believe that effort leads to improvement and learning rather than natural talent?

These things need to be *said* to students in ways that are optimistic, yet realistic—and they need to be said frequently in order to sustain an enthusiastic atmosphere.

None of these suggestions about enthusiasm is meant to convey the notion that you approach class each day as if you were selling used cars on television! Phoniness and a facade of enthusiasm will be detected quickly by students. It is difficult to sustain a "rah-rah" approach to teaching for five to nine classes a day, five days a week. Enthusiasm can be conveyed in quiet, simple ways as well as through more vocal, upbeat messages.

Don't Ignore Feeling and Emotions

Good interpersonal relations between teachers and students cannot be based solely on the regular curriculum. It is my view that learning skills is the most important aspect of a physical education curriculum, that skill in sport, gymnastics, dance, and other activities remains the major goal of physical education. But it need not be the only goal. A teacher can influence the whole life of a student, but this won't happen if the teacher does not establish a lasting relationship on

---

8.4 On Smiling!

Do physical education teachers smile often? Does it matter? The answers seem to be "No, they don't smile much " and "Yes, it can matter a great deal."

Amos Rolider (1979) experimented with physical education teacher enthusiasm. He asked 1,000 students, over 100 teachers, and several teacher education experts to list the main characteristics of an enthusiastic physical education teacher. Most of those characteristics are described in this chapter. One of the characteristics most often mentioned by students was that enthusiastic teachers smiled a lot.

Rolider then experimented with physical education teachers. Through a workshop in which they discussed, role played, and videotaped, the teachers learned how to use their nonverbal gestures to convey enthusiasm and to smile more often. They then went out and tried to do more of this in their teaching. Systematic observation revealed that they had indeed improved (increased) their nonverbal gesturing and their smiling. Did the students pick it up? Yes, indeed they did. A questionnaire given to students after each class session had several questions about enthusiasm embedded within it. When the teachers smiled more often, the students rated them as more enthusiastic.

Now, smiling isn't all that hard, is it? It could be that a little more of it in your own teaching will convey to students the enthusiasm you actually feel for them and for teaching!

a personal basis, and the latter cannot be done unless there is some interaction based on the student's feelings.

Many leading proponents of the humanistic education movement have emphasized the need to shift from an exclusive emphasis on the regular curriculum to an equal emphasis on the affective content of what transpires in schools and in the lives of students (Weinstein & Fantini, 1971). This is another aspect of teaching that is usually taken for granted; it is contended that when a teacher is sensitive and cares about students, emphasis on student feeling will take care of itself. This may not be so. One survey indicated that teachers in the study devoted less than one-half of 1 percent of their time to student feelings (Myrick, 1969).

The goal here is to interact with students in a manner that enables them to feel free to express their feelings and perceive you as someone who sincerely cares about those feelings. The major skill to be developed is that of interacting positively with students who express feelings in one manner or another. Often feelings are expressed nonverbally. A child jumps up and down excitedly. An older student has a look of satisfaction after winning a match. Another student shows signs of accomplishment after making a difficult physical effort. Teachers must look for such nonverbal cues and show approval of the underlying feelings. Following are examples of such interactions:

- I'm glad you feel good about your progress.

- It feels good to win, doesn't it?

- I'm glad you feel happy about getting that stunt right.

- I think it's fine that you feel satisfied with the good effort you made.

- I'm really pleased that you get a feeling of satisfaction from helping those students.

Notice that in each case the interaction is based directly on the feelings underlying the behavior in question. The behavior is indirectly referred to, but the object of the approval is the feeling.

Many students experience great difficulty verbalizing their feeling. Students should be encouraged to express feeling. More importantly, they should be encouraged to express positive feelings. The more a student can learn to express his or her positive emotional reactions openly, the more that student will appreciate the positive aspects of affective behavior. It is important that students learn to express their feelings in different situations. It may be one matter for a student to express a feeling in private with you, but an entirely different matter for that student to express the same feeling about the same matter in front of his or her peers. Appropriate interactions might be "I'm pleased that you feel you can share that with me," or "I'm pleased that you shared that feeling with us."

Encouraging openness will bring increased expression of positive and negative feelings. Even though an emphasis on positive feelings is most important, this does not mean that all negative feelings will disappear. Students feel badly when they are defeated. They feel anxious when called on to perform in front of their peers. They feel angry if they are inadvertently slighted in some way. They feel frightened when learning a skill that involves physical risk.

In dealing with positive feelings, your goal is to accept and encourage those feelings in the hope of increasing the experience of positive feelings and the ability to share them with others. In dealing with negative feelings, your goal is to alleviate and relieve the feeling. This is not an easy task, because many students who experience anxiety or fear, do so because of previous experiences, and these just cannot be erased. Nonetheless, the goal should be to convey to the student your acceptance of the negative feelings and your willingness to help him or her overcome this feeling.

In cases where student anxiety and fear are related to the educational environment, the instructional sequence can be arranged so that students ease into difficult learning situations gradually, thus reducing the chances that the situation will cause the student to feel anxious or fearful. Above all, it is imperative that no student be ridiculed for feelings of fear or anxiety. When a student is ridiculed or made fun of due to his or her fear or anxiety, there is a high probability that the student will come to really dislike the environment (the physical education class) in which such punishment occurred.

One word of caution: sometimes, when students are encouraged to be open in the expression of feelings and emotions, one or two students will be encouraged by the attention they receive to verbalize endlessly about their feelings, to the point where one may suspect that they are reporting feelings that are trivial or irrelevant or even inaccurate. This is fairly common among younger students, and it is not confined to the expression of feelings. For example, if you encourage children to help one another, there will inevitably be several children who, in order to get attention, will try to "help" even when the situation does not call for it. Students who overreact in this manner should not be punished or even considered in a bad light. They have not yet learned to distinguish between situations in which it might be legitimate to "help" or express feelings and those where it is uncalled for. The best strategy is to ignore all instances where you feel the expression of feeling is inappropriate (see the discussion of extinction strategy in Chapter 7). If you encourage the appropriate expression of feelings, students will quickly learn to differentiate between the two. But if you penalize an inappropriate expression of feelings through ridicule or some other form of social punishment, the student will almost certainly be less likely to express any feeling.

Establishing Rapport with Classes over Periods of Time

Good rapport with a class means that they trust and respect you and that they cooperate with you in trying to achieve the educational goals you have set for them. Good rapport makes teaching more fun and less stressful. Good rapport creates the context in which more learning can take place. As suggested in Chapter 5, good rapport with a class is sometimes achieved by reducing demands in the instructional task system—by trading those demands for cooperation with the managerial task system, and by allowing the student-social system to take over. In such cases, students are well behaved and physical education is perceived as fun, but little is learned and the experience is seldom valued by students. Your goal, however, should be to develop good rapport with classes and also develop a highly effective instructional task system.

Rapport is built over time and sustained through consistent follow through of its main components (Jensen, 1988). It is appropriate and useful to tell students that you want to have a good, productive class atmosphere, but the proof is in the building of it through consistency in attending to some important class ingredients. They are as follows.

1. *Know your students.* What is their home situation? Do they have siblings? What are their likes and dislikes? Try having them fill out 4 by 6 cards with important information.

2. *Appreciate your students.* Try to understand the pressures and difficulties they are facing—and communicate this understanding. Who in classes is the target of peer pressure? Who is faced with periodically difficult home situations, emotional or physical problems?

3. *Acknowledge their efforts.* Find time to praise them for making the effort, not only in your class but for other things, too. Write notes on occasion. Find different, quiet ways to let them know you care and appreciate them.

4. *Be a careful listener.* Try to know what's going on with your students. If they perceive you to be "up" on things, you'll have a better chance of meriting their confidence.

5. *Include students in decisions.* Start with small decisions and, as students learn to be responsible, gradually incorporate them in larger class decisions. This is not only an important learning experience but also builds student ownership for what goes on in class.

6. *Make some concessions when appropriate.* When you're doing aerobics, why not let students choose the music? If you use some "free time" or "game day" as a reward for good effort and behavior, why not let students choose the activities?

7. *Always show respect for students.* Shaming, ridicule, sarcasm, and the like are simply inappropriate for professional teachers—and they are devastating for building rapport. Make sure they show respect for each other—and for you, too.

8. *Show honesty and integrity.* Don't bend the rules. Enforce guidelines consistently. Be fair in both rewarding and punishing.

9. *Develop a sense of community, of belonging to the class.* Use language and tactics that continually create a sense of "our class." Notice absences and ask about them. Send a class note to a sick classmate. Lessen the impact of cliques within the class through careful grouping. Utilize class performance goals and feedback, both for behavior and academic performance.

You need to monitor your efforts to achieve rapport with your classes. One way to do this is to be sensitive to how they respond to your directions and activities. Do they do things quickly and enthusiastically or do they complain, ask questions, and engage in task modification? You also should monitor how they treat each other. Do they willingly share and help one another—or, do they do so grudgingly and only when prompted? How do the students react to you? Do they seek out your opinion? Do they tend to approach you with questions, or do they tend to avoid you? What are things like before and after class? Do students get there early and want to know what will be done? Are they disappointed when class ends? These are all indicators of your success in building a positive, enthusiastic rapport with your students.

How Do You Come Across to Your Students?

It is important that you try to assess how you appear and sound to your students—and to fellow teachers, administrators, and parents also. We all have some sense of how we come across to other people, but our impressions of ourselves are sometimes based on less than accurate information. As a teacher, it is important for you to understand how you look and sound, and why that is important to your success in teaching effectively and relating well to your students.

The most easily altered aspect of your appearance is your clothing and grooming. While there is no need for teachers to dress as if each day were a fashion show, I believe it is important for them to have a clean, professional look. I would not presume to suggest to you exactly the kinds of athletic gear that give you a "professional" look. On the other hand, I do believe in certain guidelines. Your clothing should be neat and clean. Your outfits should not be confused with those your students wear! Quiet, professional outfits are probably better than loud, trendy outfits. Your clothes need to be worn in a way that emphasizes the look of an active, fit physical educator. Your general dress standards should comply with those of the school in which you teach, especially if you are a student teacher or a new teacher. If you are a student teacher, then some of your ideas about what is appropriate dress will have been formed by being a member of the student subculture. You need to compare those ideas with what is considered appropriate in the professional culture into which you are moving.

Do you have any habitual patterns of movement or facial expressions that might detract from your ability to communicate effectively? Do you stand straight and sit with good posture? Do you have any nervous habits with your hands or feet? How do you look when you talk to your class as a whole? Are your facial expressions and bodily movements congruent with what you are saying to them? What kind of first impression do you make? You need to assess these and make changes where you feel necessary. The only way to do this, of course, is to see yourself, which requires videotaping. Videotaping is even more useful if you use a lapel microphone to pick up your verbalizations clearly. If you don't have access to this technology, ask a good, honest friend to watch you and provide some specific assessment.

Finally, how do you sound? How quickly or slowly do you talk to students? Are your instructions and explanations at a good pace, yet clearly understandable? Is your voice loud enough? When you try to talk more loudly, can you maintain a good tone? Do you use pauses and changes in tone and loudness to provide emphasis in your talk? Or do you talk in monotone? These are important features for a teacher, because much of what you communicate is done through talking to students as a group. You need also to make sure that you don't have nervous vocal habits. Many beginning teachers have habits such as saying "OK" or "uh-h" during their sentences, and they are often unaware that they do so. To check this, you need to audiotape yourself while you're teaching. A small cassette tape recorder in a pocket can accomplish this without using a lapel microphone. Listen to yourself. If you have repetitive verbal expressions, count them! Then try to reduce them and eventually eliminate them from your speech.

How you look, move, and sound are important ingredients of how you come across to students. You want to make sure that they are working for you rather than against you as you attempt to be an effective teacher and communicator.

Communicating Through Developing Your Teaching Space

The physical nature of the space in which you teach every day also sends messages to students. There is little you can do about the actual structural nature of the gymnasium, multi-purpose room, or outdoor play space, but you can do things to make your teaching space pleasant, informative, and motivational. The teaching space should, above all, be neat and safe. You must consider the safety issues in the space for each activity you teach. A typical elementary school gymnasium will have very different safety implications for activities such as volleyball (typically safe), indoor soccer (typically in need of strict safety rules), and gymnastics (typically in need of equipment safety rules). Equipment not in current use should be stored neatly somewhere away from the space. Only those items you need for a day's activity should be available.

In most instances, you will find that physical education spaces are not very bright and appealing. You need to make them so! The physical education space should be a happy, pleasant, motivational place to engage in physical activity. When you put up posters and messages, they should be colorful and easy to read—use big print or type and colors that contrast well with the room colors. You also need to build communication into your teaching space in ways that both motivate and inform your students. Some approaches to improving the communication capacity of your teaching space follow.

1. *A communication board.* Students should know where important daily information is listed—the first activity for the day's lesson, messages to individual students, messages about upcoming events, lost items, and other issues.

2. *A unit bulletin board area.* Whether you are teaching a fitness unit, or a team handball unit, students should get to see how the activity is done, where it is done, and by whom. Pictures of playing spaces, people of different ages doing the activity, and famous performers can all help to provide information and motivate students. This is a good opportunity to

show that gender, age, and disability are not deterrents to active participation in any activity.

3. *Critical element posters.* Every activity you teach will have skills to be learned—and each of those skills will have critical technical elements that students should know and remember as they practice. Simple, colorful posters shown at a height and in a place where students can easily see them from a distance can remind students of important technical information. You should use no more than four to six critical elements per poster and choose key words to represent them. For example, a basketball shooting poster might have the following key words listed—hand spread, elbow out, ball high, knees bent, toes pressed.

4. *Gym rules.* As indicated in Chapter 6, gymnasium rules are important for developing a successful managerial task system. The gym rules should be posted in a place that is easy to see, in large print and bright colors. Again, key words should be used rather than long sentences, and the rules should be stated positively when possible.

5. *Challenge and inspiration messages.* Messages that challenge, motivate, support, and inspire students can become relatively permanent fixtures in your teaching space. They sometimes can be painted on walls. Computers can easily generate large, long message "streamers" which can be taped to walls. Brightly colored posters can be used. The messages should be simple, positive, and optimistic. They should encourage and challenge students, and emphasize the importance of sport, fitness, and dance.

Effective Communication Skills

Another useful perspective from which to view teacher interaction skills is that of communication. When communication takes place, it always has three primary elements. First, there is a sender, the person who communicates the message. Second, there is the receiver, the person to whom the message is directed and who will later respond to it. Third, there is the nature of the message itself. The message can be sent in words, expressions, or gestures, or in some combination of each. Obviously, it is important for a teacher to be an effective communicator. When messages are not sent clearly—when there is miscommunication—the result is often confusion and misunderstanding. Such situations often lead to trouble, both for the teachers and the students.

More specifically for purposes of this chapter, teachers need to communicate certain kinds of messages effectively if a humane educational setting is to develop. Messages such a "I value you as a person," "I want you to succeed in here," and "I accept you" are crucial for establishing a humane climate. If teachers do not pay attention to these messages and are not aware of their own interpersonal communications, no such climate is likely to develop. Effective, humane communicating does not happen by chance. Nor, indeed, does it occur just because a teacher wants it to occur. Skills are involved, which need to be developed and then systematically used if the goal of a humane physical education setting is to be achieved.

Sending Skills

Effective communication exists when a listener interprets a message in the way the sender intended. The skills described in this section can ensure clearer, more accurate sending.

1. *Take ownership for what you say.* It is important that people communicating messages speak for themselves. Using pronouns such as *I, me, my,* and *mine* help to establish ownership. Beginning a message with "I think," "I feel," or "I need" identifies clearly whose idea, feeling, or need that will be expressed in the message. Vagueness occurs when messages are sent by saying, "Someone thinks . . ." or "Wouldn't it be nice if . . ." When you take ownership for what you say, you invite a sense of trust and convey a sense of openness to those who receive the message.

2. *Describe rather than judge.* Messages sent to students should describe the content of the message clearly but should do so without being judgmental. Being judgmental stifles communication. If you persist in being judgmental about students, you will be unlikely to affect them in ways that contribute to their personal growth. For example, telling a student he or she is a terrible defensive player (a judgment) has a different effect from telling the student that he or she has trouble executing defensive strategies (a description).

3. *Try to incorporate the student's viewpoint.* Each of us tends to see the world from a limited perspective—our own. If you are trying to influence the personal growth of students, it is important that you attempt to take their perspective into account when sending messages to them. To what are they sensitive? How do they react to certain things? What is their nonverbal behavior like? What are the major forces that affect their perspectives? The more the sender (the teacher) can take such factors into account, the more likely are the messages to be received well.

4. *Be sensitive to feelings.* It is very helpful to be sensitive to feelings, both your own and those of the receiver. Each of us feels differently from day to day and often differently within the same day. Those feelings quite often are expressed in our messages, *even though they may have nothing to do with the communication.* For example, you may have had some disappointment. You then communicate with some students during the next class. The students may receive a message that shows that disappointment even though it had nothing to do with them! If you are more aware of your own feelings, they are less likely to intrude into your messages. The same sensitivity and awareness should be applied to messages you receive from students. They too have factors that affect their lives and get mixed up in their messages.

5. *Be aware of your nonverbal cues.* It is virtually impossible not to emit nonverbal behavior and to have that behavior become part of the message you are sending. Often the receiver reacts more to the nonverbal components of the message than to what the words themselves convey. Effective communicators tend to have direct eye contact. They look at the

person(s) to whom they are talking. Their facial expressions tend to express messages that are similar to those expressed in the words they are saying. Body movement and alignment also communicate messages. A relaxed position with a slight lean toward the listener conveys warmth. A rigid body position tends to stifle communication. Far too few of us are sensitive to the messages we send through our posture and body movements.

Receiving Skills

Although each of us no doubt could stand to improve our sending skills, it is in the area of receiving skills that most of us are really in need of practice and improvement. More communication is probably ruined by inadequate receiving skills than by inadequate sending skills. Far too few of us are good listeners! Skilled communicators need to be as involved in listening as they are in sending. Some important skills for improving your receiving skills are described as follows.

1. *Paraphrase to clarify messages received.* The term *paraphrasing* means restating, in your own words, what the sender has just said to you, including what you perceive to be the feeling and the meaning conveyed by the sender in the message, For example, a teacher might say to a student, "Am I correct in thinking you are feeling a lack of confidence about the skills in this unit?" Paraphrasing has several benefits. First, it helps to get the message straight. Second, it provides good feedback to the sender concerning how clearly the message was delivered. Third, it makes absolutely clear to the sender that you were listening. Fourth, paraphrasing helps you to gain insight into the perspective of the person from whom the message was delivered, and helps you to see his or her point of view.

2. *Use effective attending skills.* When you listen to someone, you emit a lot of behavior, particularly nonverbal behavior. Eye contact, posture, body alignment, and facial expressions all contribute to your attending behavior. Obviously, these behaviors tell the sender how you are attending and from this, the sender tends to infer how much you care about the message.

3. *Attend to the nonverbal cues of the sender.* Often a message in words needs to be interpreted in terms of the nonverbal cues that accompany the words. Nonverbal cues give hints about the involvement of the sender, how much emotion is involved, how much it means, how angry or happy the sender might be, and a host of other possibilities. Just listening to the words, and even the tone of voice, is seldom sufficient to gauge the full meaning of the message, The nonverbal cues add the extra dimension and allow you to interpret the full meaning of the message more accurately. For example, a student might send a verbal message that he or she does not want to be on a particular team, but the emotion and stress the student displays nonverbally might cause you to consider the message much more seriously than if no emotion were shown.

4. *Take in account your own feelings and how they affect the message.* If you are nervous or preoccupied, you may not hear all of a message. If you are angry or frustrated with the sender, you may infer incorrect meanings from the message. Misinterpretation is likely when the receiver is emotionally involved with the situation or is distracted, thinking about other things. To avoid this, the sender must be sensitive to his or her own feelings, especially as they apply to the message conveyed. For example, if you are having a bad day for some reason, you might want to paraphrase more often just to make sure that you are responding correctly to student messages rather than reacting incorrectly because of your own concerns.

Roadblocks to Communication

Communications experts and counseling experts agree that efforts toward communication are often blocked and thwarted by responses from one party that tend to produce negative reactions in the other party. Sometimes the intensity and severity of the block is such that communication is completely shut off. At other times, milder blocks simply slow down communication and inhibit one or both of the communicating parties. Teachers sometimes slow down or completely block communication between themselves and students, often without even being aware of what they are doing. Sensitivity to these blocks is the first step toward eliminating them from your interaction style. Here are some examples of the more common blocks (Johnson, 1981).

1. *Ordering, commanding, and directing.* "You quit complaining and just pay attention!"
2. *Threatening.* "If you guys don't stop messing round, I'm going to have to put you on report!"
3. *Preaching or moralizing.* "You girls know better than to behave that way!" "Is that any way to behave?"
4. *Offering advice or solutions prematurely.* "You'll just have to have your mother help you to get your gym clothes ready on time."
5. *Judging, criticizing, and blaming.* "You are just lazy!" "You two are always causing problems in this class!"
6. *Stereotyping or labeling* "Don't act like a fourth-grader!" "You are acting like a baby!"
7. *Interrogating or cross-examining* "What in the world did you do that for?" "How come you didn't ask me first?"
8. *Distracting or diverting.* "Why don't we talk about it some other time?" "Now just isn't the time to discuss it."

Each of us has no doubt blocked communication by using these kinds of response with students. If your goal is to communicate more clearly and effectively and through communication to help students reach effective solutions to problems, then you should avoid such blocks. To avoid responding in this way takes patience and sensitivity—and the skill to eliminate such responses from your interaction patterns.

139

Effectively
Accommodating
the
Student-Social
System

8.5 Learning Interpersonal Skills, or "Are Your Listening Skills as Good as Your Dribbling Skills?"

Physical educators understand what needs to be done for skill development—understand what is to be done, practice it, get some feedback, keep practicing it, have success with it, and so on. This text has made the argument that teaching skills (feedback, reinforcing appropriate student behavior, asking questions properly) should be approached in the same way. Can interpersonal relations skills also be viewed in this way? Yes. Not only do I consider that possible, but so does David Johnson, whose book *Reaching Out: Interpersonal Effectiveness and Self-Actualization* (1981) is one of the leading books on developing interpersonal relations. Johnson suggests the following steps for learning and improving interpersonal skills. They should sound familiar simply because they are nearly identical to the steps suggested in Chapter 1.

1. Understand why the skill is important and how it will be of value to you.
2. Understand what the skill is and the component behaviors you have to engage in to perform the skill.
3. Find situations in which you can practice the skill.
4. Get someone to watch you and tell you how well you are performing.
5. Keep practicing.
6. Load your practice toward success.
7. Get friends to encourage you to use the skill.
8. Practice until it feels real. (Johnson, 1981, pp. 11–12)

There is no mystery about becoming better skilled in interpersonal relations, just as there is no mystery about improving your tennis game. The skills must be learned, practiced, and perfected until they are virtually automatic.

Effectively Accommodating the Student-Social System

Chapter 5 described the ecology of physical education as the interrelationships among a management task system, an instructional task system, and a student-social system. Most teachers work at developing a successful management system so that students are well behaved and not disruptive. Many teachers also try to build an effective instructional system so that students achieve real educational outcomes. The management and instructional systems will have a better chance of being successful if teachers consider how the student-social system will be accommodated within them.

Social interactions are important to students of all ages. Allen (1988) has shown that a *primary* agenda of students in schools is socializing—having fun by interacting and doing things together. Students will pursue this social agenda! How teachers respond to this agenda will not only go a long way toward determining the climate of the class but will also affect how much learning takes place. Teachers can ignore the student-social system, try to shut it off, or find ways to effectively accommodate it within the instructional task system of the class.

Some teachers ignore the student-social system—often, as it turns out, at their own peril! Students will find ways to socialize, and these "ways" often will disrupt the management system and make the instructional system ineffective. Teachers who do not recognize this and have ways of responding to it often find that they are reducing demands in the instructional system so that students keep their socializing within the boundaries of the managerial task system. The worst scenario of all, from my point of view, is when the so-called instructional system is suspended and replaced with an activity-oriented, student-social system. Physical education then becomes a free-recreation period as in the case of a teacher who allows students to do the same activity day after day—typically an activity that has little instructional value. The students are well behaved (always within the boundaries of the managerial system) and cause the teacher no problems (they do cooperate), but there is no instruction and no real learning. Socializing becomes the main agenda of the activity.

A second approach to the student-social system is to attempt to shut it off. This is typically accomplished by adopting an authoritarian approach to management and instruction, one dominated by fear of punishment. Any sign of exuberance, joy, or fun on the part of the students is mistaken as a breach of the managerial task system. When this happens, some students comply, although in doing so they also probably develop an aversion to physical education. Other students, however, will comply outwardly and look for opportunities to test the system and to engage in their social interactions. In this sense, they "go underground" and try to test the teacher. This often creates problems for the teacher, who responds with more punishment and rigidity.

A third approach seems more productive for both the teacher and the students—that is to recognize that the student-social system exists and try to allow for it within the context of the subject matter. It is clear from watching children at play and from watching adults in their leisure that play, games, sport, and fitness have a strong social component. Being on a team can enhance social relationships. Doing fitness activities together can have a strong social component. Sport, fitness, and dance should be engaged in exuberantly and joyously. Physical education teachers must channel the student-social agenda toward the instructional agenda. That is, they must create appropriate ways for students to interact socially *within* the activity. "Having fun" should be a natural outcome of participation in sport, fitness, and dance. It is a kind of social experience that students should learn about and value in their own lives. When teachers work gradually toward accomplishing this educational goal, they will find that students increasingly see their own social agendas *within* the activity rather than outside it. At that point, the student-social system will be running in tandem with the teacher's instructional system—and both will be better for it.

Summary

1. Good interpersonal relations with students make life more pleasant for teachers and contribute to a context in which more learning can take place.
2. Teachers sometimes mistake good relations with students for their primary role as teachers of a subject.
3. Research evidence suggests that interaction patterns are typically neutral; there are usually more negative than positive interactions and few signs of a nurturing, positive climate.
4. Students get messages from how you teach, and these messages are important for nurturing positive interpersonal relations.
5. Interaction skills typically need to be developed, as do other skills, instead of relying on a "be-yourself" strategy.
6. The technical aspects of interactions include consistency, focus on significant student behavior, matching interactions to tasks, interacting on nonschool factors, sustaining enthusiasm, and focusing on feelings and emotions.
7. Rapport with a class exists when students trust and respect you and cooperate in achieving goals.
8. Rapport is developed over time by focusing on primary components such as knowing students; appreciating them; acknowledging their efforts; listening; including them in decisions; making concessions; showing respect, honesty, and integrity; and developing a sense of belonging to the class.
9. Aspects of dress and grooming, speech habits, nonverbal behavior, and posture all contribute to how you come across to students.
10. The communicative features of the physical space in which you teach can be enhanced to provide information, motivation, and recognition.
11. Effective communication skills include both sending and receiving skills as well as recognizing roadblocks to communication.
12. The student-social system can be ignored or shut off, but only at risk to the class ecology. It is better to accommodate the student-social system by finding ways for students to socialize within the activities.

PART Three

Effective Teaching in Physical Education

Effective Teaching needs to enhance students' growth. It should be delivered in a way that recognizes the dignity and further develops the potential of students as human beings. Thus, Part Three, which focuses on effective teaching, begins with issues and strategies related to developing a humane physical education. A humane and growth-enhancing physical education doesn't just happen because teachers have good intentions. In addition, they need to thoroughly understand the content of what they teach and how to develop it to meet the learners' needs. They need to organize that content into units of instruction and then to deliver those units of instruction through effective teaching on a lesson-to-lesson basis. As they grow as professional teachers, they can utilize different instructional formats to suit their own talents and the needs of their students.

When you master the content in this section you should be able to discuss the purposes and features of a humane physical education, understand how content is developed and matched to learner needs, and understand how to organize content into effective units of instruction. You will also be able to discuss and analyze the generic instructional strategies that underlie teaching effectiveness and describe how these strategies can be utilized in a number of different instructional formats.

CHAPTER 9

Toward a Humane Physical Education: Ethics and Morals in the Gym

Physical education teachers do not intentionally organize their classes or treat students in ways that result in unfair participation and achievement. However, there are many teachers who unintentionally turn students off with unconscious race or sex stereotyping in physical education classes. There are teachers who ignore unfair participation patterns in class games or name-calling among students. Other teachers fail to see the anger, frustration, and hopelessness some students feel because they are not highly skilled, timid about competition, or excluded by classmates.

Griffin and Placek (1983)

CHAPTER OBJECTIVES

To distinguish between legal-ethical obligations and moral purpose in teaching

To define the characteristics of a humane physical education

To distinguish between academic and therapeutic goals

To describe the contribution of developing people as players

To describe ways sexism, racism, and motor elitism are manifest in physical education

To describe strategies teachers can use to provide gender, race, and motor equity in their teaching

To describe how community, connectedness, and ritual can be developed

To describe how self-growth can be fostered within physical education

During a volleyball unit, Mr. Pitts appoints six students to captain the teams. All the captains are white. A Black student in the class complains to Mr. Pitts that none of the three Black students in the class were picked. Mr. Pitts tells him that "I'm waiting for the basketball unit; then I'll make you all captains."

Ms. Bacon allows her eighth graders to pick their own teams for a soccer tournament. The student-captains pick the best-skilled players first and then argue whether any of the teams has to pick the three least-skilled students in the class. When the teams are finally organized and game play begins, the low-skilled students play fewer minutes and seldom touch the ball when they are in the game. Some of the lower-skilled students like it this way, but two of them complain to Ms. Bacon that they aren't getting a fair chance.

James, a skinny ninth grader, is not well skilled and very timid in game settings. During a class volleyball game, he shies away from attempting to return a shot and nearly misses the ball completely. His teammates, tired of his ineptness, start berating him. One of the boys says "You play like a fairy!" James is obviously upset by all of this. Mr. Brown, having noticed the commotion, stops the play and asks "what's going on?" The boy repeats his charge: "James plays like a fairy!"

Ms. Beatty integrates the boys and girls in her class for practice and competition, believing both that Title IX requires such action and that it is the right thing to do. A student from a nearby university is conducting an observation as part of a class project on equity. The class is toward the end of a basketball unit. The student takes notes and codes certain events. Several weeks later, Ms. Beatty gets a copy of the student's report and learns that boys in her class have 74 percent of the ball contacts and take 82 percent of the shots during the games.

Jason is a Severe Behaviorally Handicapped (SBH) student who spends most of his day in a special class but is "mainstreamed" in physical education with his regular fifth grade age group. Ms. Holloway assigns a student each day to help Jason through the lesson. The students are very helpful, but on the day they serve as "tutor" they get almost no practice themselves. Jason has difficulty doing any of the practice drills, even when they are modified. He can't be placed in a game setting because of the danger to himself and to the other children. Several parents have complained that the class is not getting the attention and activity it deserves because of Jason's presence. A few of the students are starting to complain when they are asked to be tutor for the day's lesson.

Legal, Ethical, and Moral Issues in Teaching

Each of the five cases described above presents a different set of complex issues. These issues have legal, ethical, and moral overtones. Each also requires that a teacher take some action. What actions would you suggest for each case? Your answers, and the reasons you provide to support them, would say a lot about your current perspectives on societal issues that find their ways into schools and into the lives of teachers—issues such as the education of persons with disabilities, racial stereotyping, gender equity, grading criteria, sexual orientation, and appropriate forms of punishment. Other cases could easily have been described that would have highlighted issues such as student's rights, teacher's rights, and motor elitism (discrimination in favor of the more highly skilled at the expense of the lower skilled).

This chapter focuses on the development and maintenance of a humane physical education. As such, the materials within it will necessarily touch on sensitive issues. For some of these issues, there is still evidence in our culture of cruel, oppressive discrimination and prejudice. With some of them there is also evidence of serious, thoughtful disagreement among people of good will and high ethical-moral principles. As a teacher you cannot avoid these issues! They exist in your workplace—the school—on a daily basis. You will be required to confront them and respond to them. Your actions relative to these issues will represent the largest part of your ethical and moral life as a teacher. On occasion, you will also be in situations where you have to express a point of view about disputes involving race, gender, sexual orientation, disability, and a host of other

146

Toward a
Humane
Physical
Education:
Ethics and
Morals in the
Gym

9.1 NEA Code of Ethics

Principle I: Commitment to the Student

The educator strives to help each student realize his or her potential as a worthy and effective member of society. The educator therefore works to stimulate the spirit of inquiry, the acquisition of knowledge and understanding, and the thoughtful formulation of worthy goals.

In fulfillment of the obligation to the student, the educator—

1. Shall not unreasonably restrain the student from independent action in the pursuit of learning.
2. Shall not unreasonably deny the student access to varying points of view.
3. Shall not deliberately suppress or distort subject matter relevant to the student's progress.
4. Shall make reasonable effort to protect the student from conditions harmful to learning or to health and safety.
5. Shall not intentionally expose the student to embarrassment or disparagement.
6. Shall not on the basis of race, color, creed, sex, national origin, marital status, political or religious beliefs, family, social or cultural background, or sexual orientation, unfairly—

   a. Exclude any student from participation in any program
   b. Deny benefits to any student
   c. Grant any advantage to any student.

7. Shall not use professional relationships with students for private advantage.
8. Shall not disclose information about students obtained in the course of professional service, unless disclosure serves a compelling purpose or is required by law.

issues. Some teachers seek out those opportunities to speak out because they *believe* deeply in certain points of view. What you *say* on these occasions is important. What is most important, however, is that what you *say* about ethical-moral issues is congruent with how you actually respond to them when they occur in your classes.

I take a *humane physical education* to be one in which students (1) have equal opportunity to develop their talents in the subject matter, (2) receive no unfair treatment from their teacher or fellow students that is based on gender, race, ethnic origin, religion, sexual orientation, motor-skill talent, or socioeconomic status, and (3) are encouraged to develop as independent persons who respect themselves and those with whom they interact. This definition suggests that teachers are responsible for their own actions and those of their students toward each other.

9.1 NEA Code of Ethics (continued)

Principle II: Commitment to the Profession

The education profession is vested by the public with a trust and responsibility requiring the highest ideals of professional service.

In the belief that the quality of the services of the education profession directly influences the nation and its citizens, the educator shall exert every effort to raise professional standards, to promote a climate that encourages the exercise of professional judgment, to achieve conditions which attract persons worthy of the trust to careers in education, and to assist in preventing the practice of the profession by unqualified persons.

In fulfillment of the obligation to the profession, the educator—

1. Shall not in a application for a professional position deliberately make a false statement or fail to disclose a material fact related to competency and qualifications.
2. Shall not misrepresent his/her professional qualifications.
3. Shall not assist any entry into the profession of a person known to be unqualified in respect to character, education or other relevant attribute.
4. Shall not knowingly make a false statement concerning the qualifications of a candidate for a professional position.
5. Shall not assist a noneducator in the unauthorized practice of teaching.
6. Shall not disclose information about colleagues obtained in the course of professional service unless disclosure serves a compelling professional purpose or is required by law.
7. Shall not knowingly make false or malicious statements about a colleague.
8. Shall not accept any gratuity, gift, or favor that might impair or appear to influence professional decisions or action.

I have chosen to present the material in this chapter within a two-part framework—that of the legal and ethical constraints and obligations for teacher conduct, and that of the possibility for investing your teaching with moral purpose, particularly as it regards issues related to equity. Some of what teachers do relative to important societal issues is governed specifically by law. Public Law 94.142, The Education for All Handicapped Children Act, requires that students with disabilities receive a free, appropriate education in a *least restrictive environment*. In many cases, the least restrictive environment is the "regular" class. When students with disabilities are placed in regular classes, we refer to it as *mainstreaming*. Physical education is the only school subject specifically referred to in PL 94.142. Each student with a disability must have an Individual Educational Plan (IEP) agreed to by a team of professionals and the parents of

148

Toward a
Humane
Physical
Education:
Ethics and
Morals in the
Gym

the child. PL 94.142 is a good example of how compliance with a law establishes guidelines that affect what a teacher can and cannot do with certain students.

Laws, statutes, regulations, and court decisions form the *legal* basis for teacher action. Thus, PL 94.142 affects what teachers do with students who have disabilities, Title IX has changed what can and can't be done relative to girls and women in sport and physical education, and Brown vs. the Board of Education, Topeka, Kansas, changed how and when students can and cannot be segregated by race in schools.

Teachers, however, are bound by ethical principles that go beyond the law: They are professional persons and, as such, are bound by a code of professional ethics. *Ethical* issues involve duties, obligations, rights, and responsibilities. When we talk about ethical issues we tend to use words like "ought," "should," "fair," and "right." Ethical behavior requires judgment that often goes beyond the basic facts of an issue. Sometimes, with issues where various rights are in conflict with one another, some principle of fairness or justice must be applied. Teacher organizations, such as the National Education Association (NEA), have developed codes of ethics for their members (see box 9.1 titled "NEA Code of Ethics"). Behaving ethically requires us to do as we *ought* to do even in situations where we might *want* to do something different. For example, you may have deeply held beliefs about gender—what roles males and females should play in society—and those beliefs may run counter to current statutes and ethical codes for gender equity. You are entitled to your beliefs and the values that derive from them. However, you are not entitled to allow those beliefs to affect how you arrange and carry out the physical education curriculum or how you teach boys and girls in physical education. The reason you are not entitled to is that there are statutes requiring equal access to physical education and doctrines of fairness in professional conduct for teachers. Thus, as a professional teacher in America, you are obligated, by law and by professional ethics, to provide an equitable curriculum and equitable teaching for girls and boys in your classes. The same laws and ethical guidelines also require you to make sure that students treat each other fairly and appropriately as regards issues related to gender.

Some teachers want to go beyond their legal and ethical obligations to actively promote certain values that they feel are crucial for a more humane society. For example, they may want to promote gender equity or racial harmony or sensitivity to disabilities by seeking to bring these issues to the attention of their students in ways that are designed to affect the students' views and behavior. This is what I refer to as a *moral purpose* in teaching. The distinction here needs to be made clear. For example, I believe that teachers are *obligated*, by law and professional ethics, to provide an education for their students that is fair and equitable as it regards gender, an education that is not discriminatory toward girls and women in any way, one that provides equal opportunity. On the other hand, I do not believe that teachers are obligated to make gender equity a specific educational goal in their classes. If they choose to do so—to actively promote gender equity as a specific educational goal in physical education—this, it seems to me, is perfectly legitimate and appropriate. I try to do so in my teaching. The distinction is between the legal and ethical *obligation* that pertains to all teachers and the

149

Promoting
Human
Relations in
Physical
Education

9.2 Individual and Institutional Inequities

Inequity exists at both the individual and institutional levels. Prejudice at either level is unfortunate. Since much power is vested in institutions, inequitable treatment at that level is particularly disabling. Shown below are some examples of race and gender inequities at each level.

Individual	*Institutional*
Using a racial slur to refer to someone from another race	The school providing twice the support for the boys' team as it does the girls' team
Parents allowing their son to play on teams but not their daughter	An organization denying membership to Blacks and Hispanics
Calling a young girl who enjoys sports a "tomboy"	A school newspaper devoting more space to boys' sports than girls' sports
Laughing at a racist or sexist joke	All sports administrators being white males

Can you provide other examples of inequitable treatment at the individual and institutional levels? How much of it do you believe is intentional?

(Adapted from Griffin & Placek, 1983.)

individual choice to go beyond that obligation in order to invest one's teaching with a specific moral purpose. It should be clear, of course, that teachers cannot choose to have their teaching reflect moral beliefs that run contrary to their legal or ethical obligations.

It is unlikely that any person preparing to teach physical education can discharge their legal and ethical obligations relative to equity issues without first coming to grips with their own points of view. Revealing and confronting one's own biases and prejudices is difficult, and it sometimes results in conflict. If achieving equity in our society was easy, it would have been accomplished a long time ago. It is not easy because the history of our society regarding race, gender, sexual orientation, and disabilities is filled with individual and institutional prejudice and bias.

Promoting Human Relations in Physical Education

Although teaching the subject matter of physical education in a challenging and nurturant climate can be considered to be the primary feature of humanistic physical education, it is most certainly not the only feature,. There are many ways in which physical educators can promote good human relations in physical education and, in so doing, contribute both to the development of humane individuals and the growth of a humane society. The subject matter and its

150

Toward a
Humane
Physical
Education:
Ethics and
Morals in the
Gym

concerns may be the direct and primary focus of teaching, but there are many, many other lessons to be learned within physical education. Many of these other lessons are learned indirectly, as a result of the manner in which the teacher interacts with students, helps the students to interact with one another, and directly or indirectly espouses or reinforces values and behaviors associated with issues such a sex equity, racial equity, ethical behavior, sportsmanship, cultural pluralism, and human relations in general.

As indicated in Chapter 8, the physical education program and, more specifically, the physical education teacher send certain *messages* to students. These messages are sometimes sent directly through direct verbal reference or through calling attention of students directly to an issue. But, more often than not, the messages are conveyed indirectly through the behavior of the teacher and the manner in which the teacher reacts to the behavior of students. The purpose of the remainder of this chapter is to call to your attention some important kinds of messages that teachers convey to students, particularly messages that, if properly sent, can contribute to the development of humanistic individuals and a more humanistic society. The basic assumption underlying what follows is that specific humanistic goals for teaching can and should be developed and approached systematically in a manner similar to which one approaches the achievement of subject matter goals. You may disagree somewhat with the goals chosen to illustrate humanistic teaching in physical education, but the basic thing is to understand that you will be teaching values and value-laden behavior to your students. At the very least, you ought to understand what values you are promoting and then try to make your teaching as consistent as possible with the value structure you want to convey to students.

Gender Equity

Sport and physical education do not have good records in terms of discrimination against women. Many of the limiting stereotypes that girls learn about themselves are learned on playgrounds and in game situations. For many years, girls and women were systematically denied the opportunity to learn and to participate in physical education. In other cases, the opportunities were restricted to those thought to be *appropriate*. Girls and women who dared to venture beyond what was considered to be appropriate did so at some risk.

> This risk involved is, of course that associated with concepts of femininity and masculinity. Masculinity too often means tough, assertive, and hard. Femininity too often means yielding, nonassertive, and soft. Boys play football. Girls are cheerleaders. The girls' role is supportive and noncombative. Girls who step outside their prescribed roles too often are the objects of curious glances and off-color comments. The same phenomenon is true for the boy or man who participates in dance. (Siedentop, 1980 p. 213)

The segregation of girls and women in sport and physical education was specifically prohibited in Title IX of the Educational Amendments of 1972. But eliminating illegal gender segregation does not necessarily abolish gender inequity. Griffen (1981) has suggested several ways in which inequity is apparent in physical education teaching:

151

Promoting
Human
Relations in
Physical
Education

1. In team sports, boys dominate games regardless of the skill differentials between boys and girls.
2. Teachers often group students for games through public selection in which girls are typically chosen last.
3. Teachers tend to provide more academic feedback for boys than for girls.
4. When class leaders or demonstrators are chosen, they typically are boys.
5. Teachers sometimes make sex-stereotyped statements to students ("She does well for a girl." "The boys will put the mats away." "The girls will not be able to do as many push-ups as the boys.")
6. Teachers seldom intervene to correct sex-stereotyped interactions among students (such as saying, "Billy, Jane doesn't run 'like a boy,' as you said. She runs like a girl who has practiced hard and is skilled.")
7. Teachers often (inadvertently many times) role model sex-stereotyped activity patterns.

These examples occur in gymnasiums everywhere. Obviously, they could be corrected if teachers would pay more attention to them and even work specifically to achieve sex equity goals. Teachers need to be aware of how they distribute their attention. They need to make sure that all students have equal opportunity to learning and playing time and that the quality of that learning and playing time is equal. And teachers need to be sensitive to the messages conveyed in their language and interactions with students. Teachers need to avoid the sex stereotyping of activities, such as labeling certain things as "girls'" activities and certain things as "boys'" activities.

The humaneness of the setting will be improved if teachers specifically try to break down gender stereotypes. This can be done in three ways: through teacher prompting, teacher interventions on student behavior, and role modeling.

One good way to break down stereotypes and promote sex equity is to offer clear, consistent messages (prompts) when opportunities arise. Teachers do not have to wait for inappropriate situations to develop. They can take the initiative and make comments that are intentionally not sex stereotyping: "Ron, Glenda is the best set-up person on your team. You ought to try to pass the ball to her as often as possible." For additional suggestions, see Box 9.3 "Avoiding Sexist Language in Teaching and Coaching."

A second strategy is intervening to correct student interactions that are stereotyped or reinforcing student interactions that are not stereotyped. "Jake, don't say Tom throws like a girl. Girls can learn to throw just as well as boys can." "Girls can do this every bit as well as boys can." "There is no reason why the girls won't be as capable of doing this as the boys will be." "I liked the way boys and girls worked together today. It shows that you understand that the girls can learn and play in the same way as the boys."

A third strategy is role modeling. The term **role modeling** refers to exhibiting behaviors specific to a role so that students can incorporate similar patterns into their own behavioral repertoire. The potential for sex-equitable role modeling is

152

Toward a
Humane
Physical
Education:
Ethics and
Morals in the
Gym

9.3 Avoiding Sexist Language in Teaching and Coaching

Sport has traditionally been male-oriented. Many of the common terms in sport are, therefore, male-oriented terms. There are alternatives—and they should be used.

Sexist Terms	*Nonsexist Equivalents*
Guard your man closely	Guard your opponent closely
We don't have the manpower to win	We don't have the depth to win
Second baseman	Second base player
The defenseman	The defense
Three-man teams	Three-person teams
Third man (lacrosse)	Third player
Boys' and girls' push-ups	Extended or knee push-up
Man-to-man defense	Player-to-player defense
Sportsmanship	Fair play

Can you think of other examples? And good alternatives for them? When you teach or coach, do you make some of these communication errors? How can you correct them?

(Adapted from Griffin & Placek, 1983.)

endless: a male who participates in folk dance and obviously enjoys it, a female who competes vigorously, a male teacher who lets students know that he likes to cook (or garden or collect antiques), a female teacher who rides motorcycles (or jogs or does carpentry). All these models break down stereotypes and, in so doing, tend to expand the potential for the next generation to have greater freedom. It must be emphasized, however that role modeling to deceive students will eventually prove disastrous to your credibility.

Many strategies complement direct role modeling. Pictures of female athletes can be used to demonstrate technique or to adorn a bulletin board. Poster and pictures showing men and women participating together are useful. The concepts of sport hero or heroine can be used effectively to heighten the effects of modeling. Male and female physical educators team teaching an activity can provide a direct and important message, especially if they participate together on equal terms. The combined effect of these strategies optimizes the possibilities that students will adopt and value the attitudes and behaviors in question.

Race Equity

Many of the examples and strategies cited in the previous section apply equally to racial equity. There is no need to describe or catalog the many problems our society has had during the past several decades in trying to come to grips with equal opportunity for minority groups. The prejudices and stereotypes in this area are old and deeply ingrained. They are not overcome easily, but each little step toward progress that can be made is an important one for the ultimate health of the society and the respect for the humanity of each student regardless of his or her racial or ethnic background.

153

Promoting
Human
Relations in
Physical
Education

Unfortunately, sport is an area where racial stereotyping has prevailed for far too long. For example, there are common notions about the ability of Black students to play certain positions or to achieve in certain sport areas. The first goal for physical educators must be to combat such stereotypes directly, to attempt to abolish them, at least for the students with whom they work. This can be achieved directly if you teach in an integrated setting. It can be achieved indirectly if you teach in a segregated setting.

The direct approach would be through prompting, intervening on student interactions (correcting inappropriate interactions and reinforcing appropriate ones), and modeling whenever possible. Role modeling in which members of different races cooperate and work together toward a common goal can be very effective. Many students have never had the opportunity to work constructively with a member of a different racial background. If this kind of modeling cannot be brought directly into the teaching setting (by using expert demonstrators from nearby colleges or universities, for example), then it can be done indirectly by judiciously selecting visual materials for teaching skills and decorating bulletin boards. For additional suggestions, see Box 9.4 "What Can You Do to Promote Greater Equity?"

Barnes (1977) has identified teacher behaviors that are counterproductive to the development of racial equity in educational settings. It should be noted that these kinds of behaviors often occur inadvertently—that is, the teacher does not intend them to be offensive. But they often *are* offensive. The intention is not nearly so powerful as the act itself. The following kinds of statements are counterproductive in reaching equity goals with minority students:

1. Labeling or referring to students as *disadvantaged, culturally deprived,* or *slow learners*
2. Global statements that stereotype a group, such as "you people" or "all of you"
3. Making statements that highlight differences in personal matters, such as clothing, physical appearance, or material possessions
4. Patronizing students, being overly "nice" or paternalistic or maternalistic, with a style of superiority
5. Telling racially oriented jokes or using racially oriented terms such as *Mex, Chink,* or *greaser*
6. Avoiding physical contact with minority students, keeping physical distance between you and them
7. Criticizing, judging, or in any way devaluing the culture from which minority students come
8. Stereotyping individual minority children on the basis of ethnic or racial stereotypes such as the notions that Japanese children are always good in science, Mexican American children are lazy, and Black children are irresponsible.

154

Toward a
Humane
Physical
Education:
Ethics and
Morals in the
Gym

9.4 What can you do to promote greater equity?

In daily teaching there are always choices to make. How often do you include equity in the criteria you use to make choices? The more often you think about the equity implications of what you do, the more likely you will be to provide and promote equity among your students and in your school. Here are some suggestions for promoting equity.

- Include minority and female persons in bulletin board displays.
- Mention female and minority athletes when discussing sports with students.
- Don't tell or laugh at racist, ethnic, or sexist jokes.
- Don't expect minority students to "fit in" and act just like white students.
- Sponsor multicultural activity units or sport days.
- Celebrate women's sports week.
- Don't allow students to tease on the basis of gender, race, sexual orientation, or socioeconomic status.
- Avoid "loaded" terms such as *colored, chick, whitey, queer, sissy, tomboy, jockette, klutz, and wussy.*
- Make sure that low-skilled students are not picked last or assigned tasks they can't do successfully.

Can you think of other strategies that would promote equity?

(Adapted from Griffin & Placek, 1983.)

Where racial equity is an important local issue due to school integration plans, it might be useful to consider special techniques to improve understanding and behavior among students. Teachers too can benefit greatly from strategies such as visiting the home of a minority student, visiting community play areas where minority students live, participating in community service projects that bring racial groups together, observing classes taught by teachers from the minority group(s), and generally educating yourself about the cultural background of the group with whom you have contact. Your own growing understanding will be reflected in your teaching behavior and your teaching behavior will have an effect on your students.

Equity in Opportunity to Learn

Motor elitism refers to discrimination in favor of the highly skilled students in class at the expense of the less-skilled students. This discrimination is seldom intentional on the part of the teacher. Students, on the other hand, can often be overtly cruel to their classmates who are less skilled, especially in games when the less-skilled students make mistakes that hurt a team's performance. Regardless of whether the discrimination is intentional or not, it substantially reduces the less-skilled student's opportunity to learn and grow in physical education. The learning environment needs to be a successful, nurturing setting for *all* students, regardless of their skill levels. Here are some ways that less-skilled students suffer in physical education.

155

Promoting
Human
Relations in
Physical
Education

1. Less-skilled students accrue less Academic Learning Time than high-skilled students and get fewer opportunities to respond.
2. Instructional tasks set by the teacher are too often so difficult for less-skilled students that they seldom experience success.
3. In game settings, less-skilled students make fewer responses than other players and are seldom successful.
4. Less-skilled students appear to be more often objects of criticism and ridicule from classmates for their poor performances.

Teaching a large group of students who differ markedly in their skill levels is not an easy job. Students who have low skills must be given tasks that allow them to experience success. If this does not happen, physical education will become a place where they experience consistent failure, putting in jeopardy their future interests in sport and leisure activities. Since most students try to do what the teacher asks them to do, it makes sense that a range of tasks should be acceptable. Teachers can accomplish this in two ways: They can describe different levels of the task in their initial descriptions and allow students to find where they can be successful, or they can make it clear to students that certain ranges of task modification are allowable. Teachers also need to monitor students' opportunities to respond so that they can make sure that low-skilled students are not becoming willing or unwilling nonparticipants in drills or games.

Teachers can also support low-skilled students through prompts that emphasize the relationship between effort and improvement—"See John, when you keep working hard, you do get better!" Prompts to the entire class can also emphasize the need to respect different levels of skill and for students to support each other's efforts to improve.

When low-skilled students do have success, it needs to be noted. Rates of praise and reinforcement need to be higher for low-skilled students than for high-skilled students, especially in their beginning efforts to master skills and strategies. If low-skilled students are getting left out of activities, teachers need to intervene immediately, either to emphasize full participation or to change the rules of the activity to ensure fuller participation. Interventions are also appropriate when students criticize, ridicule, or make fun of less-skilled classmates. Not only should this behavior be desisted immediately, but it should be replaced with more appropriate behaviors of respect and support for classmates' learning efforts.

Finally, role modeling is as important here as it is for other equity issues. Are the bulletin boards filled with only "super-star" athletes, or are ordinary performers shown, too? Do teachers allow only the high-skilled students to demonstrate or use them as examples? Perhaps a low-skill student could demonstrate a particular accomplishment, and the teacher could make sure that classmates understand the effort the student made in doing it. When a low-skilled student

156

Toward a
Humane
Physical
Education:
Ethics and
Morals in the
Gym

perfects the rudiments of a technique, that student's modeling of the technique is as valuable as that of a higher-skilled student.

Clearly, to develop a humane physical education, those who are less naturally talented must share in the joy and success of learning the subject matter. Teachers must make sure that every student understands that their classes are *equal opportunity* classes as regards skill levels. They must also teach their students to respect and support each other as learners and performers.

Developing People as Players— Our Primary Humanizing Contribution

We should never lose sight of the fact that our primary contribution to the humanistic education of students we serve is to help them to gain skill in and an affection for our subject matter—physically active motor play. Although it may not be apparent on the first examination, a strong and compelling argument can be made for the notion that helping students to be good at and to like basketball, gymnastics, repelling, diving, skiing, running, and dancing is a strongly *humanistic* outcome. To teach people how to play and to want to play is to enhance their potential for humanistic experience. To develop a society of players and a culture devoted to play is to contribute to a civilized, humanistic future. In *The Joy of Sports* (1976), Michael Novak has offered the most complete argument for the humanistic nature of physical education outcomes.

> Sports are the highest products of civilization and the most accessible, lived, experiential sources of the civilizing spirit. In sports, law was born and also liberty, and the nexus of their interrelation. In sports, honesty and excellence are caught, captured, nourished, held in trust for the generations. Without rules, there are no sports. Without limits, a sport cannot begin to exist. Within the rules, within the limits, freedom is given form. Play is the essence of freedom: "The free play of ideas." Play is the fundamental structure of the human mind. Of the body, too. The mind at play, the body at play—these furnish our imaginations with the highest achievements of beauty the human race attains.(p. 43)

The basic argument to be derived from such an analysis is that education is humanizing if it is carried out within a challenging, nurturant setting that is free from threat and coercion. Thus, the teacher who strives for primarily academic goals, within a warm, nurturant climate, is involved in a humanistic enterprise. So too, perhaps, is the teacher whose main goals are therapeutic rather than educational. But the tendency in recent years has been to label the therapeutic orientation as humanistic and to assume that humanistic goals cannot be achieved in settings where primarily academic goals are sought. This latter argument simply does not ring true if one considers humanism in the broad sense of fostering useful human development.

Therefore, the general view taken here is that physical educators who help students to develop skill, to understand play, and to develop an affection for play forms such as games, sports, and dance are contributing to humanistic outcomes. If they teach so that the educational climate is challenging and nurturing, then the humanistic nature of their teaching is further enhanced, and they have every right to describe what they do as humanistic physical education.

157

Building
Community:
Connectedness,
Festival, and
Ritual

Building Community: Connectedness, Festival, and Ritual

The goals of a humane physical education are most easily met when teachers build a learning community within each class and throughout the school. A sense of community involves support for others, allegiance, feelings of belonging and camaraderie, and increased motivation to participate (Jensen, 1988). Community is something that is created slowly and is sustained through attention to common goals, appropriate communication, consistent support, challenge, celebration and fun.

Building *connectedness* refers to feelings of belonging, support, and purpose within a class. Students need to feel that they are part of what goes on in the class. This can be achieved by communicating class goals, allowing students to participate in decisions, celebrating individual and group accomplishments, and setting individual and group challenges. Teachers contribute to connectedness when they are skillful in their praise and specific in their feedback. They also contribute when they make those "special" gestures that communicate support and concern to students—quiet asides, notes, special privileges. The teacher clearly sets the tone for the class, yet connectedness is more likely to develop when teachers specifically teach their students to support one another—what in coaching we would call building a "team spirit." Like most other behaviors, teachers can do this through prompting appropriate interactions, reinforcing students when they support one another, and using good student interactions as models for the class.

Festival and ritual are fundamental to the development and maintenance of a sense of community. Think for a moment how ethnic and religious communities come together and sustain themselves through festivals and rituals. One of the most compelling and attractive features of sport is its celebration of festival and ritual. Think of any important contest or competition and the sense of festival that surrounds it, the importance of ritual within it. Sadly, festival and ritual are too often absent from physical education, even though they are clearly present and important in interschool sport!

Physical educators who work to build a sense of festival in their programs and develop rituals within it contribute enormously to a sense of community within the physical education program and throughout the school. One elementary specialist used the Olympic theme to build a Spring festival around track and field. Children worked hard to learn track and field events through a decathlon scoring system. They accumulated their points to achieve individual awards based on their performances (each child won an award based on his or her own performance). At the end of the track and field season, a school-wide track meet was held for the fourth through sixth graders. In the meantime, early elementary children had been exploring their movement and skill potential through a unit

158

Toward a
Humane
Physical
Education:
Ethics and
Morals in the
Gym

that was based on the Olympic discipline of rhythmic gymnastics. Classroom teachers spent time helping students learn about the early Olympic Games. The art education specialist helped students explore Olympic art through drawings and sculptures. All of this came together in the school's "Olympic Festival." The young children started the day by leading the opening ceremonies march with an exhibition of their rhythmic gymnastics. Each of the fourth through sixth grade classes followed in the parade of "athletes," all done to the music of the Olympic Fanfare. The school-wide track meet followed with 20 parent volunteers helping—and many others in attendance as spectators. The awards ceremony ended the festival, with every child receiving an award of some kind. The effects of such efforts are long-lasting.

There are many ways to create festival and ritual in physical education. Gymnasiums can be made more attractive, more colorful. Competitions within class can be made more festive. Sport units can be taught more like sport rather than as isolated skill fragments with games at the end of the unit (Siedentop, Locke, & Mand, 1986). Students can be assigned to groups in which they cooperate toward collective goals—on teams in sport units and as members of cooperative groups in fitness or dance units. If teachers do not make participation in physical education "special" for their students, the students will tend not to consider it to be "special."

Promoting Self-Growth in Physical Education

Virtually every physical educator expresses concern about the self-growth of his or her students. Indeed, some suggest it is the primary goal of their teaching. Self-growth, however, is an elusive concept. It is more difficult to see than is increased strength, a better volleyball set, or better technique in the high jump. Although self-growth has long appeared as a major goal in physical education, it is difficult to examine the research reviewed in Chapter 3 and come to the conclusion that there is any widespread achievement of these goals in today's programs.

A humane physical education should develop self-growth as a by-product of achievement in sport, fitness, and dance activities and as an outcome of participating in an equitable, supportive learning environment. Self-growth cannot be viewed in isolation, because individuals do not exist alone. They exist as members of social groups—families, neighborhoods, peer groups, teams. Thus, self-growth must not only enhance individuals but must also help the individuals become more useful and successful members of the groups to which they belong. In terms of physical education, self-growth must first of all help each student to become a more productive member of the physical education class.

Self-growth in physical education has meaning as a set of specific behavioral skills that students can acquire and refine as they participate in the ongoing motor-skill and fitness curriculum. These skills are: having a positive attitude towards oneself, expressing positive attitudes toward others, behaving responsibly as a class member, becoming a "fair player," and behaving ethically within the context of the class.

All evidence suggests that students who experience success in meaningful activities in physical education in a nurturing learning environment will improve their attitudes toward themselves, toward school, and toward the subject matter. Beyond that most important set of circumstances, teachers can promote self-growth by helping students undertake new learning experiences with positive expectations for achievement; helping students to take appropriate risks and see themselves as "doers"; helping students to make appropriate, positive statements about themselves and their accomplishments; and encouraging students to be willing to perform in front of peers and others. The idea here is to foster an "I can!" atmosphere in your classes. (For additional suggestions see Box 9.5 "Ability, Effort, and Achievement." Prompting students to have positive expectations, reinforcing appropriate self-comments, using peer models, and public recognition of accomplishments are all strategies that help students to feel positively about their experiences in physical education and about themselves as physically competent persons.

Developing and Expressing Positive Attitudes toward Others

The *self* is always in relation to *others*. Our sense of ourselves is often determined largely by the groups we belong to and the sharing that goes on within those groups. Students need to learn to be productive members of groups. One important set of skills is that of expressing positive attitudes toward others, in this case the fellow members of their physical education class. Students being nice to each other doesn't just happen. Indeed, most student groups form cliques in

---

9.5 Ability, Effort, and Achievement

Students understand clearly that some classmates are "better" than others. To what do they attribute those differences—innate ability or individual effort? Research (Holloway, 1988) shows that most American students believe that innate ability explains most of the differences in achievement that they see in their classmates. In Japan, on the other hand, students believe that differences in effort explain most differences in achievement. While it would be foolish to deny that students differ in their natural talents for sport, it would be more foolish to suggest that success in sport is more related to heredity than to hard work.

One of the most important self-growth concepts students can learn is that sustained effort leads to achievement. Teachers have to help students make the connection between sustained effort and achievement. Setting goals, monitoring small increments of improvement, charting improvement, modeling the effort of other students, recognizing sustained effort, and generally creating an "I-can" learning environment not only will lead to greater achievement for students but will also help them to make the important connection between sustained effort and achievement.

160

Toward a
Humane
Physical
Education:
Ethics and
Morals in the
Gym

which the students are typically supportive of clique members and frequently critical of other classmates. Teachers can help students learn to be thoughtful, appreciative "complimenters" by prompting the expression of positive attitudes toward others, reinforcing it strongly when it does occur, and modeling it themselves in their own teaching behavior.

For example, at class closure each day, several students might be asked to describe one good thing they saw a classmate do that day. Players on teams can be prompted to publicly recognize contributions of teammates. Prompting students to say "thank-you's" to classmates who help them in some way can help make that kind of response a class standard. Evidence (Wescott, 1977; Rolider, 1979) in physical education suggests that this kind of behavior is infectious—once it gets started, and students get over the initial, awkward stage of being nice to one another, they grow to like being complimented and become more willing to compliment others. Part of this growing willingness to have and express positive attitudes toward others will, inevitably, result in students having an increased tolerance and respect for classmates who differ in background, appearance, or some other characteristic.

Learning to Behave Responsibly as a Class Member

One important aspect of a mature "self" is being a responsible member of a group. Behavior in this area goes beyond that of staying on-task and not creating disturbances—indeed, that is just the beginning stage of being a responsible member of a group. The important skills here are those that balance your rights and obligations as an individual with the goals of the group—between "watching out for yourself" and being a "good team player." Specific skills in this domain are learning to distinguish between fair and unfair consequences, accepting fair consequences maturely, being willing to report your own infractions or accidents, apologizing when your behavior has infringed on the rights of a classmate, taking leadership when it is appropriate, and being a good follower when it is appropriate.

Physical education is full of opportunities for students to learn what I refer to here as "responsibility" skills. Team sports require that individuals play roles, and those roles require the blending of individual assertiveness and team play. Games have rules and consequences for violating them. Many activities require the formation of groups and the exerting of leadership within groups. Some aspects of the subject matter—fitness, for example—lend themselves to individual planning and commitment. The equipment and space in physical education almost always need to be shared, often in ways that are potentially distracting and disruptive. These situations present teachers with opportunities—if they prompt responsible behavior, describe it specifically, reinforce it when it occurs, and generally make it an important class goal, then it will more likely happen. It doesn't happen automatically, however. It has to be taught just as specifically and carefully as do bump passes, forward rolls, or double-teaming.

Learning to Become a "Fair Player"

Earlier in this chapter I suggested that our primary humanizing contribution was the development of persons as players. Learning to become a fair player in the context of sport and games is an important self-growth experience. Below are lists of fair-player behaviors and unfair-player behaviors (Griffin & Placek, 1983).

Fair-Player Behaviors	*Unfair-Player Behaviors*
Plays hard to win at all times	Plays halfheartedly when behind
Says "my fault" if it was	Blames teammates for mistakes
Plays own position and role	Hogs ball or space
Respects rules	Takes advantage of rules
Supports teammates	bosses or criticizes teammates
Is respectful to officials even when questioning them	Yells at officials and blames them for team problems
Respects opponent's effort	Belittles opponents
Treats winning and losing appropriately	Sulks after defeats and gloats after victory

I am sure you could add to these two lists. The student who displays the fair-player behaviors consistently has learned how to be a mature player, and the situations through which those behaviors were acquired were important self-growth experiences. There are two important teaching requirements here. First, the behaviors themselves must be prompted, reinforced, described specifically, and modeled. Second, however, students must come to understand, appreciate, and value *why* these behaviors are important in sport and games. For example, they must understand that for a victory to have real meaning, not only must you play hard, to the best of your ability, but your opponent must do the same. If your opponent plays very hard and within the rules, then when you achieve victory, you have achieved something worthwhile and important. The role of the opponent in this equation is crucial, and opponents should be respected when they fulfill that role to the best of their abilities.

Learning to Behave Ethically in Physical Education

Learning to become a fair player (see above) is an important ingredient in the ethical climate of a physical education class and program. Yet there are ethical "skills" to acquire that go beyond sport and games; again, physical education is replete with situations where they can be learned and practiced. I will suggest four ethical "skills" that I believe are important—distinguishing truth from untruth, monitoring one's own behavior and reporting one's own infractions, not engaging in inappropriate behavior even though the opportunity exists, and applying norms of "fairness" to class events. You, no doubt, could add more.

Young students often tell stories that stretch the truth. Truth-telling is an important behavior that can be prompted, modeled, and reinforced. To learn truth-telling, students must be able to distinguish truth from untruth and to know when truth is being "stretched" to achieve an effect. Students sometimes lie to avoid punishment. Thus, truth-telling needs to be taught in association with the skill of accepting fair consequences.

162

Toward a
Humane
Physical
Education:
Ethics and
Morals in the
Gym

Needless to say, physical education is a wonderful subject in which students can learn to monitor their own behavior and report their own infractions. Rules of games are clear, and students can act as their own referees as they play. Remember, however, these skills need to be taught and teachers should not expect that students will reliably demonstrate them just because they have been told to do so.

It is easy for students to behave well when they are under the direct sanction of a teacher. On many occasions, however, students will not be under direct supervision and the opportunity to misbehave "without getting caught" will occur. Sometimes, peers will create pressure to engage in the misbehavior. Teachers need to convey to students that they understand these situations will occur and that resisting the opportunity to misbehave is a mark of maturity, responsibility, and independence. Examples can be used. When you see a student resisting peer pressure to misbehave, you must find a strong, private way to reinforce that student.

Finally, students in physical education have many opportunities within their class to learn about "fairness" and to see norms of fairness applied in the daily life of the class. Students will see these things and learn to appreciate their importance if teachers point them out and explain why they are important. Changing the rules of a game to make it fairer for all skill levels or for achieving certain skill/strategy goals is an example. So too is creating equity in a game by adjusting a rule for a physically disabled student. Applying different fitness norms based on developmental levels is yet another instance where a norm "fairness" is being applied. There are many situations in which the question "What's Fair?" can be asked, and students can learn something about fairness in each situation.

Academic and Therapeutic Goals

In the United States, the federal Constitution assigns the primary responsibility for education to the states. Thus we have no national goals for education. States often set minimum curricular standards, but leave much of the goal-setting to those at the school district level—preserving the tradition of *local control* for education. Schools, therefore, differ markedly in their goals for education. I believe it is important to distinguish between goals that are primarily academic and those that are primarily therapeutic. It is clear that most parents—and most professional educators—believe that the main responsibilities of schools are academic achievement within the various subjects taught in the school. This is not to suggest that parents or educators are unconcerned about the growth and development of children and youth, their social skills, or their ethical character. These, too, are considered to be important.

The distinction here is one of emphasis. Some professionals have suggested that schools should be devoted primarily to therapeutic goals—those of self-growth, social responsibility, and character development. They believe subject matter outcomes—being better at math, reading, social studies, or sport—to be secondary to the therapeutic goals. With societal problems such as latch-key children, single-parent families, and substance abuse growing in our society, schools have been made increasingly responsible for helping children and youth in ways that go beyond subject matter goals.

It is important to restate that the issue here is one of emphasis rather than having to choose to pursue one set of goals at the expense of the others. The research reviewed in Chapter 2 showed clearly that in classrooms and schools where academic achievement was emphasized within a supportive, nurturant environment, students not only achieved more but also had better attitudes toward themselves, toward school, and toward the subject matters they were learning. Effective teaching tends to breed both achievement and attitude gains!

The academic-therapeutic distinction is also necessary because this chapter is about developing a humane physical education. The focus here is on gender and race equity, for example, not on basketball and fitness. The focus is on persons with disabilities and low-skilled children, not tennis or team handball. While social issues are necessary and important ones for effective teachers to consider, they do not, in my judgment, constitute the main goals of physical education. I believe that social and character goals can and should be achieved through an effective physical education that has a primary focus the subject matter itself—which I take to be physically active motor play, especially those forms institutionalized in our culture in sport and fitness.

Summary

1. Teachers have legal and ethical obligations to provide equitable treatment for their students, especially as regards gender, race, ethnicity, socioeconomic status, and motor-skill talents.
2. Beyond their legal and ethical obligations, teachers may want to infuse their teaching with moral purpose as regards equity and self-growth.
3. Teachers should have a primary purpose of achieving subject matter goals, but this should not be done in the absence of or at the expense of achieving equity and self-growth skills.
4. The primary humanizing contribution of physical education is to help students gain skill in and an affection for games, sport, fitness, and dance.
5. Avoiding gender stereotyping and providing gender equity is an important human relations goal.
6. Avoiding race stereotyping and providing racial equity is an important human relations goal.
7. Providing equal opportunity for learning regardless of natural talents is an important human relations goal.
8. Building a learning-community in which persons connect positively with one another is developed through common goals, appropriate communication, and the establishment of festival and shared ritual.

164

Toward a
Humane
Physical
Education:
Ethics and
Morals in the
Gym

9. Self-growth is achieved when student achievement is fostered in a nurturant, supportive learning environment.

10. Specific self-growth skills such as developing positive attitudes toward self, developing positive attitudes toward others, behaving responsibly as a class member, becoming a fair player, and behaving ethically can be achieved through specific teaching strategies.

CHAPTER 10
Strategies for Content Development

There are no national curriculums in physical education, and there are few state or local curriculums to which physical educators are held accountable. Physical educators are therefore largely left on their own when establishing goals and instructional programs. Lack of accountability has produced much diversity. It has given the creative teacher the opportunity to more nearly match programs to student needs. It has also resulted in many poor progams— programs that have no identifiable pedagogical goals or programs that bear no relation to their stated goals.

Judy Rink (1985)

CHAPTER OBJECTIVES

To distinguish between the philosophical and technical aspects of planning

To describe the professional context for planning

To distinguish among the various views of the "good" in physical educational curricular planning

To describe issues related to planning an equitable curriculum

To describe factors affecting program-level planning

To describe guidelines for selecting activities

To formulate appropriate terminal content goals

To formulate progressions through informing, refining, extending, and applying tasks

To distinguish between well-aligned and non-aligned instructional plans

To describe planning issues related to closed and open skills

To describe various accountability strategies

This chapter focuses on program building. All of the experiences that students have in physical education in a particular school represent that school's *program*. Physical education is the subject matter, and the activities done in physical education form the *content* of that program. Everybody would agree that those experiences in physical education ought to add up to something significant in the lives of students. Thus the content of the program must be developed to achieve goals that will affect the lives of students who experience the program. While that sounds appropriate and even easy, it is not! Developing the content of a physical education program requires a set of decisions about what goals to strive for and what activities to use to achieve those goals. It also requires technical planning skills to develop a series of learning experiences for those activities—learning experiences that achieve the goals which define the program. Not all physical teachers plan well because they do not have serious goals for student learning, as Box 10.1 indicates.

To develop content for a program, therefore, you must involve yourself in two fairly distinct and different undertakings. The first—

thinking about your subject matter and establishing a set of goals—involves reflection, valuing, sensitivity to local considerations, and making tough decisions among some attractive choices. The second—technically planning the content development—involves both a thorough knowledge of the activities and planning skills such as task analysis and instructional alignment.

Planning an exciting, attractive, useful program is a fundamental aspect of becoming a skilled, professional physical educator. Putting that plan into action on a daily basis represents the important culmination of thoughtfully choosing goals and activities and skillfully planning content so that students engage in a series of learning experiences that gradually help them achieve the goals of the program. Reflection, decision making, and planning, however, should not be thought of as ends in themselves. Teachers are not good because they develop good-looking program plans or carefully devised unit plans. They are good when program and unit planning pay off in better teaching and more learning.

The Professional Context for Planning

Nearly every school district in America has a curriculum syllabus for the subjects taught in its schools. Some states also have syllabi for all subjects taught in the schools. Generally, these curriculum guides include both a set of broad objectives to be achieved in the subject and a list of activities that are thought to contribute to those objectives. The objectives for physical education are most often categorized as (1) motor skill, (2) fitness, (3) knowledge, and (4) social development. The words used as labels for these categories differ from place to place, but most objectives can be placed in these four areas. There are usually a large number of activities listed in the district curriculum syllabus (sometimes referred to as a Graded Course of Study). If teachers program activities that are not among the approved activities in the district syllabus, they are at risk for liability if an injury is sustained, because the activities were not "officially sanctioned" parts of the curriculum. Thus the most common practice is to include in district syllabi most activities that might be taught in physical education. These activities are sometimes grouped into areas such as aquatics, team sports, individual sports, cooperative games, basic movement, adventure activities, and dance. In some larger city districts, there might be a prescribed yearly program that requires teachers to follow a sequence of activity units chosen by a supervisor or district committee.

This tradition of defining a program through broadly conceived curriculum syllabi has resulted in the situation described in the quotation that opens this chapter. The fact is that most physical education teachers can, over a period of time, substantially influence the program they teach to students. The overall lack of accountability for specific outcomes in physical education allows teachers to develop programs that are very good—and can let programs deteriorate until they become very bad.

The elementary physical education specialist typically works with other specialists in a district to establish an overall elementary program. Within the general guidelines, the individual teachers are left to plan and deliver that program according to their own interests. The middle or secondary school physical educator typically works with colleagues within a school—and to a lesser extent with other middle and secondary colleagues at other schools in the same district. Again, however, the opportunity for variation exists even among teachers within the same school's physical education staff. These situations represent the typical *professional* context for developing a physical education program.

What Is the "Good" in Physical Education?

Developing the content of a physical education program starts with decisions about activities and goals. The most often cited curriculum development model (Tyler, 1949) suggests that goals should be established and then activities chosen to meet those goals. For example, following this goal-driven planning model, a teacher would first establish that cardiovascular fitness was a primary goal and *then* would examine activities to ascertain the degree to which they could contribute to that goal. Most evidence, however, suggests that teachers' primary concern in planning is with the activity chosen rather than the goals to be reached (Stroot & Morton, 1989). For example, a teacher might learn about Team Handball and decide that it would be a good activity to include in a program. Regardless of whether you begin by examining various goals to be achieved or by thinking about various activities that might be included in a program, you are, at that point, making some fundamental decisions about your views of physical education.

What is the "good" that students acquire when they experience a physical education program? Is is fitness? Skill in sport? The development of cooperation and attitudes about competition? Is it an aesthetic experience? Is there some kind of personal meaning to be derived from activity that defines the essence of physical education? Or is developing a sense of oneself as a competent mover or player the primary good to be achieved? These issues need to be confronted. They are not about the technical planning of syllabi, units of instruction, or daily lesson plans. They are about the "stuff" of physical education. They are about answers to questions like "What am I trying to accomplish?", "What am I contributing to the lives of these students?", or "How do I want my students to be different as a result of completing this program?". Answers to these questions involve values and personal visions.

Different visions of the "good" should, of course, lead to a different programs. That is where the technical skills of content development and planning units of instruction become central. Suffice it to say at this point, if you believe that the "good" is a personal commitment to and knowledge about lifetime fitness, then your program should be substantially different from that of someone who believes that the primary "good" is to play well and enjoy a variety of sports. Your program will be different still from a teacher whose personal vision is for a physical education that results in people becoming confident, competent movers.

There appears to be no consensus within the profession on what constitutes the primary "good" to be achieved in physical education. As Box 10.1 "Differing Visions of the 'Good' in Physical Education" indicates, there are at least eight curriculum models that compete in contemporary physical education, representing different visions of the "good." That may be one reason most of the "goods" described above are typically included as goals in physical education program planning. There has been a growing consensus nationally, however, that not all "goods" can be achieved in any one program—and that trying to achieve too many goals results in little achievement in any area.

> The generally accepted goals of physical education are to promote physical fitness, self-esteem, and cognitive and social development. However, the practice—the proliferation of and emphasis on teaching too many activities in too short a time—has made these goals more difficult to attain. The smorgasbord approach of requiring team sports, individual sports, dance, physical fitness activities, all within the space of one school year lessens those students' opportunities to master any one activity through which they can meet the stated goals. (Taylor & Chiogioji, 1987, p. 22)

This tradition of trying to reach multiple goals through a varied program of activities is called the *multiple activity curriculum*. It is the traditional approach to developing content for physical education. Although it has recently has been questioned seriously, it continues to represent the most common approach to programming physical education.

The arguments against a multi-activity approach have resulted in a renewed interest in what I call *main-theme programs;* that is, programs that have a clear sense of a more limited "good" and arrange sequences of activities to achieve that good.

> The (good) programs stood for something specific. We learned about good fitness programs, good social development programs, and good adventure programs. Each of the programs had a main focus that defined and identified the program. (Siedentop, 1987, p. 25)

Main-theme programs develop because the physical educators responsible for them had a vision about what was the primary "good" to be achieved and then developed content to achieve that vision. A main theme becomes an *organizing center* for a program—the central thrust around which content is developed to meet goals.

Developing an Equitable Curriculum

While a teacher's personal vision of the "good" is a powerful and legitimate influence on content development, it is also important that the physical education experience serve students equitably. One important question that all curriculum planners should ask is "What groups are best and most served by this curriculum?" Are males better served than females? Are those interested in competition better served than those interested in an aesthetic experience? I believe that curriculum planners have an ethical responsibility as professional educators to develop curricula that serve students who are

10.1 Differing Versions of the "Good" in Physical Education

Placek (1983) studied a number of physical education teachers to determine how they planned and what they saw as indicators of success in teaching. The responses led her to conclude that when students were well behaved, physically active, and having fun, their teachers felt as if they had achieved success. Achieving specific learning goals—no matter how they were conceptualized—was not how these teachers judged their success. Instead, they saw themselves as successful when students were busy, happy, and good.

Sherman (1979) also studied teacher planning in physical education and concluded that teachers planned primarily for well-managed classes and engagement in activity, rather than for specific learning outcomes.

Stroot and Morton (1989), on the other hand, studied effective elementary physical education specialists and found that student learning was clearly evident as the main objective in their planning. The visions of these elementary specialists differed; that is, each had a different view of what was most important in physical education. However, they all had a view that related directly to student learning, and they all planned activities so that students could achieve the goals of program.

Here are two activities that can help you come to grips with your own visions about physical education and examine them in light of those of classmates or colleagues.

1. Secure a physical education syllabus from a local district. Could you carry out your vision of physical education and still fall within its guidelines? Could classmates who have differing visions do the same? What does that mean?

2. Have each member of class (or colleagues) prepare a rank-ordered list of "goods" that define physical education. Limit the lists to four or five outcomes. Then collate the lists with number 1s getting 5 points, number 2s getting 4 points, and so forth. Is there consensus?

different and especially those who traditionally have not been well served in physical education. Griffin and Placek (1983) have offered the following suggestions for equity in curriculum planning.

1. Include the elimination of gender/race stereotyping and discrimination as a goal of the curriculum.

2. State curricular objectives in language that is nonsexist/nonracist.

3. Provide a balance of activities that accommodate different physical abilities and interests; for example, quickness, strength, finesse, aesthetics, strategy, power.

4. Actively encourage participation in activities that have been traditionally stereotyped by race or gender.

5. Group students by ability and size whenever possible.
6. Use evaluation strategies that do not penalize developmental differences among students.

Physical education has been a content area where certain groups have sometimes been put at a disadvantage and suffered as a result—the lesser skilled, the overweight, and females, for example. Program-level planning is one place where action can begin to ensure that this doesn't happen.

Factors Affecting Program-Level Planning

Too many programs are planned for the achievement of a wide variety of goals in ideal circumstances. Good program planners are always conscious of practicing the "art of the possible." They are aware that programs need to achieve *real* results to be valued by students, administrators, and parents. Once a program is achieving important results, it can be expanded and become more daring, more ambitious. While some program planning might start from ground zero, it is more likely that you will do program planning by selecting goals and activities from a district syllabus and then developing content to achieve those goals. Regardless, the following factors will need to be considered.

1. *Your own personal vision of physical education.* You are a professional person and have the right—the obligation—to pursue your own vision of what constitutes a good program. You are more likely to plan and teach well if your program reflects your own interests and visions. While this is not the only factor you can consider, it perhaps should be the initial one.

2. *The nature of the local district.* You will need to consider the values and norms of the community where you teach. These values and norms may favor some activities more than others, such as outdoor winter activities in the Northeast. There may be sanctions on some activities, such as religious sanctions about social dancing. Over time, a physical educator can help to change the values and norms of a community as regards physical education, but to ignore those values and norms at the outset is a mistake.

3. *Facilities and equipment.* It would be foolish to ignore facilities and equipment when developing content for a program. The size of the indoor space, the kind of surface on an outdoor space, the accessibility of a pool, and the provisions for specialized activities are important. Equipment can be purchased or made, but it takes time to build an equipment inventory. Since early success in programs is important, it makes sense to initially develop a program that "fits" your facility and equipment. However, to use limitations in facilities or equipment as an excuse to delay program development is equally foolish. The physical education literature is replete with evidence of how seemingly inadequate facilities have been developed and how activities can be modified to fit facility and equipment constraints.

4. *The educational programming within the school.* Typically, physical educators have to fit their program within the larger program of the school. Open classroom elementary schools, flexibly scheduled middle schools, alternative high schools, or modularly scheduled schools each present different programming formats for physical educators. This is one of those issues that "you can't know until you get there!" This factors requires that physical educators be able to rearrange their sense of program—especially time—to meet the schedule of the school.

5. *The status of the learners.* While in most cases teachers can assume that they are serving a normal population of students, it is possible that groups within a school or even an entire student body might have special needs. For example, fitness testing may reveal an unacceptably low level of cardiovascular fitness or very poor upper-body strength. Students may have substantial access to team sport instruction in the community but very little opportunity to learn more recreationally oriented individual and dual sports such as tennis and golf. These factors might cause you to consider a program to serve these needs better.

The combination of these influences will affect content development for your program. Considering them carefully and realistically will help you avoid problems and optimize your chances for initial success. Success in your program will build support from fellow teachers and administrators, as well as increase the interest and enthusiasm of the students you teach. From a solid base of success and support, you can then begin to work toward developing your program further. As you do, you no doubt will struggle again and again with your vision of what constitutes the primary "good" of physical education. That continuing struggle is important for you to stay alive as a concerned professional.

Choosing the Content—Selection of Activities

The organizing center of a program is the main theme that defines the "good" of physical education in that program. Once a main theme is selected, it remains to choose activities that will form the content for the program. It is precisely at this point that program planning often breaks down. Activities are sometimes chosen because they are "neat" or because it is "that time of year," rather than for the degree the activities contribute to the main theme. The following guidelines are helpful for selecting activities.

1. *An activity is "appropriate" because it contributes to program goals.* "Appropriate" in this case is a relative term. If your main theme is sport education, then golf and tennis are "appropriate" activities. If you have an adventure theme, then repelling and climbing are "appropriate" activities. Team Handball is a wonderful sport that would contribute to a sport education theme. However, golf is not an "appropriate" activity for a fitness curriculum, nor is aerobics "appropriate" for an adventure or sport curriculum.

10.2 Differing Visions of the "Good" in Physical Education

There are at least eight curriculum models that compete in contemporary physical education. Each of these models represents a different vision of how the "good" in physical education should be conceptualized and developed into a program. The eight models are as follows.

1. *Developmental education.* The traditional education-through-the-physical approach using a multi-activity program to accomplish broad developmental goals of skill, fitness, knowledge, and social development.

2. *Humanistic physical education.* A social development model in which activity outcomes are secondary to a growing sense of self, responsibility, independence, and cooperation.

3. *Fitness.* Typically, fitness models focus on lifetime fitness and emphasize health fitness and its related knowledge components of exercise and nutrition. Such programs are increasingly called "wellness" programs.

4. *Movement education.* A model in which moving competently, confidently, and intelligently become primary outcomes and aesthetic, cooperative activity is valued over competitive activity. Learner decision making is emphasized and teaching strategies are typically discovery-oriented.

5. *Kinesiological studies.* Also called the "concepts curriculum," this approach focuses on blending activity experiences with knowledge about activity that is derived from the subdisciplines of physical education. A more "academic" approach, this model emphasizes cognitive and attitudinal outcomes over skill and fitness outcomes.

6. *Play and sport education.* This model emphasizes developing competent players who understand and value the best of sport traditions and outcomes. Emphasis in this model is on strategic play rather than isolated skill development. It places students in roles as coaches, referees, and record keepers.

7. *Personal meaning.* This model emphasizes the fact that individuals derive different kinds of personal meaning from physical education, and that creating and enhancing that meaning is a primary goal. The purposes of students are given central focus in development of program content.

8. *Adventure curriculum.* This model emphasizes self-development through risk and adventure activities. Cooperation and personal knowledge are emphasized, and the natural environment becomes the primary educational space.

Sources: Jewett & Bain, 1985; Siedentop, 1990.

2. *Successful programs accomplish goals.* If you are to err in planning, it is wise to err in the direction of trying to achieve too little rather than too much. Limited goals—a fewer number of activities—are easier to achieve than a large set of goals and many activities. Doing activity units well takes time. There is reason to question whether an "exposure" program accomplishes anything of lasting value (see Box 10.3 "Does Physical Education Suffer from Overexposure?"). If you want your program to be successful, choose a limited number of goals and develop a limited number of activities to reach those goals. This assumes, of course, that the goals you are trying to accomplish are *learning*-oriented, rather than keeping students busy, happy, and good.

3. *Know what you are doing.* The activities you choose become the content of your program. Teachers should *know* their content well, because without that knowledge it is difficult to develop content thoroughly. Choosing activities you have limited experience with results in inadequately developed content. How much space does the activity take? How can it be modified? How are skills and strategy best refined? How should equipment be modified? To answers these questions typically requires that you know the activity well.

If you choose activities that do indeed contribute directly to the goals implied in your main theme, if you know those activities well enough to develop the content appropriately for the learners you serve, and if you provide sufficient time for those learners to make meaningful gains in doing the activities, then you will have taken huge strides toward establishing a successful program of physical education.

Developing Content: Knowing Where You Are Headed

Whether you are developing content for a one-year high school program or a seven-year elementary school program, you need to know what you want to happen as outcomes for the program. Content is always developed in a direction—and you should first develop the final destination so it can provide the necessary guidance as you proceed. The final destination of content is developed by establishing *terminal goals*—statements describing student performance that should occur reliably as a result of participating in the program. It is only when you know exactly what you want students to be able to *do* at the end of your program that you can begin to decide what needs to be done within the program to get them to those points.

Terminal goals should be defined as *meaningful units of performance,* which are performances that are useful for settings other than the instructional setting. For example, in programs in which the content is sport—where sport serves as an organizing center—terminal goals should be defined in terms of game settings rather than as isolated skill performances. Terminal objectives for tennis should be defined in terms of playing the game of tennis rather than as executing skills in nongame settings. This also means that "passes a test on tennis rules" is not a

Box 10.3 Does Physical Education Suffer from Overexposure?

How many times have you heard a physical educator say that his or her goal was to "expose" students to a game or activity? What is implied in such a statement is that the teacher doesn't really have expectations that students will learn a great deal or improve in the necessary skills and strategies of the game or activity, but will instead just "get to know it a little." Far too often, from my point of view, students get exposed to volleyball somewhere in the fifth or sixth grade, then exposed again to volleyball in the eighth or ninth grade, and then again in the senior high school program. Because each of the efforts is aimed at exposure, students never get beyond beginning skills and seldom can play at a level higher than that for "backyard" volleyball. I believe that this represents serious "overexposure."

One of the major lessons of recent teacher effectiveness research is that effective teachers hold high, yet realistic expectations that students will not only learn a great deal but will continue to learn and improve in whatever is the subject matter being studied. There is no thought to merely expose students to reading or mathematics. Students are expected to learn and to continue to learn and improve from day to day, month to month, year to year.

For effective teaching to occur in physical education, someone must *care* that students learn and improve. In many schools—far too many— the school administrators do not care as much as they should. Thus it is clear that if the physical education teacher does not care about learning, then quite likely few others will.

Haven't we all "exposed" students long enough to volleyball, tennis, golf, and a host of other games and activities? And, how many games of kickball and bombardment need to be played before students are "over-exposed"?

meaningful terminal goal. Instead, a goal such as "while playing, scores game correctly and identifies rule violations correctly" would be more appropriate.

Skill and strategy goals therefore should be defined in terms of game play rather than in nongame settings. Knowledge goals, too, should be defined in terms of how the knowledge should be used in applied settings, rather than displaying the knowledge in an artificial setting, such as a written test. Attitudinal, social, and emotional goals are much more difficult to define, yet the same principle needs to be used—they should be defined in terms of their meaningfulness in noninstructional settings. Developing good attitudes toward lifetime fitness, for example, can be defined in terms of students volunteering (that is, choosing) to take part in intramural aerobics or joining the school bicycle club. Developing appropriate emotional control in competitive settings can be defined by player behavior toward referees, teammates, and opponents. Social qualities such as cooperation can be defined in terms of situations in which students can help each other—and then do. Here are some examples of program-level terminal goals of meaningful student performance (defined here without specifying the activities).

175

Developing
Progressions
to Achieve
Terminal Goals:
Getting There

- During games, students will call their own violations accurately and assess the appropriate consequence (this goal includes knowledge of rules and emotional control to call their own violations).

- During games, students will execute appropriate offensive strategies called for by the situation.

- In noninstructional time, students will choose to take part in lifetime fitness activities.

- When participating in activities that involve risk, students will use appropriate safety techniques specific to the activity.

- In games, students will utilize skills appropriate to situations and will execute those skills with appropriate technique.

- When planning exercise programs, students will adjust factors of intensity, duration, and frequency to accurately reflect their current status and desired improvements.

Developing Progressions to Achieve Terminal Goals: Getting There

Once you know where you are headed, you have to decide how to best get there. To understand how to get there, you should first know where you might be starting from; that is, what will be the level of skill and understanding of the students when they will enter the program. As a trained professional educator, you will know this in a general way from your study of motor development, elementary physical education, and secondary physical education. This general knowledge will allow you to develop content by planning progressions that lead to terminal goals. The application of these progressions, however, will always be *specific* to the students taught in any particular place and time. Experienced teachers know that you can teach two fifth grade classes in consecutive time blocks and require very different progressions to adequately meet the developmental differences in the two classes. Nonetheless, developing progressions becomes an important technical skill in developing content. Developing progressions is where knowledge of content and knowledge of teaching come together—what Shulman (1987) has called *pedagogical content knowledge;* that unique blend of content and pedagogy that is the special expertise of the teacher.

Progressions are learning tasks that move students from less complex, less sophisticated performances to more complex, more sophisticated performances, and eventually to the kinds of meaningful performances that represent the goals of the program. Teachers communicate progressions to students through a series of instructional tasks within a lesson or unit, and, from year to year, across units in the same activity. Rink's (1985) model for developing progressive instructional tasks is widely used in physical education. Initial tasks serve to *inform* the student of a new skill or strategy. Subsequent tasks serve to refine the quality of the performance, to extend the performance by altering it slightly, and to apply the skill or strategy (Rink, 1985).

1. *Refining the quality of performance.* Perhaps the most neglected, yet most important kind of progression is the sequence of learning tasks through which students improve the technical quality of performance—what Rink (1985) calls *refinement tasks.* Teaching fourth- through sixth-grade children how to shoot a basketball one-handed is a typical example. One-hand shooting can be introduced with a demonstration and explanation of the four or five critical performance elements that define the skill (an informing task). Students can then practice this skill and perhaps will do so every day of the basketball units in the program. But the skill should be refined. The position of the shooting hand will not always be correct. The shooting elbow will move improperly to the side. The off-hand will be either too dominant or not act sufficiently as a guide. The flexion of the knees will be too late, too early, or not apparent. It is through a series of refining tasks that students become more aware of the technical components of good shooting so that the quality of their shooting improves. Each skill or strategy tasks that a teacher introduces will need to be refined. In refining tasks, the conditions of practice do not change. Only the focus of student attention changes as different technical elements of the skill or strategy are emphasized. Success in skill and strategy requires quality performance, and that should become the teacher's goal. Refining tasks can't always be fully anticipated. Teachers must use information about the performance of their students to develop progressive refining tasks.

2. *Within-task progressions.* Both skills and strategies need to be simplified to begin with and then gradually made more complex. Think of building content in the track and field part of a program; for example, the shot put. The basic task—putting the shot—will not change, which means that right from the outset a legal "put" rather than a throw is taught. However, few would begin to teach shot putting by having students start at the back of a shot put circle and then teach the glide and put in their mature forms. Instead, a series of *within-task progressions* are taught—Rink (1985) refers to this as *intratask development.* You might begin with an implement that is lighter than a standard 6-pound elementary shot and students stationary in the final putting position, focusing on hip and shoulder rotation to provide force for the put. Regardless of where you begin, you would have to refine the skill demanded in *that* task before you extend the skill with a slightly more complex task, which then would again require refinement before moving to still another more complex task. Rink (1985) refers to within-task progressions as *extending tasks,* those that change the complexity of performance. The refining-extending cycle, repeated over

and over again, forms the central core of content development in physical education. Knowing what to refine and how much to extend—for the specific learners you are working with—is perhaps the most important ingredient of expert planning.

Table 10.1   Examples of Refining Tasks and Extending Tasks

Situation: Basketball, one-hand shooting, novice or young learners. Initial informing task: Square to basket, ball in possession, stationary position, close to basket.

Refining tasks:

- Shooting hand spread behind ball.
- Off-hand supporting (not pushing or leaving go too early).
- Elbow toward basket (not toward side).
- Ball at head level (not brought down).
- Knee bend to generate force (rather than just with arms).
- Press toes to generate force (keep ball high).
- Emphasize wrist snap with ball "rolling" off fingertips.
- Coordinate knee bend and toe press.
- Extend wrist and flex elbow as knees are bent.
- Keep eye on rim.

Extending tasks:

- Pivot away, pivot back to square up position and shoot.
- Receive pass from teammate, square up and shoot.
- Shoot from different angles, but always squared up.
- Gradually extend distance from basket.
- Back to basket, pivot, square up and shoot.
- Move to spot, receive pass, square up and shoot.
- Dribble to spot, square up, and shoot.
- Shoot from spot, move to next spot, receive pass, square up and shoot.

Note: Keeping a class shot chart where students keep track of their shooting practice each day can produce the accountability needed to keep students on-task.

3. *Between-task progressions.* When planning a program that begins with either novice learners or young learners, it is necessary to consider progressions between tasks that are thought to be related. For example, moving from the scissors jump to the Fosbury style in developing high jump content, from a one-hand set shot to a jump shot in developing basketball content, or from 3-versus-3 strategy in soccer to a full-sided game with more players in a larger space all represent different tasks rather than variations of one major task. The progressions among them become important building blocks in developing content for a program. Between-task extensions need to be thought through carefully. Teachers sometimes assume that tasks are progressions when they are not. To be a

progression, one task would have to be related to another in terms of common, critical performance elements (see section on task analysis—page 189). I would argue that the underhand volleyball serve is not a progression for the overhand serve—even though the underhand serve might be used for young or novice volleyball players. The technical demands of the two skills are too different for them to be a skill progression. The scissors high jump, on the other hand, contains virtually all of the beginning technical elements that students will need when they eventually learn the Fosbury style, so those two tasks are a legitimate progression.

Instructional Alignment: Doing the Right Thing

Progressions should be thought of as instructional tasks that lead to terminal performance goals. Earlier in this chapter, I argued that terminal performance goals should be developed as *meaningful* units of performance, which were defined as performances useful for students in settings other than the instructional settings; that is, playing games well, skillfully negotiating wilderness settings, participating competently in fitness activities, and the like. As refining and extending tasks are designed to help students progress toward terminal goals, it is important that instruction be aligned so that they have the best chance for success.

Instructional alignment exists when there is a match in the stimulus conditions of intended outcomes, instructional processes, and instructional assessment. In other words, instructional alignment requires a match between goals, practice, and testing. There is substantial evidence to suggest that well-aligned instruction produces achievement results that are two to three times stronger than nonaligned instruction (Cohen, 1987). To understand the concept, let's first examine a nonaligned situation—a mismatch. Suppose you state terminal goals for volleyball that focus on the appropriate execution of skills and strategy in game play. However, most of your instructional practice tasks are isolated skill drills whose conditions do not reflect the conditions of game play. Your testing consists of forearm passing against a wall, set-passing with a partner, and a serving test for accuracy. In this example, the stimulus conditions of practice and testing are seriously nonaligned with those described in the terminal goals.

Developing volleyball content so that better instructional alignment exists using the same "game play" terminal goals—requires that instructional task progressions be defined by the conditions of the game situations in which they might occur. Isolated skill practice is replaced by different kinds of "mini-scrimmage" situations. Testing or evaluation is done during game play rather than in isolated skill-testing situations. Either a qualitative assessment of skill and strategy during game play is made, or statistics are kept on players (serve percentages, returns, sets, kills, blocks, and so forth) and those are used for assessment purposes, much as they are on volleyball teams.

The concept of instructional alignment requires teachers to think seriously about the nature of the goals they have for their students and how they can

Box 10.4 Instructional Alignment Exercise

Here is an exercise to help you practice and understand the concept of instructional alignment. Assume you are developing content for basketball. You are at that point where you are thinking about designing progressions for the skill of passing. Assume, too, that your terminal goals are for students to execute passes appropriately in game settings.

If you were planning to begin instruction with novice learners or with fifth grade children, where would you begin with this skill? Remember, the notion is to arrange the *conditions* of practice tasks so they match the conditions stated in your terminal goals.

Would you allow students to "travel" as they begin practicing passing; that is, allow them to drag a pivot foot as they pass?

Would you ask them, as an extending task, to use the "other foot" as a pivot foot in practicing passing tasks?

What kinds of passes do you most often see in a game at the middle or junior high school level? Would you spend more time practicing *those* passes rather than a two-handed chest pass to a partner who is not far away and with no defender present at all?

How and when would you introduce the presence of a defender? How would you gradually increase defensive pressure, or would you just allow it right away?

What are the most important critical technical elements of passing that you would need to plan to refine?

What are the most common passing errors made by beginning learners? Finally, do you think you know basketball well enough to complete this exercise with confidence?

---

arrange task progressions that meet *those* goals. Using assessment procedures that are highly aligned with the goals helps to ensure a better match. "Teach what you test and test what you teach" is an old adage in education. It is often violated in physical education.

It is worth repeating that to effectively refine student performance of skill or strategy and to carefully align the conditions of outcomes, instruction, and assessment, you must know a great deal about the activity for which you are planning. As Cohen has suggested, this need to know quite well the subject you teach brings us full circle to the issue that began this chapter.

Teaching what we assess, or assessing what we teach seems embarrassingly obvious. The fundamental issue is: *What's worth teaching?* This is the same question as: *What's worth assessing?* We can either know what we're doing, or not know what we're doing, but in either case, we'll be doing something to other people's children. Do we not have an ethical obligation to know what we're up to? (Cohen, 1987, p. 19)

If instruction is well aligned with goals and assessment procedures, then it will allow students many opportunities to practice relevant skills and strategies *in situations similar to those in which they will be used.* Rink (1985) has referred to these kinds of tasks as *applying* tasks. It is clear that a particular instructional task can serve both to refine a skill or strategy and still be an applying task; that is, the stimulus conditions of practice can be such that they are aligned with terminal goals, even though the major purpose of the practice might be to refine or extend the performance of a skill or strategy. Thus both refining and extending tasks can be defined so that they serve as applying tasks, too—and, when they do, instructional alignment is more likely.

Closed and Open Skills

If the execution of skill and strategy, as in sport performance, becomes important content in your sense of appropriate physical education programming, the distinction between closed and open skills should affect how you develop that content. Closed skills are performed under standard environmental conditions (Gentile, 1972). The shot put is a good example. The size of the ring, the weight of the shot, the dimensions of the sector into which it is put, and the rules for putting are all standard. Open skills are performed under changing environmental conditions, so that responding effectively to the changing environment becomes most important. A basketball guard dribbling down court to initiate an offense is a good example. The guard contends with differing defensive configurations, each of which might cue a different set of offensive options. Defensive pressure changes, as do the conditions of the game itself—time remaining, score, and the like.

The closed-open distinction is best understood as a continuum, with the most skills performed under most constant conditions at one end and skills performed under most variable conditions at the other. Sport skills are placed on the continuum according to the conditions under which they are performed, as shown in the following diagram.

Closed				*Open*
Shot put	Foul shot	Golf putt	Tennis forehand	Soccer dribble

Developing the content of closed and open skills differs markedly. The more closed the skill, the more emphasis will be on refining technique. The goal is to develop a consistent, high level of technique that is performed invariably. The more open the skill, the less time will be spent on technique and the more time will be spent on extending tasks that cover the variety of situations where the skills will be used. The goal is to develop performance that is appropriately responsive to the changing demands of a game setting. One of the major errors—an error in instructional alignment—physical educators make when developing content for open skills is that they treat them as if they were closed skills, with the conditions of practice constant instead of variable.

Accountability: Driving the Instructional Task System

In Chapter 5 it was shown that instructional task systems are driven by formal and informal accountability—and that in the absence of accountability the instructional task system can be suspended. What happens in the total absence of accountability for performance in the instructional task system depends on two things: (1) the focus of the managerial system in which students might have to look like they are making an "effort" and (2) the interests and motivations that the students have for the subject being taught.

Accountability refers to all of the practices teachers use to establish and maintain student responsibility for task involvement and outcomes. The clearest form of accountability is the grade-exchange opportunity—what we typically refer to as *testing* or *assessment*. Grade exchanges occur infrequently in most physical education classes, often only at the end of a unit. Effective teachers utilize many different kinds of accountability mechanisms to keep students strongly on-task and motivate them to improve their performance. Among these accountability mechanisms are:

- Public challenges with result reporting, such as "Shoot from the six spots with your partner rebounding" and then "How many made 3? 4? 5? 6?"

- Recording scores, such as keeping records of time on a fitness circuit and recording daily results on a class poster.

- Carefully supervising practice and noting successes publicly, such as monitoring the practice of a volleyball bump and set drill and, at the end, noting the several practice groups who did particularly well.

- Carefully supervising practice and providing specific feedback and general support, such as monitoring the practice of a serve-and-return tennis practice task and providing support for students working hard and technical feedback to students making errors in critical elements of the skills.

- Building accountability into the practice task, such as designing a dribble, pass, trap, and tackle soccer task into a mini-game by providing students a way to keep "score."

The point to be made in including a discussion of accountability along with the planning is that teachers need to build accountability into their task progressions if they expect students to stay on-task and be motivated to improve their performances.

Accountability should not always be thought of as an "extra" but, instead, should be integrated with the instructional task itself. Eventually, if instructional tasks are designed so that practice conditions are aligned with meaningful terminal goals, students will become more and more motivated by doing the task itself—which is typically referred to as *intrinsic motivation*.

Extending your Program in Nonattached Time

As you develop content for a physical education program, you will begin to repeat one phrase again and again—"There's not enough time!" Physical educators everywhere feel as if they don't have enough time to meet program goals. There are only two ways to react to this fact of professional life. First, you can adjust your terminal goals downward to realistically fit the amount of time assigned for instructional classes. Second, you can try to extend your program time by having students participate in nonattached time. *Nonattached time* refers to school time that is not part of regularly assigned physical education class time. Examples are recess time in elementary school, intramural time, study period time in high schools, or club and special activity time.

In a recent study of effective elementary physical education specialists (Jones, et al., 1989) it was found that weekly allotted class time was between 45–80 minutes, well below what is thought to be appropriate for the elementary school. However, each teacher studied had found ways to extend his or her program to nonattached time. If you want your *program* to have a greater impact on students, then extending its influence to nonattached time becomes an important goal.

There are several prerequisites for effectively extending your program to nonattached time.

1. Students must be motivated to participate, because participation in nonattached time is not required. Thus you must make your program attractive and find "reasons" for students to participate. For example, you might give class soccer teams extra points in their competition if they practice as a team at recess time. You might have track and field events to practice during the time you are doing track and field as a class unit—and if students can improve their performance in nonattached time, it will "count" for their class performance. You might have interclass competitions within sport units. You might develop a mass aerobics session three times per week, train student leaders, and let students choose their own music.

2. To benefit from practice during nonattached time, students must be on their way toward being independent learners. Activity during nonattached time is only minimally supervised. To stay on-task and benefit from practice during nonattached time, students must know what to do and how to do it, without having to be told by their teacher. This suggests that activities during nonattached time should be familiar, and the routines necessary to practice should be well established.

3. Students like the social nature of affiliation with a group. Practice during nonattached time seems to work better when students have membership in a group. For example, the class team that practices during recess forms an affiliation and has social implications. Belonging to a weight-training club that meets twice per week allows for social interaction and membership. Being able to go to aerobics with your "friends" becomes an informal group membership. These affiliations not only make social interaction more likely and fun for students (don't forget the student-social system) but also create moderate pressures for students to attend regularly and take part.

Summary

1. Developing content for a program requires you to choose goals (a reflective task) and to plan to meet those goals (a technical task).

2. Most school districts have subject-specific syllabi that are periodically revised by teachers in the district.

3. Various visions of the *good* compete for curricular allegiance in physical education, but the standard approach is to include all possible goals in a nulti-activity curriculum.

4. Main theme programs focus more time and resources on a particular vision of the *good* in physical education.

5. Curriculum planners should examine their efforts to ensure an equitable curriculum based on gender, race, and ability levels.

6. Factors such as the personal approach of the teacher, nature of the local district, facilities and equipment, educational programming, and status of the learners all affect program planning.

7. Successful programs accomplish limited goals by selecting activities relevant to those goals.

8. Content should be developed by establishing terminal goals as meaningful units of performance, thus providing a clear end product to strive toward.

9. Progressions are developed through informing, refining, extending, and applying tasks, both within and between task progressions.

10. Instructional alignment exists when there is a match between the conditions stated in outcomes, those arranged for practice, and those of testing or evaluation.

11. The requirements for progressions in open and closed skills differ markedly and should not be confused.

12. Accountability drives instructional task systems, and teachers should plan to incorporate various accountability strategies in their task-development planning.

13. Successful programs extend into nonattached time but work best when students are motivated, have independent learning skills, and are affiliated with a group.

CHAPTER **11**

Developing Effective Units Of Instruction

Most students (perhaps over 90 percent) can master what we have to teach them, and it is the task of instruction to find the means which will enable our students to master the subject under consideration. Our basic task is to determine what we mean by mastery of the subject and to search for the methods and materials which will enable the largest proportion of our students to attain such mastery.

Benjamin Bloom (1980)

CHAPTER OBJECTIVES

To describe and discuss reasons why teachers plan

To distinguish between plan-dependent and plan-independent teachers

To describe strategies for determining entry and exit levels

To distinguish between process and product objectives

To formulate appropriate motor, cognitive, and affective goals

To conduct appropriate procedural and hierarchical task analyses

To describe practical factors related to unit planning

To describe a well constructed unit plan

To describe a well constructed daily lesson plan

To describe equity issues in unit planning

To describe and discuss issues related to grading

To construct appropriate instructional objectives

The focus for this chapter, which is planning units of instruction, was chosen for three reasons. First, most teachers consider unit planning to be their most important planning task (Clark & Yinger, 1979). Many teachers work on a daily basis from their unit plan, rather than having individual daily lesson plans. Second, teachers who prefer to plan at the daily lesson level typically do so by planning all the daily lessons for a *unit*. Thus the unit again appears to be the most functional way to think about planning. Third, focusing on unit plans requires that you think about progressions that build across daily lessons and move toward the achievement of unit objectives. Even though it is the daily lesson through which a unit is taught to students, it is the series of daily lessons (the unit) that should make sense as a whole.

Why Teachers Plan

There are four main reasons teachers devote time and attention to planning for instruction (Clark & Yinger, 1979; Stroot & Morton, 1989).

1. To assure that a progression is followed both within and between lessons.
2. To help the teacher to stay on-task and to use time as planned.
3. To reduce teacher anxiety and maintain confidence as they teach.
4. To fulfill a building or district policy.

Not all teachers plan for all these four reasons, nor do all these reasons influence teachers in the same way. Some principals require that teachers leave lesson plans for the next day on their desk when they leave school in the afternoon. This is done because teachers, because of illness or some unforeseen emergency, may need substitutes the next day.

In their study of effective elementary physical educators, Stroot and Morton (1989) found what many have noted from observing teachers work: Some teachers are very dependent on plans, while others seem to be nearly independent of plans. They referred to these two extremes as *plan-dependent* and *plan-independent teachers*. For example, one teacher in their study said "I would feel incredibly uncomfortable if I did not have them (plans), and I carry them around on my clipboard everywhere I go" (Stroot & Morton, 1989, p. 219). Another teacher taped the daily plan on a wall of the gymnasium where it could be referred to easily if needed, even though observation indicated that the teacher seldom referred to it. Still other teachers go through an entire day's teaching without referring to plans, needing only to glance at them in the morning to refresh themselves about what they intend to do in their classes that day. The difference between plan-dependent and plan-independent seems to be one of personal comfort, reduction of anxiety about lessons, and maintaining confidence as the teaching is actually done. Remember, in this study, these were all *effective* teachers, so that there is no suggestion here that plan-dependent teachers are more or less effective than plan-independent teachers. It seems a matter of personal style, although less experienced teachers tend typically to be more plan-dependent. The plan-independent teachers obviously do their work from mental recall of their previous planning and experience with the activity being taught.

The same study found, as have most others, that somewhere back in time, all the effective teachers had worked hard to plan good units of instruction. The work they did when they initially planned units of instruction is similar to what will be presented in this chapter. Thus no matter whether the teachers were, at the moment of the study, plan-dependent or plan-independent, they had all gone through extensive planning when initially developing units—and they continuously upgraded and modified those initial plans based on their experiences teaching them. If the teachers perceived themselves to be in an activity unit in which their own background was "weak," they tended to become more plan-dependent than in those units where their own skills and experiences were stronger.

Effective teachers plan! No matter what method they use to teach or how independent they become of actual, physical lesson plans, they all carefully consider objectives and activities, progressions, equipment and space needs, safety and managerial issues, and evaluation. Thus the skills and strategies presented in this chapter appear to be central to effective teaching

Determining Entry and Exit Levels:
The Starting Place for Unit Planning

As described in Chapter 10, unit content should be developed so that terminal objectives represent meaningful units of performance. What is obtainable as end-of-unit performance, however, strongly depends on the physical abilities, skill levels, and experience of students as they begin the unit. End-of-unit skill goals in activities like gymnastics depend on the strength and flexibility of students when they begin. Skills on a high bar require arm and shoulder strength. If students can't support themselves on a high bar for more than a few seconds, then it becomes nearly impossible to work toward skill goals.

Likewise, students who have little experience as game players will have a difficult time learning even beginning concepts of defensive coverage, offensive spacing, and the like. Students who have not developed mature throwing skills, no matter what their age, will have great difficulty learning basic skills of striking in activities such as badminton. To teach students to play the game of soccer requires that they have sufficient cardiovascular endurance to sustain moderate activity for periods of time.

The great problem of planning physical education units, especially when students are grouped only by grade level, is that some students will have all the limitations described above, while others will have the physical capacity, skills, and experience for higher-level instruction. Most teachers tend to plan their units at or just below what they consider to be the average for their classes and then attempt to adjust the instructional task system so that it accommodates students who vary markedly in their readiness for those tasks. Many of the instructional strategies described in Chapters 12 and 13 are relevant to meeting the needs of diverse learners within the same class.

Recalling from Chapter 10 that effective programs accomplish real goals, it makes sense to plan units so that ample time is provided for limited goal accomplishment. Many students will need a large number of successful repetitions to develop skills to the point where they can be used in applied settings. Strategic concepts will have to be practiced to the point where students can execute them reliably in modified game settings. Repetitions of skill and strategy practice take class time, often more than planners are willing to allocate. The result, far too often, is classes that rush through skill and strategy practice so quickly that the skills can't be performed well in applied settings and the strategies are nowhere to be seen once game play begins. Of particular interest at this point is the research in physical education (Marks, 1988; Son, 1989) that reveals that teachers seldom use refining tasks during their skill instruction. Again, recalling from Chapter 10, it is through repeated cycles of refining and extending tasks that skill develops and the execution of strategy becomes reliable. This refining-extending cycle takes time, especially if all students are to get enough repetitions to be able to perform the skills and strategies in applied settings.

The choice of end-of-unit objectives is important because they form the basis from which unit planning should be done. Therefore, those terminal unit objectives should be defined with the entry-level status of learners clearly in mind and with a realistic appraisal of what can be accomplished in the time available.

187

End-of-Unit
Objectives as
Goals and
Evaluation
Targets

End-of-Unit Objectives as Goals and Evaluation Targets

A teacher's choice of end-of-unit objectives describes both the teacher's goals and how those goals should be evaluated. To the degree that the objectives are fuzzy or written poorly, it will become difficult to know exactly what the goals are or how they can be evaluated. The section on writing goals and objectives that appears later in this chapter describes how to construct clear goals and objectives and how to write them properly.

When developing content for units, it is important that you consider what you want to achieve in three educational domains. The *motor domain* includes skills, the execution of strategy, motor-performance fitness, and health-related fitness goals and objectives. The *cognitive domain* includes knowledge related to the activities, including knowledge about oneself as a learner, mover, or performer. The *affective* domain encompasses goals and objectives that focus on students' attitudes and values. Traditionally, physical education has been conceptualized as a subject field that contributes to outcomes in all three domains. If it is important to you to achieve goals that extend beyond the motor domain, then you must plan specifically to achieve those goals. Knowing about personal fitness, valuing fair play in games, or feeling confident about yourself in risk activities isn't likely to just happen! Like most other valuable educational goals, these goals are more likely to be attained when they are carefully considered in the planning process. Box 11.1 shows examples of end-of-unit objectives in the three domains.

End-of-unit objectives can be described as process objectives, product objectives, or a combination of the two. A *process objective* focuses on how something is done. In the motor domain, for example, the execution of skills can be defined in terms of the presence or absence of critical performance elements. In the affective domain, fair play can be defined and assessed in terms of how players respond to situations in games. A *product objective* focuses on the outcome of an action rather than how the action is done. In the motor domain, for example, you might describe objectives in terms of number of rebounds or assists in a basketball game or the time it takes a student to run one mile. In the cognitive domain, you might expect that students will be able to assess important health fitness parameters and use that information to plan a personal fitness program, or they might describe correctly how a particular offensive strategy is executed in volleyball. In the affective domain, you might have an outcome objective for a soccer unit that more students will voluntarily choose to sign up for school intramural soccer, or that after a jump rope unit, students will choose to join the jump rope club.

11.1 Examples of End-of-Unit Objectives in Three Domains

Motor Domain

- Demonstrate critical performance elements of bump and set passes in 3 *vs.* 3 game play (process).

- Ninety percent of class will achieve 50th percentile on mile run (product).

- Catch 90 percent of foam balls thrown from a distance of 25 feet using appropriate technical elements for above- and below-waist catches (process and product).

- Perform three folk dances to music without cues using correct step sequences without errors (process and product).

- Play at least two positions in 2–3 zone defense, making appropriate adjustments during 5 *vs.* 5 game play (process).

- Complete a 5-element floor exercise routine with a minimum score of 2.0.

- Seventy-five percent of serves received in backline result in bump-set-hit sequence (process).

Cognitive Domain

- When called on, explain and demonstrate appropriate techniques for three traps.

- Describe correctly the procedures for determining the threshold level for cardiovascular training effect.

- Describe why fair play among participants is fundamental to good competition.

- Explain the technical elements that contribute to force production in the shot put.

- Recognize and call fouls and violations correctly in 3 *vs.* 3 basketball games.

Affective Domain

- Call fouls and violations on themselves correctly when playing in non-refereed games.

- Students do not defer to others in skill opportunities during game play in ways that are based on gender or skill levels.

- When opportunities arise, more skilled students volunteer to help less skilled students.

- Share equipment and response opportunities equitably without teacher prompting.

Once end-of-unit objectives are chosen, the planner has to decide which progression of activities can best achieve those objectives. The success of the unit is evaluated by the degree to which members of the class achieve the objectives. If clear objectives are developed, and a progression of activities that represent progress toward those goals is arranged, and if the evaluation of student performance is directly related to the objectives, then the planner will have achieved the kind of instructional alignment described in Chapter 10—and, if the lessons in the unit are delivered as planned, the result is likely to be a very high degree of achievement. Having chosen end-of-unit goals, how does one decide what task progressions need to be developed? This is best accomplished through task analyses, which are described next.

Using Task Analysis to Sequence Content

Once end-of-unit objectives are developed as meaningful units of performance, the actual planning of the unit develops by working *backward* from the final performance description to where the unit begins. The instructional design skill used in this procedure is called *task analysis*. Two kinds of task analysis are used in planning: the procedural task analysis and the hierarchical task analysis.

A procedural task analysis describes a chain of events that together define a meaningful unit of performance. Activities such as bowling, shooting arrows in archery, vaulting in gymnastics, running a three-lane fast break in basketball, and the long jump in track and field are typical of those skills for which a procedural task analysis is useful. Procedural analyses of the long jump and fast break are shown in Figures 11.1 and 11.2.

Goal: Long jump with proper approach, takeoff, and landing.

Running Approach $\longrightarrow$ Last Stride and Foot Plant $\longrightarrow$ Take Off from Board $\longrightarrow$ Flight $\longrightarrow$ Landing

Figure 11.1 *Long jump procedural analysis*

For skills in which a procedural task analysis is useful, the individual elements of the chain (the foot plant, the takeoff, and so on) can be learned somewhat independently and then put together to form the chain. Usually, the individual elements of the chain are fairly easy to learn. It is the "putting together" that represents the crucial aspects of the instruction. The final outcome requires that each element of the chain be performed smoothly and in an integrated fashion. A breakdown at any element tends to ruin the entire performance.

A procedural task analysis is useful for identifying the points at which instruction should be focused, both in identifying the elements of the chain and in pinpointing the crucial spots at which the elements have to be linked together smoothly for a skilled performance. The long jump represents a short, fairly simple chain; rebounding and initiating a fast break in basketball represents a considerably more complex set of elements. A procedural task analysis of a fast break is shown in Figure 11.2. Notice how the analysis allows the designer or planner to identify the important learning tasks (the elements of the chain) and also the points at which they need to be put together smoothly for a skilled performance.

The second type of analysis, a *hierarchical task analysis*, is a description of all of the subskills that must be learned in order to perform the terminal skill. In a hierarchical task analysis, there is a necessary relationship between the skills. One skill must be learned before the other can be learned (unlike the procedural task analysis, where elements can be learned independently). In a hierarchical analysis, the designer or planner starts with the terminal goal and asks the question "What will the student have to be able to do in order to accomplish this task?" This question is asked again and again until the basic entry skills for the task are reached. A hierarchical task analysis would be diagrammed as shown in Figures 11.3 and 11.4.

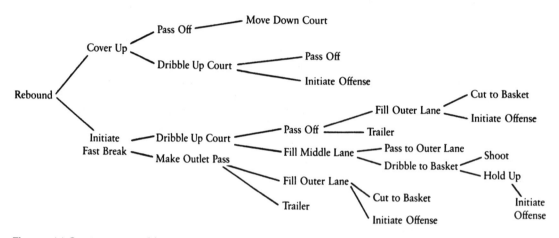

Figure 11.2 *Some Possible Fast-Break Behavior Chains for a Basketball Player Rebounding*

The hierarchical task analysis identifies only those skills *necessary* for accomplishing the higher-level skill. With practice, designers and planners become competent at identifying relevant subskills and adjusting the size of the subskill steps so that they are best suited to the needs of the learners. The size of steps from one subskill to another is crucial to the success of the design. If the steps are too large, students will experience failure too often and lose interest and enthusiasm. If the steps are too small, they might become bored. The designer or planner works to establish steps that are large enough to be continually challenging and small enough so that students have frequent success.

Unit goals for the cognitive and affective domains are likely to require a hierarchical rather than a procedural task analysis. If the goal "students will correctly call their own fouls and violations in modified games without arguing" is adopted, then the teacher has to ask herself what tasks need to be designed to achieve that goal by the end of the unit. The goal described involves a cognitive component because the students must know the fouls and violations and the appropriate consequence when they are committed. The goal also involves an

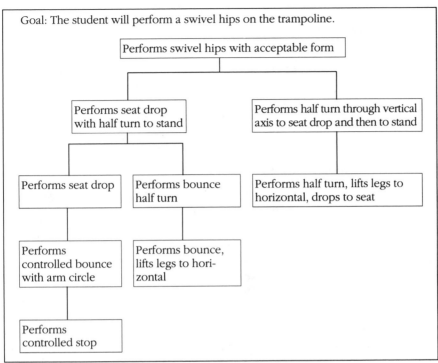

Figure 11.3 *Hierarchical Task Analysis (I)*

affective component in that the students are willing to make calls on themselves and do so without arguing. The teacher might decide that "calling your own violations and fouls" in all skill drills will become routine. This introduces the need to know the rules and also get students accustomed to doing so in less intense situations than an actual game.

Once unit goals have been identified and the relevant task analyses completed, most of the actual content for the unit is developed. The subskills and elements that have been identified become the informing and extending tasks for the unit. Most tasks will require refining along the way. Applied tasks should be inserted regularly to sustain students' enthusiasm and show them how their developing skills and strategies are put to use. It is at this point, when the many tasks needed to achieve success in terminal goals have been identified, that planners realize how much there is to be done in the time allotted. The great temptation is to include too many tasks and not plan for sufficient time for achievement at each point in the progression. The inevitable result of succumbing to this temptation is that end-of-unit goals become impossible to achieve.

Practical Factors Related to Unit Planning

The most important instructional design goal for unit planners is to identify relevant content through task analyses and identify the refining and extending tasks that will be necessary for a particular set of students to achieve success in

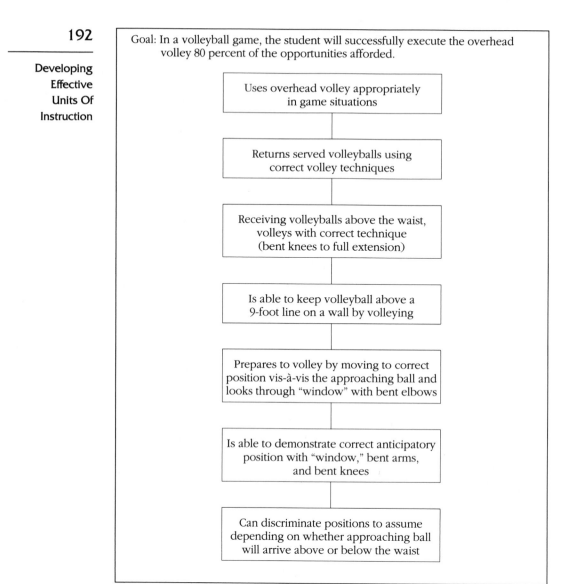

Goal: In a volleyball game, the student will successfully execute the overhead volley 80 percent of the opportunities afforded.

Uses overhead volley appropriately in game situations

Returns served volleyballs using correct volley techniques

Receiving volleyballs above the waist, volleys with correct technique (bent knees to full extension)

Is able to keep volleyball above a 9-foot line on a wall by volleying

Prepares to volley by moving to correct position vis-à-vis the approaching ball and looks through "window" with bent elbows

Is able to demonstrate correct anticipatory position with "window," bent arms, and bent knees

Can discriminate positions to assume depending on whether approaching ball will arrive above or below the waist

Figure 11.4 *Hierarchical Task Analysis (II)*

the major tasks. However, you must also consider certain practical factors as you translate those unit-level tasks into daily instructional tasks for students to do. You need to identify the skills for which practice routines can be developed, consider how equipment could be modified, think about the usage of space, consider the ratios of equipment to students, think about how to modify applied-performance conditions, and consider how to set up effective accountability mechanisms.

1. *Building routines for fundamental skills.* Nearly every unit of instruction will have skills that are considered to be fundamental to success in the activity. It is often difficult for students to participate successfully in applied

activities unless they have achieved a certain level of mastery in the fundamental skills. For example, passing, catching, and pivoting are fundamental to success in basketball. It is difficult to imagine how a student could experience success in a modified basketball game without being able to do those skills quite well. To achieve an adequate level of performance in applied settings, fundamental skills need to be practiced often. One way for teachers to accomplish this in units is to develop routines for practicing fundamental skills. *Skill routines* are designated ways of practicing skills. These skill routines are like managerial routines in the sense that students can do them quickly and correctly with only minimal instructions. You could easily see how three or four skill routines might be developed in a basketball unit, perhaps one for the passing/catching/pivoting combination, one for shooting, one for dribbling, and one for defensive movement. On a simple command, students would immediately organize and begin the routine. If groupings were sufficiently small (partners, triads, and so forth) students could practice each routine for 30 seconds. In two minutes a rather large number of successful repetitions could be achieved. Like managerial routines, however, these skill routines have to be done both quickly and accurately to achieve their intended effect, which is a high amount of good practice in a short period of time.

2. *Modify equipment to achieve intended outcomes.* Instructional tasks can be made easier or more difficult by modifying the equipment students use. Often, successful repetitions are very difficult to achieve with full-sized equipment. It is much easier to learn good stroking skills with rackets that are shorter and lighter. Slightly deflated soccer balls or foam balls make it easier to learn kicking and trapping. Even a commercially produced elementary school discus is typically too large for fourth or fifth graders to grip and hurl—a shuffleboard disc is more appropriate. Any game or activity that requires students to anticipate the flight of an object can be made much easier by slowing down the object or causing it to stay in the air longer. Often students can execute skills in controlled settings (partner pass), but not when the action goes more quickly. The problem is that they don't have enough experience to anticipate the flight of the object and move to be in position to execute the skill. Thus, using beach balls for beginning volleyball-type skills or raising the net in badminton-type games to keep the object in the air longer, gives students more time to anticipate and move to the proper position. The overall point is that student performance outcomes for units are often dependent on the equipment used in the unit.

3. *Design space-skill relationships to emphasize success.* The difficulty of learning skills is often related to the space the skill is performed within. In ball-striking games, a very small court requires too much control of shots for many successes to occur. Activities requiring guarding are often easier in larger spaces. On the other hand, activity or game spaces that are too large often result in only a few participating. Teachers should try to design

spaces that produce an optimum level of challenge and success relative to the skill levels of the students. As students increase their skillfulness, the spaces can be modified to continue to make the activity challenging.

4. *Optimize equipment/student ratios.* Few instructional factors have as much influence on student response rates as does the ratio of available equipment to students. More good responses lead to more achievement. Other things being equal, a class with a 2:1 equipment ratio will get twice the number of response opportunities as a class with a 4:1 ratio. The equipment/student ratio should be a major factor in planning unit performance outcomes. The higher the ratio, the less you can expect to achieve. This is an especially important factor for all individual skill practice. When skill practice purposely takes place in groups, then the appropriate consideration is the equipment/group ratio. This factor needs to be kept in mind when designing applied tasks such as games.

5. *Modify applied-performance-conditions to ensure high, successful participation.* It is important for teachers to plan tasks that are challenging and plan appropriate culminations for task development progressions. This is especially true for game playing, because in many units games will represent the most frequent kind of applying task. How many "hits" does a sixth grader get in a 6 *vs.* 6 volleyball game that lasts 12 minutes? According to research (Parker, 1984; Lawless, 1984; Brown, 1985), the answer depends on how skilled the student is relative to others in the class. A relatively skilled student will get a reasonable number of hits. A less-skilled student will get very few hits, often no more than one or two decent hits per 20 minutes of game play. Games like softball produce even more disastrous response rates for most players. Modifying applied performance conditions requires planners to consider together the issues described in points 2, 3, and 4 above; that is, equipment modifications, space arrangements, and equipment/student ratios. What is the "best" kind of volleyball game? Probably a 3 *vs.* 3 game with net height, court size, and ball modified to fit the skills of the students. Most experts argue that volleyball is a series of three-person strategies, so the 3 *vs.* 3 configuration preserves the fundamental nature of the game and also allows for more hits per unit of time.

6. *Creating accountability mechanisms to ensure high rates of on-task behavior and achievement of goals.* Two kinds of accountability need to be considered when planning: daily accountability aimed at on-task behavior and unit-level accountability aimed at achievement of end-of-unit objectives. Teachers need to hold students accountable for staying on-task on a daily basis (see page 181 for a discussion of various accountability measures). Some activities, such as a check-list for gymnastics stunts, lend themselves to peer monitoring of performance. Some activities lend themselves to group challenges with resulting public recognition. Some teachers rely on active supervision, prompts, and feedback to keep students on-task. While daily on-task behavior is crucial to goal achievement, teachers would do well to consider a unit-level

accountability system that is contingent on achievement of end-of-unit objectives. In some cases this might take the form of a test, such as a fitness test at the end of a fitness unit. For other activity units, students might work toward awards, such as performance awards for various events in a track and field unit. In a sport education format (see page 172) teachers have had great success developing seasonal awards based on performance throughout the sport unit—awards such as a fair-play award, most improved award, best out-of-class practice record award, coaches' awards, as well as team championship awards. Children enjoy signing their names to posters that reflect goal achievement; for example, a poster at the end of a horizontal climbing wall can be signed when the wall is negotiated appropriately. In Chapter 5 it was shown that accountability drives instructional task systems. Strong motivational and incentive schemes, tied to unit objectives, can create the necessary climate for a high degree of goal achievement.

Constructing the Unit Plan

There is no one "best" way to actually write a unit plan. Eventually, teachers adopt formats that prove to be most useful for them in their daily teaching. Remember, it is the class lesson that gets taught to students. The unit plan, therefore, should be constructed using a format that provides the necessary guidance at the lesson level. To be most helpful to teachers who will use unit plans again and again, the following elements should somehow be addressed in the plan.

1. *End-of-unit objectives stated as performance outcome measures that serve also as evaluation measures.* The best way to ensure a high degree of instructional alignment (see page 178) is to have your performance goals also serve as your evaluation measures. If teachers have goals in all three domains, then they should be included at this point. Decisions about process or product goals/evaluation also need to be made.

2. *The sequence of instructional tasks considered necessary to achieve the unit's objectives.* These will come from having done the relevant task analyses for each end-of-unit objective.

3. *Distribution of instructional tasks to lessons within the unit.* The construction of a good unit will not be achieved by simply starting at the beginning of the instructional task list and moving toward the end. Remember, the unit is really a series of lessons! Each lesson should make sense, too. You probably will want to begin most lessons with review tasks. You probably will want to have initial tasks serve as "warm ups," too. Tasks requiring vigorous activity might need to be alternated with less vigorous tasks. Many teachers like to have a culminating task (typically an applying task) for each lesson, one that is exciting and motivates students. The unit plan should have anticipated instructional tasks blocked by lesson so that day-by-day teaching progressions will be clear, and each lesson can be

judged as an independent entity as well as being part of a series of lessons comprising the unit.

4. *Specification of special managerial routines for the unit.* Are there specific managerial routines needed for this unit that go beyond those that are in operation throughout the school year? In gymnastics, for example, many teachers establish routines for rotating among apparatus. With limited equipment, you might need a special routine for sharing.

5. *Anticipating safety issues and establishing special rules.* When planning an archery unit or a gymnastics unit, you will have special safety considerations that are specific to that activity. Your regular class rules will need to be expanded for that unit. Remember, these will be "new" rules, and they will require teaching and vigorous enforcing at the outset until they become established.

6. *Creating organizational arrangements to save time.* For most instructional tasks there will be a preferred organizational arrangement (practicing alone in self-space, partners, triads, and so forth). Moving from one organizational arrangement to another takes time. Planning tasks within lessons, therefore, should take into consideration the transitions between organizational arrangements. Moving from self-practice, to partners, to quads represents a series of easy transitions that should take little time. Grouping practice tasks within one organizational framework also makes sense; for example, doing a series of practice tasks using partners before moving on to a different organizational arrangement.

7. *Organize and prepare the accountability materials.* Do you need posters, charts, ribbons, or homemade certificates? The unit plan should include both a list of materials and a copy of each.

Developing Lesson Plans from the Unit Plan

For many experienced teachers the unit plan, if it has instructional tasks blocked by lesson, will be sufficient for teaching each lesson. For some experienced teachers and nearly all beginning teachers, a daily lesson plan will prove to be very helpful, particularly to help them stay on a time schedule and to create the confidence that comes with having a good plan to refer to when needed. Again, there is no "perfect" format for lesson planning. Most teacher-educators would agree that at a minimum a lesson plan should include:

1. The anticipated progression of tasks with a time allotment for each task. It is most helpful to the teacher if the time allotment is listed cumulatively for the length of the lesson.

2. Descriptions for how each task will be communicated to students. Some feel that at the outset the exact words should be written on the lesson plan.

3. The organizational arrangements for each task.

4. Any teaching cues or prompts the teacher wants to remember to help the students master the task. These might be critical elements of skills or just

reminders to "speak slowly and enunciate clearly" if you have been experiencing difficulty with students understanding your explanations and directions.

5. Some way of recording reactions to what took place so that the next time the lesson is taught or when the unit is revised, you have information about what went well or what might be changed.

Anticipating Equity Issues in Unit Planning

Planning for an equitable experience for all students requires not only that equity be considered at the program or curriculum level (see page 168) but also at the unit level (Griffin & Placek, 1983). In some cases, the nature of the activity related to the students participating might produce equity concerns that can be anticipated to plan for some affirmative strategy to prevent inequities from developing. Box 11.2 "Anticipating Equity Problem in a Weight Training Unit" shows an example of this kind of proactive analysis and strategy-development from a weight training unit for tenth graders.

A more general equity analysis can be done for all units planned. This is best accomplished by applying a list of questions to the completed plan. Are students grouped for practice and play by skill rather than gender or race? Is student participation distributed without regard to gender, race, or skill level? Do applied-performance activities such as games have rules that require position rotation and disallow better skilled students from dominating? Are promotional and motivational materials equitable in terms of race, gender, and disability? Appropriate answers to these questions will help you to feel confident that you have planned an equitable unit.

Grading

In most school districts, the school year is divided into "marking periods" and grades are compiled for each period. The yearly curriculum block plan for physical education often may not correspond to the school's grading periods. If students receive a grade for physical education, it will be the teacher's obligation to submit grades for each marking period. What contributes to that grade and how it is calculated is often decided by the physical education staff, as in a high school, or the elementary specialists within a district. A common grading format for all schools in a district is typical.

Considering the information presented in this chapter, it would seem obvious that a major portion of each student's grade would be determined by the degree to which the student met the end-of-unit objectives. Those objectives should be constructed so that evaluating performance relative to the objective is clear and unambiguous. It is my strong conviction that students in physical education should be evaluated primarily on the degree to which they achieve the outcomes intended in the program. It is also my conviction that students in physical education should achieve goals that go beyond good behavior, participation, and having fun (see Box 11.3).

Clearly, some physical education teachers believe their major objectives are to keep students "busy, happy, and good" (see page 169). If those are legitimate

11.2 Anticipating Equity Problems in a Weight Training Unit

A tenth-grade weight training unit is planned to achieve goals related to identifying major muscle groups, accurately describing weight training principles, designing and following a personal fitness program, and appreciating the divergent needs of individuals relative to fitness goals and programs. Students will be evaluated with a written test, development of their personal program, and evidence of following their program, as well as their behavior toward each other in the weight room (etiquette, cooperation, helpfulness).

The following equity problems might be anticipated.

- Competition among stronger boys and teasing of weaker boys
- Girls' fears about muscularity and teasing of stronger girls
- Students segregating voluntarily by gender
- Girls being embarrassed in front of boys
- Parents of some students objecting to participation
- Girls having less experience in weight training and weight rooms

The following are some strategies to affirmatively reduce the occurrence of problems.

- Describe social behavior clearly and develop a point system to reinforce compliance and punish offenses.
- Create positive expectations for all students.
- Use individualized task sheets and programs (maybe contracts).
- Use both boys and girls to demonstrate.
- Prepare bulletin board with pictures of boys and girls in strength training.

Make physiological differences between genders part of the knowledge base for the unit.

- Send home a flyer to parents emphasizing personal goals and development as objectives for the unit.
- Strongly reinforce progress of less confident students.
- Point out examples of helping, sharing, and cooperating.

(Adapted from Griffin & Placek, 1983, pp. 229–230)

objectives for a school subject taught by a professional teacher, then grading solely on the basis of attendance, appropriate behavior, participation, and attitude is fully acceptable. Those are the goals, and the evaluation is based on achieving the goals. If, however, the goals are not acceptable, then the evaluation isn't, either.

11.3 Is Grading on Subject Matter Performance Appropriate?

I know of one school district where the School Board has a policy that students in physical education cannot be graded on the basis of skill development or other such performance measures. The reasons for this policy are unclear, although there is some thought that participation is most important and no student should be denied academic honors by a low grade in physical education. Still, the physical education teachers in that district have found many informal methods of accountability to promote skill development and other performance outcomes in their classes.

The point is that accountability in classes is not always related to grading. Grading is one form of accountability, but certainly not the only form and, one might argue, in physical education not the most important form. On the other hand, if physical education is a legitimate and important school subject, shouldn't it be treated similarly to other subject areas?

What do you feel should most contribute to the grade in physical education? Should grading in physical education be like grading in algebra or literature classes? Should elementary children be graded in physical education as they are in their classrooms? If your answer is "no," why do you choose that answer, and why is physical education different? If your answer is "yes," why do you choose that and how would you suggest implementing it?

I believe that concepts such as "effort" and "fair play" can be made into end-of-unit objectives for which student performance can be evaluated. If social skills such as sharing, cooperation, and helping are important to you as a teacher, then they should be written as end-of-unit objectives related to the activity you are teaching; for example, sharing and cooperation will be different in a gymnastics unit than in a soccer unit. Students should know what they have to do to earn a high evaluation, and they should be held accountable for behaving according to those specifications.

I believe that performance in the activity is important, too. There are ways to evaluate improvement in student performance as well as evaluating on absolute standards of performance that make grading equitable for all students. If your program has an equitable range of activities (see page 169), then students of differing body types and abilities will find units in which they can earn a high evaluation. Over the course of a school year, student grades should represent a fair estimate of their performance, effort, and improvement in the program.

Constructing and Writing Instructional Goals/Objectives

An *instructional objective* is a statement describing a task, the conditions under which it will be performed, and the criteria or standards by which it will be judged to have been completed successfully. Instructional objectives are often referred to as *behavioral* or *performance objectives.* They are identical in format to what I have described as end-of-unit objectives or student performance outcomes. Instructional objectives are used widely in education, for several purposes. They are often included within lesson plans as indicators of the main outcomes of a daily lesson. They are, in some form, common to unit plans, as indicated in this chapter. They also are used extensively in physical education for describing learning tasks to students in the style of teaching referred to as "task teaching" (see Chapter 13).

The purpose of an instructional objective is to communicate an instructional intent by describing what will happen as the result of an instructional experience. In teaching volleyball, it is standard procedure to list on a lesson plan the objective of learning the overhead pass. The overhead pass is an observable task, but simply stating that the student will "learn" this skill is not sufficient. In writing an instructional objective for this task, the conditions under which it will be performed and the criteria by which it will be judged must be included. Where does the student stand? How does the ball come to him or her? How high does it have to be hit? Where does it have to go? How many attempts does he or she get? How many successful passes have to be completed? Consider the following two examples of instructional objectives (Rushall and Siedentop, 1972):

> Standing in the back center of the court, the student will toss the ball to herself and execute four of five overhead passes that reach a minimum height of 10 feet and land in the front left section of the court.

> Standing behind a line drawn 12 feet from a wall, the student will make eight continuous overhead passes that hit the wall within a designated target area drawn at a height of 10 feet.

All the questions posed in the previous paragraph are answered in these two objectives. The learner knows the situation, the task, and the criteria by which the task will be judged. It is useful to construct objectives in terms of these three components. The second objective has the following components:

Situation	*Task*	*Criteria*
Standing behind a line drawn 12 feet from a wall	Eight continuous overhead passes	Hit the wall within a target area drawn at a height of 10 feet

It is important to make sure that an instructional objective excludes skills that the teacher does not want developed. To develop a task for serving in tennis that states only, "The learner will serve four of five legal serves" allows the student to complete the task by hitting a "bloop" serve, which no doubt is not the intent of the instructor. This can be avoided in at least two ways. First, the criteria could require that the serve must pass between the net and a string stretched parallel to and above the net at a height that would require the student to serve with sufficient velocity to make it a good serve. Second, the criteria could require that the serve must land beyond a certain line on the first bounce, thus guaranteeing a measure of velocity in the serve. The instructional intent is for the student to learn to serve accurately and with a certain velocity. This is achieved when the criteria are stated so that the only way the student can complete the task is by serving in a manner that is consistent with that intent.

There are two ways of making instructional objectives for any given task more or less difficult: (1) by manipulating the conditions under which the task is performed and (2) by manipulating the criteria by which the task will be judged. For example, a bump pass task could be made progressively more difficult by holding the criteria at a given level (reach a height of 10 feet and land within a designated target area) and manipulating the conditions in the following manner:

- Condition 1: Bump pass by throwing ball to yourself.

- Condition 2: Bump pass a ball lobbed to you by a partner standing 10 feet away.

- Condition 3: Bump pass a ball thrown across the net.

- Condition 4: Bump pass a ball served by an opponent.

The changes in conditions make the task gradually more difficult, even though the task is the same and the criteria for successful completion are the same.

The same purpose can be accomplished by holding the conditions constant and varying the criteria. If the task is the bump pass and the conditions are a "ball served by an opponent," the task can be sequenced by changing the criteria in the following manner:

- Criterion 1: Reach a minimum height of 8 feet and land within bounds on your side of the court.

- Criterion 2: Reach a minimum height of 10 feet and land within the front half of the court.

- Criterion 3: Reach a minimum height of 15 feet and land within a specified target area in the front left or front right of your side of the court.

These criteria allow for a gradually higher and more accurate bump pass. Obviously, by combining changes in the conditions and criteria it is easy to sequence a series of instructional objectives to develop the instructional task of bump passing.

Objectives can also be sequenced by changing the performance requirements; the conditions and criteria might be held constant. Consider the following sequence of balance tasks:

- Instructional Objective 1: Balance on one foot for 10 seconds with your arms in any position.

- Instructional Objective 2: Balance on one foot for 10 seconds with your arms folded across your body and your knee held high.

- Instructional Objective 3: Balance on one foot for 10 seconds with your eyes closed.

- Instructional Objective 4: Balance on one foot for 10 seconds with your eyes closed and your arms folded.

In each of these objectives, the conditions are the same (standing on a line or standing on a beam) and the criterion remains constant (10 seconds). The performance becomes slightly more difficult in each objective. Thus, instructional objectives can be sequenced by changing conditions, altering the task itself, or changing the criteria by which the performance is judged. The combinations available with these three options allow for a wide variety of methods of sequencing objectives to achieve the completion of instructional tasks.

Instructional objectives can be written for skill, strategy, knowledge, and social outcomes. The value of analyzing a task in terms of instructional objectives is that it helps you and the learner understand precisely what is to be learned. Suppose you are teaching a basketball unit and you want your students to "understand" the 1-2-2 zone defense. The verb *to understand* is not acceptable in writing instructional objectives because it does not specify exactly what the task is. The following three objectives might reflect a certain level of "understanding":

- The student will diagram a 1-2-2 zone defense.

- On direction by the instructor, the student will take the correct position in a 1-2-2 zone defense.

- Given diagrams of zone defenses, the student will correctly identify the 1-2-2.

The first objective could be done from memory and is a memory-level task. The second objective refers not to a paper-and-pencil understanding of the defense, but to taking up a proper position (low left wing, upper right wing, point, or whatever) when instructed to do so. The third objective represents a higher order of understanding because the student must identify the 1-2-2 from among other zone defenses, which requires him or her to differentiate the 1-2-2 from the 2-3 or 1-3-1. When constructing objectives for knowledge and strategy outcomes, make sure that you are reaching the level of understanding that you desire.

Instructional objectives should be evaluated on the basis of four qualities. First, the situation should be clearly specified so the student knows what will or will not be available to him or her. Second, the task should be stated so that it refers to an observable behavior. Verbs such as *identify, underline, label, dribble, pass, run, swim free style,* and *high jump* refer to tasks that will be recognizable to the student. Verbs such as *understand, appreciate, know, know how to do,* and *learn* do not refer to tasks that students can easily translate into action. The degree to which a task is properly stated is judged by the kind of verb used in the objective. Verbs that do not have behavioral referents will result in students coming to you seeking further information. If a verb is not sufficiently specific, the solution is usually found in the criterion. The following objective uses a verb that is unclear and has no criterion:

The student will learn the overhand serve.

This confusion can be cleared up by stating a specific criterion such as the following:

The student will learn the overhead serve, as demonstrated by his or her ability to hit three of four legal overhand serves that pass between the net and a string stretched parallel to and 4 feet above the net and land within the court boundaries.

Any objective that uses an unclear verb usually has to have an "as demonstrated by" clause attached to it. It is even easier to remove the imprecise verb and state the objective directly:

The student will serve three or four legal overhand serves that pass between the net and a string stretched parallel to and 4 feet above the net and land in bounds.

The criterion is judged by how clearly it expresses the standard by which the task will be judged. Often, as indicated in some of the objectives shown on previous pages, the criterion is an implied 100 percent. If students are supposed to walk on a pool deck, mount a trampoline only when four spotters are in place, watch demonstrations, or refrain from pushing ahead in lines, it is implicit that this behavior should occur all the time.

Objectives should not allow for performance that is not the intent of the instructor. Students should not be able to complete serve objectives by hitting "bloop" serves. Students should not be able to complete push-up objectives by doing incorrect push-ups. Students should not be able to complete analysis objectives simply by memorizing material. This problem is best avoided by stating the criterion in such a way that in order to complete the objective the student would have to perform somewhere within the boundaries of the instructional intent.

Although most instructional objectives are written using product criteria for judging successful completion, it is perfectly legitimate to utilize objectives that involve process criteria. In a throwing and catching unit for second graders, for example, it would be a good idea to develop objectives that have the technical critical elements of good throwing and catching form as criteria, along with objectives that are product related. Likewise, it would be legitimate to write an instructional objective for a high school golf class that focused on making swings in which the front arm is kept extended throughout the backswing.

It is also possible to arrange performance criteria so that the task cannot be successfully done unless the appropriate form is used. For example, in a golf unit it is important for students to learn to "hit down and through" shots, especially short irons. Rather than write a process criterion related to the critical elements of the swing, you could construct an objective in which a product criterion could not be achieved without using the appropriate form. Here is an example objective: "Standing 50 yards from the green, hit four of five nine-iron shots that land on and remain on the green." It would be difficult for a student to achieve that objective without hitting squarely down and through the ball on the nine-iron shot, because it is that action which produces backspin on the ball and allows it to land on and stay on the green rather than rolling through the green as it would if it didn't have the backspin.

Summary

1. Teachers plan to ensure progressions within and between lessons, to use time efficiently, to reduce anxiety and build confidence, and to fulfill building or district policies.

2. While teachers may be plan-dependent or plan-independent as they teach, evidence suggests that all effective teachers originally plan units thoroughly.

3. Determining entry and exit levels is the starting place for unit planning.

4. Ample time should be allocated for limited goal accomplishment.

5. End-of-unit objectives should both describe goals and the means for evaluating them.

6. Objectives can be written for motor, cognitive, and affective domains.

7. Process objectives focus on how something is done, while product objectives focus on the outcome of activity.

8. A procedural task analysis describes a chain of events that, taken together, form a meaningful unit of performance.

9. A hierarchical task analysis is a description of all the subskills necessary to perform the terminal objectives.

10. Unit plans are more practical when routines for fundamental skills are taught; equipment is modified to achieve outcomes; space-skill relationships ensure success; equipment/student ratios are optimized; applied-performance conditions ensure high, successful participation; and accountability mechanisms ensure high rates of on-task behavior.

11. Elements such as end-of-unit objectives, sequences of instructional tasks, distribution of tasks to lessons, specific managerial routines, anticipated safety issues and related rules, time-saving organizational arrangements, and accountability materials should be in unit plans.

12. Elements such as task progressions, task communications, organizational arrangements, teaching cues, and reactions for purposes of revision should be present in daily lesson plans.

13. Equity problems in units should be anticipated and strategies to ameliorate them incorporated in the unit plan.

14. Grading should be related to accomplishment of end-of-unit objectives.

15. If concepts such as fair play and effort are important for grading, they should be incorporated into the unit objectives.

16. An instructional objective is a statement describing a task, the conditions under which the task is to be performed, and the criteria or standards by which the task will be judged as successfully completed.

17. Instructional objectives can utilize process or product criteria, or some combination of both.

CHAPTER **12**

Generic Instructional Strategies

The teacher's job involves many roles besides that of instructing students. At times the teacher will serve as a parent surrogate, an entertainer, an authority figure, a psychotherapist, and a record keeper, among other things. All of these are necessary aspects of the teacher's role. However, they are subordinate to and in support of the major role of teaching. Important as they are, they must not be allowed to overshadow the teacher's basic instructional role.

Jere Brophy & Thomas Good (1974)

CHAPTER OBJECTIVES

To explain the relationship between teaching and learning for purposes of evaluation

To describe the instructional functions related to tasks that comprise a lesson

To describe why and how the learning environment must be made safe: physically, psychologically, and intellectually

To describe effective and efficient task communication

To describe how task information can be embedded in the environment

To describe the purpose and effective use of guided practice

To differentiate among various forms of feedback

To describe the purpose and effective use of independent practice

To describe teaching functions during applying tasks.

To describe various strategies for monitoring student practice

To describe various strategies for accountability

To describe the purpose and effective use of closure

Chapters 12 and 13 focus on teaching, particularly the manner in which an instructional task system is delivered to students. In Chapter 12 we will consider the main instructional functions that are necessary in effective teaching, no matter what "format" the teacher adopts. Regardless of whether you are utilizing an "active teaching" format or a "task" format, you still will need to communicate instructional tasks and organize student practice, and you still will have to ensure a safe instructional climate and develop a way to monitor student performance. In Chapter 13 we will focus on the specifics of the various formats of teaching that are found in physical education.

Research on teaching has shown clearly that teachers do make a difference! Who your teachers are and what they do in class will affect how much you learn, how you feel about the subject, and how you feel about yourself as a learner. Teachers can, on occasion, also touch the lives of students, influencing them in very fundamental ways. The main role of teachers, however, as the opening quote to this chapter suggests, is their role as instructor. It is through this role that physical education teachers provide a quality, equitable education for all students.

Although this chapter and the next focus on the instructional task system, we should not forget that an effective managerial system sets the stage for effective instruction (see Chapter 6). Effective management saves valuable time that can be used for instruction and practice. Effective management reduces the chances of off-task or disruptive behavior. He also sets the orderly, supportive climate in which students can be successful at learning tasks.

Teaching and Learning

Effective teaching should be evaluated primarily by observations of student work involvement (process) and student outcomes (product). For example, when a teacher improves the amount of academic learning time her students are accruing on a daily basis, she has, other things being equal, improved her effectiveness. This represents a process approach to evaluating instruction. If students have significantly increased the distance they can cover in a 12-minute run test at the end of a cardiovascular fitness unit, this too represents a measure of effective instruction. The same is true for students who not only can successfully do folk dances at the end of a unit but also demonstrate new knowledge about the countries where the dances originated. If the students ask if the folk dance unit might be extended for a few days because it's so much fun, this too is evidence of effective instruction.

Evaluating instruction only through observations of the teacher can be misleading (see Box 12.1 "How Much Time? How Much Information?"). Well-explained tasks and a pleasant rapport with students that do not translate into high rates of work involvement are of little value from an achievement perspective. Do not misunderstand this caution. How teachers instruct is important, because it has been shown that some kinds of instruction are more likely to produce effective student work involvement, and effective work involvement has been related to achievement and attitude gains. The point is that evaluating instruction must include evidence about what students do as well as evidence about what teachers do.

Teachers teach—students learn. Teachers cannot learn for the students. Students learn through their involvement with the subject matter. What teachers can do is influence the kind of work* students do and the intensity and duration of their work. This involvement, on a lesson-by-lesson-basis, is the key to understanding effective teaching. This is true whether the work involvement is related to motor, cognitive, or affective objectives. It is also true regardless of whether the teaching style is direct, or task-, or discovery- oriented, or whether

---

* I use the word *work* here not to oppose it to "play" but because student "work" is a phrase used commonly in teaching research. I have long been associated with the view that physical education is best understood as a form of play education. I believe we can talk about student work and still understand that helping students to play better is an important goal.

the involvement is teacher-directed or self-directed. The line of influence, therefore, should be understood as in the following schematic.

Teacher
instructional   ◄──────►   Student
strategies   work
                            involvement   ──────►   Student
                                                    motor, cognitive, and
                                                    affective outcomes

If you want to improve your students' skills, fitness, knowledge, or attitudes, the way you do it is to influence the kind of work they do in class (and out of class, too) and the intensity and duration of their involvement. In attempting to do so, you must also recognize that students, through the nature of their involvement, will influence your instructional strategies. As shown in Chapter 5, there is a two-way influence between teachers and their students. Chapters 10 and 11 focused on how to decide and plan for the "kind of work" students do, including making judgements about the value of that work. Chapters 12 and 13 focus on how to influence the intensity and duration of their work involvement.

12.1 How Much Time? How Much Information?

Situation. A junior high instructor is introducing some advanced tumbling skills (handsprings). As the class begins, the instructor asks a student to bring over a projector and then threads a film loop. The students are shown an assisted handspring while the instructor explains and discusses the skill. Then the students are shown two other film loops on the other handspring skills. During each showing, the instructor details the execution of the skill.

Results. The students are given far too much information, and far too much time is spent in the presentation.

Analysis. The equipment is not ready. The repeated showing of film loops is questionable. The verbal explanation is probably far too detailed for an introduction. No live demonstration is given. Students have to sit for a long time. The question is "When they finally get up to try the skill for the first time, will their attempts be much better because of the detailed presentation?" The answer is probably no!

Prescription. The students need to have an overall visual impression of what the handspring looks like, with their attention drawn to the two or three crucial aspects of execution. Then they need specific beginning objectives to get them started practicing the skill and specific feedback about their performance. The presentation gives the illusion of high-level teaching, but is actually contrary to principles of effective instruction.

Lessons as Arrangements of Tasks

Lessons should be viewed as arrangements of tasks. This is a useful way to view lessons because it focuses on what students *do* in the lesson. Every lesson has managerial and instructional tasks, and teachers should never forget that students always have social tasks to accomplish (see Chapter 5 for an explanation of task systems). Students will enter the gymnasium or need to move to an outdoor space (transition tasks, entry tasks, initial activity tasks). They will have to be informed as to what content will be practiced for the lesson (informing, refining, extending, and applying instructional tasks). They may have to organize differently for different instructional tasks (transitional tasks, equipment replacement tasks). At some point they may have to gather and disperse to receive instruction and return to practice. The lesson will eventually culminate with a closure, and students will transition to their classrooms or to a locker room. How all of these tasks are implemented determines the success or failure of the lesson from an instructional point of view.

What follows are the main elements of a typical physical education lesson showing the tasks students do and the important instructional functions related to those tasks. The lesson assumes an "active teaching" style, but the functions would not differ markedly for different styles.

Student Task	*Instructional Function*
1. Enter gym and engage in initial practice task.	Develop and teach entry routine for practicing familiar tasks.
2. Gather for instruction and receive instruction for a new skill.	Gathering routine and well-planned demonstration that culminates in clear communication of informing task.
3. Practice the informing task.	Guided practice.
4. Disperse for independent practice—practice task.	Dispersal routine and supervision of independent practice.
5. Refine task being practiced.	Attention routine, clear refinement communication.
6. Extend task by changing conditions of practice, followed by practice.	Attention routine, clear communication of extending task, followed by active supervision.
7. Refine task, continue practice.	Attention routine, clear refinement communication, followed by active supervision.
8. Gather students to explain applying task.	Attention and gathering routines, well-planned explanation and demonstration.
9. Explain organizational format for applying task and disperse students for practice.	Dispersal routine followed by guided practice.

| 10. | Applying task practice for 10 minutes. | Active supervision. |
| 11. | Gather for closure. | Gathering routine followed by closure. |

As can be seen from examining the right-hand column, there are instructional functions that get repeated throughout the lesson. The managerial functions described have already been addressed in Chapter 6. The instructional functions of explanation/demonstration, task communication, guided practice, active supervision of independent practice, and closure will be addressed in this chapter, along with monitoring systems and various strategies for holding students accountable for performance.

Ensuring a Safe Learning Environment

A major responsibility of every physical education teacher is to provide a safe learning environment for students. Safety should be considered when planning, but it is in the implementation of a lesson that safety must be foremost. Whenever a potentially hazardous activity is being undertaken, the teacher should emphasize clearly the *rules* that have been established with regards to the hazard. These rules should be described, prompted often, and students should be held accountable for obeying them. To do less is to risk both student injury and a lawsuit.

This is not to suggest that activities involving risk should not be used in the physical education program. Quite the contrary, one goal of the program should be to help students learn to take some risks and want to participate in activities. Many sport activities have the potential for injury. What needs to be emphasized are the rules regarding safety in terms of the specific activity and the space within which it is practiced and played.

Psychological safety is also important for a good learning environment. Students not only need to *behave* safely but they also need to *feel* safe about what they are doing. This means quite simply that they should feel comfortable about their participation, should be willing to participate fully. They will have psychological safety to the degree that their efforts are supported and are not met with ridicule and negative comment.

Students will also feel comfortable, and tend to behave safely too, if they have experienced an appropriate progression to shape their skills and if they have a background of related successes. If they have experienced the proper progressions, they will be challenged by current tasks and feel able and willing to do them safely.

Finally, the teacher must be constantly alert to unsafe student behavior. Students are not mature adults. Often, in the excitement of an activity, they do not behave in fully mature ways. Teachers need to be aware of student behavior that jeopardizes the students' own safety or the safety of others. Unsafe behavior should be desisted immediately, and specific feedback should be given as to why the behavior is unsafe. Active supervision (discussed later in this chapter) is the best strategy to help teachers keep in close contact with what their students are doing.

Ensuring an Intellectually Challenging Learning Environment

Although physical education should be an activity experience rather than an intellectual discussion experience, every teacher should encourage discussion related to the development of skill and playing of games. Students may ask why one technique is better than another. This allows you not only to give feedback with an information and value content, but also to interact strictly on the basis of the question asked (that is, you can provide the proper feedback and then compliment the asking of the question). Students may comment about previous experiences or they may want to express ideas about how to play a defense, how to solve a problem, how to develop arm strength, or how to measure the beat of a musical selection. You should not only answer their questions, but you should also find ways to let them know that you value questioning, commenting, and the expression of ideas. This is one of those "hidden messages" that the learning environment sends out to students.

Questioning and commenting should generally be encouraged, but you must be careful with younger students not to encourage this kind of behavior strictly for the attention the student gets for it. I am not suggesting that you cut a student off immediately if you feel that he or she is just asking or commenting in order to get attention. This is a natural thing for younger students to do, and it will diminish if you have some patience and use your interactions carefully. Students must learn how to distinguish between those situations in which questions are relevant and comments are called for and those situations in which they are not. You can easily teach them this by reacting in a positive manner to appropriate questioning and commenting, and usually ignoring what you consider to be attention-getting questioning and commenting. This is another situation where the information and value content of the feedback can be very helpful. For example, instead of just saying, "That was a good question, Jack," you might say, "That was a good question because it brings up a confusing rule, and by answering it we can help others avoid violating the rule in the future." The information and value content not only strengthens the general predisposition of students to question and comment, but also teaches them what an appropriate question is and why it was important to ask it and have it answered.

Communicating Tasks to Students Effectively and Efficiently

Both managerial and instructional tasks need to be communicated to students. If the tasks are informing tasks, the communication will sometimes need to be fairly extensive. Task communications should be evaluated by their effectiveness and efficiency. *Effective task communication* means that students will attend to and comprehend the information you present and that information will be sufficient for them to initially do the task as it has been described. *Efficient task communication* means that only as much time will be used as is necessary to ensure effective communication.

211

Communicating
Tasks to
Students
Effectively and
Efficiently

Most physical education teachers probably spend more time than is necessary in task communication. They often provide more information than students can use when they begin to practice the task. Most experts agree that students learn most effectively when they have a good general idea of what is to be accomplished and are aware of major technical features of the skill or strategy, but not the details. The "details" of task development are accomplished through a series of refining tasks, not by including all the details in the informing task.

Motor skill and strategy tasks should be introduced by establishing the importance of the task or linking it to previous work. Students should then see what the whole task looks like. They should then be told what to look for in terms of the few elements being emphasized for that task practice. Teachers often have students passively watching for these task presentations, but there is much to be said for having the students actively involved. Particularly in skill tasks, students can be "shadowing" you as you describe the elements being emphasized.

Before beginning practice, you should check to see if the communication was received accurately. Students as a group can show you a kind of choral responding. Students can be chosen to show an element or to describe an element. This check for understanding will not only serve as a signal to you that the task has been communicated effectively but also serve as an accountability mechanism to keep students attending to your presentation. This check for understanding should include the elements of the skill or strategy to be practiced as well as also the organizational conditions for practice.

The following are suggestions for developing effective task communication skills.

1. Plan carefully. You need to communicate all the necessary information but no more. Writing a main task description on your lesson plan in the words you will use with your students is a big help.
2. Include necessary information to make it a complete task description. Too many teachers focus on details of the skill or strategy itself and neglect a complete description of the conditions the task will be practiced under and some measure by which students can judge task success or completion.
3. Use language students can understand. Appropriate language will take into account age level and experience with the activity. Technical terms should be used only after they have been taught.
4. Talk enthusiastically but slowly. Remember, you know the material better than students do. They need time to process the information. Don't try to save time by rushing through an explanation; that is, don't try to achieve efficiency at the cost of effectiveness.
5. Demonstrate a skill or strategy under conditions as close as possible to the way it will be used. Demonstrate the set pass in volleyball near the net. Demonstrate goal keeping in soccer at the goal.
6. If it is important for students to see the skill or strategy from more than one view, provide the appropriate views. For example, in emphasizing the

elbow lead of the one-hand shot in basketball, show it from a front view and a side view.

7. Make sure the demonstration is accurate. It doesn't have to be "elite" from a skill point of view, but the elements that are emphasized should be done accurately.

8. If safety is a particular issue with the task, make sure that the dangerous elements are stressed and appropriate rules and routines are understood.

9. As much as possible, involve students in the task description and demonstration rather than have them passively observing.

10. Check for student understanding before beginning guided or independent practice.

Tasks need to be communicated both to students gathered to receive the information and, on other occasions, to students dispersed in some practice format. You should usually gather students for tasks that require new information or more lengthy explanations and demonstrations. This means that these tasks will be preceded by attention and gathering routines. Most refining tasks and some extending or applying tasks can be communicated to students at their dispersed positions, without first gathering them. Communicating tasks to a dispersed class requires you to place yourself where all students can see and hear the explanation. Dispersed task communication also requires that you use a good, strong voice. If the conditions of task practice have been changed, as they often are with extending tasks, then you should check that the students understand them before they return to practice.

Embedding Relevant Task Information in the Environment

Learning time is a precious commodity that should be used judiciously. Much of the information communicated from teacher to student during class time could be communicated just as effectively in another manner without using class time. Mimeographed handouts are inexpensive, provide the learner with a permanent record of instructional intent, and reduce the possibility of students misunderstanding a verbal presentation. Instructional objectives, rules, diagrams of playing fields, diagrams of defensive and offensive maneuvers, and other matters can be communicated to students through handouts. Of course, it is useless to provide handouts for students if there is no mechanism in your instructional system to ensure that they use the handouts. An informal method of ensuring this is to intermittently ask students questions that pertain directly to the handouts. If you provide a handout listing instructional objectives at the end of Monday's class, at the start of the next class you might ask several students what the criteria for certain objectives are. If you hand out a diagram of a badminton court, you can ask a student to show the back boundary line for the doubles serve. Students' understanding of the material should be formally assessed only if the handout is of sufficient importance to warrant taking time for this. Thus, you might administer a short rules test before beginning actual game competition in a new activity. If students have a handout on the rules and if they must pass a short quiz in order to gain access to the game, then chances are they will learn the material. Thus the game can proceed at a much higher level, because the situations in which rules will need to be clarified will be minimal.

Posters using cue words to describe the critical elements of the skills that are being practiced can be placed around a gym so that students can look at them when they need them. Pictures of players with the critical elements emphasized can provide another source of information. Diagrams of strategic movements can also be used. Thus, when students need to have this information they can get it without taking the time of the whole class. For example, if one group is having problems practicing a particular skill, they could be sent briefly to a poster and picture to refresh themselves about which elements to emphasize and see what those elements look like in action.

Guided Practice

When a new task has been introduced (informing tasks) or when the conditions for task practice have been changed substantially (extending tasks), it is important that a period of guided practice occur after you have the task communicated. *Guided practice* is a period of teacher-led, whole-group practice that functions to (a) correct major errors in performance, (b) reteach if necessary, and (c) provide sufficient practice so students can participate in independent practice successfully (Rosenshine & Stevens, 1986).

Guided practice usually occurs in a whole-group formation with the teacher in a position to see and be seen by the entire class. As students practice the task, the teacher provides prompts and cues to emphasize the major technical features of the task and the way the task is to be practiced. The organizational format allows the teacher to check to see if major errors are being made. If so, time is taken to reteach the skill or strategy, emphasizing the elements related to the errors. Checks for student understanding are frequent, both by visually monitoring performance and by asking questions.

Teacher feedback during guided practice typically focuses on the technical aspects of performance, particularly the critical performance elements emphasized during the task communication. Feedback relative to these critical elements should be specific, and you should strive to achieve a balance between correcting errors and reinforcing appropriate performance (see Box 12.2 "Subject Matter Feedback: Types and Examples" for an explanation of various forms of feedback and Box 12.3 "Feedback Related to Student Responses" for correctives related to student errors). You should also ensure that the conditions for student practice are being followed; that is, that the student practice is congruent with the task description. For example, if the practice task requires a "feeder," a player delivering thrown or passed "sets" to practice spiking, the type of "feed" should be monitored also, with supportive or corrective feedback provided for students feeding correctly and incorrectly.

Response rates during guided practice should be as high as possible, and there should be enough practice trials for you to feel confident that students can be successful when shifted to independent practice. If initial student responses during guided practice result in too many errors, then you should either reteach, emphasizing the elements being performed incorrectly, or shift practice to an easier task that will act as a building block for the current task. Once you are sure that tasks can be performed successfully as intended, then students can be shifted to independent practice.

12.2 Subject-Matter Feedback: Types and Examples

General positive feedback: Purpose is to support student effort and build a positive learning climate.

Nice shot.	Good effort.	That's the right idea, Mary.
Tough defense, Jim.	A-1, Roberto.	Tremendous pass, Bob.
That's better, Jill.	Very nice.	Squad 1 did really well.

Nonverbal positive feedback: Same purpose as above. Can accompany verbal statements.

Clapping hands	Thumbs-up signal	Pat on the back
The "OK" sign	Scruffing hair	Raised, clenched fist

Positive specific feedback: Purpose is to provide specific information about what was done appropriately.

Good feed, Bill, it was exactly the right speed and height. That was nice. Your circle was different from anybody's. Beautiful! You really had your knees tucked that time. Everybody in this circle made the switch to the step-hop exactly on beat. Much better. Your front arm was straight throughout the backswing. Well done, Squad 2. Your timing on the cuts was good.

Corrective feedback: Purpose is to correct errors with specific information.

Denise, you need to keep your position longer before you move. Start from the legs, Joe. You're just shooting with your arms. OK, but you did that last time. Try to find a different way now. Squad 3 needs to cover the wings of the zone better. Anticipate! Jane, you had an open alley and should have tried a passing shot.

Specific feedback with value content: Purpose is not only to provide information but also to connect performance with outcome.

Way to help on defense, Pat. When you cover like that, we can take some chances.

That's better. When your head is up, you can see your teammates.

Good effort, Jane. When you work hard like that you will improve very quickly.

Thanks, Wanda. When you provide that kind of help, Jesse's going to learn a lot.

Independent Practice

The purpose of *independent practice* is for students to integrate the new task into previously learned material and to practice the task so that it becomes automatic. Students need sufficient practice so they can use the skills confidently and quickly in conditions under which the skill or strategy will eventually be used. Time is a precious commodity in physical education, and many teachers feel that they have to cover a large number of activities. Subsequently, teachers often do not allow enough time for students to practice tasks to the point where they can do them successfully and automatically. The result is that students have covered many skills, strategies, and activities, but can't do any of them well enough to enjoy the context they are used in. Students need to have sufficient command of skills and strategies to utilize them effectively in game settings. Students need to know dance steps and transitions well enough to do the dances to music without prompts. They also need to be strong and fit enough to do sustained strength or aerobic activities.

Independent practice should provide the successful repetitions necessary to ensure those kinds of performances. While guided practice is used to correct major errors and to ensure that students can practice successfully, independent practice is used to produce high rates of successful repetitions of the task. The teacher's role during independent practice is different than during guided practice. Typically, students are dispersed for independent practice, utilizing all the space and equipment available. For example, a teacher may introduce the one-hand shot in basketball to a class gathered at one basket, but independent practice should take place using all of the baskets available throughout the space.

The major instructional function during independent practice is *active supervision*. The major purposes of active supervision are to (a) keep students on the task as assigned and (b) to provide supportive and corrective feedback where necessary. The following are key features and elements of active supervision.

1. Keep all students within sight. Moving around the perimeter of a space is usually better than moving through a space, especially at the outset when you are trying to establish a strong on-task focus.
2. Scan frequently. Don't get caught up for too long with any student or group. Briefly scan the entire class frequently.
3. Don't get predictable. Moving down a line of tennis courts or clockwise around a gymnasium gets predictable. Some students, when they can predict you are far away, will be more likely to go off-task.
4. Use your voice across space. It is important that students know that you are aware of their behavior even though you are not near them. Quick prompts and feedback across space help to accomplish this goal. Try to balance the supportive and corrective comments; that is, don't respond only to the off-task students all the time.
5. Be aware of unsafe or disruptive behavior and stop it immediately.

6. Try to distribute your attention equitably. Make sure that time and interactions are not predictable on the basis of gender, race, or skill level.

7. Use opportunities to build expectations for a successful learning-oriented climate.

Don't Forget to Teach During Applying Tasks

Many teachers plan to have a culminating applying task for each lesson. Units are often planned so that they build to a series of applying tasks toward the end of the unit. Applying tasks can be games, dances, gymnastic performances, and the like. With the approach to planning advocated in this text, the entire unit should be devoted to "getting students ready" to participate successfully in the applied contexts for which the skills are relevant.

There is evidence, however, that many teachers design applying tasks, such as games, and then refrain from any teaching while the students are practicing the task. (Metzler, 1979; Ormond, 1988). To consider what teaching functions might be accomplished during applying tasks, it will first be helpful to distinguish between the concepts of scrimmage and game. A *scrimmage* is a set of conditions that are very like those of an applied context, such as a game, but in which the teacher stops and starts action to engage in brief teaching episodes and also engages in interactive teaching during the activity. A *game* is an applied context in which the stops and starts are determined by the nature of the activity rather than the teacher's judgments. In this general sense, the concepts of scrimmage and game are applicable to activities such as gymnastics and dance; that is, a "scrimmage" for a folk dance lesson would be to perform the dance to the musical accompaniment but with brief stops and starts for the teacher to provide instruction, while the "game" would be the folk dance performed in its entirety without breaks.

Several things seem clear from the descriptive research literature in physical education. What I described above as scrimmage occurs infrequently in physical education. Most physical education classes move from practice tasks into game conditions without the intervening benefit of scrimmage situations. Curiously, the evidence for interschool sport teams is nearly opposite (Rate, 1980; Ormond, 1988). In those settings, coaches use scrimmage very frequently.

Research suggests that in both physical education and coaching settings, frequent prompting may be the best teaching function during scrimmages and games (Ormond, 1988). A *prompt* is a teacher intervention that serves to guide performance in one direction rather than another. Prompts are often brief, typically single cue words or phrases. Think, for example, of the prompts used in teaching a folk dance. Hand-clapping or a drum beat can be used to accentuate the underlying beat that serves to cue the various steps in a dance. Teachers also often use verbal prompts to cue the steps, especially during initial practice. Transitions from step to step are often highlighted verbally. Although these prompts are gradually faded as students get more proficient and come under the control of the musical prompts, they do not have to be eliminated completely.

Game play, culminating activities, gymnastic routines, and dances are meant to be fun and exciting. Students typically look forward to them, often asking when they enter the gymnasium, "Are we going to play a game today?" There is no reason, however, for teachers to abandon their instructional role during these applying activities. Quite the contrary, these are the activities in which performance needs to be polished and elements put together so that the entire performance is successful, be it a game or a dance. Teachers can prompt behavior and support successful performance without interfering in the activity itself. Likewise, "scrimmage" tasks can be arranged when "game" conditions are present, but frequent yet brief teaching episodes can be interspersed to emphasize key points and correct key errors.

Monitoring Student Performance

If students are to be held accountable for performance in the instructional system, then some means for monitoring their performance must be implemented. If performance measures are to be used for grading rather than for

---

12.3 Feedback Related to Student Responses

Although it seems logical to suggest that teacher feedback should be directed at the main elements of tasks being practiced, it doesn't always happen that way. Occasionally teachers prompt a student to focus on one element of performance, the student does so successfully, and the teacher corrects another error rather than reacting positively to the successfully performed element. Some have referred to this as the "correction complex" in teaching physical education. Here are some types of student responses and hints for relating your feedback more appropriately.

1. Student responses that are correct, quick, and firm. Support positively with brief reactions that do not disturb the momentum of practice.
2. Student responses that are correct, but hesitant. Support positively with brief reactions, but add some specific information related to technical elements.
3. Student responses that are "careless" errors. Briefly correct the error and prompt better concentration or effort.
4. Student responses that show lack of knowledge or skill. Give corrective feedback targeted to specific elements and support for continued effort. Take time to reteach or reassign to component tasks if necessary.

(Adapted from Rosenshine & Stevens, 1986)

Students	Level C Objectives								Level B Objectives						Level A Objectives			
	Short Serve	Long Serve	Underhand Clear	Overhead Drop Shot	Overhead Clear	Rallying	Matches	Knowledge	Overhead Clear	High Doubles Serve	Smash	Underhand Drop Shot	Backhand Clear	Net Shot	Overhead Clear	Backhand Clear	Push Shot	Drive Serve

Figure 12.1 *Checklist for Completion of Badminton Tasks Needed to Achieve Grades of C, B, or A (Badminton)*

end-of-unit testing, then a formal monitoring system must be used to produce a reliable record of student performance throughout a unit. *Monitoring*, then, refers to informal and formal ways of observing and assessing the degree to which student performance meets specifications.

Tasks	Students and Date Completed
Dribbling obstacle course	
Jump shooting	
Free throw shooting	
Driving lay-ups	
Defensive movement	
Passing	
Rebounding	
Strategy	
Game play	

Figure 12.2 *Checklist for Student Completion of Tasks in a Basketball Unit.*

The primary form of informal monitoring in physical education is active supervision by the teacher (see page 215), in which the teacher responds positively to task accomplishments and corrects task errors. Monitoring is also a part of informal accountability mechanisms such as "challenges" by the teacher. For example, a teacher assigns a partner-passing task in volleyball and then "challenges" the students to see how many pairs can make 10 consecutive legal hits across the net in a 20-second period. After the student performance, the teacher then asks how many pairs met the challenge. Another form of monitoring performance is to have students respond publicly, as when a teacher says "Squad 5 did that drill very well, and I want you to watch them repeat it."

Formal monitoring systems produce a record of student performance relative to instructional tasks. The task checklist is often used for this purpose. Task checklists can be completed by individual students about their own performance, by partners who monitor the performance of each other, by squads with one member designated as "recorder," or by the teacher. When students monitor their own performance or the performance of peers, it is important that the teacher ensure that students are accurate and reliable in their assessments. This is one of those many situations in physical education where concepts of "honesty" and

I can do	It took me ____ times	I can do	It took me ____ times
V-sit		Assisted handspring	
Bridge		from mat	
Arching		Handspring	
Jump and tuck		walkout	
Jump and turn		Roundoff	
Russian dance		Forward walk	
Leg circles		Backward walk	
Front scale		Hops	
Side scale		Side cross step	
Blind balance		Turn	
Crab walk		jump	
Donkey kick		one leg	
Front roll		cat walk	
Forward roll		Knee scale	
Dive roll		Front scale	
Backward roll		Side scale	
straddle		V-sit	
jackknife		Backward roll	
extension		Straddle stand	
Cartwheel		Split	
Neckspring		Needle scale	
Headspring		One-leg balance	
straight leg		Front walkover	
from walk		Squat balance	
to seat		Head balance	

Figure 12.3 *Checklist for Completion of Gymnastics Tasks with Provision for Recording Number of Trials per Task.*

"reliability" can be taught and supported. Figures 12.1, 12.2, and 12.3 show checklists for badminton, basketball, and gymnastics. Each of these checklists provides for recording information about the completion of instructional tasks.

There are many other ways to monitor student performance formally and use monitoring systems as incentives and rewards for students. Many elementary physical educators use "I can" posters that children sign when they complete important tasks; for example, being able to climb to the top of a rope or reaching the top of a climbing wall course. Using a map to track accumulation of miles completed riding a bicycle produces a record and also acts both as a visual incentive for children and as a reward when they reach new destinations on the map. There are now many computerized fitness-reporting formats that allow teachers to produce permanent records of fitness accomplishments and report to parents (Stroot & Baumgarner, 1989).

In sport units, an important way to monitor performance is to keep records during competition. In a basketball unit, records could be kept on points scored, rebounds, free-throw percentages, and assists. Students can be taught to do this recording, not just as an aid to the teacher's monitoring system, but because being able to recognize and record those kinds of performances is a worthy objective for students to achieve. In tennis units, results of mini-game round-robin tournaments can be kept. In gymnastics, points can be awarded for meet performance, just as they are when gymnastics is competed in interschool programs.

All of these formal monitoring systems produce records of performance that can be used for grading. When records of student performance relative to end-of-unit objectives are made available through a monitoring system, then end-of-unit testing becomes irrelevant. A student's grade relates to his or her performance throughout the unit rather than to how the student does on one day at the end of the unit.

Accountability Related to Supervision

In Chapter 5 it was suggested that accountability drives task systems, and in the absence of accountability, student performance relative to instructional tasks is determined by the students' interests and motivations from day to day and from moment to moment within each class. Types of accountability were described on page 181. The monitoring systems described above are, of course, strongly related to accountability in the sense that no accountability is possible without some kind of monitoring system.

Accountability, too, can be viewed as informal or formal. The major form of informal accountability in physical education is active supervision by the teacher, accompanied by strong support for on-task behavior and strong sanctions against off-task behavior. Remember, however, that the strong support and sanctions provide the accountability. Active supervision is only a means of providing that support and those sanctions when and where they are needed. Without support and sanctions, active supervision is much less effective in producing a highly on-task learning environment.

You should now begin to recognize and understand that the need for active supervision—as a monitoring and accountability mechanism—is related *inversely* to the presence and strength of a formal accountability system. If you have defined unit tasks appropriately, developed a monitoring system to record student completion of those tasks, and designed an incentive system to motivate students to accomplish the tasks (grades, certificates, ribbons, privileges, and so forth), you will have much less need to actively supervise student practice. The accountability system will motivate students to practice and achieve the goals. If, on the other hand, there is a weak accountability system—or none at all that is related to daily work involvement—then active supervision will be needed to keep students on-task.

The Functions of an Effective Closure

Closure refers to the end-of-class time when teachers bring together the parts of a lesson to make it whole for students, to make sure students understood the important elements learned in the lesson, to reestablish the importance of the elements, and to assess and validate students' feelings relative to the lesson. Many teachers do not plan for or implement closure because they feel it is not important, don't want to waste time with it, or simply run out of time before they get to it. I believe closure is an important ingredient of a lesson and that it should be planned for and implemented carefully.

An effective closure can accomplish many things. While not all should be attempted for every class closure, the following represent some goals and strategies for effective closures (Jensen, 1988; Marks, 1988).

1. *Closure means completion.* Students should be made aware of what was accomplished in the lesson. This can often be done by asking a few pertinent questions, using the answers both to check students' understanding and to underscore their important accomplishments.

2. *Closure is an opportunity for recognition.* How did the class as a whole do? What students did well? What students provided help to others?

3. *Closure is an opportunity to check students' feelings.* Which activity was best liked? How do students feel about their progress? Use this opportunity to make sure that students feel good about their real accomplishments.

4. *Closure can be a review.* What critical elements were learned today? Show me how the cartwheel is done correctly. Students can respond verbally, but they can also *do* the task to show their understanding.

5. *Closure can provide a transition from intense activity to locker room or classroom behavior.* Lessons often culminate with an applying task, which is often very active and intense. Students then have to go to a locker room to change or return to their class. In either case, closure provides a transition time for students to "cool down" physically and psychologically.

Maintaining the Pace of a Lesson

Every lesson has a pace—the forward momentum of the various managerial, transitional, and instructional tasks, as well as the smoothness of those events.

The pace can be very slow to very fast. Smoothness can range from being very jerky to very even. Research has shown that a strong, smooth pace is very important to effective teaching (Kounin, 1970).

Clearly, effective planning is an aid to creating and maintaining smoothness and momentum. Knowing where you are headed and how much time each lesson element should take will increase your chances for effective pacing. A briskly paced, smooth lesson conveys the message to students that this is an orderly, important learning environment. Regardless, however, of how well lessons are planned, it is in their implementation that pace is established and maintained. Especially important to pace is organization and transitions.

Managerial routines (see Chapter 6) are important to briskly paced lessons because they get things done quickly with as little fuss as possible. Transitions between instructional and practice elements of the lesson should be done quickly. Teachers should expect students to "hustle" during transitions, and noncompliant students should be held accountable. Equipment changes should be accomplished without producing "down time," which means they have to be planned for so that equipment will be ready and easily accessible to students.

Practice tasks should be such that students remain active. Waiting for turns to practice and doing activities that produce "down time" for students means that you risk losing lesson momentum. More and less intense practice activities can be sequenced so that students can continue to practice without having fatigue produce slowdowns that destroy the lesson's pace.

The biggest enemy of lesson pace is student waiting. In Chapter 4 it was shown that "wait time" typically accounts for the single largest chunk of time in physical education, sometimes accounting for half the lesson time. However, research on effective physical education teachers has also shown that wait time can be less than 7 percent of lesson time (Eldar, Siedentop, & Jones, 1989). Lessons with high amounts of wait time cannot possibly have the brisk pace required for teacher effectiveness. Teachers need to communicate expectations that students hustle, support those who do, admonish students who don't, and generally convey a sense of energy to the students.

Summary

1. Effective teaching should be evaluated by observations of student work involvement and student outcomes.
2. Teachers influence student work, and observations of teaching without reference to student work can be misleading.
3. *Lessons* are arrangements of tasks, each of which requires some instructional function.
4. Teachers need to ensure a physically and psychologically safe learning environment.
5. How teachers respond to questions and discussions with students will send a message about the intellectual nature of the learning environment.

6. Tasks are communicated *effectively* when students attend to and comprehend information that is sufficient for beginning practice. Tasks are communicated *efficiently* when no more time is used than is necessary.

7. Task communications should be planned carefully and include only the necessary information for practice. They should be stated in language students can understand, be delivered slowly but enthusiastically, and be done accurately in a situation where the task will be performed. When communicating tasks, be sure to stress safety if necessary, involve students, and check them for understanding.

8. Relevant task information can be embedded in the environment through posters, pictures, and diagrams so it is there for students when they need it.

9. *Guided practice* is a period of teacher-led whole-group practice that functions to correct major errors, reteach if necessary, and provide sufficient practice so students can participate successfully in independent practice.

10. Feedback can be general-positive, nonverbal, specific-positive, and corrective. It can also have value content.

11. In independent practice, students integrate the new task into previously learned material and practice it so that it becomes automatic.

12. In active supervision, teachers should keep students in sight, scan frequently, avoid predictable movement, use their voice across space, stop unsafe behavior immediately, distribute attention equitably, and use opportunities to support student efforts and build expectations.

13. *Scrimmage* is an applying task in which teachers stop and start practice frequently but briefly for teaching and feedback, while a *game* is an applying task in which teachers do not stop and start activity.

14. During applying tasks, teachers should direct student practice through frequent prompts rather than through feedback.

15. *Monitoring* refers to informal and formal ways of observing and assessing the degree to which student performance meets task specifications.

17. *Closure* is an end-of-class task in which teachers complete the lesson, recognize student performance, check student feelings, review critical learnings, and change from a more to less active mode.

18. Effective lessons have a brisk pace that is not slowed down but maintains its forward momentum, especially during transition and management tasks.

CHAPTER 13

Instructional Formats

Teaching functions are usually performed within an instructional framework—a delivery system for getting content to the learner. This instructional framework is called a teaching strategy. Many factors influence the choice of a teaching strategy, including the content itself, the characteristics of the learner, and the objectives and preferences of the teacher.

Judy Rink (1985)

CHAPTER OBJECTIVES

To describe Mosston's Spectrum of Styles

To match various formats to context issues

To differentiate between instructional format and teaching style

To describe and analyze active teaching

To describe and analyze task formats

To describe and analyze teaching through questions

To describe and analyze peer teaching formats

To describe and analyze cooperative learning formats

To describe and analyze self-instructional formats

To describe strategies for instruction of mainstreamed students

Different approaches to the teaching of physical education have been promoted, analyzed, and sometimes hotly debated since Mosston (1981) introduced the Spectrum of Teaching Styles in 1966 (see Box 13.1 "Mosston's Spectrum of Teaching Styles"). Mosston's original model suggested that student growth and development was increasingly fostered as teachers moved from "command" styles of teaching to "discovery" styles of teaching. Throughout his several revisions of the "Spectrum," as it came to be known, the claim that a teacher's choice of instructional format was directly related to student growth was dropped, as it became more and more clear that the appropriateness of alternative styles was more related to contextual factors, such as the content being taught, or to personal preferences of teachers. For example, when Ms. Jones uses task teaching for a gymnastics unit, it works well because gymnastics lends itself to a task format, and Ms. Jones likes and does well with that format. Unfortunately, many physical educators persist in believing that "command" styles are authoritarian and inappropriate, while "discovery" formats are more

---

13.1 Mosston's Spectrum of Teaching Styles

The Spectrum of Teaching Styles differentiated among various strategies on the basis of who made decisions (teacher or student), how students were grouped, and how learning activities were paced (teacher- paced or self-paced).

- **Command Style** Instruction and practice controlled directly by teacher.

- **Task Style** Some instruction and most practice embedded in tasks that can allow for individualization of content and pacing.

- **Reciprocal Teaching** Students work in pairs with some instructional functions taken over by student, especially feedback and support.

- **Small-Group Teaching** Student roles in instruction and practice further differentiated as doer, observer, and recorder.

- **Individualized Teaching** Content individualized based on student abilities.

- **Guided Discover** Teacher guides students through a series of problems in which students make decisions and explore alternative solutions.

- **Problem Solving** Teacher poses problems that students must solve on their own with alternative solutions valued.

(Adapted from Mosston, 1966)

---

humanistic. There has been a tendency to confuse "teaching style" with "instructional format" (see Box 13.2 "Style and Format: What's the Difference?"). As used here, *instructional format* refers to the way a teacher organizes and delivers instruction and provides practice for students. *Teaching style* refers to the managerial and instructional climate of the learning environment, especially as reflected in the interaction patterns of the teacher.

Matching Format to Context

Education is most effective when teachers adapt instructional formats to the contexts within which they teach. Instructional formats should reflect sensitivity to (a) personal skills and preferences of teachers, (b) characteristics of the learners being taught, (c) the nature of the content being taught, and (d) the context within which teaching takes place. Some teachers feel more comfortable with some formats rather than others. Personal preference is a legitimate factor in the teacher's choice of which format to adopt, especially when that preference derives from a professional belief in the validity of a format. Teachers no doubt tend to perform better when they work from a format that they believe to be effective, one with which they are comfortable. Nothing is worse for teachers than to feel they are being forced to adopt an instructional format that they do not believe in and cannot perform adequately. The beliefs of teachers about instructional formats can change, and teachers can learn to utilize new formats, often easily when they become convinced that a different format will help them achieve their goals better. These changes, however, should be the result of professional development and reflection, rather than administrative imposition. Box 13.5 "The Teacher I Want to Be—The Teacher I Am" (later in this chapter) contains a reflective exercise that will help you clarify your own position relative to instructional format and teaching style.

The choice of instructional format should also be sensitive to the characteristics of the learners. Clearly, when learners have had substantial experience in an activity, you will approach the teaching of that activity differently than if the class were all beginners. Children with disabilities may require a more direct format. Having children mainstreamed in your classes may warrant consideration of a peer-teaching or cooperative learning format. Classes that are well behaved give teachers more options for choice of format than do classes that require more attention to managerial and behavioral issues.

Content is also a factor. Gymnastics, climbing, soccer, and folk dance might lend themselves to different instructional formats. Teaching basic skills in any activity is a different issue than teaching higher-level strategies to learners who already have mastered the basic skills. For example, fitness problem solving is best preceded by acquisition of basic knowledge about fitness and basic techniques for measuring fitness. Thus, a teacher might change instructional formats from a whole-class, active teaching format for basic knowledge and skills to a group-oriented problem-solving format for higher-order knowledge and skills, all within the same fitness unit.

The context for teaching is also important to the choice of format, particularly the facilities. If the facility for teaching tennis consists of six courts, all in one row, then the problems of gathering and dispersing along that row of courts might compel a teacher to use a task or individualized format rather than an active teaching format. Safety issues in a beginning archery class taught outdoors might suggest active teaching with visible teacher control at the outset. If one teaching format is "better" than another, however, it is only "better" within a particular context, and only then because it matches the needs of that context in a particularly effective way.

It is important to remember that effectiveness of any instructional format needs to be judged in terms of student process and outcomes. Do students achieve the goals of the unit? Are there large amounts of academic learning time in the lessons? Do students grow in their appreciation of the activity and their desire to participate? Answers to these questions should determine whether the teaching format meets the needs of the context in which it is used.

13.2 Style and Format: What's the Difference?

It is not uncommon for laypersons to confuse teaching style with instructional format. As used in this text, *instructional format* refers to the different ways teachers organize for the delivery of instruction and, particularly, how the student role changes as a result of the changing format. A number of different formats are described in this chapter.

Teaching style refers to the instructional and managerial climate for learning; it is often most easily seen through the teacher's interactions. The climate for teaching can range from clearly negative to clearly positive with a neutral climate in the middle. Teachers can be "upbeat" or "laid-back." They can be frequent interactors or infrequent interactors. They can be very challenging or very supportive, or even both at the same time. Students experience the teacher's "style" through the interactions the teacher has with the class as a whole, with groups, and with individuals. The amalgam of these many interactional features produces each teacher's distinctive style. Terms such as *warm, caring, businesslike, demanding, aloof,* and the like are used to describe teaching styles.

It should be clear that format and style are basically unrelated phenomena. It is easy to imagine a quietly supportive and laid-back teacher succeeding in active teaching as well as in task or problem-solving formats. It is just as easy to imagine an upbeat, energetic teacher succeeding with different formats.

What is your style? How would you describe yourself as a teacher? Do you think that makes you better suited to one format rather than another?

Active Teaching

The dominant format for effective teaching in American schools, especially for children and beginners at any level, is active teaching. In *active teaching*, teachers provide direct instruction, either to a whole class or small groups, followed by guided practice in which major errors are corrected, followed by independent practice in which student work is actively supervised, all within a supportive climate in which high, realistic expectations are set for student work and students are held accountable for performance. In active teaching, content is communicated by the teacher rather than through curricular materials. The pacing of the lesson is brisk and teacher-controlled. Students get many learning opportunities and experience high success rates. Active teachers are skilled managers, relying on managerial routines to optimize time for learning and reduce opportunities for off-task and disruptive behavior. The review of research on teaching effectiveness in Chapters 2 and 3 presented more complete descriptions of active teaching.

Active teaching is also referred to as *direct instruction* (Rosenshine, 1979), *interactive teaching* (Rink, 1985), and *explicit instruction* (Rosenshine & Stevens, 1986). Active teaching also provides the main components for Instructional Theory into Practice, popularly known as the Hunter model (Housner, 1990).

Active teaching has been shown to be differentially more effective than other instructional formats for well-structured subjects, such as reading, mathematics, and physical education. Part of the success of active teaching can be attributed to the organizational and supervision aspects of the format that allow teachers to manage student engagement.

In active teaching, the teacher chooses the content and arranges the progressions, which are typically sequenced in small steps. Feedback and evaluation are done by the teacher, with active supervision as the necessary intermediate function. The instructional functions necessary to do active teaching were described at length in Chapter 12.

Task Teaching

For several different reasons, teachers often find it useful to have more than one task being practiced at the same time. When this is done, it is typically accomplished through a task-teaching format. *Task teaching* refers to organizing the learning environment so that different students can engage in different learning tasks at the same time. Task teaching is also referred to as *station teaching* (Rink, 1985). The availability of gymnastic apparatus, for example, might prompt a teacher to design tasks for each apparatus and rotate students among the various pieces of equipment.

Task teaching is not limited, however, to situations where limited equipment is the dominant contextual factor. Consider the possibilities for teaching a strength development unit or a volleyball unit. In strength development, several major muscle groups need to be worked on regularly. In volleyball, several fundamental skills need to be practiced regularly. Both of these could be accomplished through an active teaching format with the teacher pacing students through the series of strength or skill tasks, all students doing the same task at the same time. Both could also be accomplished through a task format in which the various strength and skill task stations are spread throughout the learning space and students rotate among the task-stations during the lesson.

In task teaching, it is inefficient for a teacher to communicate the content of each task to students. Teachers sometimes try to provide descriptions and demonstrations of each task at the outset of a lesson, but this strategy, to be effective, requires that tasks be very simple and easily remembered. Introducing of new tasks is difficult in a task format. Sometimes teachers use active teaching to introduce tasks in the early lessons of a unit and use task teaching to practice these tasks as the unit progresses. Students then know the tasks and can practice them without lengthy teacher explanations and demonstrations.

Most teachers who use task formats design task cards for students or task posters for each station. With cards or posters, the task is communicated through brief, simple descriptions. Task posters can also use pictures or drawings. The student reads the task description, perhaps looks at a picture of correct technique, and begins to practice the task. Obviously, this approach lends itself to either simple tasks or ones with which students are basically familiar. Figure 13.1 shows a sample task poster.

SPOT SHOOTING

Task: Shoot one shot from each spot, starting with an outside-close spot and moving either clockwise or counterclockwise. Have your partner rebound and feed a pass to the next spot. Count the number made of the six tries and record your score. Then rebound for your partner while he or she shoots.

Remember !!!   Square up
Knees bend
Push from toes
Elbow leads
Follow through

Figure 13.1 *Task Poster for a Basketball Unit*

One advantage of the task format is the possibility for accommodating different skill levels at one station. A major problem in teaching large groups of students is that they often have marked differences in ability and experience with the activity. In active teaching, the teacher typically communicates one task and students respond. Occasionally, very effective teachers find ways to communicate variations in the task that accommodate different skill levels. A task poster, however, might list a progression within that task, and students would then do the task that fits their entry level. If the task at one volleyball station, for example, were to practice the set against a wall, different levels of skill could be accommodated by having different height lines on the wall to hit the ball above, having different distance lines from the wall, and using different balls. Students would be instructed to do the task they thought they can accomplish successfully and then move up or down the task sequence, depending on their initial trials.

Another advantage of task formats is that teachers can set up their physical space ahead of time in ways that help learners master content. In badminton, for example, a teacher might want specialized learning aids to help students learn specific skills. In an active teaching format, these aids would have to be set up and taken down as the tasks changed throughout a lesson. With a task format, they can be set up for the entire lesson, with students rotating through the task stations. One station might be for the short and long serve with a string stretched above the net to provide feedback for the short serve and target areas on the floor. Another station might have similar aids to the clear and drop shots. A third station might be used for doubles play.

Task progressions between stations are more difficult and represent a general weakness of this format. The problem is that with six stations and five students per station, all stations have to be used at the outset, with students rotating throughout the lesson. If Stations 1 through 6 represent a progression, then some students will be starting at the last part of the progression and moving to the early part. Thus the task format is typically used for tasks that do not represent progressions.

Most teachers who use task formats signal changes in stations and have student groups rotating on signal. It is possible, however, to have students rotate after having met some particular performance criterion, whether it be volume of practice (25 trials) or quality of practice (five consecutive hits above the line). The problem with criterion-based rotation is that several stations tend to get crowded, with resulting problems of equipment sharing and active involvement.

To use task formats well, students need to have good self-control skills. Teachers can actively supervise task environments just as they would independent practice of any kind. They can provide more feedback and teaching, however, if students are generally well behaved and on-task. Task formats work best when tasks are clearly and completely described (a situation for performing—performance—qualitative or quantitative indicators of success or completion) and when there is a strong accountability system other than teacher supervision, such as accumulating points toward individual awards or competition among the rotating groups based on collective scoring.

Teaching through Questions

Teaching through questions refers to an instructional format in which tasks are communicated to students through questions, questions that guide student activity toward particular goals or questions that pose problems to be solved. In physical education this approach has been widely used in teaching young children, particularly within the curricular emphasis known as movement education (see Box 10.2 "Differing Visions of the 'Good' in Physical Education" in Chapter 10). Teaching through questions in a movement education format is really a variation of active teaching because a whole-group format is typically used and teachers tend to control the pacing of the lesson by presenting a sequences of tasks through questions. The questions most often represent refining and extending tasks, but ones that allow students to explore options rather than to reproduce a skill as shown by the teacher. With older students, teaching through questions can be used in connection with most instructional formats to add a problem-solving characteristic to the learning environment.

The distinguishing characteristic of this format is the way in which the task is presented to students and how that changes the student's role in the learning process. In active teaching, tasks are described carefully, including the conditions for practice, the task itself, and some measure of success. In teaching through questions, the common strategy is to describe conditions for practice and some measure for success, but to leave the performance itself open for student exploration and interpretation. For example, a teacher says: "Maintaining your self-space, can you find a different way to balance on three body parts?" Balancing on three body parts indicates the successful completion of the task, but there are different ways students can be successful. The nature of the task presentation encourages them to explore different combinations. One solution might be followed by the question: "Can you find another way to do it?" The decision of what to do to fulfill the task is left to the student rather than trying to reproduce what the teacher has explained and shown as the right way to do a task. When teachers prepare a series of task questions that help students progress toward specific skill goals, the format represents what Mosston described as *guided discovery.*

While teaching through questioning is most prevalent as a format for movement education with young children, it is by no means limited to that context. Most activity units could be taught using the teaching-through-questions format. Box 13.3 "Types and Examples of Questions" shows types of questions and examples from a basketball unit.

When teaching through questions is used with older students in connection with other teaching formats, the result is most often referred to as a *problem-solving approach.* Problem solving is often associated with what is called a "foundations" or "concepts" approach to curriculum (see Box 10.2 "Differing Visions of the 'Good' in Physical Education" in Chapter 10). In these approaches, cognitive goals are often as or more important than motor-skill and strategy goals. Figure 13.2 shows this approach for part of a high school unit on cardiovascular endurance.

Peer Teaching

Research has shown that as the size of a learning group gets smaller, achievement increases (Cooke, Heron, & Heward, 1983; Bloom, 1984), with the most dramatic achievement gains resulting from one to one tutoring. Bloom (1984) outlined a number of strategies that could help teachers working with normal-size classes approximate the gains that are achieved through tutoring. Among the more promising of these instructional formats are those in which peers play an active role in the instructional process through what is referred to here as *peer teaching.*

Peer teaching can be done in pairs, triads, or small groups, depending on the needs of the activity. When done in pairs, it represents what Mosston (1966) described as *reciprocal teaching.* It should be pointed out that using peer teaching formats does not eliminate the teacher's responsibility for the design and implementation of instruction. The teacher is responsible for planning and implementing a learning environment where instructional goals are achieved efficiently and in a way conducive to student growth and good

13.3 Types and Examples of Questions

Questions can be organized into four types according to the cognitive activity involved. Questions from each category are used for different purposes. To use questions as part of an instructional format, it is important that they be consistent with the purposes for which they are used.

1. *Recall questions.* Require a memory-level answer. Most questions that can be answer yes-no are in this category.

   - Where should your eyes be when you are dribbling?
   - Which hand should be up on defense against a right-hand dribbler?
   - Which foot should you push off from when cutting?
   - Should you keep your elbow out while shooting?

2. *Convergent questions.* Analysis and integration of previously learned material. Requires reasoning and problem solving. Typically has a range of correct and incorrect answers.

   - Why should you stay between your opponent and the basket?
   - What are your responsibilities if your opponent shoots and moves to the right to rebound?
   - What should you do if the defender steps out to guard you on a pick and roll?

3. **Divergent questions.** Requires solutions to new situations through problem solving. Many answers may be correct.

   - What ways could you start a fast break off a steal?
   - What could you do if caught defending a taller player in the post?
   - What passing options do you have when double teamed?
   - What strategies would you suggest when 3 points ahead with 2 minutes left in a game?

4. **Value questions.** Requires expressions of choice, attitude, and opinion. Answers are not judged as right or wrong.

   - How do you react when you are fouled but the referee doesn't call it?
   - How do you feel about intentionally fouling opponents at the end of a game?
   - What gives you more enjoyment, scoring a lot or playing on a winning team?

Problems:

1. What effect does posture and speed of movement have on heart rate?
2. What is your minimum threshold of training?
3. What activities best develop CV endurance?

Directions: Do all activities with a partner. Activities except calisthenics and volleyball, which will be done as a class, can be done separately. Do each of the activities, then immediately calculate your working heart rate at the end of the activity. Rest between activities so that your heart rate returns to normal.

Activities: (take pulse and calculate heart rate after each).

1. Lie down for five minutes and relax.
2. Sit up, then take pulse after one minute.
3. Stand rigidly at attention for two minutes.
4. Slow walk for two minutes.
5. Fast walk for two minutes.
6. Slow jog for two minutes.
7. Medium run for two minutes.
8. Sprint for 30 seconds.
9. Jump rope for one minute.
10. Calisthenics for five minutes.
11. Volleyball game for five minutes.

   - What happens to heart rate as you change body positions?
   - How did your heart rates differ from those of opposite sex in class?
   - What is your personal target zone for CV endurance work?
   - What might your target zone be if your were 45 years old?
   - How do the heart rates you achieved compare to what you do in daily activities?
   - What options might you have to get appropriate CV work each day?

(Adapted from Lawson & Placek, 1981)

Figure 13.2 *Laboratory Task Sheet for Cardiovascular Fitness*

interpersonal relations. But this does not mean that the teacher has to be the sole or even major agent of instruction, demonstration, or feedback. In peer teaching, these instructional roles are shifted to students.

While it is clear that students can teach each other through peer-teaching formats, it is equally clear that students need to be prepared to act as tutors, and that the content has to be well designed.

> Research clearly indicates that children can effectively teach each other skills. These gains are optimized when the peer tutoring program is highly structured, when there is an emphasis on repetition, when learning reaches mastery levels before the tutee advances, when a review system is incorporated, and when tutors are trained. (Cooke, Heward, & Heron, 1983, p. 2)

Peer-teaching formats have several strengths. First, the tutors benefit from having to teach things to their peers. Second, students divided into smaller groups can have instruction more individualized to their own needs. Third, groups can progress at a pace conducive to mastery of the content. Fourth, the one-to-one instruction typically results in higher numbers of correct responses because of the evaluation and feedback provided by the tutors. Fifth, it is quite likely that students learn responsibility acting as tutors and also learn a great deal about the learning process in physical education.

The liabilities of the peer-teaching formats are the time needed to train students to act as tutors and the time needed to individualize content so that student groups can progress at different rates. Another potential liability is that with student pairs, for example (one member responding, the other observing), the overall response rates would not be as high as they might be with an active teaching format (all students responding). This limitation might be less important if successful response rates were higher due to the frequent feedback from tutors to tutees. The key to success for peer-teaching formats is the working relationships among tutors and tutees. Students need to know how to help one another, and they have to be willing to work together cooperatively, both in leadership roles as tutors and in their role as student-tutees. Tutors have to learn how to be supportive and clear in their directions and feedback, as well as how to analyze a performance to provide accurate feedback. This latter function is made much easier with well-prepared materials. Figure 13.3 shows a tennis task sheet for use with pairs, and Figure 13.4 shows a soccer task sheet for use with triads. Notice that task sheets include help for the tutor in terms of the skill analysis function that precedes tutorial feedback.

When teachers utilize peer-teaching formats, they expend more time and energy planning lessons and developing materials. Once the students have been taught how to perform the various instructional functions and the necessary managerial routines have been developed, the teacher's primary function during the lesson is to supervise the tutoring process. Like most of the instructional formats described in this chapter, peer teaching can be used as the primary instructional format for a lesson or a unit, or it can be used in combination with other instructional formats.

Acc = Accomplished
n.t. = Needs more time

| Task/Criteria* | doer 1 | | | | doer 2 | | | |
| | 1st set | | 2nd set | | 1st set | | 2nd set | |
	Acc	n.t.	Acc	n.t.	Acc	n.t.	Acc	n.t.
1. Stand with left side turned to the net, with weight on the right foot. (If left-handed, do the opposite.)								
2. Swing the racket back at about hip height, after you throw the ball upward. Keep eyes on the ball.								
3. Transfer your weight onto the front foot, and swing the racket on a fairly straight line to the ball.								
4. Watch the ball until it is hit by the racket. Bend the knees slightly through the stroke.								
5. The racket contacts the ball when it is even with the front foot.								
6. Keep wrist firm and swing with the whole arm, from the shoulder.								
7. Rotate the trunk so that the shoulders and hips face the net on follow through.								
8. Follow through with the racket, upward and forward in the direction of the hit.								

*In some tasks, the specific description of the "parts" constitutes the "points to look for."

Figure 13.3 *Peer Teaching Tennis Task Sheet for Pairs (Source: Mosston and Ashworth, 1986, pp. 68–69)*

Name _____

Class _____

Date _____

Partner _____

Soccer—long throw-in

Work in groups of three—doer, retriever, and observer. Doer executes the task 10 times to a distance of approximately 15 yards. The retriever returns the ball, while the observer offers feedback to the doer by comparing the performance to the criteria listed below.

Long throw

Point A
(for long throw)

Criteria:

1. Both hands are used as ball is swung to point A behind the head.
2. Player takes one or two quick steps forward to gain momentum.
3. Body is bent backwards, with a slight bend at the knees.
4. A whipping action of the body and a forceful straightening of legs develops thrust.

   Note: Both feet must stay on the ground until ball is released and it must be thrown in the direction the thrower is facing.

Figure 13.4 *Peer Teaching Soccer Task Sheet for Triads (Source: Mosston and Ashworth, 1986, p. 95)*

Cooperative Learning

Educators are always on the lookout for instructional formats that seem to improve achievement while at the same time having important social benefits for students. One such new instructional format in recent years has been cooperative learning, which appears to have strong research support for both achievement and social growth (Slavin, 1988). Physical education teachers have begun to use cooperative games in their classes, games in which outcomes are determined by team members cooperating to achieve a goal. Cooperative learning, however, refers to the format for instruction rather than the activity being pursued (Kagan,

1990). In *cooperative learning*, student work is structured so that it requires interdependence in the achievement of group goals but also provides individual accountability for members of the group. A common structural format in cooperative learning is student teams.

Teams are most often formed with students of differing skill levels so that the teams as a unit are reasonably equal in performance capability. The group is judged by its success as a group; that is, by a team score, for example. Yet in successful forms of cooperative learning, the team score is a collection of the individual scores, requiring that the team work hard to optimize the performance of each team member. While cooperative learning has been used widely in classrooms, particularly from grades K–9, and has been extensively researched (Slavin, 1990), it has as yet made little impact on instruction in physical education.

Three common cooperative learning structures are the "pairs-check," "jigsaw," and "co-op co-op" formats (Kagan, 1990). In the pairs-check format, students work in groups of four with two partner-pairs in each group. Student pairs work on an instructional task with one coaching the other, as in peer teaching. The two pairs then get together to check to see if they are achieving the same goal, solution, or outcome, with further feedback and practice as a result. In the jigsaw format, students on teams each become an "expert" at one element or skill by working with members from other teams who are "experts" on the same element or skill. They then return to their own teams, and experts teach other team members the element of skill they have learned. Thus, all the bump or set "experts" in a volleyball unit might work together to master that skill and then return to their own teams to teach it to their teammates. In the co-op, co-op format students work together in groups to produce a particular group product in which each student makes a particular contribution that can be evaluated. The groups then present their work-product to the rest of the class. This format might be successful in developing acro-sport demonstrations or learning folk dances.

Cooperative learning is intended to produce social and affective outcomes as well as content mastery outcomes. The research evidence suggests that when used appropriately, cooperative learning results in social gains among racial groups and across skill levels, as well as in more acceptance of mainstreamed students and increased friendships among students in general (Slavin, 1990). Classroom teachers often utilize cooperative learning formats for student practice of instructional tasks after having used an active teaching format for initial instruction. Cooperative learning, which has some elements of peer teaching within it could also be used in a task format. The sport education curriculum model described in Box 10.2 "Different Visions of the 'Good' in Physical Education" in Chapter 10 represents a form of cooperative learning within the context of sport, and it could easily be adapted to become a full-fledged cooperative learning model. As Box 13.4 "When Teaching Least is Teaching Best" indicates, cooperative learning is one of the instructional formats that puts the student at the center of the learning environment.

When we think about "teaching," our first thoughts typically are about the things teachers do in class. Too often when we think about evaluating teaching, we think about watching what the teacher does. A consistent message in this text has been that the best evaluation of teaching comes from watching what *students do*. Teachers do not have to be at the center of the stage for good instruction to take place. Indeed, arguments can be made that for student growth toward becoming responsible, independent learners, the teacher must move off stage, so that the students themselves can occupy the central roles. There are several instructional formats in this chapter that can accomplish that goal better than others.

Responsible, independent learners can no doubt develop from many of the variations of peer teaching and self-instructional formats. While responsibility and independence are important qualities, one might also argue that learning to work together toward collective goals is also an important, humanizing experience. Some peer formats and most cooperative learning formats would be appropriate for this goal.

It is "OK" for teachers to get off and stay off the center-stage role in the instructional format. Enough is now known about classroom management for teachers to work gradually toward implementing instructional formats that not only promote independence and responsibility but also require collaboration and responsibility for others, and allow students to experience the multiplier effect that can be achieved through communal effort toward collective goals.

The formats through which these goals can be achieved are not easy to implement. Teachers need highly developed class management skills to develop an orderly environment where students can learn to function effectively in these student-centered formats. Even then, it must be recognized, there are probably situations where active teaching might still be the preferred format, because format needs to be adapted to goals and context.

Self-Instructional Formats

Self-instructional formats allow students to progress through a sequence of learning activities without the physical presence of a teacher. These are really a family of formats that share the common feature of allowing the student to work without the immediate direction and supervision of the teacher. Among the formats in this "family" are individualized instruction, contracting, and Personalized Systems of Instruction (PSI). Self-instructional formats embed all of the teaching functions in materials and typically use a formal accountability system.

Teachers who plan self-instructional formats spend a great deal of time developing and improving those materials and maintaining records of student performance in an accountability system.

Self-instructional formats can be used within a traditional class setting, or they can be used for students to pursue learning independently from a class setting. Self-instructional formats are widely used in high school physical education for courses that take place away from the school, such as in a local bowling alley, indoor tennis arena, or area golf course. Due to the nature of physical education content, self-instructional formats often require that students work in pairs, triads, or small groups to complete the learning tasks. Thus, self-instructional formats are often used in conjunction with peer-teaching formats. Also, because of the need to develop clear and explicit materials for learners, self-instructional formats take on many of the characteristics of task teaching.

The strengths of self-instructional formats are the flexibility allowed learners and the possibility of matching learning tasks to student abilities more than is possible in a whole-class, active teaching format. The flexibility of good self-instructional materials is that they can be used within a class or outside a class. There is also much to be said for students having the responsibility of completing a learning sequence "on their own" by following the materials prepared by the teacher.

Self-instructional formats rise or fall on how specific and appropriate the materials prepared for students are and the degree to which the accountability system motivates the students to complete the tasks. The self-instructional materials need to be complete and explicit, providing students with the help they need at the point when it is needed. Figure 13.5 shows self-instructional materials for the skill of volleying in soccer. These materials are typical of self-instructional materials to be used within a class.

Contracting is a form of individualized instruction in which students sign a learning contract to complete a sequence of learning tasks according to a predetermined set of criteria. Contracting is a popular self-instructional format for physical education courses completed at sites other than the school and under the jurisdiction of persons other than the physical educator. Thus, students might complete a golf unit or a bowling unit at local sites on their own without the supervision of the teacher. The contract specifies the learning tasks to be completed, the amount of practice required, and the criteria for performance necessary for a particular grade or fulfillment of a requirement. An example of a learning contract is shown in Figure 13.6.

Personalized Systems of Instruction (PSI) is a self-instructional format in which content is divided into small units that require mastery before moving on to other units. PSI formats require developing specific instructional tasks and clear mastery criteria. Students then practice the tasks until they meet the criteria; they then move on to the next task. PSI allows for individual progress through a series of learning tasks. At the end of a PSI unit, students will differ in terms of *how much* they have learned rather than *how well* they can perform. Grading is typically done in terms of how many tasks are completed

VOLLEY

Purpose:

To redirect an aerial ball strategically.

Skill Analysis:

1. Align body part with approaching ball.
2. Focus the eyes on approaching ball.
3. Move total body and body part toward ball.
4. Apply firm body part to center of the ball.
5. Follow through toward intended flight direction.

Kinds: Foot, knee, shoulder, and head.

Task Learning Experiences:

1. In partners, A throws the ball toward B's shoulder and B volleys the ball executing a shoulder volley. Repeat five times from a distance of 10 feet. Reverse. Repeat from 15 feet.
2. Repeat Task #1 preceding the volley with two or three steps. Reverse.
3. Repeat Tasks #1 and #2 directing the ball to the left, right, and toward center.
4. Repeat Tasks #2, #2, and #3 executing a knee volley.
5. Repeat Tasks #2, #2, and #3 executing a foot volley.
6. In partners, A throws the ball underhand so that it arches and drops toward B's head. B executes a head volley. Repeat three times from a distance of 10 feet. Reverse.
7. Repeat Task #6 directing the ball to the left, right, and toward center.
8. Stand 10 to 15 feet from a wall and kick the ball into the wall. Volley the rebound with different body parts according to the level of rebound. For a more forceful rebound, precede the kick with two or three steps. Different levels of rebound can be achieved by contacting the ball at various points below the center. Repeat 10 times.

Figure 13.5 *Self-Instructional Materials for Volleying in Soccer* (Adapted from Zakrajsek and Carnes, 1986, *Individualizing Physical Education: Criterion Materials [Second Edition].* p. 186. Reprinted by permission.)

within the time constraints of the unit. PSI could also be used away from the time demands imposed by class periods during school days. If so, then students who need extra time to master a series of tasks could do so. Figure 13.7. shows a single task from a PSI tennis unit. The unit is composed of a series of such tasks.

Requirements:

1. Practice at a local course for a total of 20 hours.
2. Complete test on golf rules at score of 90 percent or better before playing on course (test is available in PE office).
3. Play 36 holes of golf and turn in completed score cards.
4. Maintain a diary describing problems encountered in skill practice and play. Turn in at completion of unit.
5. Play a final 18 holes at the end of the unit.

Practice tasks: (20 hours minimum).

1. On practice range, hit 9 iron, 5 iron, and 1 or 3 wood 20 times each. Utilize critical element checklist for each practice. If possible have a partner observe and complete checklist.
2. On practice green, hit 25 9-iron pitch and chip shots. Utilize critical element checklist as you practice.
3. On practice green, put 50 putts of varying lengths and slopes.
4. As you improve, spend more time practicing the tasks you are having most difficulty with.
5. Have practice times attested by a partner or course employee.

Playing tasks: (minimum of 36 holes).

1. Play at least nine holes at a time.
2. Play following all official and local rules.
3. Complete score card and have score attested.
4. Record thoughts and reactions in your diary.

Grading criteria:

C = Completion of all requirements.
A or B = Negotiated on basis of improvement in score from practice rounds to final 18 holes.

Figure 13.6 *Self-Instructional Golf Contract*

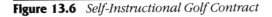

Providing Effective Instruction for Mainstreamed Students

Public Law 94.142, The Education for All Handicapped Children Act, passed by Congress in 1974, requires that students with disabilities be educated in the *least restrictive environment* relative to their disability. In many school districts, the least restrictive environment for the physical education of students with disabilities is considered to be the regular class. When students with disabilities are mixed with regular students in regular classes, the result is referred to as *mainstreaming.*

243

Providing
Effective
Instruction for
Mainstreamed
Students

UNIT 4—Rules and Rally

Terminal Objectives

1. Student will demonstrate knowledge of tennis rules by scoring 80% or more on a written test.
2. Student will demonstrate the ability to move from a ready position to the forehand and/or backhand ground strokes só that a Rally is continued for 6 consecutive hits, and the balls remain within a singles court.

Learning Tasks

1. Student will read handout provided and answer questions on a worksheet.
2. Student will participate in "home base" drill so that six consecutive balls are hit between singles boundaries.
3. Student will participate in "ground stroke" scramble until six consecutive balls are hit within singles boundaries.
4. Student will participate in "two-on-one" drill until the student can rally six consecutive times within singles boundaries.

Figure 13.7 *Learning Task from a High School Tennis Unit.* (Source: Tousignant, 1983, p. 34. Reprinted with permission from the Journal of Physical Education, Recreation & Dance.)

Mainstreaming is an effort to allow students with disabilities to experience as normal an education as possible, especially in terms of the social dimensions of education. As a result, it is now common for physical education teachers to have one or more mainstreamed children in their regular classes. The presence of mainstreamed students often requires the teacher to modify instruction in one or more ways.

Students with physical disabilities typically require that activities be modified so that they can take part with the rest of the students. This often requires modifying equipment for practice activities and changing rules for group activities and games. In a basketball unit, for example, if one student has to participate in a wheelchair, a lowered basket, smaller ball, or both, might be necessary for practice. During games, every effort should be made to secure the use of another chair so that the opponent would be on equal terms. Rules for those two players would have to be modified. If no chair is available, a scooter might be used. In a soccer unit, a disabled student with limited mobility might play goalie.

Students with mental or behavioral disabilities often present different and sometimes more difficult problems for the teacher. In these cases, using some of the instructional formats described in this chapter could be helpful. For example, a student tutor might be assigned to each "special" student to help them engage in some modified form of the task being done by the class. A different student

13.5 The Teacher I Want to Be—The Teacher I Am

The purpose of this exercise is to help you to evaluate the congruency between your own views of teaching physical education and where you now stand relative to those views. The material in this chapter and from Chapter 10 will be helpful in completing this exercise.

Part One: The teacher I want to be

Write a description of what kind of physical education teacher you want to be. Include in the description (a) your concept of the "good" in physical education (see Box 10.2 "Differing Visions of the 'Good' in Physical Education in Chapter 10), (b) your preference for instructional format, and (c) the teaching style you want to achieve. Describe how the goals of physical education you value, the instructional format you like best, and the style you would like to communicate to students come together to make you the teacher you want to be.

Part Two: The teacher I am

This part of the exercise requires records from observations of your teaching, an observer to produce a current record, or a videotape that you can evaluate yourself. You might want to utilize some of the observation formats described in Chapter 16. To determine if students are achieving the kinds of goals you believe represent the "good" in physical education, observe their behavior. What do they do? How often do they do it? Are they successful? How would you describe the instructional format? Does it achieve what you expect it to achieve relative to your goals? To determine your "style," observe and evaluate your interactions with students. Do you communicate high, realistic expectations? Is there evidence of providing support for students' efforts? Are you primarily positive? Corrective? Do you convey energy?

Part Three: Congruency evaluation

Now, put Parts 1 and 2 together. How close are you to achieving your vision of the teacher you want to be? At what points are there discrepancies? What might you do to improve in those areas?

might serve as tutor for each new class period. Or, student groups might be formed in which students with disabilities are integrated within the groups in a cooperative learning format, making all members of the group responsible for the active participation of the disabled student.

Summary

1. *Instructional format* refers to how a teacher organizes instruction and delivers practice to students, while *instructional style* refers to the managerial and instructional climate of the learning environment.

2. Mosston's spectrum of styles described ways of teaching—from command to discovery—that were supposedly related to student growth.

3. Instructional format should match the context for teaching, which reflects the teacher's personal preferences, characteristics of learners, the content, and the context within which the teaching takes place.

4. *Active teaching* is a direct format in which the teacher controls the pace of the lesson, providing ample guided and independent practice, producing high rates of successful student participation in a supportive climate.

5. *Task teaching* is a format in which different students are engaged in different tasks at the same time, typically rotating among the tasks stations throughout the lesson.

6. *Teaching through questions* is a variation of active teaching in which student responses are not prescribed, typically taking a guided discovery or problem-solving approach.

7. Questions can be recall, convergent, divergent, or value, depending on the type of response required.

8. *Peer teaching* is a format in which students take on instructional roles, typically pairs, triads, or small groups, and peers are prepared to do the roles well, especially the feedback role.

9. *Cooperative learning* is a format in which student work is structured so that it not only requires interdependence in the achievement of group goals but also provides individual accountability for members of learning groups.

10. Teachers do not have to be center stage; good instruction and learning often takes place with students occupying more central roles.

11. *Self-instructional formats* allow students to progress through a sequence of learning activities without the immediate presence of the teacher, with teacher-prepared materials important to successful implementation.

12. *Contracting* and *PSI* are self-instructional formats used both in regular classes and in independent study classes or experiences.

13. Students with disabilities are required to be educated in the least restrictive environment, which often means mainstreaming.

14. Mainstreamed students change the instructional demands for the teacher and can be accommodated through variations of formats such as peer tutoring or cooperative learning.

PART Four

Becoming a Professional Teacher

Teachers work in schools. To survive and grow as a professional, a teacher has to understand what schools are like from a teacher's viewpoint, how schools operate, and what issues are most relevant to productive and happy professional growth. Many obstacles to growth tend to decrease effectiveness and force compromises that can result in decreased productivity and even unhappiness as a teacher and as a person. The possibilities of this negative scenario occurring for you are lessened the more you understand the culture of the school and the salient organizational, legal, and professional issues within which teaching is embedded. Providing that understanding is the purpose of Part Four.

When you master the content of Part Four, you should understand and be able to discuss how issues such as organization, liability, professional ethics, and the like affect teachers. You should know what things you can do to optimize the chances of having a successful induction into teaching and then continuing to grow as a professional person. You should also understand and be able to discuss obstacles to effective teaching in physical education and what can be done about them. Finally, you should understand systematic observation and be familiar with a number of instruments and the varying purposes for which they are used.

CHAPTER 14

Learning about Schools: Transition from Student to Teacher

We need have no fear that good teachers will be driven off by close examination of the teaching role. The attractions are genuine and powerful. So long as they have not been promised a rose garden, most people can be happy with a plot of wild pasture—just so long as the annual crop of roses outnumbers the annual crop of brambles, even by only one.

Larry Locke (1975)

CHAPTER OBJECTIVES

To describe the formal and informal organization of schools

To describe the major features of being a new teacher

To describe the major problems faced by beginning physical educators

To describe the major themes derived from teachers' views of life in schools

To describe the characteristics of effective schools

To describe the characteristics of effective school-wide discipline programs

To describe and discuss suggestions for surviving in schools

To describe the teacher's responsibilities for providing a safe and responsive physical education

To define terms and concepts related to legal liability

To describe how and why teachers organize and bargain collectively

To define terms and concepts related to collective bargaining

Teachers live a large part of their lives in schools. They live among students. They exist in a bureaucratic structure. It is not surprising that the organizational characteristics of schools and the nature of the minute-by-minute life within them dramatically affects the kind of person a teacher becomes over the years. Most teacher educators recognize that what they do on campus is of less importance than what happens to interns during student teaching, and even less important than what happens to a first-year teacher. This is not to suggest that teacher education experiences, even those on campus, are unimportant—only that they typically do not have the same power to influence the prospective teacher as does the experience in school.

It is important that prospective teachers learn about schools *before* they begin to teach full time. This is true for two important reasons. First, if you know a lot about schools, the manner in which they operate and the power of influences they have over teachers, then you can adapt more readily to them and your initial teaching experiences will be less frustrating and more successful. Second, if you should choose to try to effect some change in schools, then a knowledge of how schools work is essential to the success of your change effort. Thus, whether you want to be an "adapter" or a "change agent" or some combination of the two, it will be to your advantage to learn about schools.

Schools as Organizations

Schools are organizations. As such they tend to be unavoidably bureaucratic. There are policies, forms to fill out, and reports to be made. Small elementary schools in small systems can sometimes avoid this feeling of bureaucracy. Large schools in large systems too often are dominated by the feeling.

The formal organization of schools is hierarchical. Principals report to a superintendent; teachers report to principals. The lines of authority are clear and often rigid. As systems grow larger, the number of administrators increases and the hierarchical nature of the formal organization is emphasized.

Schools respond to many divergent interests, so there are many divergent interest groups within schools. Schools respond to parents, school boards, state departments of education, to teachers' organizations, professional organizations, and students. The formal organization takes all these interests into account, but not always to an equal degree. Because of the need to respond to different interest groups, it is unlikely that all members of a school organization will agree about the major goals of the school. They are unlikely to be "pushing in the same direction" at all times. This can frustrate and complicate life for the naive teacher who enters a school assuming that all policies and all decisions are based on "what's best for the students." Life in schools is not quite that simple.

Schools also have *informal organizations,* which are patterns of influence that exist outside, and sometimes in conflict with, the formal, hierarchical structure of school administration. Informal organizations develop in different ways and are seldom the same from school to school. You won't read about them in the school district's official description of the system. You are more likely to learn about them in the teachers' lounge. Some things in schools get done through the formal organization. Other things get done through the informal organization. Teachers can suffer, at least potentially, until they learn which organization is best for getting certain kinds of tasks done.

Although schools are like other organizations in many respects, they differ in certain important ways (Tumin, 1977). Schools are most often public institutions financed through public funding. They are controlled by school boards, elected by local citizens. Maintaining *local control* of schools is a cherished American tradition, even though it means very different things in small rural districts and in large urban districts. Some states have hundreds of districts and therefore have hundreds of local school boards. Hawaii has only one school district—the whole state. Therefore, it has only one school board. Thus, local control means something very different in each state and often within states, depending on the size of the school district.

The fact that schools are often so thoroughly public means that their actions are highly visible—what they do is often in the public eye. Parents, politicians, and local media people feel quite at home in scrutinizing what goes on in schools

250

Learning about
Schools:
Transition from
Student to
Teacher

and sharing their feelings in public. In that sense, at least, the organization of the school is highly accountable to a number of public interests.

A second way in which schools tend to differ from many other organizations is that their success as an organization is very hard to define. People disagree, often vigorously, about what should happen in schools. If people disagree as to what the goals of schools should be, then it is clear that they will also disagree on what criteria should be used to judge schools. Some believe that schools exist to teach basic tool skills such as language, mathematics, and knowledge of democracy. Others see schools as vocational training. Still others believe that self-growth and self-actualization are the most important goals. The differences are sometimes so great that to achieve one set of goals almost prohibits reaching another set of goals—such schools are in a "no-win" position.

Schools, as organizations, need to communicate to their many constituencies clear and consistent messages about the many goals they seek and the degree to which they are successful in doing so. This should happen at the school district level, building level, and subject matter level. Thus, physical education teachers need to find ways to communicate to parents and other interested parties the goals of the district physical education curriculum from K–12 and the degree to which those goals are being achieved.

The New Teacher

Teachers come in all sizes and shapes. They differ in many respects. Yet they enter teaching with many of the same characteristics, expectations, and problems. Most often, the new teacher is also a new adult, in the sense that he or she is entering a professional career for the first time (career shifts among adults are no longer uncommon, but the feeling of first entry still holds for a majority of first-year teachers). This means that a new phase of life is beginning as well as a new career.

New teachers often have to relocate. For some it means leaving home for the first time—perhaps even making that final move of independence that establishes a person as an adult in our society. The relocation often means new friends, a new place to live, and new responsibilities. Thus, the adjustments of the first year of teaching are made even more difficult by the accompanying transition away from university life and into adulthood.

New apartments and new friends may represent one kind of transition, but the first-year teacher encounters a far more profound transition in the school in which he or she is employed. Schools have different value structures from university and college teacher education programs. Universities tend to be places where idealistic values are supported, often preached in teacher education programs. Schools tend to be more conservative, most often reflecting the values of the community in which they are located. In addition, public schools are not typically tolerant of people who question the values implicit in school policies and procedures, especially when the questioners are first-year teachers fresh from the university. The result is often conflict—and, conflict appears to be something with which first-year teachers live on a daily basis.

The first year of teaching is often complex and even bewildering. There is never enough time to prepare. What you thought was adequate preparation turns out seldom to be exactly that. Students sometimes test new teachers, and if the test reveals weaknesses, the students are sometimes not above trying to probe those perceived weaknesses even further.

Discipline often becomes the major focus of the first-year teacher's effort. Although the preparation program might have taught good teaching techniques and even good planning strategies, there is typically less done to teach good discipline techniques. True, you might know about some discipline skills, such as those described in this text, but you probably have had little opportunity to actually try them out. This is true quite simply because preparation programs cannot, in fairness to students, set up problem situations for trainee teachers in order for them to get practice at discipline skills.

The new teacher is also socialized rather quickly into the teaching profession. Often there is a decision to be made about whether to join a teachers' union (sometimes called a professional organization, but functioning as a union). In this case, too, there probably has been little that preparation programs have done to help a trainee teacher to be ready to handle the decisions required by professional socialization during the entry year of teaching.

One of the more difficult aspects of first-year teaching is getting accustomed to the school routines and the extra duties they require of teachers, many of which are part of the organizational bureaucracy referred to earlier. Teachers take attendance and report it to a central office, they pass on school notices, they collect money, they send home for permissions, they do hall duty, they do lunchroom duty, and they become involved in a host of other quasi-administrative chores—chores that tend to take time away from their planning and preparation for teaching.

None of this is to suggest that first-year teaching is always a horror story and that the new teacher is inevitably headed for disappointment. One must always remember that new teachers also have their own classes for the first time—really their own! They can teach in their own style without having to please a college instructor or a school cooperating teacher. They have time to get to know student with the knowledge that the relationship may extend over years. They also encounter the joys of actually helping students to achieve and grow.

The degree to which the first year of teaching is viewed from a primarily positive or negative perspective depends on the balance that is achieved by all the forces described in this section, as Box 14.1 shows. The outcome is hard to predict. Many, many teachers leave the profession after just one year—leave it of their own accord, feeling that they simply cannot or do not want to deal with the many problems encountered. Others have their aspirations reaffirmed and become even more committed to a career in teaching. What is absolutely clear is that the first year would be considerably easier if teacher education programs would better prepare their students for the realities of school organizations and life in schools. That, in effect, is the purpose of this chapter and the next.

Much of the blame for the difficulties encountered in first-year teaching must be placed on the teacher education programs from which the teachers graduated.

252

Learning about
Schools:
Transition from
Student to
Teacher

14.1 Diary of a Beginning Teacher

September 1, 1966

Am I tired!!! Everyone told me I would be, but I didn't really believe it. Things went better today than I had expected, although I did mess up my attendance. The classes went pretty well except for the last period. All the other classes were only 30 minutes long but sixth period was 55. I hadn't realized this and didn't really have enough to fill up the extra time—I guess I'm not practiced at the gentle art of stalling. I've got so many things running around in my head that I have to remember, especially paperwork, that I'm sure I'll never remember it all.

The secretary in the office must shudder every time she sees me coming. I have so many problems with all of the records.

I feel guilty because I haven't got any long-range plans for my class, but I'm still too confused.

Postscript, May 10, 1968

Although my official record says that I have now had two years of teaching experience, it might be more accurate to say that I have had one year of experience and one year of teaching. My first year of employment seems to fit much better under the category of pure experience. My second year has been nothing like the first. For every one problem I have had this year, I had 15 or 20 last year. My first year, more often than not, was defeating, depressing, and exhausting. All this, however, was for a purpose: the second year and the years to come. From the first it was obvious that I was learning a great deal more than I was teaching. I would not give up a moment of my experiences last year (well, maybe one or two moments) because every mistake, every crisis, made this year easier.

As I reread the diary which I wrote last year, many half-forgotten events came back and many unforgettable ones were relived. I was amazed by some of the things which I didn't know or thought I did. Yet, it is not really amazing at all. Last year was for me a year of learning. The clicheé says that experience is the best teacher. Well, experience *makes* the best teacher too, and last year was an experience.

Source: Morris, J. Diary of a beginning teacher. *Bulletin of the National Association of Secondary School Principals,* October 1968, p. 6–22.

I have tried to identify the major skills for effective teaching and explain them clearly, suggested strongly that they need to be practiced often, and provided observational suggestions through which feedback can be provided to the teacher education student. The skills emphasized in this book are precisely those most needed by new teachers—they are first-year survival skills in that sense! The following summary comment from a study of first-year teachers in inner-city schools (Hayman & Moskowitz, 1975) points to skills that have been emphasized in this text:

> Confirmed strongly in the present study was the finding that the struggle for effective instruction (and learning) in the inner-city junior high school is effectively won or lost at the very beginning of the school year. The first meeting with the class, in fact, appears to be crucial in this regard. Successful teachers establish a productive climate at the very start, and they do it with specific types of orienting and expectation-setting behaviors. Few new teachers have the knowledge or the skills needed to effectively take control at the very beginning, and they suffer frustration as a result. . . . Successful teachers were also much more adept at engaging in reinforcing, motivating behaviors than were new teachers, and their superiority persisted throughout the school year. (p. 14)

On the other hand, it is not possible to create experiences for trainee teachers that are exactly like those they will face as first-year teachers. Thus, survival skills are "bets" in the sense that they are the best way to prepare trainees to "win" the first-year experiences.

The new teacher's attention during the first year is often focused on discipline more than teaching. Classroom management has often been cited as the new teacher's biggest concern and greatest source of anxiety (McDonald & Elias, 1983). This is no doubt due to the fact that classroom management and discipline are often under-represented in teacher education programs. Although discipline and class management continue to represent the largest source of problems for first year teachers, it does not have to be so. O'Sullivan (1989) investigated the successes and problems of two first-year physical education teachers who had been prepared in a program that emphasized class management and discipline skills. These new teachers gained almost instant credibility in their schools because of their success in skillfully managing classes and handling discipline problems quickly and positively. Midway through their first year of teaching, these physical educators were being approached by other teachers for advice and help in management and discipline problems. While their first year was not without problems, they gained early acceptance in their schools because of their skill in class management.

The Beginning Physical Education Teacher

Most of what was suggested in the previous section would be true for all teachers regardless of the subject they teach. One of the "new" experiences for most beginning physical education teachers is to find themselves as part of a school faculty, spending time in teacher's lounges, lunchrooms, and committee meetings with elementary classroom teachers, history, science or math teachers, and other "specialist" teachers such as the art or music specialist. Learning to be a faculty colleague with teachers from other subject areas represents a special problem for physical educators for various reasons, namely the lack of accep-

254

Learning about
Schools:
Transition from
Student to
Teacher

tance of their subject matter, their isolation from colleagues in the elementary school, and their after-school duties in coaching at the middle and secondary levels.

Most physical educators seem to share one common problem: Too few people in their schools value their subject matter. While the new physical educator might be liked and appreciated as a person and considered to be a good beginning teacher, it is still doubtful that many teachers, administrators, parents, and students will view physical education as one of the important subjects in the school. Competent and professional physical educators often find themselves in a constant battle to provide legitimacy for their subject matter (O'Sullivan, Stroot, & Tannehill, 1989). If persons in positions of authority within school organizations don't view physical education to be as important as other subjects, then physical education teachers will face difficulties involving scheduling facilities, securing equipment, and a host of other issues. If parents don't view physical education as important, they will influence their children both in direct and subtle ways, many of which create problems for the physical education teacher. Perhaps most of all, if students don't view learning in physical education to be important—seeing it instead as just a fun time for activity— they won't be motivated learners.

Elementary physical education specialists share one important common problem: They are too often isolated from interactions with other physical educators who also teach children (O'Sullivan, 1989). The elementary physical education specialist is often isolated within the elementary school. With seven to nine classes per day, the specialist can often go for hours without talking to another adult. While classroom teachers can discuss common concerns about curriculum and student learning, the physical educator is most often without a peer-teacher group that can speak relevantly to issues related to teaching fitness, movement, sport, and dance. Because of this isolation, it's a good idea for beginning elementary physical education specialists to form networks of peer-teachers in other schools and districts to share concerns and ideas—and, sometimes, just for being able to talk and listen to someone who is going through similar experiences.

Middle and secondary physical educators typically have physical education colleagues to talk with on a daily basis. Their major problem, aside from establishing the legitimacy of their subject matter, is their general lack of integration into a school faculty because of coaching commitments and the role conflict that develops between teaching and coaching demands. Middle and secondary physical educators often have coaching commitments, sometimes for two of the three sport seasons of the school year. These commitments require them to be with their teams immediately after school, especially in the autumn and spring when indoor spaces do not have to be shared. However, most teacher groups and school committees meet immediately after school. The physical educator, therefore, is often unable to even attend these meetings, let alone play any leadership role in a teacher's organization or school committee.

Most new physical educators enter schools thoroughly *unprepared* to play an important role in collaborative decision making that affects their programs and their lives as teachers (Locke, 1986). If physical education is ever to achieve a more central role in the school curriculum and if physical educators are ever to achieve a more influential role in the organization of the school, then participation in the life of the school is essential.

> Some lack of visibility is inevitable for special subject teachers, especially those who move from building to building within a district. It is also true that some nonparticipation results from the need to limit involvements and conserve energy in an exhausting daily schedule. Nevertheless, being relegated to the periphery of school life is related to the fact that physical education teachers sometimes fail to take full membership in the school community. Such membership can be sustained only be being present when and where decisions are made, by participation in the dialogue and debates, and by persistently behaving as though teaching physical education is just as central to the mission of the school as teaching any other subject. (Larry Locke, 1986, p. 62)

In a sense, teaching is like being part of a sports team. You can't expect to show up and play a "star" role. You have to be part of the team, attend the practices, go through the training, and learn to get along with your teammates. The fact is that in terms of active membership in the collaborative work of teachers, too many physical educators have decided to "not play in that game" and, in the long run, physical education pays the price for this noninvolvement.

Teachers' Views of Life in Schools

Several important studies have attempted to obtain information about the perceptions teachers have about what they do each day in schools. The two most notable of these studies have been reported in Lortie's *Schoolteacher* (1975) and Jackson's *Life in Classrooms* (1968). Through interviews and questionnaires, an immense amount of data were gathered and then analyzed. There were five major recurring themes in the views of the teachers. The views of teachers about what they do are an important source of information to consider when trying to learn more about schools.

A major recurring theme in the data from these two important works was the here-and-now urgency of teaching, the immediacy of events in the daily life of the teacher. A teacher who has to deal with a number of classes, each of which contains a large number of students, has little time for reflection and contemplation. Attention is riveted on the here and now—at least it had better be, if success is to be achieved. Eventually, this "present-ism" changes teachers. If you are required to always attend to immediate events, you are less likely to be contemplative and reflective. You become a somewhat different person. This is clearly a major effect of living in schools as a teacher.

A second theme was that of informality. Rather than define specific styles of teaching, teachers tend to narrow that issue down to formal versus informal teaching. The distinction usually rests on the manner in which the teacher chooses to use his or her authority, his or her managerial style. A strong desire

256

Learning about
Schools:
Transition from
Student to
Teacher

for informality was apparent, yet it clearly meant less formal rather than *not* formal—a difference in degree rather than in kind. Informality often is related to "being accepted by the students" or "getting along with the kids." It seems clear that this influences teachers to understand and adapt to current language and dress styles among students.

A third recurring theme was the concern expressed about threats to professional autonomy. This general concern was expressed in many ways, such as having to implement an inflexible curriculum, being required to plan to far in advance, and being observed too often by supervisors and administrators. The investigators felt strongly that concerns for autonomy did not reflect a desire for total independence or a desire to be "left alone." Teachers feel strongly about the collective nature of school life. The concerns about autonomy evidently reflect the desire to be free from inspection while performing major instructional duties. Teachers want help. They most often like the idea of working together with specialists from other areas. On the other hand, they also want to feel in control of their own classroom.

A fourth theme emerging from the data was that of individuality. Criteria for success in teaching are terribly vague. Teachers, therefore, tend to use individual judgment to develop success criteria for themselves. These success criteria are much more often focused on what individual students do rather than what happens to the group. The individualization of success criteria also tends to make teachers resistant to outside accountability and to suggestions for change.

The final theme extracted from the studies is that of conservatism, not necessarily the political kind of conservatism but rather a "maintenance of status quo" kind of attitude. Most teachers seem to believe that limitations on their success are due mostly to institutional constraints and to lack of support. They view improvement as the removal of constraints and the addition of support. They are skeptical about new methods simply because they believe that they are well equipped to do the job if proper support were forthcoming. Individualism also contributes to this conservative ethic, because so many judgments about success are reduced to individual judgment. The very nature of life in schools, therefore, tends to promote and strengthen this conservative view, which is very often difficult to deal with when attempting to effect change in schools.

The point to be made from this brief review is that these forces in schools will affect you, too. Regardless of the attitudes you have when you enter teaching, the nature of life in schools will tend to push you in the direction of the attitudes and values just described. To the extent that you understand these attitudes, you have a chance to protect yourself against them if you should so desire.

Characteristics of Effective Schools

An effort was made in the early chapters of this text to define and describe the more effective teacher and distinguish what more effective teachers do that is different from strategies used by less effective teachers. The same kinds of analyses have been made for schools; that is, with the school as the unit of analysis rather than individual teachers and their classes. Indeed, some researchers believe that student achievement and growth can be explained better by a "school effect" than by individual "teacher effects."

> In sum, school effect is more powerful than the teacher effect. This does not mean that individual teacher behavior is not a critical determinant of the quality of teaching and learning. It merely means that the school as a total environment has the capacity to elevate or depress individual teachers' capacity for effective or ineffective teaching. (Edmonds, 1983, p. 78)

In this research field, effectiveness is judged much as it is in teaching research; that is, by the achievement of students in the school and various indices of the quality of their behavior and their social/emotional growth. If the character of the school you teach in has the potential to make you a more or less effective teacher, then it is in your best interests to understand what makes a school effective and how you might make your school more effective.

The characteristics that define effective schools are amazingly similar to those that define effective teachers (Mann & Lawrence, 1981).

1. Principals provide strong leadership and are assertive and direct, but still provide support for teachers. They communicate high, yet realistic expectations for teachers and students.
2. Teachers are task-oriented, feel responsible for student achievement and growth, and maintain learning-oriented classrooms.
3. The school atmosphere is orderly and highly disciplined, with strong morale among teachers and students.
4. The instructional emphasis is on clear learning goals. There is both pressure and support for achievement and excellence.
5. Student progress toward these learning goals is carefully monitored. Student work is frequently evaluated.

There appears to be a consistent belief underlying all of these characteristics: All students can learn and achieve if we—the teachers and staff—create and maintain a climate conducive to achieving those goals. This belief tends to pervade the teaching and administrative staff, so much so that it can be seen and felt when visiting such schools. This is typically what is meant when the term *school climate* is used.

Effective schools view discipline as a school-wide issue rather than as an issue for the individual classroom and individual teacher. In effective schools there are school-wide rules and consequences, and these are enforced consistently from class to class and from one teacher to another. The elementary physical educator teaches and enforces the same rules as the second grade classroom teacher in an elementary school; the secondary physical educator enforces the same rules as the math teacher.

Rules and their enforcement lie at the heart of effective school-wide discipline programs. Box 14.2 "Characteristics of Effective School-Wide Discipline" shows the way rules are developed and enforced in effective schools.

258

Learning about
Schools:
Transition from
Student to
Teacher

14.2 Characteristics of Effective School-Wide Discipline

How rules are developed and enforced, and how they are treated by teachers in the school, determine the effectiveness of a school-wide discipline program. The following characteristics can typically be seen in the school-wide discipline programs of effective schools.

1. Rules are developed collaboratively with administrators, teachers, students, and parents involved.
2. Consequences for breaking or following rules are also developed collaboratively, with the same groups involved.
3. There is typically a school-wide recognition program for following rules just as there are consequences for breaking them.
4. Rules are publicized widely within the school. Parents are made aware of the rules early in the school year and reminded of them frequently as their support for enforcing rules is sought.
5. Procedures are developed for consistent enforcement of rules among teachers and staff, as well as for consistent application of rewards and punishments related to rule-following and rule-breaking. Some form of due process to protect student rights is part of the procedures.
6. The rules (and their consequences) are treated as curricular issues. Special orientations are provided to incoming students and transfers.

The physical educator will have special rules for the gymnasium and activity spaces, as well as special rules for some activities, such as gymnastics or archery (see Chapter 6). These rules must be taught and enforced within the general guidelines suggested by the school-wide discipline program. Your credibility as a beginning teacher will probably be more highly related to your managerial and discipline skills than to your teaching skills. If you want the support of your teaching colleagues and the approval of your administrators, then developing your own managerial system *and* knowing and strongly supporting the school-wide discipline program will be a major priority.

Surviving in the Organization

To grow and prosper in schools, first you have to survive. You have to earn tenure. You have to learn how to handle the work load—and enjoy it, too. There is no one set way to survive in schools. The first level of survival is wanting to stay in the profession. From 20 to 25 percent of the teachers who enter schools each year leave after their first year! For whatever reasons—often very complex and sometimes having little to do with the teaching experience itself—they do not survive. They choose to leave.

A second survival point is tenure. Granting tenure is usually a decision made by school administrators after the third year of teaching. At that point your fate is in the hands of a principal or some other administrator.

No single set of suggestions should be taken as complete when discussing how to survive in the organization of the school. Tumin (1977) has suggested some "rules" for surviving in schools. They are included here because they are realistic in terms of what is known about life in schools and because they are practical.

1. Don't make big fights over little matters. You cannot exert real influence until you have credibility. You will not achieve credibility if you challenge every point made by a colleague. Don't be afraid to challenge—just make sure it is an issue for which it is worth putting yourself on the line.

2. Until you are tenured, let more experienced teachers take the lead in matters that are viewed as adversarial by administrators. Schools are conservative organizations. Administrators do not take kindly to people they view as "troublemakers." You can help. You can express yourself. But try to do so in a way that allows others to assume the major leadership roles—at least until you have tenure. Then you can become more assertive and active.

3. Administrators tend to judge you in terms of your loyalty to them and the manner in which you contribute to goals they see as vital to *their* success. It would be nice if all administrators were first of all concerned with how well you are teaching. Some are. Many are concerned, but not as much as they should be.

4. Do not burden administrators with unnecessary problems. They have enough problems dealing with budget, school boards, and parents. If you are always transmitting your problems to your administrator, you will probably be viewed as someone who can't handle the job.

5. Conduct an orderly class. Administrators often have difficulty distinguishing creativity from chaos. Far too often they see orderliness and assume that a great deal of learning is going on. As you know, both perceptions can be inaccurate because they confuse classroom or gymnasium climate, management of student behavior, and management of learning tasks. It helps here to know your administrator—or at least the degree to which he or she tends to confuse those elements of classroom life.

6. If colleagues and administrators are going to form negative judgments about you, make sure it's over something important. Teachers are not different from other people. They gossip. They make value judgments on trivial matters. They attribute major personality and character defects to people who dress or talk differently from the way they do. Every local school exists in a community that has norms and standards of behavior that are considered to be acceptable. You will survive more easily to the extent that you can accommodate those local norms. Of course, if the norms violate a principle that you feel is really important, then of course you should hold your ground and be willing to take the consequences.

260

Learning about
Schools:
Transition from
Student to
Teacher

7. Don't make snap judgments about your colleagues, and try not to deal in stereotypes. Older teachers are not always conservative. People who dress differently than you do are not always "out of it." Administrators are not always people who have no real interest in students. If you do not want colleagues to stereotype you, then don't do it to them.

8. Don't expect all teachers to share your views on the right way to do things. You have just come from a preparation program where you have, hopefully, learned the latest approaches to teaching and to curriculum in physical education. Some of your colleagues will have been prepared in a different program, one in which perspectives on teaching and curriculum might have been very different. You will need their help and support. You cannot hope to get it by unduly criticizing their approaches or by implying that they are "out of touch" and that you have the real truth.

9. Try not to learn from teachers who have retired on the job. You will soon encounter teachers who do very little—or at least as little as possible. They may have burned out—only to retire on the job. They may be victims of role conflict and may have chosen coaching as their major priority. They may be disillusioned. You will no doubt wonder how they continue on in the organization, but every organization has them and an organization with a guarantee like tenure probably has more than most. Don't imitate them!

10. Don't develop patterns of teaching primarily to "get in" with students. Every suggestion in this text can lead you to more productive, positive, humane interaction patterns with students. But such interactions are done to promote learning and student growth, not to gain acceptance in the student culture. Friendly, surely. Warm, of course. But do it as an adult.

11. Try to avoid taking on roles for which you have no expertise. You are unlikely to be an expert in all things. This is especially true for roles as counselor and analyst. Students go through developmental stages that can be fraught with problems. If students have real problems, they should be referred to the appropriate person who can provide the relevant help. Learn to distinguish between those problems for which you can provide legitimate help and those where your involvement might be counterproductive, both to the student and to yourself.

12. Be very careful when you attempt to be a change agent. It is to be hoped that every new teacher will try to bring some change to the school in which he or she first works. This has always been one of the most important sources for continuous change and updating in schools, the infusion of new ideas and strategies that accompany new teachers. But be careful about how you do it. Make sure that the change is in the best interests of the students and not just your own personal trip. Realize that schools are highly resistant to change and particularly so to new educational fads. Innovations have come and gone from schools with great rapidity over the past 10 years—and schools have stayed remarkably the same. To be a change agent, you have to have credibility

and support. Change is seldom brought through adversarial strategies. Every change tends to imply that the status quo is not good enough. Someone will have some of him- or herself invested in the status quo you will be trying to change. Be careful!

If all these suggestions tend to rub you the wrong way or tend to offend your sense of "being yourself," then you had best look carefully at the kind of school you want to become involved with for your first job. You can be yourself in every truly important way if you survive! You can effect change if you do it through the organization. But you cannot impose change on unwilling colleagues. That just isn't the way schools work.

Providing a Safe and Responsible Physical Education

A major responsibility for the new teacher is to ensure that students have a safe environment in which to learn. Remember, you are *responsible* for the students entrusted to you when they enter the gymnasium. That responsibility cannot be assigned to anyone else, nor is ignorance of some part of that responsibility a valid argument against being held accountable for safe teaching.

It is a fact of life in America that the judicial system has played an increasingly important role in the work of all professional persons over the past several decades. We have become accustomed to hearing about "medical malpractice," and it now appears that we are in the beginning stages of legal suits brought against teachers for "educational malpractice." It is increasingly important, therefore, that new teachers understand the issues related to legal liability in teaching as well as legal principles related to education that affect teachers. Box 14.3"Terms and Concepts Related to Legal Liability for Teachers" shows definitions of important legal terms related to teachers' liability issues.

Physical educators have always been conscious of legal liability because they work in settings in which there are potential safety hazards. Trampolines, ropes, obstacle courses, bats, shots, arrows, and other pieces of equipment can be hazardous unless used and supervised properly. Teachers have always been cautioned to establish safety rules, to instruct students carefully in the proper use of potentially dangerous equipment, and to use good safety techniques such as spotting properly in gymnastics.

What is new is a tendency to sue not only because of specific safety considerations but also because students were not provided with proper prior instruction—thus the educational malpractice. Spotting improperly is one thing. But not providing the necessary progressions for a student to safely take part in an activity is an entirely different matter. It opens up to judicial scrutiny the planning and teaching efforts of teachers. You should take this very seriously. Being sued for $1 million is no joke. It has happened with increasing frequency during the past few years, and there appears to be no reason to suspect that the trend will not continue.

262

Learning about
Schools:
Transition from
Student to
Teacher

14.3 Terms and Concepts Related to Legal Liability for Teachers

You cannot acquit yourself responsibly as a teacher related to issues in liability unless you understand some basic terms and concepts that are fundamental to laws related to liability.

- *Liability* is the breach of a duty, most often through a negligent act.

- *Negligence* is conduct that falls below an established standard of care to protect others against unreasonable risk. Negligence can occur through acts of commission or omission.

- The *but for* test refers to establishing negligence as a causal factor in injury; that is, the injury would not have happened *but for* the negligent act.

- *Duty* is the responsibility to protect others from unreasonable harm and to avoid acts of omission that produce harmful situations.

- Being a *professional* means you undertake to provide services in the practice of a profession and that you are required to exercise the knowledge and skill typically demonstrated by members of that profession who are in good standing in similar communities.

Risk is typically assigned on the basis of the facts and circumstances involved in the individual situation. In school cases, risk is based on the following practices:

1. The student (person exposed to the risk) is given the highest value.
2. The reason for taking the risk; that is, did undertake the activity voluntarily with knowledge of the potential consequences, or was the student doing what the teacher said to do?
3. The magnitude of the risk, which relates to the potential for physical harm.
4. The utility of the risk.
5. The necessity of the risk; that is, was there some other activity that might have produced the same instructional outcome with less risk?

(Adapted from Drowatzky, 1978)

Parents and students are increasingly willing to use the courts to redress their grievances against schools and teachers. Teachers cannot afford to be ignorant of the basic principles over which schools and teachers are sued. That you "did not know" is no defense!

McDaniel (1979) has recently reviewed the school law principles that appear to have the widest applicability in schools today. Here is a brief explanation of them.

1. *Worshipping in educational settings:* Prayer, worship services, or Bible reading intended to promote a religious belief are prohibited. Any act by

a teacher intended to promote a religion is probably a violation of the neutrality principle that has guided most court decisions.

2. *Academic freedom:* Democracies try to protect freedom of expression, and both teachers and students have been afforded protection in this area. When reasonable judgment has been used, teachers can take on controversial issues. Allowing all sides to be heard seems to be an important consideration in this legal area. Increasingly, courts are protecting free expression in terms of hair length, beards, and symbolic demonstrations such as the wearing of badges, buttons, and arm bands. Controversial literature can be used if teachers can show that they have exercised god judgment and that it is relevant to the topic under study. A typical test is to judge the appropriateness of the literature to the age and maturity of the students.

3. *Engaging in private activities:* Teachers can engage in private activities to the extent that they do not impair teaching effectiveness and they are not illegal. Teachers can write public letters of criticism, engage in public debate, belong to unpopular organizations, and have private lives—all without having it held against them by the school.

4. *Due process:* Teachers are entitled to due process. So too are students. Teachers who deny students due process may be liable to lawsuits. Increasingly, courts are willing to look at issues of unfair punishment for student violations of school rules. Specific guidelines now exist for things such as expulsion from school.

5. *Punishing by using academic penalties:* Schools may discipline students. Academic penalties can be given—but they must be for academic violations, clearly related to the offense. Academic penalties cannot be used for violations of school rules that are nonacademic in nature. Students cannot be kept from graduating or have their grades reduced because they have violated school rules. Grades related partially or solely to attendance are questionable. Academic evaluations should be based only on academic performance.

6. *Corporal punishment:* Some states prohibit corporal punishment entirely. Even in states where it is permitted, local school districts often decide to bar it completely. Where it is used, it must be used according to clear guidelines. The punishment must never lead to permanent injury. The punishment must be fair in terms of the offense and must not be an act of revenge. Schools that want to use corporal punishment should have clear procedural guidelines that protect both the students and the teachers.

7. *Neglecting safety concerns:* Rules for safety should be established and enforced consistently. Teachers are responsible for monitoring student activity so that safety is maintained. Violations of safety rules need to be acted on immediately. Above all, be where you are assigned to be! You cannot supervise adequately if you are not even at the site.

8. *Slandering or libeling students:* Students have rights. Teachers cannot treat students any way they want to and be free from lawsuits. Derogatory terms, ridicule, maintaining the confidence of students, refusing to make

264

Learning about
Schools:
Transition from
Student to
Teacher

subjective judgments of character, and violating student privacy through searches are all areas in which teachers need to be very careful.

9. *Knowing the law:* Again, ignorance is not a permissible defense. Teachers should ask their administrators to make clear what policies and procedures have been developed for the school. The better informed a teacher becomes, the more likely he or she is to avoid situations in which problems might arise. Some of the laws referred to here are for the protection of teachers. Some are for the protection of students.

The Courts

The courts are not "out to get" teachers. In fact, many current judgments have been made for teachers. Recently, the *NEA Reporter* (1980) announced the following judgments, in which teachers were supported by NEA (National Education Association) legal resources:

- A home economics teacher in Texas was awarded $71,000 for back pay, emotional stress, and injury to reputation. The jury decided that her rights had been violated when her school board had dismissed her for circulating an Ann Landers questionnaire.

- A Denver teacher was granted $11,000 by a jury which decided that his activities as an NEA association member had been taken into account as part of his school's decision not to renew his contract.

- A Columbus teacher won a court decision which required that a letter be removed from his permanent file. A principal had written the letter criticizing him for his activities on behalf of a teacher's organization.

- The Montana Education Association won a class action suit against the Montana School Boards Association. The suit required that school boards throughout the state put an end to dismissal of nontenured teachers for vague reasons.

The point is that the courts and the judicial system are not "out to get" anybody—except those who by their actions violate the Constitution. Most educational organizations and teacher's organizations have strong liability protection programs. In some cases, teachers receive liability protection by belonging to their teachers' organization or the local or state educational organization. Liability insurance can also be purchased independently, often as an addition to home owners' insurance. To be without it today is a big mistake.

Why and How Teachers Organize

Teachers organize to promote and protect their professional interests. There was a time in American education when teachers were severely underpaid and completely under control of local school officials. The contract shown in Box 14.4 "The Teacher as an Indentured Servant" is humorous by today's standards, but you should not ignore the implications of school officials being able to control the lives of teachers in ways implied by that contract. Traditionally, individual

14.4 The Teacher as Indentured Servant

Why do teachers organize to bargain collectively for benefits, salary, and professional issues? When you read the provisions of a contract for a female teacher in 1923, the answer will become clearer to you.

Teaching Contract—Tucson Public Schools—1923

This is an agreement between Miss _____, teacher, and the Board of Education of the _____ school whereby Miss _____ agrees to teach in the school for a period of eight months beginning September 1, 1923. The Board of Education agrees to pay Miss _____ the sum of $75.00 per month.

Miss _____ agrees:

1. Not to get married.
2. Not to keep company with men.
3. Not to loiter in downtown ice cream stores.
4. To be home between the hours of 8:00 p.m. and 6:00 a.m. unless involved at a school function.
5. Not to leave town at any time without the permission from the Chairman of the Board.
6. Not to smoke cigarettes. This contract will become null and void immediately if the teacher is found smoking.
7. Not to drink beer, wine, or whiskey. This contract becomes null and void if the teacher is found drinking beer, wine, or whiskey.
8. Not to ride in a carriage or automobile with any man except her brother or father.
9. Not to dress in bright colors.
10. To wear at least two petticoats.
11. Not to wear dresses less than two inches above the ankles.
12. To keep the schoolroom clean.
13. Not to use face power, mascara, or paint the lips.
(Adapted from Tucson *Arizonian*, March 21, 1983)

teachers signed contracts with school districts. The conditions of employment and compensation might differ from teacher to teacher. Women were paid less than men. Teachers in some subjects paid more than those in other subjects. Extra duties might be required of many teachers with no extra compensation. Teachers could be dismissed without any due process or protection.

During the twentieth century, the move toward labor unions and professional organizations dramatically affected teachers. Two major organizations, The National Education Association (NEA) and The American Federation of Teachers (AFT), came to represent more and more teachers. Today, the vast majority of

266

Learning about
Schools:
Transition from
Student to
Teacher

teachers belong to a professional organization that serves as their agent in collective bargaining agreements with school districts (see Box 14.5 "Terms and Concepts Related to Collective Bargaining"). Laws that govern collective bargaining generally operate at the state level. These laws typically recognize teachers' rights to organize and bargain collectively, describe provisions within the school district for teachers to determine which agent shall represent them in bargaining, describe the procedures for bargaining between the teachers' agent and the school board, and describe a procedure to follow should an impasse occur in the negotiations.

14.5 Terms and Concepts Related to Collective Bargaining

1. For collective bargaining to take place, the school board must agree or be required by statute to accept a group or organization as the *authorized representative* of the professional staff for purposes of negotiation.

2. Where a majority of teachers are members of an organization, and no other organization makes a competing claim, the NEA and AFT may agree that the majority organization be granted *exclusive recognition rights.*

3. In a *union shop*, all teachers are required by the collective agreement to become members of the organization and to remain members as a condition for employment.

4. In a *modified union shop*, some teachers might be exempted from the membership requirement.

5. In an *agency shop*, all teachers who do not join the organization are required to pay monthly dues, typically the equivalent of organization dues.

6. The *negotiating team* typically consists of officers of the organization and a negotiating committee. Attorneys and/or consultants can be hired.

7. When the negotiating team and the school board cannot reach agreement on one or more issues, they have reached an *impasse.*

8. In cases of impasse, teachers might seek *mediation* by a state or federal mediation agency, appoint a *fact-finding board* to make recommendations for a settlement, submit to *binding arbitration* by an impartial third party, or decide to proceed with a work stoppage through a *strike.*

What are the collective bargaining laws in your state? What organizations do most teachers in your area belong to? Can teachers strike? How are negotiation impasses solved locally?

(Adapted from National Parent Teachers Association, *The Role of Collective Bargaining in Public Education.* Washington: NPTA, 1979)

It is no longer uncommon to read about teachers striking because their negotiations with a school board have reached an impasse. In many states, strikes by teachers are still prohibited by laws which also allow for the dismissal of striking teachers. Strikes, long a major strategy in labor negotiations in industry, have played an increasingly important role in teacher organizations.

Beginning teachers face several important decisions relative to the teachers' organization in their districts. The first is "Shall I join the organization?" In some organizations, membership will be required because the benefits of collective bargaining apply to all teachers. The second decision is "Shall I actively participate and promote the organization?" This decision will reflect your views of your professional commitment, unions, and collective bargaining. The third decision may be relative to supporting the organization during times of impasse in negotiations. Would you pass out flyers door to door in support of the teachers? Would you picket in support of teachers? Would you be willing to strike? If not, would you be willing to cross picket lines to continue to work? These issues stir deep emotions among teachers and laypersons alike. There is much disagreement among teachers on the degree to which their professional organization should behave like a "union." It is fair to suggest that many parents resent teachers' organizing when collective bargaining issues result in higher tax bills or the threat of strikes disrupts the education of their children.

The result of collective bargaining between the agent for a teachers' organization and a school board is typically referred to as a *master contract*. It covers all of the provisions decided through the negotiation process. Teachers negotiate for many things, including salary, benefits, paid leave, sick days, compensation for extra duties, limits on meetings, limits on class size, maternity leave policies, teachers' rights, grievances, and support for inservice and advanced education.

It is to your advantage to examine the master contract in a district you might join as a teacher. Once you have accepted a job, you should know the provisions of the master contract very well. In most districts, regardless of your own personal views about unions and organizations, your welfare as a teacher is fundamentally bounded by the provisions of that contract.

Summary

1. The formal organization of schools is hierarchical, with clear lines of authority. The organization responds to divergent interest groups.
2. The informal organization of schools has patterns of influence that exist outside and occasionally in conflict with the formal organization.
3. The dominant control of schools is local. Much of what happens is highly visible to the public. The success of the organization is viewed differently by constituent groups.
4. New teachers are quickly socialized into school life. Discipline dominates first year-concerns.

268

Learning about
Schools:
Transition from
Student to
Teacher

5. Beginning physical educators face problems in being isolated from other subject specialists, legitimating their subject field, and taking part in the organizational and decision-making apparatus of the school.

6. Life in schools is dominated by presentism, informality, threats to professional autonomy, individual criteria for success, and maintenance of the status quo.

7. In effective schools, principals provide strong leadership, teachers are task-oriented, the school atmosphere is orderly with strong morale, there is a strong instructional emphasis, and student progress toward learning goals is carefully monitored.

8. Effective school-wide discipline programs have rules and consequences that are developed collaboratively. They also have a school-wide recognition program for good behavior. They provide frequent publicity about the program specifications, support procedures for consistent application of rules and consequences, make available some mechanism for due process for students, and integrate the program into the curriculum.

9. Survival in school organizations requires a sensitivity to the formal and informal mechanisms. You should also be careful in your judgments about when to bring problems forward and careful in judgments about colleagues. Other survival qualities are tolerance for views different from your own, a willingness to participate but only in roles for which you are prepared, and conservativeness in attempting to effect change.

10. Teachers are required to provide a safe and responsible physical education for students in ways that show knowledge of legal liability within the context of teaching physical education.

11. Teachers need to be aware of school law principles and avoid behavior that clearly contradicts them.

12. Most teachers are organized and collectively bargain for salary, benefits, and conditions of work.

13. Issues about being a member of a teacher organization need to be considered carefully with a knowledge of concepts related to collective bargaining.

CHAPTER **15**

Maintaining and Improving Your Effectiveness

For each teacher the question must be, "Is it worth the effort?" Is there enough possibility in a given school setting to encourage the long struggle? If the answer is even "perhaps," that is sufficient, for then we have at least a place to begin. Avoiding professional isolation, taking full membership in the school community, and helping administrators give effective support—those are the steps that can move us through the struggle for excellence.

Larry Locke (1986)

CHAPTER OBJECTIVES

To describe and assess guidelines for surviving the first year of teaching

To describe and assess obstacles in the struggle for excellence

To describe and assess ways teachers cope with obstacles

To describe and assess how effective teachers stay alive with their teaching

To describe concepts and issues related to teacher/coach role conflict

To describe and assess ways the system can be changed to facilitate teacher growth

It has been my aim to present important teaching skills in a realistic manner. The topic of professional role development tests that aim, because it is very easy to slip into quite unrealistic discussions of the professional development of the "perfect" teacher. Too many texts present an idealized portrait of a selfless person dedicated totally to the development of each student, not caring unduly about the financial implications of his or her professional role, willing always to go the extra step with students and colleagues, forever attempting to upgrade his or her knowledge of subject matter, possessing a highly developed service motive to school and community, and embodying the finest qualities of the ideal American citizen. Historically, the teacher has been considered a paragon of virtue in the community, and, from time to time, when people have discovered that teachers are ordinary human beings, the result has often been cruel treatment and dismissal. Fortunately, the past several decades have seen a shift to a far more realistic view of what a teacher is and should be. Indeed, with the rash of teacher strikes that seem to accompany the opening of school each fall, it is common to hear people describe teachers as noncaring, totally mercenary, cynical, and un-American.

As a teacher in training, you know that neither the idealized version nor the totally critical version of your motives is correct. The purpose of this chapter is to help you examine some of the forces that have influenced and will continue to affect your development as a professional teacher, thereby helping you arrive at some realistic assessment of what your professional role is or may become, and what kinds of factors will affect that role as you begin your teaching career.

In teaching more than any other occupation, the trainee preparing for a career suffers from what Ryan and Cooper call "overfamiliarity." The teacher trainee has spent the better part of his or her life in a school. The trainee has known literally hundreds of teachers of all shapes, sizes, and personalities, and has seen dozens of different teaching styles. The problem is that the trainee too often assumes that this wealth of experience has taught him or her all that there is to know about what it means to be a teacher. The fact that he or she does not know all there is to know about teaching may come as a jolt!

> Most of the 200,000 or so new teachers who enter American schools each year receive a rude awakening. Although the routines—homeroom, clubs, bells, books, and ball games—are all familiar to the new teacher, there is much about life in school he doesn't fully appreciate. Most new teachers, for example, have had relatively pleasant experiences as students. If they had not succeeded in school, they probably would not be in a position to become teachers. As a result, new teachers are frequently astounded by how difficult learning is for some children and how unhappy many children are in school. Many students are difficult to reach and apparently unconcerned about learning. Beginning teachers are surprised at the amount of administrative and clerical work that goes with the job. Nor did they realize that good teaching takes so much time-consuming preparation. Another shock for many is the amount of energy, both physical and emotional, teaching requires. Somehow these facets of teaching rarely get communicated to the audience of students. (Ryan & Cooper, 1972, p. 136)

The problems to which Ryan and Cooper refer, as well as other aspects of professional role development, will begin to confront you daily. Listen to the professional matters you hear discussed in the teacher's lounge, at lunch, or during a departmental or faculty meeting. If things follow their natural course, these are the matters that you will become concerned about as you grow into a professional teacher.

This chapter has two themes. The first is the examination and identification of ways in which a teacher can control his or her own performance in the gymnasium and playing field. This theme deals with the continued development and maintenance of good teaching. The second theme deals with exploration of the realities of the professional teaching role. The first theme can be approached directly, and suggestions are made as to how to achieve control over your own teaching performance. The subject is one in which answers can be found and definite statements made. The second theme is quite different. In this text it is approached in an exploratory fashion, without attempts to moralize or otherwise impose on you any preconceived notions of the ideal professional role.

Surviving and Growing in Your School

Skilled, knowledgeable, and caring teachers are among our nation's most valuable resources. Effectiveness and expertise in teaching doesn't just happen—it is the result of a long, sometimes difficult struggle to be good at what you do and to continue to care about the students you teach. The first obstacle in that struggle is the often difficult transition from student to teacher that typically encompasses the first year of teaching. Doing well in your first year of teaching is important not only in terms of the advancement of your career, but also because you must gain satisfaction from teaching if you are to stay involved in the process of becoming a more effective professional.

How do new teachers survive the first year intact and grow into effective, caring physical educators? While there is obviously no formula for professional growth, there is sufficient evidence to suggest some guidelines that deserve to be considered seriously. This evidence, from the study of distinctive teachers (Earls, 1981), excellent secondary physical educators (Templin, 1983), and effective elementary specialists (Siedentop, 1989), as well as profiles of teachers who struggle in difficult situations (Locke & Griffin, 1986), is not theoretical but instead is drawn from the real-life situations of teachers and their reflections on their work. The following guidelines seem particularly relevant to the survival period during the first year of teaching.

1. *Manage well.* Most teachers who fail do so not because they don't know their content well enough but because they don't manage well. The initial impressions that teachers and administrators form about your work are based predominantly on how you manage students. Management and discipline continue to be the problems most often cited by first-year teachers, but the examples of the elementary specialists described in Chapter 14 show that first-year teachers can earn strong reputations in schools by managing well from the outset.

2. *Choose an instructional format you can carry out effectively and efficiently.* To increase your chances of having a good year of *teaching*, you should adopt an instructional format that you know you can do effectively and that will not require an extraordinary amount of extra preparation, either in time or materials. For most teachers this will be an active teaching format (see Chapter 13). Since you will get to teach each lesson several times, because of multiple sections or classrooms at the same grade level, you will have opportunities to improve your teaching on a daily basis.

3. *Communicate your efforts to others.* Much of what students, parents, co-teachers, and administrators learn about your teaching will come from various types of communications. Even though many of these communications are directed at students, others see them, too! Posted gymnasium rules, neatly done pairings for a class volleyball tournament, "I can" posters in elementary schools, a bright, interesting bulletin board on the Olympics, or a list of captain or squad leader responsibilities are all

done for your students but are also *seen* by other students, teachers, administrators, and parents. Together they communicate important messages about your teaching. Direct communications to parents through publications such as a "PE Newsletter" can also be effective.

4. *Make your spaces and programs attractive to students.* It is important that students respect and like your teaching and your program. Developing an attractive environment helps to achieve this goal. If you don't believe this, take a look at the private sector sport/fitness clubs in your area. They are clean, bright, and attractively decorated—fun places to be! People of all ages voluntarily spend their money to go to those places. The programs offered at those places are partially based on "client needs and desires." Although you, as a professional, are required to make judgments about the needs of your students, it is foolish to ignore their own sense of what would be good to do in physical education and to provide a setting that is attractive to them.

5. *Monitor your teaching behavior and students' learning behavior.* Throughout this text there has been an emphasis on how effective teaching skills are related to productive student work. Teacher behavior can be monitored in terms of time or events—how much time in instruction, how many specific feedback statements, how many statements of positive expectations for learning. Student behavior can also be monitored in terms of time or events—how much academic learning time, how many successful response opportunities, how much time spent in transition or waiting. The techniques for observing these phenomena are described fully in Chapter 16. It would be to your advantage to monitor your own classes on a regular basis through self-monitoring, videotaping, or having a non-participating student do the observations. We each form "impressions" as we teach, but there is no substitute for having good data. Also, any supervisor or principal who comes to observe you could not help but be impressed with a new teacher who regularly monitors his or her own behavior, especially if there is accompanying evidence that the data have been used to improve teaching.

6. *Begin to be involved in the formal and informal structures of the school.* No one expects a first-year teacher to take leadership roles, but there is an expectation that you will begin to take part. By taking part, you will learn how the organizations work and what you will have to do to begin to exert influence to improve your own program and the status of your subject matter within the school and district.

7. *Seek a mentor.* Increasingly, school systems are developing mentoring programs where experienced teachers are assigned to provide mentoring services for new teachers. If your district does not have such a program, you might ask, when you are employed, for suggestions as to which physical educators in the district might be willing and able to serve as a mentor to you. Mentors teach you the "ropes" of the organization. They are there when you need them to answer questions and to provide advice. Often, they serve you best by listening and supporting you.

8. *Develop a network.* You should make every effort to learn about and make contact with physical educators in your area who are highly regarded for their teaching and their programs. Most teacher organizations have bargained for "professional days," and a certain number of these will be available to you. One of the best uses of a professional day is to visit an area teacher to see them work and discuss issues with them. Not only are these visits valuable, but the contacts are even more important because they can help you develop a network of colleagues that can serve to combat the isolation physical educators typically experience.

The suggestions listed above represent a *pro-active* approach toward survival and professional growth. I believe such an approach is necessary. As Box 15.1 "Poor Teachers Are Made, Not Born!" argues, teachers need to be as much in control of their programs and their own teaching situation as is possible. Control, however, is not simply given to you. Increased control over your program and your teaching situation is typically earned by doing the kinds of things suggested above.

Obstacles in the Struggle for Excellence

Most teachers enter the profession expecting that they will teach well to begin with and continue to develop their effectiveness as they gain experience. They no doubt see themselves improving gradually but surely from their initial point as a first-year teacher to some future point as an experienced teacher. Even for those who do grow into excellent teachers, however, the line of improvement from novice to effective veteran is seldom straight. There are sometimes periods of "flatness" where little improvement is seen. There are occasionally periods of "regression" where the teacher is less effective. Many of the flat periods and regression periods are due to obstacles that stand in the way of growth toward excellence. There is evidence that these obstacles will occur in the careers of most physical educators. The degree of severity of these obstacles will differ from district to district. In some cases, the obstacles will be so severe that the teacher and program become debilitated. In other cases, the obstacles will be less formidable and will often be overcome with individual initiative from the teacher. What follows are the six obstacles to professional growth and program excellence that seem most prevalent and serious.

1. *Isolation.* It has been shown consistently that many physical educators suffer from professional isolation, an insufficient number of contacts and amount of time with other physical educators, and, in some cases, with adults in general. Bill, a mid-career elementary specialist thinks about program ideas but has no opportunity to discuss them with others in the district.

> I don't even know how many physical education teachers there are in the district. I never see the other elementary teachers unless I call them to say "Hi." I *never* see the high school teachers, and I don't know what they're doing there. The children come back (to visit) and give me some idea, but I really don't know. (Schwager, 1986, p. 43)

15.1 Poor Teachers Are Made, Not Born!

American teachers have often been criticized for their lack of initiative and their seeming willingness to "give in" in the face of pressure. In 1904 John Dewey criticized what he saw as teachers' "tendency to intellectual subserviency." In 1936, in the book *Are American Teachers Free?* Howard Beale charged that American teachers are "dominated by cowardice and hypocrisy." In 1970 Charles Silberman, in his influential book *Crisis in the Classroom*, said that "what is mostly wrong with the public schools is not due to venality or indifference or stupidity but to mindlessness."

Vincent Crockenberg (1975) has argued that critics have misunderstood the nature of the problem in schools—that the focus should not be on the teachers as people but rather on the organizational characteristics of schools, the conditions under which teachers work. He suggested that "teachers are denied the conditions necessary for the development of mind because of the way in which schools are organized and controlled" (p. 189). Crockenberg argued that teachers will continue to "give in," to act mindlessly, until they gain significant control over the determination of school practices and school policies. He concluded his argument with the following analysis:

If teachers are to overcome mindlessness, if they are to teach purposefully and intelligently, they must be allowed to work in a context where they do not simply act on the purposes and decisions of others (often unseen others). They must be allowed to formulate their own purposes, initiate their own actions to further those purposes, and then modify their purposes and their practices in the light of the consequences. (p. 196)

To be a professional is to be in control. Physical educators have the opportunity to make these kinds of decisions—if they want to badly enough! Teachers are not inept—but the context within which they work often tends to produce mental dullness over the years. If you know that this is a possibility, then you can guard yourself against it. It all depends on what kind of a professional teacher you want to be—poor teachers are most often *made*. They were not born that way.

Eleanor is a veteran teacher in a large district with very few resources and little support. She never sees the district physical education coordinator and hardly ever has contact with other physical educators. The district has inservice education each month, but Eleanor stopped going long ago because principals never focused on physical education. Eleanor is alone! Within the limitations of her context, she teaches what she wants, when she wants, how she wants—a set of rules that provide a kind of autonomy, but at a substantial price.

> Digging a little deeper, however, there are several consequences of playing by these rules that affect all the players. The flip side of Eleanor's autonomy is isolation. Because Eleanor rarely interacts with other physical educators, has never been evaluated, and has no "home base," she is left to solve all her problems alone, relying only on her own resources. (Griffin & Locke, 1986, p. 41)

As long as physical educators remain isolated in their work, the chances for them to improve the conditions of their work and the degree to which their subject matter is valued remain very low.

2. *Lack of teacher and program evaluation.* Does this surprise you? You may think of "evaluation" mostly in terms of testing and grading. Try instead to think of it in terms of incentives, recognition, and collaborative program improvement. When you do that, you will see how a lack of evaluation can be a serious obstacle to growth, individually for the teacher and for the program as a whole. Eleanor had been in her district for 18 years and had never been evaluated! In some schools there is periodic evaluation, but it is too often less substantive than it should be, based too much on generalities and social relationships than on effective teaching and program development. The result of such perfunctory evaluation is that expectations are low and there is little recognition for truly effective teaching and programming.

Susan is by most standards a truly excellent physical educator. Her situation is not unusual—she is highly valued as a person and gets good evaluations, but few of her colleagues know what really goes on and little support is provided for improvement.

> Susan's students experience excellence in the teaching of each class, but the rest of the world pays scant attention. Although her principal says, "Susan's great," there is little evidence that he knows what she does that is so wonderful. Certainly there are no clear standards or high expectations used to inspire the other physical education teachers who have worked at the school. (Lambdin, 1986, p. 37)

High standards for physical education and strong support for teachers and programs cannot happen without evaluation. Lack of strong, substantive teacher and program evaluation stands as a real obstacle to professional growth.

3. *Boredom and routine.* Teaching is one of the few professions where one's job description does not change across the years. Veteran teachers with 20 or more years of experience are likely to have identical assignments to first-year teachers. The sameness of assignment from year to year produces a numbing routine that often results in serious boredom. The boredom too often translates into reduced effectiveness and what is called "teacher burn-out." The truth is that many teachers are "bored-out" rather than "burned-out." Many teachers who face the obstacle of boredom overcome

it not within their profession but outside it. Kim, a 15-year veteran, who has had an effective program and great enthusiasm for teaching, has changed over the past several years.

> For two and one-half years, Kim has maintained a part-time business on weekends and during the summer months. Though she originally began moonlighting simply to generate extra income for her family, she now finds her second job more fulfilling because it provides both the challenges and rewards she once found in teaching. (Faucette, 1986, p. 45)

Many physical educators find this challenge and reward not in a job outside the profession, but instead in coaching school sport teams. The role conflict created by this widespread practice is examined in detail later in this chapter.

Bill, the veteran mentioned above, has taught six classes a day in the same school for 15 years. The school staff has not changed in over a decade, and Bill finds himself still the youngest teacher on the staff. When asked what the toughest part of his job is, he responds: "Fighting boredom." His reaction is not unique. Instead, it represents a common obstacle to professional growth in physical education.

4. *Lack of administrative support.* Many physical educators experience a frustrating lack of administrative support for their programs. Even among effective physical education teachers who are highly regarded by their principals, there is a lack of support when it comes to their programs rather than themselves as persons.

> They often questioned the value of their input when decisions were made by the administration that seemed to have ignored their expressed concerns. It seemed that while the veterans were respected by their principals, this respect was for them as persons and professionals and did not automatically transfer to respect for their subject matter. Despite the prestige of its advocates, physical education was not considered to be of central value when tough curricular decisions were called for. (O'Sullivan, Stroot, & Tannehill, 1989, p. 264)

Susan, described earlier, reflects a sadly typical situation, having worked hard to overcome many obstacles in the improvement of her program, but being unable to seriously affect what she saw as the largest obstacle.

> Susan has overcome many hurdles and has improved the teaching situation in many ways, but she has not been able to overcome the most important barriers to her own success and her students' learning. She is blocked by the lack of real support for physical education in the school and by isolation from the administrative decisions which create the day-to-day reality of her workplace. (Lambdin, 1986, p. 37)

When physical educators choose not to become involved in the formal and informal organizations of the school, the results described above are inevitable—and somewhat deserved. The sadder note is that even when physical education teachers do become involved, the results are sometimes disappointing.

5. *Context factors.* For many physical educators, obstacles to professional growth are found in classes that are too large, facilities that are old and in disrepair, inadequate equipment, and a yearly budget that is too small to begin to change any of those factors. These context factors often make it impossible to deliver a sequential curriculum that is devoted to student learning. They often result in a series of compromises at best and a total abandonment of learning goals at worst. Eleanor, who had experienced nearly all of these context obstacles, now does a day-to-day curriculum in which each lesson forms a unit, hoping that children enjoy themselves and experience some success each day.

> Eleanor has learned to cope with the system as it is. She no longer believes the system can be dealt with rationally about curriculum and instruction issues. She has learned that she cannot change the system; she must accommodate to it. Eleanor has identified what she believes she can and cannot change and has adjusted her priorities and goals to match these realities. Having abandoned progress as a concept, Eleanor doesn't try to teach a sequential curriculum of activities focused on skill progressions and student learning. Instead, she has worked hard to gain control over the aspects of her day-to-day work that are within her power to direct. (Griffin, 1986, p. 40)

The hope for quality, daily physical education for children and youth remains a vision for the profession. It must seem like a romantic fairy tale for many teachers who struggle with serious context obstacles in their day to day work.

6. *Lack of legitimacy for the subject matter.* Griffin (1986) has argued that lack of care and concern about the subject matter underlies most of the obstacles described above and is made manifest by the system's lack of responsiveness to these obstacles.

> To summarize, unresponsiveness is a consistent thread running through the systemic obstacles identified. In most cases, the schools did not intentionally limit what could be accomplished in physical education. Instead, they practiced benign neglect. The tendency of everyone to ignore physical education presented what seems to have been the most formidable obstacle to excellence. (Griffin, 1986, p. 58)

Mr. P's situation is not unusual. He is well respected as a teacher. The school administrators speak highly of his work. Parents seem satisfied with his program. Students appear to like him. Everyone seems happy, even though examination of the program reveals that little learning takes place and that physical education has become mostly a supervised recreation period.

Students at this school do not actively dislike physical education, but it is largely a social activity. They appear to tolerate the physical demands in order to secure the social time. The program asks very little of students in terms of motor skills, and close observation confirms that they give very little in return. The program reflects precisely what people in the school and the surrounding community hold as expectations for physical education. Mr. P is an accurate and sensitive judge of what will work smoothly within such a system. It is not an accident that everyone seems satisfied. (Rog, 1986, p. 56)

If those around you are willing to tolerate this level of effort, especially those who control budget and curriculum, then it is little wonder that many physical educators eventually succumb to this obstacle of neglect and allow their lessons to become socially oriented recreational periods.

Coping with Obstacles—Staying Alive in Teaching

The obstacles described above no doubt differ in degree and quantity in each school. How teachers respond to the unique set of obstacles they encounter as they attempt to grow professionally will also differ from person to person. Some teachers quit! Estimates are that 30 percent of all new teachers don't make it to their fifth year of teaching (Rosenholtz, 1987). While there are many reasons teachers leave the profession, no doubt many of them feel as if the obstacles to successful teaching are too formidable.

Other teachers stay in the profession and continue to hold a teaching position but gradually give up on trying to achieve real learning goals—what we have referred to as the *nonteaching teacher*. Some teachers don't give up on teaching their students, but have to compromise in ways that goals are reduced or altered. These teachers are what Griffin (1986) referred to as "tinkerers,"—those who direct their energies to making changes in their teaching to accommodate the obstacles they can't change in their own situation. Still other teachers overcome most of the obstacles and grow as effective teachers, often developing unique and highly valued programs in their schools.

It needs to be noted that the above characterizations are as much or more about the obstacles teachers face than about the teachers themselves. Some teachers who compromise would not do so in less difficult situations. Many teachers who overcome the obstacles in their settings might have quit or become nonteaching teachers under other circumstances. Many who are successful tinkerers would have developed into highly effective teachers under less difficult circumstances. What follows are brief descriptions of how teachers cope with obstacles.

1. *The nonteaching teacher.* Simon is a 15-year veteran physical educator, popular with his students, admired by his colleagues for his managerial skills, and trusted by the parents of his students. His classes are always well

behaved. When Simon began teaching, he was full of enthusiasm for student learning, but the struggle to improve his teaching situation has changed him.

> Maintaining a high level of student cooperation has required some compromises. Simon values a warm, relaxed atmosphere in which neither he nor the children have to struggle with difficult tasks. To accomplish that goal, he finds it inappropriate to press too hard for less salient objectives such as skillful performance, physical fitness, conceptual learning, and student accountability for intensive engagement in learning tasks. Physical educators like Simon exert great energy in attempts to improve the quality of their programs, but eventually their passion cools and they learn simply to cope with what is, rather than struggle for what might be. (Tousignant, Brunelle, & Morency, 1986, p. 52)

There is an important point here. Nonteaching teachers typically keep children busy, happy, and good. In many cases their gymnasiums and play spaces are filled with well-behaved, active students. Many who see these settings, including school administrators, mistake what they see for sequential learning. Closer analysis, however, reveals that students do not have to learn to earn a high evaluation. More typically, students have to be on time, dress appropriately, behave well, and appear to be cooperating in the activities. If they do this, they earn a high grade (Tousignant & Siedentop, 1983).

Many teachers who compromise to the point of nonteaching find satisfactions in other work. Some hold second jobs outside education. Many other physical educators seek and find their satisfaction in coaching. The role conflict created by the coaching and teaching assignments no doubt contributes to their tendencies to compromise their teaching and their striving for important learning outcomes. Role conflict will be addressed later in this chapter.

2. *The tinkerers.* Many teachers react to obstacles by changing what they can change and learning to live with what they can't change. This typically requires them to adjust their goals for their program and their approach to teaching. Bill, battling boredom at midcareer, tends to change the activities in his program often, choosing activities that include a lot of action and motion, but not a lot of equipment. He "psyches himself up" and tries to do the same for his students. He knows that he is not accomplishing all that can or should be accomplished in physical education.

> Bill performs his job as teacher in response to the demands put upon him. He is praised and rewarded for doing exactly what he is doing. Even though he has much more to offer, no more is expected of him. By the usual standards of our profession Bill is a successful practitioner, but there is little satisfaction in that achievement. (Schwager, 1986, p. 43)

Eleanor, described earlier, faced a situation that is about as bad as it gets. She had compromised for what she called "lesson-units," a new activity each day. Yet within those lesson-units her students got good activity, learned to behave well and cooperate, achieved some limited success, and enjoyed themselves. And, within all these limitations, she continues to care for her students and derive satisfaction from them.

> On the contrary, Eleanor loves her job. Observations of her teaching confirm this impression. In a system where it seems no one cares, she has a remarkable reservoir of energetic, good-natured, patient, and caring interactions with children that extend from the first class in the morning to the last one in the afternoon. (Griffin, 1986, p. 41)

3. *Those who overcome the obstacles.* There are many excellent physical education programs in our schools, at all levels. I have argued elsewhere (Siedentop, 1987) that a consistent factor in exemplary programs at all levels has been the leadership of a dedicated, skilled physical educator. I also believe that one key to the success of these programs has been their ability to secure administrative support. Kim, described earlier, is a highly competent teacher who had worked for two kinds of principals. One she described as a "dictator who treated me like a bootcamper" (Faucette, 1986, p. 46). The other had facilitated the growth of her program and helped her to become a viable member of a team of teachers, all working to enhance the program goals of the school. That experience prompted Kim to suggest that a good, fair principal is a teacher's strongest ally. In the next section, we shall consider some of what has been learned about physical educators who are highly effective, those who have stayed alive in teaching despite the obstacles.

How Do Effective Teachers Stay Alive with Teaching?

Most of this text has been about effective teaching. The purpose of this section is not to describe what effective teaching looks like—you should already have a clear understanding of that—but instead to examine how effective teachers have stayed alive and continued to struggle to improve their effectiveness and their programs. As before, there is no suggestion that all of these characteristics and strategies apply equally to all effective physical educators, only that they appear to represent common themes among teachers in varied contexts who have managed to stay alive despite the obstacles.

1. *Being motivated by student accomplishments.* Physical educators who stay alive with their teaching tend to like students and are rewarded in many ways by how students respond to their programs. Job satisfaction is often equated with how much students learn—a finding highlighted in a year long study of seven effective elementary specialists.

Children were the major source of satisfaction for our seven specialists, as revealed by several examples throughout the monograph (i.e., "kids make me feel important," or the joy of hearing children tell "what they learned in gym today"). These teachers are committed to what they do, as reflected in Missy's statement, "I'll fight the system to do what is best for my children." (O'Sullivan, Stroot, & Tannehill, 1989, p. 265)

281

How Do
Effective
Teachers
Stay Alive
with Teaching?

The flip side of this motivation is that successful teachers find rude, uncaring students to be major sources of dissatisfaction, which may partially explain why these teachers all seem to be strong managers and consistent, effective disciplinarians.

David is a successful high school physical educator and coach who teaches both regular classes and classes for students with disabilities. His own search for excellence in teaching is clearly reflected in how he reacts to students who also begin to realize their own potential.

For David, some of his most satisfying moments come when students see their improvement, feel the accomplishment, and are proud. His successes—and his proud students are many—students with no running experience build up to and complete the mile run without walking; an adaptive student turns on to golf, archery, or fencing by pursuing it on his/her own time; a special student once afraid of height walks the length of the balance beam. It is rewarding to observe the growing pride and involvement of David's students as they strive for their individual excellence. (Mancuso, 1983, p. 26)

The important point here is that teachers who stay alive not only like children and youth, but also like them *as teachers should*: as young persons and as learners who achieve and strive to improve. Their satisfaction derives not only from what they see happening on a day-to-day basis but also from the awareness of their long-term impact on the lives of their students (Earls, 1979).

2. *Not having to deal constantly with discipline problems.* Every study of effective physical educators shows that they all are strong class managers and effective disciplinarians. The important point here is that staying alive with teaching is nearly impossible if discipline problems dominate your teaching day. The elementary specialist study cited above showed virtually no off-task behavior in any of the seven teachers' classes. Reports of excellent teachers nearly always begin with descriptions of their well-run classes (see Templin, 1983). The description of Sandy, a female teacher in an inner-city high school, is very much like that of others in different contexts.

Sandy teaches a prescribed curriculum in health and physical education. For them she has specific goals and high standards, designing developmentally sequenced learning tasks. There is little time wasted in transitions, standing around, complaining, or in so-called free play. Her lessons, both in health and physical education, are businesslike and purposeful. Her pace during class is vigorous. (Goldberger, 1983, p. 21)

Most of these effective teachers discipline well, but do so within a positive climate for learning. As mentioned several times throughout this text, there is no evidence that effective teachers are negative or abrasive with students. Quite to the contrary, the bulk of evidence shows they are quite positive. However, they do not tolerate disruptive behavior, and they are quick and consistent in dealing with it when it does occur.

3. *Staying alive with program and teaching.* In many cases, it appears that teachers who overcome obstacles do so partially by staying alive with changes in their own approaches to teaching or by developing a unique program. Sandy developed a PSI teaching program in a desegregated, inner-city high school (Tousignant, 1983). Sue got involved with making her teaching of high school classes more equitable (Woods & Dodds, 1983). Nearly all reports of such teachers emphasize how jealously they guard time and how conscious they are of using each moment of class wisely, which shows they have examined their own teaching in terms of its managerial implications.

One of the ways physical educators stay alive is to develop programs that reflect their points of view about their subject and how it should be taught. Many of these teachers develop "main theme" programs (see page 168). While these teachers believe that the programs they develop meet student needs—and there is no reason to doubt that they do—it is also no doubt true that the programs reflect personal interests and enthusiasm. The three veteran teachers in the elementary specialist study had all gradually developed their programs over time so they represented some particular theme. Gary developed a strong adventure education focus in his curriculum. Chris did most of her sport teaching using the sport education model (see page 172). Bobbie focused often on "Olympism" both in activities chosen (Team Handball, Rhythmic Gymnastics, for example) and in special events (an Olympic assembly, winter Olympic play days).

It doesn't seem to matter whether the focus is fitness, sport education, adventure, or social development. What matters is that the physical educator is developing a program he or she truly believes in and that this project captures their imagination and sustains their enthusiasm for teaching.

4. *Working within the system.* Much of what effective physical educators accomplish can be attributed to having worked in the formal and informal school organizations to the point where they have achieved a substantial status, which brings their programs more attention and more favorable administrative support. They also pay attention to parent and community groups in ways that gradually earn support for their efforts. They have paid their dues by taking part and by doing it effectively. The special programs

cited above don't just happen. They typically require support—financial support from the community, parents' groups, and school budgets, and administrative support on issues such as scheduling.

Duane and Anita were secondary physical educators who had a dream of developing an ideal weight-training facility and program for boys and girls (Kneer, 1983). They solicited donations from private sector weight clubs, involved students in fund-raising projects, applied for and won grants from private foundations, got local print shops to donate workout cards, had a local community office put mirrors on the walls of the new facility, and finally got the school administration to agree to remodel the spaces necessary to produce a first-class facility. They eventually achieved their dream—and then some! The facility was opened to the community. Self-instructional videotapes were produced to individualize instruction and workouts. Computers were purchased to instruct students and to keep records. The program became widely known and highly regarded and brought much exposure to the school, which in turn created even more favorable community, parent, and administrative support. It can happen!

5. *Drawing the line.* Does a long-term commitment to effective teaching in physical education require that your entire life be devoted to your professional endeavors? Not only is the answer to this question a clear "no," but studies of distinctive and effective veteran physical educators reveal that they tend to draw a clear line between their professional commitments and outside interests. Earls (1979), in a study of distinctive physical educators, found that they engaged in summer activities that were entirely different than teaching, allowing them to come back to the start of each school year refreshed and ready to go. The veteran teachers in the elementary specialist study referred to earlier each had extensive involvement with activities outside the school. These outside activities seemed to be a positive force in their professional and private lives.

> These teachers do not allow their involvement with outside activities to adversely affect their teaching or their program. On the contrary, it seems to have had quite the opposite effect in all three cases. Outside interests have provided the veterans with many rewards. All three veterans have "drawn the line" about doing a good, solid professional job and "consuming themselves" with it, which none of them do. Their outside interests act to re-energize them, albeit for reasons that are highly specific to each individual, for the demanding work of teaching and their role as teachers. (O'Sullivan, Stroot, & Tannehill, 1989, p. 265)

Staying alive with teaching, it would appear, is related to a full and satisfying outside life that serves to invigorate and refresh the teachers so they can return to their school responsibilities with the energy and enthusiasm to continue the struggle.

Role Conflict

Physical education teachers are often also employed as coaches (see Box 15.2). Far too often, indeed, men and women are hired first of all for what they can coach and only secondarily for their teaching expertise. It is probably true that many undergraduate physical education majors have coaching as their first interest and teaching as a secondary interest (Locke, Siedentop, & Mand, 1980). For these students, teaching on a daily basis is a secondary career choice.

A case has been made in this text for the fact that teaching, when well done, is a complex set of actions that requires the full attention and devotion of the person doing the teaching. When this difficult role is placed against a person's role as a coach, the result is often a serious case of role conflict.

A role is defined as a pattern of expected behaviors for a specific position in some segment of society (Locke & Massengale, 1978). Each of us has been in a student role and a son or daughter role. Some of us have been in roles as parents, teachers, and coaches.

Three kinds of role conflict are particularly bothersome in physical education. Interrole conflict exists when one person occupies different roles that require incompatible patterns of behaving. A physical educator experiences interrole conflict when practice interferes with a teacher's meeting, when scouting interferes with family obligations, when planning for practice interferes with planning for daily teaching, and so on.

Intrarole conflict occurs when one person must respond to incompatible expectations from different people or groups. Thus, a coach must deal with some parents who want only to win and with others who see school athletic participation as a developmental experience. The teacher must deal with those who expect a "fitness first" approach and those who are most interested in group sport skill development.

Finally, *load conflict* refers to the incompatible expectations that arise from the combined loads of teaching and coaching. This conflict often interacts with interrole conflict, especially when the person is away from home often, is under psychological stress, and becomes physically exhausted from the sheer length of the work day. Teacher coaches often arrive at school between 7:30 and 8:30 A.M., teach a full complement of classes, and begin coaching at 4:00 P.M. The practice session might end at 5:30 or 6:00, but by the time that equipment is put away and students have showered and left the premises, the coach usually cannot leave until 7:00. During a competitive season, this hectic schedule may be made even worse by scouting trips and away game travel dates.

The roles of teaching physical education to regular students during the day and coaching athletes in interscholastic sport teams differ in a number of important ways (Locke & Massengale, 1978). The two roles most often differ in terms of the relevance of each to the professional's career advancement. The two roles tend to differ in the level of technical preparation and competence perceived necessary for successful entry. There certainly seems to be a difference in the way in which people view the need for continuous upgrading of expertise in the two roles. Conventional wisdom supports the notion that the requirements of daily preparation differ in the two roles. Certainly, in one of the roles, the person's

15.2 How Real and Prevalent Is Role Conflict?

Chu (1981) studied teacher coaches and reported that 87 percent felt that their school administrations compelled them to coach in order to maintain their positions as teachers. One teacher coach put it this way:

> I think it is assumed that if you're in physical education, you are responsible for coaching teams. If I gave up the varsity baseball job, I would probably lose the physical education position. There was one guy who refused to coach because of the low extra pay and they took him out of physical education and made him a permanent driver's education teacher—the administration, the principal did that. (p. 40)

A majority of subjects in this study also indicated that they would have to "put up with" teaching physical education classes in order to coach.

Segrave (1981) studied 267 teacher coaches and reported that 62 percent of the total sample indicated coaching as the preferred role rather than teaching. For those who had been varsity athletes while in college, 71 percent indicated coaching as the preferred role. For those who had not been varsity athletes, 53 percent indicated coaching as the preferred role.

Massengale (1981) suggests that teacher coaches are seldom fired for teaching inadequacy, yet demonstrated skill and competence in teaching seldom compensate for coaching a losing team. Noncoaching teachers do not work under the unequal reward system that so strongly affects the lives of teacher coaches. Thus, they seldom can appreciate the conflict experienced by the teacher coaches.

The answer to the question is that role conflict is very real and is prevalent in American schools.

performance is regularly evaluated, often by people who become very much involved themselves in the performance (other students, parents of students, administrators, and so on). Regular evaluation of performance entails general agreement as to what constitutes good performance in at least one of the roles.

The students served in the two roles also tend to differ. They tend to be homogeneous in one and heterogeneous in the order. They are always volunteers in one and seldom in the other. They have different levels of skill, the one group being an elite group in the school. The kind of contact the person has with students in the two roles differs markedly. In the one, the contact is often with large numbers for short periods of time, in a fairly relaxed and not very intimate setting. In the other, the contact is frequent, with large amounts of time devoted to it, and the teacher coach shares important kinds of experiences with the students that are intense and often intimate.

As you might have guessed, the roles seem to be very different, with a much more powerful set of contingencies applying to the coaching role than to the teaching role. Although this does not always hold true (one must always be careful not to stereotype individuals), the general picture of these differences seems to be strongly in favor of the coaching role as the dominant role. The differences can be characterized as shown in Table 15.1.

It needs to be stated again that this characterization does not hold true for all physical education teachers. But it does fit the traditional stereotype of the "coach" who "rolls out the ball" during his or her instructional responsibilities and generally loafs through the day, only to turn into a human dynamo at athletic practice. It has often been said that the interscholastic coach does the best job of teaching in the school and the physical educator the worst job—*and they are the same person!* Table 15.1 explains why that stereotype is sometimes accurate:

Table 15.1 *Differences Between the Roles of Teacher and Coach*

Role Characteristic	Teacher	Coach
1. Relevance of role to career advancement	Low	High
2. Technical preparation required for successful entry	Low	High
3. Need for continuous upgrading (clinics, etc.)	Low	High
4. Requirements for daily preparation	Small	Large
5. Frequency of public evaluation of performance	Seldom	Often
6. Emotional involvement of evaluators	Low	High
7. Consensus about desired outcomes of performance	Low	High
8. Extent and intensity of contact with students	Low	High
9. Homogeneity of students worked with	Low	High
10. Degree of voluntarism among students	Usually low	Always high
11. Motivation of students worked with	Differs greatly	Mostly high
12. Skill level of students worked with	Differs greatly	Highest in school
13. Intensity and intimacy of contacts with students	Mostly low	Often very high

Locke and Massengale (1978) found this caricature to be more accurate than inaccurate:

It is clear, however, that load conflicts and teacher/coach conflicts constitute widespread and intensively experienced role problems for the teacher/coach. In the case of load conflict more than one half and in the case of teacher/coach conflict nearly a third of all respondents judged those problems to have "great" or "very great" significance.

Furthermore, their data indicated that role conflict for the physical educator coach was higher than for the classroom teacher coach. The literature on role conflict indicates clearly that when conflict exists, people tend to select one role as the major role. They then use the demands and expectations of this role to provide the basic framework within which they make decisions about the other role(s). If a teacher coach chooses coaching as the dominant role, then he or she makes decisions about teaching within the framework of expectations and needs of the coaching role. The teaching role becomes secondary and the time and effort devoted to it become more and more commensurate with its lowered status in the person's life. The literature also suggests that making decisions about the relative priorities of the two roles tends to reduce the tension and anxiety that was created by the role conflict.

Although the official policies of the school suggest that teaching is the top priority, the facts seem to indicate that the realities differ considerably from the official rhetoric (see Box 15.3). Massengale (1981, p. 51) has made the following observation based on a review of the available evidence: "For all practical purposes, it appears that most teacher coaches fail to resolve their occupational role conflict, attempt withdrawal, and then make a large commitment to the coaching portion of the role and a small commitment to the teaching portion." This commitment to coaching is often tacitly encouraged by departmental or

---

15.3 Coaching Interscholastic Sport Teams: The Pay Is Low and the Hours are Long

The most common method for reimbursing teacher coaches for the extra work they do as coaches is to provide them with supplementary pay through a supplementary contract. Chu (1981) reports that teacher coaches in his study received between $1.74 per hour and $0.32 per hour for the time they devoted to their coaching. It appears that the average pay for a coach is somewhere near $1.00 per hour for the time he or she puts into the coaching assignment—not exactly a get-rich-quick strategy!

How much time do they spend? The following data from the Chu (1981) study indicate the imbalance of time devoted to teaching and coaching:

Hours During the Coaching Season

	Males			*Females*	
Class Contact	*Class Preparation*	*Coaching*	*Class Contact*	*Class Preparation*	*Coaching*
18.4	2.7	44.2	18.8	4.1	27.2

Hours During the Noncoaching Season

Class Contact	*Class Preparation*	*Coaching*	*Class Contact*	*Class Preparation*	*Coaching*
18.4	2.7	2.5	18.8	5.4	3.7

One interesting point in these data is the fact that teachers and coaches do not seem to devote more time to preparation for their teaching in their noncoaching seasons.

school administrators through the adjustment of assignments (Templin, 1981). For example, coaches are often assigned a "planning" period during the final period of the official school day. Although planning periods are supposed to be used for the preparation of teaching, everybody clearly understands that the teacher coach will use it to prepare for the day's practice session. Teacher coaches are also often given study hall or hall duty assignments in lieu of classes with the understanding that the lightened responsibility will give them time to plan for practices, review films, and attend to other aspects of their coaching assignments.

That is not a pretty picture. It is believed to be an accurate picture. And it is most probably related to the current phenomenon in teaching known as *burnout*—the point at which the total demands of being a professional educator exceed the abilities and resources of the person to continue productively in his or her many roles.

There is no answer to role conflict in physical education. The most desirable solution would be a different pattern of staffing in schools, one that would allow those who are primarily interested in teaching to do that, without having to worry about "saving themselves" for an afternoon practice. However, to expect such a dramatic shift in staffing patterns in the near future is unrealistic. Perhaps the best that can be done now is to sensitize future teacher coaches to the problems of role conflict and to impress on them the need to sustain a responsible teaching effort. To provide only this knowledge and some "cheerleading" about a continued effort in teaching will not do the job. If dual roles are to continue to be the status quo, then strong accountability mechanisms for good teaching need to be developed in American schools.

Improving the System

Education has been under attack, for one reason or another, for many years. Will schools get better? Most of us will respond to that question with a quick yes simply because we have been raised to believe that things do get better and because we no doubt believe that we can help them to become better. But improvement does not *necessarily* occur with the passage of time. Schools may get worse, public support may continue to wane, programs and facilities may continue to deteriorate, dissatisfaction may become more widespread, and critics may become even more vocal and strident. It is only when this latter view is taken seriously by each of us that we can begin to think seriously about improvement.

The new teacher has always been a major source of improvement in schools. The new teacher brings new ideas, a fresh enthusiasm, and infectious optimism. But there are fewer new teachers each year than has been typical for most of this century. Teachers tend to stay longer in their positions simply because economic conditions have decreased their mobility. Lack of funds in local districts has caused administrators to cut back on teaching staffs, often leaving vacated positions unfilled. Still, there is much the new teacher can do to improve schools *if* he or she decides that effecting change is part of being a professional teacher. As Ryan (1970) has argued forcefully, the chances for change are small if new teachers do not seize the opportunity:

The first year of teaching is the beginner's initiation into the profession. Like other initiation rites, whether into the role of infantryman or fraternity man, it is a period of intense learning and also a trial. . . . In particular, initiations make defenders and believers. This is true of the first year teacher, too. Having passed the test . . . the survivor is no longer as critical of the system. This allegiance to the status quo is particularly unhealthy at this time. Presently there is a growing awareness within the larger community that the schools need fundamental changes if they are to be a vital force in the lives of our children. If the beginning teachers are not the agents of reform, the chances for real change are small. (p. 190)

The major problem with this scenario is that most first-year teachers have not *prepared* to be change agents! Without the skills necessary to effect change, the first-year teacher tends to be less effective than would be possible if he or she had some developed change skills and some experience as a change agent.

Can our schools get better? Of course they can! As Goodlad has suggested, however, it will not happen without the leadership of educators; that is, we shouldn't expect that anybody is going to make schools better for us without our direct involvement.

Our schools can and should be better. But educators must take the lead, together, to make them so. Large numbers of parents and students are ready to join us, I believe, in making our schools, one by one, better places in which to live and work. The slogans for improvement are, for the most part, rhetoric. Our schools must be reconstructed, one by one, by citizens and educators working together. Nothing less will suffice. (Goodlad, 1979, p. 9)

Aside from their individual efforts to continue to struggle to overcome obstacles to excellence in physical education, teachers must work persistently to develop *systemic mechanisms* which facilitate professional growth. The point here is that the *system* has to change so it is more facilitative of teacher growth and program development. What follows are brief descriptions of four important changes in the education system that would help to achieve this goal.

1. *Principals trained to evaluate physical education.* Evaluation is a key ingredient in the development of teachers and programs. Therefore, it is important that those who evaluate physical education teaching and programs be better educated about good programming and effectiveness in the motor skills and fitness area.

2. *Induction and mentoring systems.* Learning to teach effectively is a long process of which preservice teacher education is just the initial phase. Many experts consider the first several years of teaching—referred to as the *induction years*—as crucial to the long-term success of teachers. Mentoring programs, where new teachers are paired with veteran teachers, would do much to ease the transition to teaching and reduce the anxieties that are encountered in the early phase of teaching full time. Mentoring and induction systems would be even more effective if first-year teachers could be given a reduced load, providing time to

engage in the kinds of activities that would better ensure their growth as teachers.

3. *Staff development.* Most professions have ongoing programs of inservice education that require members to stay abreast of latest developments in their fields and to continuously upgrade their professional skills. The tradition in teaching has been to accept college and graduate school credits as evidence of professional development experience. Teachers must have more specific programs of staff development that are keyed to their particular subject matter. Staff development tends to work best when it is a collaborative effort among teachers and administrators in a district, rather than a program decided by administrators and imposed on teachers.

4. *Collaborative work.* The idea of professionals working together to help each other, often cutting across institutional lines, is a good idea that has been difficult to achieve. There are, however, several good examples of collaborative models in physical education. The "Second Wind" program sponsored by the University of Massachusetts offers collaborative staff development for individual teachers, for the physical education staff in a school, for the entire K–12 physical education staff in a district, and for networks of teachers that cut across districts (Griffin & Hutchinson, 1988). The focus of the staff development can be teaching improvement or curriculum development. A different model was developed from Teachers College, Columbia University (Anderson, 1988), bringing together administrators and physical educators from six school districts to form a Physical Education Program Development Center. Program development is the main focus of this collaborative effort, and the involvement of administrators makes it an appealing model.

Teachers work best when they are in better control of the forces which affect their teaching. As Box 15.1 "Poor Teachers Are Made, Not Born!" argues, poor teachers develop that way in response to conditions. The systemic improvements described would create conditions for professional growth that can empower teachers to gain better control over the factors that tend to curtail program development and teaching effectiveness. Teacher empowerment, however, must be accompanied by accountability for performance. As we move into the 21st century, it appears that mechanisms for providing greater accountability in education will be more prevalent. If this occurs, it is imperative that educators work together to create conditions for teachers that provide them with work conditions within which they can perform to meet the new accountability.

Summary

1. The typical teacher trainee has been successful in school and suffers from overfamiliarity with school experience that provides a false sense of knowing about teaching.

2. New teachers enhance their chances of surviving and growing in their career by managing well, choosing an initial instructional format they can be successful with, communicating their early efforts to others, making their spaces and programs attractive, monitoring their behavior, and involving themselves in the formal and informal structures of the school.

3. Obstacles in the struggle for excellence for physical education teachers include isolation; lack of evaluation; boredom and routine; lack of administrative support; contextual factors such as poor facilities, class size, and inadequate equipment; and lack of legitimacy for the subject matter they teach.

4. Obstacles force some teachers to leave the profession, while others become nonteaching teachers or tinkerers, or find ways to overcome the obstacles.

5. Effective teachers who persist in developing their careers and programs are motivated by student accomplishments, manage so well that discipline problems become infrequent, stay alive by trying new teaching and program approaches, work within the school system to gain support for their programs, and find satisfaction in nonschool activities.

6. Physical educators who also coach often suffer from role conflict, of which there are three kinds—interrole conflict, intrarole conflict, and load conflict.

7. Teaching and coaching roles differ in a number of ways. Rewards for coaching are typically far stronger than those for teaching.

8. Continuing role conflict typically leads emphasizing time and effort in one role at the expense of the other role.

9. The education system is mostly likely to improve by changes in systemic mechanisms that facilitate professional growth, such as: principals trained to evaluate physical education, induction and mentoring systems, subject-specific staff development programs, and collaborative work with other professionals.

CHAPTER 16

Instruments for Measuring Teaching and Its Outcomes

To recapitulate, recording is the terminal event of a complex series that begins with defining the response class of interest, proceeds through observing, and culminates in creating a permanent record of the behavior....The permanent record that remains after defining, observing, and recording have taken place is the only evidence that measurement actually occurred, and the quality of the entire process cannot exceed the characteristics of that record.

J. Johnston & S. H. Pennypacker (1980)

CHAPTER OBJECTIVES

To define *reliability* and explain its importance in systematic observation

To explain strengths and weaknesses of traditional methods for assessing teaching and its outcomes

To explain and provide examples of systematic observation methods

To combine observation methods into a system to accomplish a specific purpose

To explain the steps necessary to develop an observation system

To explain how observers are trained

To calculate the reliability of observational data accurately

To differentiate among purposes of various observation systems

To observe teacher and student behavior reliably

Teaching skills will improve to the extent that trainee teachers have a chance to practice specific skills and get reliable feedback about progress toward goals. To expect such improvement without feedback is wishful thinking. The research literature in teacher education is not very helpful when it comes to the outcomes of intern experiences such as student teaching. There is no evidence to defend the proposition that merely putting trainee teachers into a real setting will *automatically* improve their teaching. Quite to the contrary, there is evidence to support the notion that the teaching skills of student teachers actually (in terms of the skills emphasized by the training program) deteriorate.

For teaching skill to improve, there should be goals, feedback on a regular basis, and a chance to improve. This implies that practice teaching experiences need to be supervised, at least in the sense that the experiences must be observed and data collected in order to provide feedback for the trainee teacher. But supervision must also include the *systematic* collection of data if it is to be useful. Supervision that is done intuitively, with little more than note taking to collect data, is unlikely to be powerful enough to account for improvement. That is not just an opinion. It is a statement of fact backed by a substantial body of research. The research on traditional forms of supervision is so dismal that Mosher and Purpel (1972, p. 50) concluded their review of it with the statement that "the inescapable conclusion to be drawn from any review of the literature is that there is virtually no research suggesting that supervision of teaching, however defined or undertaken, makes any difference."

In recent years it has become clear that teachers can improve their teaching, often dramatically and quickly, when they have specific goals to reach, when their teaching is observed, and when they receive regular feedback based on those observations (Siedentop, 1986). A similar research literature with similar results exists in a number of areas, including counselor education. All of these advances have occurred as a result of wider use of systematic observation instruments. The number of instruments now available is substantial, so much so that a textbook focusing solely on instruments for various purposes in physical education and sport is available (Darst, Zakrajsek, & Mancini, 1989).

The Reliability of Observational Data

Reliability in observational data collection is of great importance. The term *reliability* has many meanings in scientific literature; in this text it is defined as the degree to which two people, using the same definitions, looking at the same person, at the same time, record the same behavior. Why is reliability important? Suppose that a peer or instructor observes your teaching during the first week of a teaching experience and records the behavioral interactions and feedback statements you make to your students. This becomes your baseline performance. Suppose another observation is taken the next week, and your interaction and feedback rates are considerably lower. Now the question is "Who changed—you or the observer?" If the observer changed (perhaps interpreting the definitions differently or perhaps just not being as accurate), then you will get misinformation and maybe even a poor evaluation. That is why it is important for the data collected on teaching to be reliable—so that it can reasonably be assumed that the data reflect faithfully what actually happened during the teaching episode. This chapter discusses techniques for collecting reliable information on teaching.

Most data gathering in science is accomplished by automatic recording systems. Exercise physiologists automatically record the heart rate of subjects prior to, during, and after exercise. The behavior in this case is the heartbeat, and it is made observable by placing electrodes on the skin and transmitting the impulse to a machine that continuously and automatically prints out the fluctuations in heart rate. Kinesiologists collect data on action of the muscles in much the same way. These data are accurate and reliable and provide a convenient permanent record of some crucial aspects of human behavior. But the behaviors of importance in teaching cannot be recorded by transmitting impulses via electrodes. Most often the behaviors in question must be observed by another human being. It is probably true that most socially significant behavior is seldom convenient, in that it is not easily observable, and this lack of convenience creates measurement problems that often demand the use of human observers.

When one human is used to observe the behavior of another human it is important that steps be taken to ensure the reliability of the observations. If psychology has told us anything in the past 50 years, it has told us clearly that the facts and our perceptions of the facts may differ considerably. If I observe your teaching skills, I may be viewing them from my history of experience and interpret things differently from the way someone else would. If during subsequent observation sessions I detect some change in your teaching performance, it is important that steps be taken to assure that the change occurred in your teaching performance and not in my observations. As you well know, we all have a tendency to see what we want to see, and we are particularly susceptible to the influence of suggestion. If your cooperating teacher tells your supervisor that you have "really improved" in some aspect of your teaching, all evidence indicates that your supervisor will tend to see you as improved whether or not any change has occurred. Therefore, it is important to collect data that give reliable evidence of your progress and are not susceptible to the whims of suggestion or the distortions of perception that so commonly plague inadequate observation systems. Methods for assessing the reliability of observations are presented later in this chapter.

Traditional Methods for Assessing Teaching

For many years teacher educators and teaching researchers attempted to assess teaching and its outcomes through a variety of methods such as intuitive judgment, eyeballing, anecdotal records, checklists, and rating scales. In teaching research, these methods have long been abandoned because they were shown to be unreliable and not valid as measures of teaching. But for some reason they are still widely used as methods for gathering data on teaching for supervisory purposes. Even though experts and texts consistently caution against using such methods, they are still used more often than is systematic observation. The main features of these traditional methods and their shortcomings are described as follows.

Intuitive Judgment

The method of *intuitive judgment* implies that an experienced supervisor, knowledgeable about teaching, watches a teacher teach and then makes a careful, overall judgment about what was seen. The intuitive method implies a wealth of knowledge about teaching research and about the realities of daily teaching in schools, all brought to bear on the events of a teaching session in such a way as to be able to evaluate it sensitively and usefully. This global approach to supervision is simply inadequate if it is the main method used. Trainee teachers do not need overall estimates as much as they need specific information. Also, intuitive methods tend to focus far too much on the teacher and not enough on the students. Intuitive judgment becomes useful only when it is used as an addition to a systematic observation methodology.

Eyeballing

The most common form of feedback used in preparing teachers is what I refer to as *eyeballing*. The supervisor or cooperating teacher simply watches you teach for a period of time. No notes are taken, no checklist is used, no data are recorded. After the session, the supervisor discusses the teaching performance with you. Some very specific incidents may be brought up. Some very valuable information may be brought to your attention, but it is unlikely that any information will be passed along that will help you improve your teaching skills systematically. As an observation method, eyeballing is very susceptible to errors in perception due to misconceptions, previous history, or suggestion. Far too often feedback generated from eyeballing is insignificant and is useless for improving teaching skills.

Eyeballing can be a a valuable technique if it is used in addition to a systematic method of observing and recording behavior. Eyeballing has potential value because the observer is usually a trained professional, a master teacher, who can see complexities of interaction during teaching that are too subtle to be picked up by a systematic observation program. But if eyeballing is the primary observation source from which feedback is generated, then it is unlikely that a sufficient amount of reliable information will be made available to you.

Anecdotal Records

If an observer keeps notes on what goes on during an observation session and uses these notes to discuss the session with you, the system is referred to as the use of *anecdotal records*. Anecdotal records are a more extensive and reliable method of eyeballing. The observer relies exclusively on general perceptions of what is going on, but these perceptions are written down. This assures that valuable information will not be lost during the observation session. It provides a much sounder base for conducting an interactive feedback session. Depending on the thoroughness and complexity of the note taking, this can be a valuable source of information for precisely the same reasons that eyeballing can be valuable; that is, the person taking the notes is usually an experienced professional who can see the sometimes subtle and complex elements that contribute to a successful teaching performance.

Anecdotal records suffer from the same problems that plague eyeballing. The fact that a piece of information is written down does not ensure that it is an accurate perception of what is going on. Furthermore, it is highly unlikely that information generated through anecdotal records is sufficiently precise to allow you to gauge your progress toward highly specific goals. Anecdotal records appear to have their greatest potential when used in addition to the systematic observation format that generates precise information on well-defined performance categories.

Checklists and Rating Scales

In the past the most common method of systematic observation was the use of checklists. A *checklist* is a list of statements or characteristics about which an observer makes a judgment. The judgment is often a yes or no decision. Sometimes it involves use of a scale so that the space between the yes-no points is graded to allow for a range of possible responses such as *often, sometimes, infrequently, never.*

The checklist method has one dubious advantage and a number of very serious drawbacks. The advantage is that it provides the appearance of a true data-based approach to the improvement of teaching skills. By using a checklist as a terminal evaluation instrument, the supervisor is giving a pseudo-scientific wrapping to a very casual approach to evaluation. If the checklist is used in successive observation sessions as a learning tool rather than strictly as a terminal assessment tool, the same advantage is gained. The benefit gained from the use of checklists is derived primarily by the supervisor; it provides a false sense of security, the illusion that the feedback given the intern is based on some hard evidence rather than mere eyeballing.

Checklists are **notoriously unreliable**. The statements or characteristics on the checklist are not defined sufficiently to ensure reliable observations. To make a rating on the initiative shown by an intern is virtually impossible unless the characteristic labeled *initiative* is defined so that the intern, the supervisor, and other interested parties have some common understanding of its meaning and some examples of initiative and lack of it.

Rating scales are often thought to be more precise and sophisticated if they involve a large number of choice points. The rating scale shown here has nine choice points ranging from always to never.

Always 1 2 3 4 5 6 7 8 9 Never

This kind of rating device is **highly unreliable**. The illusion of greater precision and sophistication is gained at the cost of reliability. The fact is that the fewer the choice points, the more reliable the ratings. However, this is balanced by the fact that fewer choice points provide less precise information. One is left with a dilemma: a choice between reliable, imprecise information and more precise yet less reliable information. Neither is acceptable as a primary data collection format for a program that is serious about helping interns improve their teaching skills.

Rating scales are useful when information generated from simple choice points is of sufficient value to help improve teaching skills. In this case, rating scales are quick, efficient, and reliable. Checklists are useful for recording tasks completed. They serve as good reminders of the number of tasks to be completed, the nature of those tasks, and the time at which they are completed. But this use of checklists is little more than record keeping and should not be seen as a substitute for actual data collection.

Systematic Observation Methods

The systematic observation of teachers teaching has revolutionized teaching research and has led to important discoveries about the nature of effective teaching (See particularly Chapters 2 and 3). Systematic observation is the foundation on which teaching research has been built. It should also be the foundation on which teaching skills are developed. Systematic observation is simple to do—it requires only some basic understandings and a little practice. The data produced through systematic observation become the information used to help teachers to improve. In most cases, a simple summary of the raw data is all that is needed. No sophisticated statistical analysis is necessary. Adding, subtracting, and dividing are all that is required to develop very meaningful and useful information about teaching. The primary techniques of systematic observation are event recording, duration recording, interval recording, group time sampling, and self-recording.

These methods for observing and recording behavior have been used extensively in many areas of research dealing with human behavior. Having been used extensively, their reliability is well demonstrated. These methods are included also because they are easy to learn and easy to use. They require no apparatus more sophisticated than a tape recorder or a stopwatch. They have been used reliably by researchers, teachers, and students (Siedentop 1981).

Reliable use of these methods depends a great deal on how well the various performance categories are defined. Given adequate definitions, the methods are easy and reliable. They can usually be learned in one or two practice sessions. Most difficulties in using the methods arise more from problems in definition of performance categories than from technical errors associated with the observation systems.

Event Recording

Once a performance category has been defined adequately, it can be observed most simply by making a cumulative record of the number of discrete instances that it occurs within a specified time period. This results in a frequency count of the events as they occur (Hall, 1971). Your supervisor may record the number of your positive interactions with students. Your cooperating teacher may count the number of times students break specified class rules. You may count the number of trials that two students have at a skill during a class session. Event recording produces a numerical output that can easily be converted to a rate per minute. The value of converting to rate per minute is that performances from different occasions can be compared because they are classified in common units—that is, rate per minute.

Event recording is one of the most useful methods of collecting meaningful data; any action or reaction of a student or teacher and any aspect of interaction between student and teacher that can be defined can be measured by counting the number of times it occurs. Concepts such as cooperation, competition, competitive effort, sportsmanship, and aggressiveness can be given new meaning by defining them in terms that can be observed and then by counting them as they occur.

Event recording can be done continuously; that is, several categories of teacher behavior can be observed via event recording for an entire teaching session. The length of a session is easily determined, and the data can be converted to a measure of rate per minute. Often it is too time consuming and fatiguing to do event recording for an entire session. Also, other observations may need to be made. A valid measure of teacher behavior can be obtained by doing event recording for a short time period and repeating it at intervals throughout a teaching session. For example, it is usually quite satisfactory to do 3-minute periods of event recording and to do five such intervals in a teaching period. If the five recording intervals are spaced throughout the period, a valid sample of the teacher's behavior is gained even though only 15 minutes of the session are devoted to the data collection. This concept of sampling behavior rather than recording it continuously is important to any data-based approach to the improvement of teaching.

Duration Recording

Event recording is useful if the most meaningful understanding of a behavior can be gained by having some idea about the frequency with which it occurs. For example, one way to better understand the efficiency of a learning environment is to have some idea about the number of trials that students need to practice a skill. Event-recording intervals placed periodically throughout a session give valid and reliable information that can be seen as number of trials per minute.

Sometimes, however, the frequency of a behavior does not yield the most useful information. Suppose that you want to get some measure of the degree to which a student is participating in your class. The first task would be to define participation and nonparticipation. It would not be appropriate to use event recording to study participation. One single participation (an event) might last for a long time, and another single participation (another event) might last for a short time. To know that two events occurred would not help you understand a student's rate of participation. It would be far better to record the amount of time a student spends in activity that you have defined as participation. A stopwatch could be turned on and off according to a student's participation; the resulting cumulative time would be the most accurate measure of participation.

Duration recording uses time as a measure of behavior. The raw data derived from duration recording is expressed in minutes and seconds. A student might participate for a total of 21:30 in a 30-minute class (21 minutes and 30 seconds). These raw data can be converted to a percentage figure that permits comparisons among students and among various sessions. The data are converted by dividing the total time of a recording session into the time derived from duration recording. The resulting measure is expressed as a percentage of total time spent in participation.

As with event recording, it is often inefficient to do duration recording continuously for an entire teaching session; samples can be done with duration recording. Three 5-minute samples of duration recording spaced periodically throughout a teaching session provide valid information about the percentage of time spent in any defined behavior. In this case the percentage figure is derived by using the total time of the recording intervals rather than the total time of the class. The output is still in percentage of time spent in a defined behavior category.

Duration recording is useful for any behavior category in which the length of time spent engaged in the behavior provides the best estimate of the importance of the behavior. This is true for both teacher behavior, such as the amount of time spent giving instructions to the class, and student behavior, such as the amount of time spent in managerial activity or participation.

Interval Recording

Another technique for providing meaningful data on teaching is interval recording. The term *interval recording* refers to observing behavior for short time periods (intervals) and deciding what behavior best characterizes that time period. For example, the total time period might be divided into 10-second intervals. In the first interval, the teacher is observed. In the second 10-second interval, the observer records the behavior category that best represents what he or she just observed. In interval recording, consecutive intervals are used to first observe and then record. Intervals should be small, usually no longer than 20 seconds and sometimes as small as 6 seconds. The observation interval does not have to be of the same length as the recording interval. Usually, the recording interval can be shorter, especially, as observers grow more skilled or when a small category system is used in which fewer decisions are necessary.

The data generated from interval recording are expressed as a percentage of intervals in which each behavior occurs. However, because the intervals represent a precise measure of time, the interval technique can also be used to estimate time involvements. Interval recording has the advantage of being highly reliable. The instructions as when to observe and when to record can be preprogrammed on a cassette and the observer cued through an ear jack on the tape recorder.

Interval recording has been used successfully to observe teacher behavior, student behavior, and measures such as academic learning time. Observers should strive to use as short an interval as can be and still have reliable data. The only problems usually encountered using interval techniques are when the intervals are so long that several behaviors can occur and the observer has a difficult time deciding which behavior to record. A short interval (6—12 seconds) normally avoids that problem. If a 10-second observe and 10-second record interval system is used, there will be one data point gathered every 20 seconds, three per minute, and 90 per 30-minute teaching episode. The total of 90 data points is usually sufficient to ensure the validity of the behavior being observed; that is, what is recorded faithfully represents what actually happened in the setting.

Group Time Sampling

One technique used to gather periodic data on all members of a group (typically a class or specific subset of a class) is *group time sampling.* Group time sampling has also been referred to as *Placheck recording* (Planned Activity Check). At regular intervals throughout the observation session, the observer quickly scans the group and counts the number of students engaging in the behavior category of interest. This scan typically takes no more than 10 seconds, even for a fairly large class. A smaller group could be scanned in 5 seconds. Once a student is counted, the observer does not return to that student even if her or his behavior changes. The goal is to observe each individual at a moment in time and to record the number of the total group engaged in a particular behavior category. Behavioral observations for categories such as effort, participation, productivity, and appropriate behavior lend themselves well to the group time-sampling technique. Periodic measures of criterion variables such as academic learning time could also be taken in this way.

The group time-sampling method is used as follows. The observer always scans in a specified direction, usually from left to right. A specified amount of time is taken for the scan (usually 10 seconds). However, this is dependent on the total number in the group, because with larger groups progressively more time is required to complete the scan. The number of people engaged in the behavior category is counted. It is always easiest to rate the behavior category in which the fewest are engaged. For example, if you are rating productive and unproductive behavior, and most students are engaged in productive behavior, it is easiest to count those engaged in unproductive behavior. The number engaged in productive behavior can be calculated simply by subtracting the number engaged in unproductive behavior from the total. Again, it is best to convert these raw data into a percentage figure. This is done by noting the size of the total group and dividing the total into the appropriate figure. Thus, a percentage of students engaged in productive behavior can easily be calculated by dividing the total number of students into the number engaged in productive behavior.

Group time samples should be spaced periodically throughout a class session. Because they take only 10 seconds to complete, they need not prevent the observer from doing other observations during the time between intervals. Eight group time samples spaced evenly through a 40-minute session will take only 1:20 of observation time (1 minute, 20 seconds) yet they will yield valid information concerning the behavior of the group.

Self-Recording: Producing Data Regularly

Data on teaching and its outcomes can be collected as a regular part of the teaching process. Chapter 12 showed examples of how students could record their own performance, both the number of attempts (a process measure) and the actual performances themselves (outcome measures). Performance on routine practice tasks can be recorded on a lesson-by-lesson basis. For example, the basketball shooting task poster shown on page 230 is a routine task that could be used to produce a daily record of shooting performance. The same could be done for gymnastics stunts completed, the amount of time to complete a fitness circuit, or daily performance "bests" in a track and field unit.

Teachers can also self-record behaviors that are important to them. In Chapter 15, I indicated that producing a regular record of important teaching behaviors was a positive growth strategy for new teachers. This can be done in several ways that do not detract from your teaching. For example, you could use a small tape recorder to record your verbal behavior. You could later listen to it and systematically analyze it for a number of important variables such as prompts, use of student names, behavior statements, and skill feedback statements. Chronographs are so inexpensive and popular now that you can easily keep track of how time is spent in a class, using divisions such as instruction time, management time, and practice time. Tallies of events can be kept on clipboards or in a notebook. Some teachers have used wrist counters (typically available in golf stores) to tally events.

Many schools are equipped with video equipment, so it is sometimes possible to tape a class and then analyze it in a number of ways. It is very helpful, when videotaping, to have a wireless microphone to wear so that your voice comes through clearly on the videotape.

Combining Observation Techniques in One System

The choice of an observation technique should make sense in terms of the behavior being observed. Feedback from a teacher to a student is best observed with event recording—the most meaningful measure of feedback is either as a rate (number of feedbacks per minute or per a 30-minute teaching lesson) or as a ratio (percentage of total feedbacks that were delivered accurately or percentage of total feedbacks that had specific information content). Useful information about feedback can also be developed through an interval format. But duration recording doesn't give useful information about feedback. Knowing the length of a feedback interaction doesn't tell us much about it.

Student learning opportunities can be gauged as a measure of time using duration recording or interval recording. Thus, total amount of time spent in active learning is a very meaningful piece of information. So too is the percentage of intervals in which a student was engaged in academic learning time. Student learning opportunities can also be observed through event recording, accrued by counting the number of trials per 30 minutes that occur among members of a class.

Variables such as student on-task behavior can be observed in a number of ways, through event recording (number of instances of off-task behavior), duration recording (percentage of total time spent on task), interval recording (percentage of total intervals spent on task), or group time sampling (percentage of students off task). The choice of which one to use will most often be dictated by considerations such as reliability and economic use of the observer's time. The goal should be to get the most reliable data possible with the most efficient use of the observer's time (using less time to get reliable data on on-task behavior leaves more time to observe something else).

Many observation systems incorporate more than one kind of observation technique. This can be done quite easily through sampling the various behaviors in question. The goal should be to sample them regularly and to have the samples spread out across the entire time period. If all the teacher behavior data were collected in the first 15 minutes of a teaching episode and all the student behavior data in the second 15 minutes, the data would not yield a true picture of what went on throughout the entire period. It is much better to sample a small amount of teacher behavior, then move to student behavior, then back to teacher behavior, and so on throughout the entire observation period. For example, the following 4-minute cycle of observations uses event recording for teacher behavior and group time sampling for student on-task behavior and student learning time:

10 seconds	Group time sample number of students off task
10 seconds	Record
10 seconds	Group time sample number of students in ALT-PE
10 seconds	Record
20 seconds	Rest
60 seconds	Event record teacher behavior
10 seconds	Group time sample number of students off task
10 seconds	Record
10 seconds	Group time sample number of students in ALT-PE
10 seconds	Record
20 seconds	Rest
60 seconds	Event record teacher behavior
4 minutes	Total time

With this format, the 4-minute cycle could be repeated seven times in a 30-minute observation period, leaving 2 extra minutes for rest. The seven cycles would produce fourteen group time samples for off-task behavior, fourteen group time samples for academic learning time-physical education, and fourteen minutes of event-recorded teacher behavior data. Because each cycle was distributed well across the total time, together they represent a very faithful picture of what actually happened.

This is all accomplished with just one observer. That observer is aided tremendously (and the data made more reliable) if the particular patterns of observe and record are preprogrammed on a cassette tape with simple cues such as "Observe student off-task behavior," "Record student off-task behavior," "Begin one minute of teacher behavior event recording," "End teacher behavior event recording" and "Begin one-minute rest." An ear jack should be used so that the cues are heard only by the observer and therefore are not intrusive in the setting where the observations are taking place. Ideally, a very small tape recorder could be placed in a pocket, so that the entire apparatus would be as unobtrusive as possible. The tape recorder should be battery powered so that the observer is free to move about. Batteries should be checked often so that the time intervals on the tape are as accurate as possible.

By sampling behavior rather than observing it continuously and with the development of multitechnique observation systems, the amount of information collected by one observer can be substantial. This observer can be an instructor, a peer intern, a helping student, a cooperating teacher—or the teacher him- or herself, if the session is videotaped.

Important Decisions in Developing an Observation Strategy

An observation system should serve a specific purpose. Often, a teacher, or students and faculty in a teacher education program, may want to produce information on a few specific teacher or student variables. If so, a small, specific system should be tailored to the goals of the experience. On other occasions, a more comprehensive observation system is needed, but it too should be developed so that it produces information relative to the more comprehensive goals. The point is clear: You should develop an observation system to produce information about established goals rather than choosing an existing system and then letting the goals develop from that choice.

Once the observational techniques of event, duration, interval, and time sampling are understood and mastered, adapting existing observational systems or developing new systems becomes quite easy. If proper attention is paid to appropriate behavior sampling and if the categories are well defined, observation systems from the very basic to the quite complex can be developed and refined. What follows are steps that should be followed in developing observational systems.

1. **Define the goals the observational data will be used for.** The more carefully and specifically this is done, the easier will be the remaining steps in the process. Suppose you want to get information about teacher feedback. Should you attempt to assess the accuracy of the feedback; for example, the degree to which the information relayed to the student was based on an accurate performance diagnosis? Are subcategories of general positive, positive specific, and corrective sufficient? Do you want to further subdivide to find out how many feedback statements are directed to boys and girls or high- and low-skilled students?

2. **Decide what teacher and/or student behaviors will give the most valid information relative to your goals.** This step is fairly easy if the goal is to produce information relative to class time spent in managerial and transitional activities. It is more difficult if you want to produce a measure of class climate or teacher enthusiasm. In this part of the process, very explicit, behavioral definitions are extremely important. Problems in producing reliable observations are almost always related to incomplete or "fuzzy" definitions of behavior categories.

3. **Decide what observation technique to use.** Some behaviors, such as teacher prompts, clearly lend themselves to event recording, while others, such as student waiting, lend themselves to duration recording. On the other hand, interval recording can be used for almost all behavior categories. Thus, as the number of goals to be achieved through an observation system increases, decisions have to be made about the combination of observation techniques that best produce a valid record of behavior related to those goals. The coding format for advanced management skills (see Figure 16.7) and the general supervision instrument shown later in this chapter (see Figure 16.11) both utilize several observation techniques combined to produce a number of different data sets.

4. **Decide how much can be observed reliably.** The complexity of observation is related to the number of decisions the observer has to make relative to his or her experience in observation. A five-category teacher behavior system is quite easy, even for a beginning observer. A 24-category teacher behavior system is much more difficult, because every time the teacher does something, the observer has to decide from among many categories

which category to use to record that behavior. If duration and event recording are being used, the complexity increases because the observer's attention may be focused on two things at once. Generally, it is more important to produce less data that are highly reliable than it is to produce more data with lower reliability. The generally accepted convention in applied research is that independent observers should achieve 80 percent agreement for data to be considered reliable.

How to Build the Observation System

The first step in building a system is to choose the variables to be observed. This process was explained in the preceding section. The second step is to choose the observation technique; that is, to decide whether the variables chosen would best be observed through event recording, duration recording, interval recording, or group time sampling. This decision is made on the basis of two factors: (1) the *match* between the technique and the variable and (2) the integrating of the various techniques into a total system. If the observation system is small, limited to only one or a few variables, then the match between the technique and the variables should guide the decision. This means that, first, most teacher behaviors are best observed through event recording. Second, certain analytic units such as managerial episodes are most meaningfully observed through duration recording (merely counting the frequency of managerial episodes doesn't reveal much of interest—it is their length that counts!). And, third, an overall criterion process variable such as ALT-PE is best observed through interval techniques in which the intervals are quite short.

But if there are several variables to observe, then the system must be built in such a way that allows one observer to do several things. In this case, measures of ALT-PE might best be gathered with group time sampling because it requires less observer time than does interval recording. The time saved can be used observing other variables through other techniques.

Once variables have been chosen, carefully defined, and observational techniques chosen, the next step is to develop the actual coding instrument. A coding instrument is a record sheet that enables an observer to record observations most efficiently. Several examples of coding instruments appear in this chapter. They should be developed for observer efficiency, which means that they make the process of transferring the observation to the coding sheet as easy as possible. For example, after several years of using duration recording and transferring durations to coding sheets in columns, one research group discovered a much easier process, that of building a *time line*. The use of a time line enables an observer to make a simple mark across the line to show when one kind of activity stops and another starts. This was not only simpler for the observer but provided a much more useful *picture* of what had happened and was more easily interpretable to the person for whom it would become feedback.

A portion of a time line is shown in Figure 16.1. This time line is six minutes long and is divided into 10-second units. The observer merely draws a line

16.1 What to Observe: Assessment of Teaching and Its Outcomes

It will be helpful to review Figure 4.1, the assessment model and the information in Chapter 4 relative to process and outcome variables. What follows are examples of the teacher and student variables that can be observed.

Teacher process variables

Managerial prompts per managerial episode
Positive/negative behavior reactions
Distribution of attention—boy/girl, high/medium/low skilled.
Expectation statements
Skill feedback analysis
Time spent in explanations of skills and strategies
Number of managerial routine prompts at beginning of school year
Clarity of instructional task statements
Sequence of refining, extending, and applying tasks

Student process variables

Time spent waiting
On-task time during management, instruction, and practice
Responses to instructional tasks (congruent, modified, off-task)
Analysis of skill responses (appropriateness, success, etc.)
Instances of disruptive behavior
Appropriate help and support for fellow students

Teaching units

Managerial episodes
Accuracy of prompt—student response—teacher feedback cycle
Latency and congruency of initial student task responses
Relationship of supervisory patterns to on-task behavior

Criterion process variables

Academic learning time—physical education
Opportunity to respond (appropriateness and success of responses)

Student outcome variables—short term

Scores on Physical Best fitness test
Game statistics from end-of-unit class tournaments
Scores on knowledge tests

For long-term student outcomes variables, please review Box 4.2.

305

Important
Decisions in
Developing an
Observation
Strategy

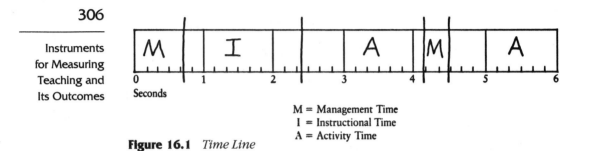

Figure 16.1 *Time Line*

through the time line when one activity, such as a management episode (M), ends and an instruction (I) activity begins, or when a transition (T) activity ends and a practice (P) activity begins. Later the time line can be examined to calculate total time spent in the various activities. This method is simple and efficient. It also is a useful format for providing feedback because the teacher can then actually *see* the flow of activities as they occurred in the lesson.

Like observation instruments, coding sheets should be developed for specific, local purposes. It is unlikely that a coding sheet developed in one place will be exactly what is needed in another place. The point is to develop and instrument that reflects as precisely as possible the decisions made concerning the goals of the teaching episode and the techniques through which the variables will be observed.

Coding sheets such as the general supervision instrument shown on page 322 provide a large amount of information on one sheet. Several techniques are used, and a place is provided in which to summarize the information. This provides useful feedback for the teacher and a convenient way of storing collected data on teaching for future reference. There should always be an area on the coding sheet itself (either at the top or on the back) to provide relevant information concerning the teacher, the setting, students, duration of the total observation period, and other pertinent information. If this information is included, the completed coding sheet becomes a valuable record that can be used for feedback, for research, and for eventually establishing realistic goals and expectations for future experiences.

How to Do the Observations

Choosing relevant variables, matching observation techniques to the variables, and developing the coding sheet for transferring the observations to a permanent record represent the actual building of an observation instrument. What remains is to put it into use, to ensure that it can be used reliably.

Preprogramming an audiotape to cue the observer is an important contribution to systematic observation, especially for systems that use different techniques, sample behavior, or are interval systems. Of course, if you are simply using a five-category event-recording instrument to monitor teacher feedback, the audiotape feature is unnecessary. But, if observers need to sample behavior, switching from the observation of one variable to another, or switching from teacher to students, the cues on a preprogrammed tape can greatly simplify the task for the observer and thus increase the chances of obtaining reliable data.

The observer should be as unobtrusive as possible and still be in position to get the necessary data. If teacher verbal behavior is being observed, then the observer should plan to move around, keeping in close proximity to the teacher, yet staying as inconspicuous as possible. Students will react to the presence of an observer, but will react less and less the longer the observer is in the setting. Teachers too will react—and tend at the beginning to be on their "best behavior." Across time, however, the demands of teaching are such that teachers will tend to behave more normally, attending to the needs of their students and the immediate situation rather than thinking constantly about being observed. Still, unobtrusive observation should be sought.

The observer should have all that is needed to complete the observations, including (1) extra coding sheets, (2) extra pencils, and (3) a clipboard or some other firm surface on which to place the coding sheet, (4) strong batteries if a portable tape recorder is being used to provide preprogrammed cues, and (5) copies of all definitions for categories under observation. The observer should be at the setting in plenty of time to be prepared for the beginning of the teaching session. The data can be summarized while the teacher is ending the class and taking care of after-class supervision. The data can then be used as feedback when the teacher has the time available to study them and react to them. Supervisory conferences should be based on the data and should use the data as a foundation from which to examine and interpret what went on.

Training Observers

This text has emphasized that observational skills are easily acquirable and that reliable observations can be made by peers, instructors, cooperating teachers, supervisors, or by teachers themselves if the teaching sessions are videotaped. In each instance, the observer, no matter who it might be, needs to have sufficient training to ensure the collection of data that meet minimal reliability standards. Most of the observation techniques described in this chapter and the observation systems shown as examples can be learned to an adequate degree of reliability in a short period of time, often as little as two to four hours. More complex systems will take a little longer. The steps in training observers are clear-cut and have received widespread agreement in the literature concerning systematic observation:

1. Observers learn definitions from printed materials. Definitions should contain sufficient examples so that distinctions among categories are clear. Good definitions are the single most important ingredient in collecting reliable data. When observers are having problems, the difficulty is almost always traceable to definitional problems.
2. Observers study a written transcript of a teaching lesson and categorize the behaviors from the transcript. This process can be done as "homework" and tends to eliminate many errors and remedy major misconceptions.

307

Important
Decisions in
Developing an
Observation
Strategy

3. If useful, observers discuss the categories, the examples, the transcript, and other issues.

4. Observers practice observations on a videotape. The tape should have been coded by an experienced observer so that the trainee can compare his or her data with that of an experienced observer. This process helps to establish observer accuracy. The term observer accuracy refers to the degree to which an observer agrees with a precoded standard.

5. Observers practice in the field. Observers should always practice in pairs so that interobserver reliability can be calculated. The term *interobserver reliability* refers to the degree to which two independent observers working with the same definitions viewing the same subjects at the same time record similar data. The two (or more) observers can then discuss discrepancies and resolve issues.

6. Throughout the training process, a decision log should be kept. A *decision log* is a record of observer disagreements and how they were resolved. Periodically, the definitions should be reviewed in light of the information developed through the decision log and changes made to fit the decisions concerning how to handle various situations.

7. Observers practice until they have met a minimal reliability standard. In behavioral observation research, using interobserver agreement calculation techniques (see next section), a criterion of 80 percent is typically required before observers can begin to collect data that are used for research. A slightly less stringent requirement is no doubt acceptable if the purpose of the observation is to generate feedback for teachers in training.

8. Reliability should be checked often to ensure that observers are applying the code accurately. This is analogous to calibrating a weight scale regularly. The observer needs to be "calibrated" too.

Calculating the Reliability of Observation Data

There are several reasons why it is important to ensure that observations are reliable. First, reliable observations indicate whether or not the definition of a teacher or student performance category is sufficiently clear and adequate. A poorly defined teacher or student performance category almost guarantees unreliable observations. When a reliability check indicates a low reliability, the situation is most often remedied by clarifying the definition of the performance categories.

A second reason for estimating reliability is to make sure that changes noted in teacher or student performance are due to the teacher or student and not to the observer. Observers often tend to see what they want to see, either consciously or unconsciously biasing the observations by their feelings about how they want the experience to turn out. This does not mean that an observer is unprofessional or incompetent. It does mean that all of us are subject to this tendency.

A third reason for checking reliability is to ensure that the changes noted in the observations do indeed reflect what is going on in the class. If observations

309

Important
Decisions in
Developing an
Observation
Strategy

indicate that a teaching intern decreases management time from one week to the next, he or she can take pride in the improvement to the degree that the observations are known to be reliable. If they are not reliable, then the results hardly differ from those generated by eyeballing.

This text emphasizes a data-based approach to improving teaching skills. If this model is used and certain improvements occur in your teaching skills, it is crucial that you, the school in which you teach, and the college or university at which you study have confidence that these improvements are real. Such confidence is directly related to the reliability of the recordings made during the intern experience.

The term *reliability* refers to the degree to which independent observers agree on what they see and record. In this sense the term *independent observers* can be taken to mean that one observer could not detect recordings being made by another observer. This criterion is usually satisfied by having observers placed far enough apart so that no visual or auditory cues could be used to detect the observations being made. If a tape recorder is used for a coding format, reliability checks can be made by splicing an extra ear jack into the ear jack line and allowing for sufficient cord to have the observers sit approximately 10 feet apart.

The general formula for computing reliability is

$$\frac{Agreements}{Agreements + Disagreements} \times 100 = \% \text{ of agreement}$$

For event recording, duration recording, and permanent produce measurement, reliability can be calculated by dividing the data of the observer who has the lower number of instances or time by that of the observer who has the higher number of instances or time.

If event recording is being used to judge the number of social interactions that a student has during a period, and one observer records 14 while a second observer records 12, the reliability would be computed as follows:

$$\frac{12}{14} \times 100 = 86\% \text{ reliability}$$

If duration recording is being used to measure the amount of time a teacher spends verbalizing to the class, and one observer records 12:30 while a second observer records 13:10, the reliability would be computed as follows:

$$12:30 = 750 \text{ seconds}$$

$$13:10 = 790 \text{ seconds}$$

$$\frac{750}{790} \times 100 = 95\% \text{ reliability}$$

If attendance is being self-recorded by students as they enter class, the teacher, student helper, or observer can unobtrusively check the students as they record their attendance. If such an observer agreed with each student as he or she checked in, the reliability would be 100 percent. If, in a class of 30 students, the

Table 16.1 *Sample Data from Independent Observers for Two Students*

	Observer A		Observer B	
Interval	*Student 1*	*Student 2*	*Student 1*	*Student 2*
1	U	P	U	P
2	U	U	U	P
3	P	P	P	P
4	U	P	P	P
5	P	P	U	U
6	P	P	U	P
7	P	U	P	U
8	P	P	U	P
9	U	U	P	U
10	P	P	P	P
11	P	P	P	P
12	U	P	P	P

Note: P = Productive.
 U = Unproductive.

monitor disagreed with the check-in of 2 students, the reliability would be computed as follows:

$$\frac{28}{30} \times 100 = 93\%$$

For interval and group time-sampling recordings, reliability is determined by estimating the degree to which the independent observers agree or disagree for each interval or sample recorded. Suppose that interval recording was used to rate the degree to which two students were engaged in productive learning behavior during a physical education class. The raw data of the time sample might appear as in Table 16.1.

To compute reliability, the observations by interval for each student must be compared. Any interval for which the observers have recorded the same rating indicates agreement. Any interval for which they have recorded different ratings indicates disagreement. If the raw data are rearranged so that the observations of the two observers for each student can be compared, the agreements and disagreements become immediately apparent.

Table 16.2 shows observations that are clearly in disagreement. For student 1, the seven circled intervals indicate seven disagreements. For Student 2, the two circled intervals indicate two disagreements. There are 12 intervals, so the reliability would be computed as follows:

Reliability for Student 1　　　　　　　*Reliability for Student 2*

$$\frac{5}{5+7} \times 100 = 42\%$$　　　　　$$\frac{10}{10+2} \times 100 = 83\%$$

Obviously there is some problem with these data. A reliability of 80 percent is usually considered necessary for research purposes. With a low number of intervals

Table 16.2 *Sample Data Scored for Disagreements Between Observers*   311

Important
Decisions in
Developing an
Observation
Strategy

	Student 1		Student 2	
Interval	Observer A	Observer B	Observer A	Observer B
1	U	U	P	P
2	U	U	U	P
3	P	P	P	P
4	U	P	P	P
5	P	U	P	U
6	P	U	P	P
7	P	U	U	U
8	P	U	P	P
9	U	P	U	U
10	P	P	P	?
11	P	P	P	?
12	U	P	P	?

(12), a reliability of 75 percent would probably suffice. But these data indicate a substantial discrepancy and must be considered unreliable. The observers should attempt to clarify the definitions of productive and unproductive learning behavior, using examples of each to come to a greater agreement about the performance category they are observing.

Reliability for group time sampling (GTS) is determined by computing how much the independent observers agree for each group time sample recorded. Suppose that you want to check the degree to which your students are engaged in active learning. After defining what you consider to be active learning, you could conveniently sample this category using GTS. Suppose that you do one group time sample every 3 minutes during a 30-minute period. This would provide ten samples per period and would give you a good idea of the degree to which your students were involved in active learning. Let's assume that you have 24 students in your class and that your cooperating teacher is doing a reliability check. The raw data for the group time sample recordings might appear as in Table 16.3.

Table 16.3 *Group Time Sample (GTS) Data*

	Your Observation	Cooperating Teacher
GTS 1	12/24	14/24
GTS 2	18/24	19/24
GTS 3	17/24	17/24
GTS 4	14/24	14/24
GTS 5	10/24	12/24
GTS 6	12/24	10/24
GTS 7	14/24	14/24
GTS 8	20/24	21/24
GTS 9	22/24	22/24
GTS 10	20/24	20/24

Reliability is computed most easily by counting the disagreements for each GTS. Because you recorded 12 active learners in the first GTS and the cooperating teacher recorded 14, there were two disagreements; because there are 24 students in the class, there were 22 agreements. In the 10 GTS shown there is a total of 8 disagreements, which subtracted from the total possible of 240 (10 × 24 class members) shows 232 agreements. The reliability is computed as usual:

$$\frac{232}{232 + 8} \times 100 = 97\%$$

This shows a very high reliability, which should give you confidence that your observations of the degree to which your students are engaged in active learning are accurate. Incidentally, the hypothetical data show that during the middle portion of the class session the percentage of students engaged in active learning was barely 50 percent, a fact that might encourage you to examine what in the

---

16.2 Progress Check

Compute reliabilities from the following data.

1. Using a time-sampling format, you and an independent observer record 48 agreements and 11 disagreements.
2. Using duration recording, two independent observers record 8:34 and 9:01. (Don't forget to convert the data to seconds for computation.)
3. Doing GTS's on your class, one observer records 21 students on task while a second observer records 17 students on task.
4. Your supervisory team is checking the positive and negative feedback statements you make to your students. The cooperating teacher records 14 positive feedbacks and 8 negative feedbacks. The supervisor records 15 positive feedbacks and 7 negative feedbacks. (After you compute the reliabilities, convert the data to rate per minute, assuming that the observations were made during a 20-minute observation period and that the data collected by the cooperating teacher are used.)

Answers

1. 81% reliability
2. 95% reliability (Did you convert the minutes to seconds before starting?)
3. 81% reliability (Notice that you can compute reliability without having to know the number of students in the class.)
4. Positive feedback = 95% reliability   Rate = .7 per minute
   Negative feedback = 88% reliability   Rate = .4 per minute

organization of the class caused half the students to be inactive for such a substantial portion of the instructional time.

Examples of Observation Systems

What follows are examples of various systematic observation instruments. The coding for these instruments will be *event, duration, interval, time sampling,* or some combination thereof. The observation protocols have been chosen to show a variety of these recording techniques and to show systems that focus on a few basic behavioral categories as well as more comprehensive systems.

1. *Student time analysis.* Information concerning how students spend time can be useful for making judgments about the general effectiveness of a class. Time analyses require duration recording. Figure 16.2 shows a simple, three-category time analysis in which blocks of time spent are listed in the appropriate columns of *teacher talk, management,* and *active learning.* Data such as these are best expressed as a percentage of total class time, thus allowing for comparisons across classes of differing lengths. You will notice in this example that the total of teacher talk and management is more than the time spent in active learning.

Record of Time Allotment in Class

Class: **9TH GRADE/MR ALLEN**   Date: **1/9**   Time: **2:00–2:40**

Teacher Talk (Demonstration and Instruction)	Management	Active Learning
3:06	1:17	6:18
1:08	1:24	5:20
4:30	0:46	3:50
2:06	0:40	4:25
1:10	2:50	19:13
12:00	1:50	
	1:00	
	0:20	
	8:47	

Figure 16.2 *Student Time Analysis in Columns*

2. *Student time analysis using a time line*. The following example uses five categories, thus allowing for a more detailed analysis of time than was possible in the previous example. Also, the use of a time line preserves a visual record of the sequence of various blocks of time across the lesson. Teachers can look at a completed time line and see immediately where the management blocks occurred and where in the lesson students spent time waiting. On the other hand, the data on the time line are slightly more difficult to count and summarize than the simple column approach shown above.

Teacher _____ School _____ Activity _____ Date ____

Grade Level _____ Time Begun _____ Finished _____ No. in Class _____ No. Participating ___

Time Analysis

Wait (W) Periods of no activity and no movement between activities.

Transition (T) Periods of change from one activity to another (includes lining up or quieting down for the next activity).

Management (M) Time related to class business unrelated to instructional activity.

Activity (A) Students are participating in skill practice, scrimmage, game, fitness, or other activities related to the lesson's objectives.

Receiving Information (I) Students are attending to teacher directions or demonstrations, or other class-related information.

Figure 16.3 *Student Time Analysis Using a Time Line*

3. *Teacher reaction analysis using event recording*. Teachers respond to students often during classes and in many different ways. These events occur so frequently and often so quickly that teachers seldom have a good

Teacher: **Longlin**   Date: **3/9**   School: **Desert H.S.**

Activity: **Track**   Time started: **9:05**   Time ended: **9:40**

Length of observation: **35**   Observer: **Cusimano**

Definitions:

1. *Providing exact commendatory information on performance. (motor)*
2. *Words supporting students' motor response.*
3. *Providing commendatory statements on behavior, other than motor.*
4. *Teacher comment to terminate a behavior.*

1 Pos. Skill Fb. (Specific)	2 Pos. Skill Fb. (General)	3 Behavior Praise	4 Desists
JHT JHT JHT I	JHT JHT JHT JHT JHT JHT JHT JHT JHT JHT JHT III	JHT II	JHT JHT JHT JHT III

Totals: **16**   **58**   **7**   **23**

Data Summary:

Behaviors	Total frequency	Rate per minute
1 Pos. Skill Fb. (S)	16	.45
2 Pos. Skill Fb. (G)	58	1.65
3 Praise	7	.20
4 Desists	23	.65

Comments:

★ You seem more specific toward male students.

★ Let's work on behavior praise! (crucial this time of year)

★ Be firm when you desist!!

Figure 16.4 *Teacher Reaction Analysis Using Event Recording* (Source: From "Basic Recording Tactics" by H. van der Mars. In *Analyzing Physical Education and Sport Instruction* by Darst, et al., 1987. p. 25. Reprinted by permission)

idea about the general pattern of their reactions. Thus it is often helpful to record these events and provide the feedback to the teacher. We have found it useful to distinguish between reactions to social/managerial behavior and reactions to substantive, subject-related behavior such as skill attempts or game play. Examples of these can be found in Table 7.2 and Box 12.2. Event recording systems could be developed to observe any combination of these behaviors. The following example uses four important categories, two for skill feedback and two for behavior feedback. You should note that this systematic observation of teacher reactions could be further categorized to show the direction of the feedback (such as boy/girl, high/medium/low skilled students, and so forth).

4. *Student or class analysis using group time sampling.* When developing an observation format for student behavior, a decision needs to be made whether to observe one student, several students, or the entire class. The decision should be made on the basis of what kind of information will best serve the goal of the observation. On occasion, it is useful to get information relative to an entire class of students. The example below uses group time sampling to assess the degree students are behaving appropriately (for example, on-task regardless of whether the focus is managerial or instructional), engaged in subject matter activity, or engaged in subject matter activity at a high success rate, as is required for ALT-PE. When you review Box 3.2 you will see that the three measures of involvement used in this system provide very important information for the teacher. The observation strategy is group time sampling, where periodically the class is scanned and the number of students involved according to the three category definitions is recorded. In Figure 16.5, the time sampling is done once every four minutes. The data in this example show a class that is well behaved (98 percent appropriate), engaged in the subject matter activities at a high rate (69 percent), but not always successfully (38 percent).

Student Behavior Analysis											
Class: 5TH PERIOD/VOLLEYBALL		Teacher: BROWN					No. in Class: 30				
Start Time: 1:30		End Time: 2:10			Length of Observation: 40 MINUTES						
Student Behavior	Appropriate	20	30	28	26	20	30	30	30	30	20
	Engaged	4	26	16	18	20	30	28	26	24	16
	ALT-PE	0	0	14	18	0	24	26	22	0	10
Appropriate = 98%			Engaged = 69%					ALT-PE = 38%			

Figure 16.5 *Observation Form for Analyzing Student Behavior*

5. *Analysis of managerial episodes.* Managerial episodes are important "teaching units" (see page 57). The total time spent in management is crucial, as is the effective direction of each managerial episode. The following observation system was developed to focus exclusively on

managerial episodes; thus the structure of the observation format is by episode. Figure 16.6 uses event recording for the number of positive and negative teacher interactions within each episode, duration recording for the length of each episode, event recording for the number of managerial behaviors in each episode (such as, prompting, directing), and group time sampling (GTS) for a measure of the appropriate behavior of the class during the episode. This example is from baseline measurement, so it is prior to an attempt to change, which is good because the teacher is clearly too negative and the episode lengths are too long.

Behavioral Interactions												
Three- or Five-Minute Event-Recording Periods		+	–	+	–	+	–	+	–	+	–	+	–
		//	LHT /	/	///		////		LHT ///	/	////	//	LHT
Managerial Episodes	Length	2:47		0:58		3:16		1:42		1:36		2:30	
	Number of Managerial Behaviors per Episode	LHT		///		LHT //		///		LHT		////	
GTS for Appropriate Behavior per Episode		22/28		25/28		24/28		21/28		26/28		22/28	

Class: JONES 8TH GRADE   Date: 11/7   Starting time: 9:30   Ending time: 10:10

Data Summary

Rate of + reactions per minute = 0.27

Rate of – reactions per minute = 1.67

Ratio +/– reactions = 4/15 = 1/4

Total time in management = 12:49

Average time per episode = 6/769 = 128 SECONDS = 2:08

Average number of managerial behaviors per episode = 4.5

Percentage of appropriate behavior = 184/224 = 82%

Comments: BASELINE – 2ND OBSERVATION
BEGINNING AND ENDING MANAGEMENT MUCH TOO LONG
FOCUS ALMOST TOTALLY ON NEGATIVE INTERACTION
IT APPEARS THAT LONG MANAGEMENT EPISODES CONTRIBUTE TO
INAPPROPRIATE BEHAVIOR

Figure 16.6 *Analysis of Managerial Episodes*

6. *Analysis of managerial skills.* Figure 16.7 shows an observation system that can be used to assess and improve managerial skills. It has some of the features shown in 16.6, such as the length of each managerial episode and a group time sampling of appropriate student behavior by episode. It also includes a much more detailed analysis of behavioral interactions with four main categories (general, specific, general-value, specific-value), with recording further categorized by the direction of the feedback (to individuals, small groups, and group as a whole) and including separate coding of nonverbal interactions (facial, gesturing, contacting). There are specific spaces for the observer to rate modeling, use of extinction,

appropriate targeting of reactions, and timing of reactions, as well as a space to comment on the teacher's use of voice and variety of interactions. The system requires use of event recording (done in this case in five-minute intervals for 20 minutes), duration recording, and group time sampling.

7. *Descriptive analysis of teacher and student behavior.* One of the primary functions of systematic observation is to provide detailed "pictures" of what happens during a class. In Figure 16.8, interval recording is used to provide a description of both teacher and student behavior. The interval "boxes" are each divided so that the code for teacher behavior can be entered to the left of the diagonal line and the code for student behavior can be entered to the right. This particular system was developed to observe the behavior of fifth and sixth graders and their teachers at a school camp, showing that systematic observation need not be confined to gymnasia, playing fields, or classrooms. The teacher and student categories are listed at the bottom of the coding sheet because there are so many of them that observers would need to be able to glance at them often as they make their

Behavioral Interactions

Length of Event-Recording Time = FOUR 5-MINUTE INTERVALS' 20 MINUTES

	Positive (+)							Negative (−)						
	Direction			Nonverbal			Initiated by + Behavior	Direction			Nonverbal			Comments
	I	S	G	F	G	C		I	S	G	F	G	C	
General	///		𝍸 ///	//	/	///	~~𝍸~~ /	/		////	///	/		STARING DOWN
Specific	𝍸 𝍸 /					///	/// NOT ENOUGH HERE	////		𝍸 /				
General—value	/	/	///											
Specific—value	///	///	𝍸 /				//	//		///			//	

Voice and Variety: GOOD JOB—𝍸 // TOO MANY VOICE GOOD ON GROUP DIRECTED

Managerial Episodes	Length	0:32	0:47	0:16	1:02	0:18	—	—	—	—
	Number of management behaviors	//	///	//	///	//	—	—	—	—
GTS for Appropriate Behavior		22/24	24/24	21/24	22/24	20/24	23/24	24/24	—	—

Use of modeling: MUCH BETTER-USE OF JOHN TO MODEL FOLLOWING INSTRUCTIONS WELL-DONE-MOST GROUP FEED-BACK HAS INFO AND VALUE CONTENT 𝍸

Rating of targeting: MORE POSITIVE SPECIFIC FOR GETTING ORGANIZED QUICKLY—MORE POSITIVE FOR BILLY AND WALTER

Use of extinction: STILL HAVE TROUBLE IGNORING NANCY ///

Rating of timing: MUCH BETTER—WATCH "STARING DOWN" REACTION-GOOD DESIST ON CLASS DURING DRILL CHANGE

Class: CHAPMAN 4TH Date: 3/16 3RD OBSERVATION AFTER BASELINE Starting time: 1:10 Ending time: 1:52

Data Summary

+ interaction/minute = 2.4
− interaction/minute = 1.3
Ratio of +/− = 48/26 = 2/1
% of interactions initiated by + = 23%

% of interactions nonverbal = 15/74 = 20%
Contact nonverbal/noncontact = 8/15 = 50%
% of interactions—specific = 43/74 = 58%
% of interactions—value = 26/74 = 35%

Total time in management = 2:55
Average time per episode = 0:35
Management behavior per episode = 2.4
% of appropriate behavior = 156/168 = 93%

Figure 16.7 *Analysis of Managerial Skills*

choices. This is interval recording, so within each interval the observer makes a judgement as to what the teacher was doing and what the targeted student was doing (the coding convention could be altered so the student behavior decision was based on what best characterized the group as a whole). Typical of this kind of system would be a 8–12 second interval. Making these observations will require the kind of tape-recorded prompting described earlier in this chapter.

8. *Analysis of ALT-PE.* Academic Learning Time—Physical Education is one of the criterion process variables most often used to judge teaching effectiveness in physical education. The most common observation format for it is the interval recording system shown in Figure 16.9 (Siedentop, Tousignant, & Parker, 1982). The coding format is divided into intervals, with each interval "box" having an upper and lower level. The top level is

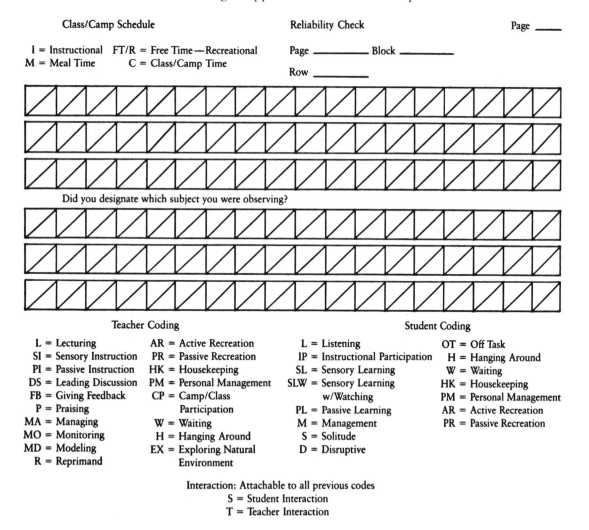

Figure 16.8 *Analysis of Teacher-Student Behavior Using Interval Recording*

used to describe the context of the interval, and the ten choices are from general content, subject matter knowledge content, and subject matter motor content. This decision is made on the basis of what the class as a whole is doing; for example, are they involved in warm-up, a lecture on strategy, or skill practice? The lower level of the interval box is used to describe the involvement of one student, with choices from the categories described as not motor engaged and those described as motor engaged. The letter code for the appropriate category is placed in the appropriate part of the interval box. This system provides a total picture of what the class does throughout a lesson and a finely grained picture of the involvement of several students. Typically, the suggestion is to observe three students of differing skill levels and to alternate observing them every interval. Those interval boxes marked as motor appropriate (MA) are ALT-PE intervals, and their total reveals the total ALT-PE for that student during the class.

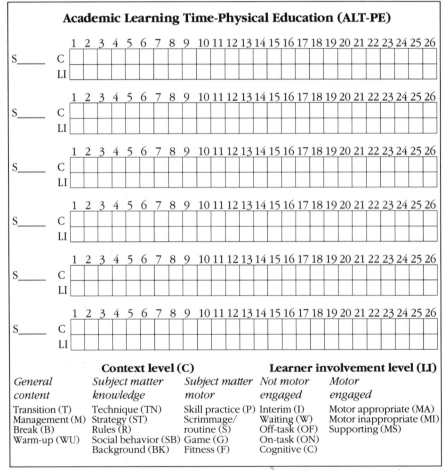

Figure 16.9 *Analysis of ALT-PE Using Interval Recording (Source: Siedentop, Tousignant, & Parker, 1982)*

9. *Analysis of OTR.* Opportunity to respond is another criterion process variable that is related to effective teaching. In OTR analyses, student responses are evaluated as they occur using an event recording format. In this example (Brown, 1989), the topographical form of the response is evaluated as acceptable (A) or unacceptable (UA), and the success of the response within its context is evaluated as successful (S) or unsuccessful (US). This example shows skill codes for soccer and volleyball, so that a record can be made that is specific to the skill attempted by the student. The example also shows the time during the lesson that the response was

Soccer		Volleyball			
Trap—T	Throw—C	Serve—S	Spike—I	Counter start	0268
Kick—K	Goalkeep—G	Pass—P	Block—C	Counter stop	1396
Dribble—D	No response—N	Bump—B	Dink—K	Timer stop	16:41
	Uncodable—X	Dig—D	No response—N	Timer start	1:25
				Total time	15:15

Volleyball/Soccer Class # __1__ of 20   Date of lesson _4/26_ Modification _4_

Observer: __Brown__   Date of observation __2/17__

Subject: __James__   Subject: __Sally__

Response sequence		Skill code	Topography		Results		Response sequence		Skill code	Topography		Results	
			A	UA	S	US				A	UA	S	US
1	1:29	P	1		1		1	1:35	P		1	1	
2	2:13	P		1	1		2	1:46	B		1		1
3	2:25	N					3	1:54	N				
4	2:33	N					4	2:08	N				
5	4:20	P		1	1		5	2:12	P		1	1	
6	6:59	P		1		1	6	2:14	P		1		1
7	8:24	P		1		1	7	2:25	N				
8	8:42	P		1		1	8	3:47	S		1	1	
9	9:23	P		1		1	9	4:02	S		1	1	
10	9:45	P	1		1		10	4:06	P		1	1	
11	12:12	P		1		1	11	5:37	P		1		1
12	14:14	S	1			1	12	5:52	P		1	1	
13	15:01	P		1		1	13	6:43	S		1		1
14							14	8:21	S		1	1	
15							15	9:20	S		1	1	
16							16	9:45	P		1	1	
17							17	10:42	S	1			1
18							18	11:12	P		1		1
19							19	11:58	S		1		1
20							20	14:11	N				
21							21	15:20	P		1	1	
Totals			3	8	4	7	Totals			1	16	10	7

Figure 16.10 *Analysis of OTR Using Event Recording* (Source: From "Systematic Observation of Student Opportunities to Respond (SOSOR). by Will Brown. In *Analyzing Physical Education and Sport Instruction [Second Edition]*. Darst, et al., 1989, p. 192. Reprinted by permission.)

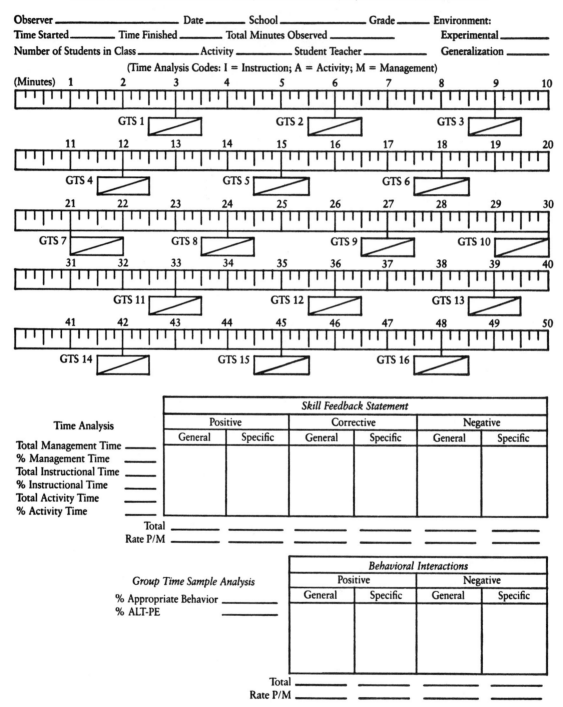

Figure 16.11 *A General Supervision Instrument*

made. Obviously, this kind of observation cannot be done for an entire class. The typical procedure is to observe two or three students of varying levels of skillfulness. The coding sheet in Figure 16.10 shows observations for two students in a volleyball class.

10. *A general supervision instrument*. During field experiences and student teaching, it is often useful for a program to adopt a general supervision observation system that will be used for all interns. Such a system serves several functions: It provides needed emphasis for achieving the major goals of the program, a means for evaluating program-level progress toward those goals, a means for evaluating individual interns, and a means for comparing the relative performance of different interns. The observation system shown in Figure 16.11 uses event recording for teacher reactions (skill feedback and behavior interactions), a time line for duration recording of the important aspects of how class time is used (instruction, management, and activity), and group time sampling once every three minutes to assess two important features of class behavior (the number of students behaving appropriately and the number of students in ALT-PE). The appropriate summary statistics are presented toward the bottom of the coding sheet. This supervision coding system can be used by one observer—either the university supervisor, the school cooperating teacher, or a peer intern. The data developed are important indicators of effectiveness, yet can be coded reliably and summarized quickly for conferencing with the intern who was observed.

Summary

1. For teaching to improve, specific goals must be defined, appropriate practice provided, and relevant, accurate feedback given.
2. Data are reliable when two independent observers using the same definitions and observing the same teacher at the same time produce similar records.
3. Traditional methods for observing teaching have been intuitive judgments, eyeballing, anecdotal records, and checklists or rating scales. Each of these has problems of observer bias and tends to lack reliability.
4. Systematic observation techniques include event recording, duration recording, interval recording, and group time sampling.
5. Teachers can self-record their own teaching behavior and important learning-related behaviors of their students.
6. Observation techniques can be combined to produce a multidimensional observation system that focuses on both teacher and student behavior.
7. Decisions in developing an observation system include what goals are being sought in the teaching episodes, what teacher and student behaviors are valid indicators of those goals, what observation techniques

are best suited to measure those indicators, and how much can be observed reliably.

8. Observation systems are built by matching the observation technique to the variable observed and integrating the various observation techniques in a workable system.

9. Observers need to have all materials needed to complete the observations as well as technological aids to cue their observations. They should be as unobtrusive as possible.

10. Observers need to be trained carefully and systematically, moving from understanding the category definitions, to video practice, to live practice in the field, and finally to establishing reliability with a trained observer.

11. The reliability of various observation techniques is calculated by comparing the observation records of the independent observers and calculating a percentage agreement score.

References

Alexander, K. (1982). Behavior analysis of tasks and accountability. Unpublished doctoral dissertation, The Ohio State University, Columbus.

Allen, J. (1986). Classroom management: Students' perspectives, goals, and strategies. *American Educational Research Journal.* 2(3), 437–459.

Anderson, W. (1978). Introduction. In W. Anderson and G. Barrette (Eds.), *What's going on in the gym. Motor Skills: Theory Into Practice.* Monograph #1.

Anderson, W. (1980). *Analysis of teaching physical education.* St. Louis: C.V. Mosby.

Anderson, W. (1988). A school-centered collaborative model for program development. *Journal of Teaching in Physical Education.* 7(3), 176–183.

Anderson, W., and Barrette, G. (1978). *What's going on in the gym. Motor Skills: Theory Into Practice.* Monograph #1.

Armstrong, R., Cornell, R., Kraner, R., and Roberson, E. (1970). *The development and evaluation of behavioral objectives.* Worthington, OH: Jones.

Aufderheide, S. (1983). ALT-PE in mainstreamed physical education classes. *Journal of Teaching in Physical Education.* 1(3), 22–26.

Baird, H., Belt, W., Holder, L., and Webb, C. (1972). *A behavioral approach to teaching.* Dubuque, IA: Wm. C. Brown.

Baley, J. (1965). *Gymnastics in the schools.* Boston: Allyn & Bacon.

Banathy, B. (1968). *Instructional systems.* Belmont, CA: Fearon Publishers.

Bane, M., and Jencks, C. (1972). The schools and equal opportunity. *Saturday Review of Literature.* 55, 37–42.

Barnes, W. (1977). How to improve teacher behavior in multiethnic classrooms. *Educational Leadership.* 35, 511–515.

Beale, H. (1936). *Are American teachers free?* New York: Scribner's.

Becker, E. (1967). *Beyond alienation*. New York: Braziller.

Berliner, D. (1979). Tempus educare. In P. Peterson and H. Walberg (Eds.), *Research on teaching: Concepts, findings, and implications*. Berkeley, CA: McCutchan.

Berliner, D. (1985). *Reform in teacher education: The case for pedagogy*. Occasional paper #1. Association for Colleges and Schools of Education and Land Grant Colleges and Affiliated Private Universities.

Berliner, D. (1986). In pursuit of the expert pedagogue. *Educational Researcher*. 15(7), 5–13.

Birdwell, D. (1980). The effects of modification of teacher behavior on the academic learning time of selected students in physical education. Unpublished doctoral dissertation, The Ohio State University, Columbus.

Biscan, D., and Hoffman, S. (1976). Movement analysis as a generic ability of physical education teachers and students. *Research Quarterly*. 47(2), 161–163.

Bloom, B. (1978). Learning for mastery. *Evaluation Comment*. 1, May.

Bloom, B. (1980). The new direction in educational research: Alterable variables. *Phi Delta Kappan*. 61(6).

Bloom, B. (1984). The 2 sigma problem: The search for methods of group instructions as effective as one-to-one tutoring. *Educational Researcher*. June/July, 4–16.

Bloom, B. (1986). Automaticity. *Educational Leadership*. 43(5), 70–77.

Boehm, J. (1974). The effects of competency-based teaching programs on junior high school physical education student teachers and their pupils. Unpublished doctoral dissertation, The Ohio State University, Columbus.

Boyer, E. (1981). Education issues. *New York Education Quarterly*. Summer, 12, 2–4.

Brophy, J. (1981). Teacher praise: A functional analysis. *Review of Educational Research*. 51, 5–32.

Brophy, J., and Good, T. (1974). *Teacher-student relationships: Causes and consequences*. New York: Holt, Rinehart & Winston.

Brophy, J., and Good, T. (1986). Teacher behavior and student achievement. In M. Wittrock, ed., *Handbook of research on teaching*. New York: Macmillan.

Brown, W. (1986). The effects of game modifications on children's opportunity to respond in soccer and volleyball. Unpublished doctoral dissertation, The Ohio State University, Columbus.

Brown, W. (1989). Systematic observation of student opportunities to respond. In P. Darst, D. Zakrajsek, and V. Mancini, eds., *Analyzing physical education and sport instruction*. Champaign, IL: Human Kinetics.

Burlingame, M. (1972). Socialization constructs and the teaching of teachers. *Quest*. 18, 40–56.

Cassidy, R., and Caldwell, S. (1974). *Humanizing physical education*. 5th Ed. Dubuque, IA: Wm. C. Brown.

Cheffers, J. (1977). Observing teaching systematically. *Quest*. 28, 17–28.

Cheffers, J., and Mancini, V. (1978). Teacher-student interaction. In W. Anderson and G. Barrette, eds., *What's going on in the gym*. *Motor Skills: Theory Into Practice*. Monograph #1.

Chu, D. (1981). Functional myths of educational organizations: College as career training and the relationship of formal title to actual duties upon secondary school employment. In V. Crafts, ed., *1980 National Association of Physical Education in Higher Education Proceedings*. Champaign, IL: Human Kinetics.

Clark, C., and Yinger, R. (1979). Teachers' thinking. In P. Peterson and H. Walberg, eds., *Research on teaching: Concepts, findings, and applications*. Berkeley, CA: McCutchan.

Cohen, A. (1970). Technology: Thee or me? *Educational Technology*. 10, 57–60.

Cohen, S. (1987). Instructional alignment: Searching for a magic bullet. *Educational Researcher*. November, 16–20.

Cooke, N., Heron, T., and Heward, W. (1983). *Peer tutoring*. Columbus, OH: Special Press.

Cooper, J., Heward, W., and Heron, T. (1987). *Applied behavior analysis*. Columbus, OH: Merrill.

Costello, J., and Laubach, S. (1978). Student behavior. In W. Anderson and G. Barrette, eds., *What's going on in the gym. Motor Skills: Theory Into Practice*. Monograph #1.

Cramer, C. (1977). The effects of a cooperating teacher training program in applied behavior analysis on teacher behaviors of physical education student teachers. Unpublished doctoral dissertation, The Ohio State University, Columbus.

Crockenberg, V. (1975). Poor teachers are made, not born. *Educational Forum*. 39, 189–198.

Cruickshank, D., and Applegate, J. (1981). Reflective teaching as a strategy for teacher growth. *Educational Leadership*. 38, 553–554.

Darst, P. (1974). The effects of a competency-based intervention on student-teacher and pupil behavior. Unpublished doctoral dissertation, The Ohio State University, Columbus.

Darst, P., Zakrajsek, D., and Mancini, V. (1989). *Analysing physical education and sport instruction*. 2nd Ed. Champaign, IL: Human Kinetics.

DeKnop, P. Relationships of specified instructional teacher behaviors to student gain on tennis. *Journal of Teaching in Physical Education*. 5(2), 71–78.

Denemark, G. (1973). Goals for teacher education: A time for decision. *Time for decision in teacher education*. Washington, D.C.: American Association for Colleges of Teacher Education.

Denemark, G., and Espinoza, A. (1974). Educating teacher educators. *Theory Into Practice*. 13, 187–197.

Dodds, P., and Rife, F., eds., (1983). Time to learn in physical education. *Journal of Teaching in Physical Education*. Monograph #1, Summer.

Doyle, W. (1979). Classroom tasks and students' abilities. In P. Peterson and H. Walberg, eds., *Research on teaching: Concepts, findings, and implications*. Berkeley, CA: McCutchan.

Doyle, W. (1980). *Student mediating responses in teaching effectiveness*. Denton, TX: North Texas State University (ERIC No. ED 187 698).

Doyle, W. (1981). Research on classroom contexts. *Journal of Teacher Education*. 32(6), 3–6.

Drowatzky, J. 91978). Liability: You could be sued! *Journal of Physical Education, Recreation, and Dance*. 49, 17–18.

Dubey, R., Endly, V., Roe, B., and Tollett, D. (1972). *A performance based guide to student teaching*. Danville, IL: Interstate.

Duke, D. (1978). Looking at the school as a rule-governed institution. *Journal of Research and Development in Education*. 2, 116–126.

Dunkin, M., and Biddle, B. (1974). *The study of teaching*. New York: Holt, Rinehart & Winston.

Earls, N. (1979). Distinctive physical education teachers: Personal qualities, perceptions of teacher education and the realities of teaching. Unpublished doctoral dissertation, University of North Carolina, Greensboro.

Earls, N. (1981). Distinctive teachers' personal qualities, perceptions of teacher education and the realities of teaching. *Journal of Teaching in Physical Education*. 1, 59–70.

Edmonds, R. (1983). The context of teaching and learning: School effects and teacher effects. In D. Smith, ed., *Essential knowledge for beginning educators*. Washington, D.C.: American Association for Colleges of Teacher Education.

Eldar, E., Siedentop, D., and Jones, D. (1989). The seven elementary specialists. *Journal of Teaching in Physical Education*. 8(3), 189–197.

Emmer, E., and Evertson, C. (1981). Synthesis of research on classroom management. *Educational Leadership*. 38, 4, 342–347.

Evertson, C. (1989). Classroom organization and management. In M. Reynolds, ed., *Knowledge base for the beginning teacher*. Washington, DC: American Association of Colleges for Teacher Education.

Evertson, C., Anderson, C., Anderson, L., and Brophy, J., Relationships between classroom behaviors and student outcomes in junior high mathematics and English classes. *American Educational Research Journal*. 17, 43–60.

Evertson, C., Hawley, W., and Zlotnik, M. (1984). The characteristics of effective teacher education programs: A review of research. Unpublished paper, Peabody College, Vanderbilt University, Nashville, TN.

Faucette, N. (1986). Educational reform—enough is enough. *Journal of Physical Education, Recreation and Dance*. 57(4), 44–46.

Fink, J., and Siedentop, D. (1989). The development of routines, rules, and expectations at the start of the school year. *Journal of Teaching in Physical Education*. 8(3), 198–212.

Fishman, S., and Tobey, C. (1978). Augmented feedback. In W. Anderson (Ed.), *What's going on in the gym. Motor Skills: Theory Into Practice*. Monograph #1.

Gage, N. (1972). *Teacher effectiveness and teacher education*. Palo Alto, CA: Pacific Books.

Gage, N. (1978). *The scientific basis for the art of teaching*. New York: Teachers College Press.

Gallahue, D. (1987). *Developmental physical education for today's elementary school children*. New York: Macmillan.

Galloway, C. (1971). Teaching is more than words. *Quest*. 15, 67–71.

Gentile, A. (1972). A working model for skill acquisition with application to teaching. *Quest*. 27, 3–23.

Glasser, W. (1965). *Reality therapy*. New York: Harper & Row.

Goldberger, M. (1983). A teacher with boundless expectations. *Journal of Physical Education, Recreation and Dance*. 54(7), 21–22.

Goodlad, J. (1969). Can our schools get better? *Phi Delta Kappan*. January.

Graham, G. (1985). Commitment to action: Looking at the future through rear view mirrors. In H. Hoffman and J. Rink, eds., *Physical education professional preparation: Insights and issues*. Washington, D.C.: American Alliance for Health, Physical Education, Recreation and Dance.

Graham, G., Parker, M., and Holt-Hale, S. (1987). *Children moving*. Mountain View, CA: Mayfield.

Griffin, P. (1981). Observations and suggestions for sex equity in coeducational physical education classes. *Journal of Teaching in Physical Education*. 1, 12–17.

Griffin, P. (1986). Analysis and discussion: What have we learned? *Journal of Physical Education, Recreation and Dance*. 57(4), 57–59.

Griffin, P., and Hutchinson, G. (1988). Second wind: A physical education program development network. *Journal of Teaching in Physical Education*. 7(3), 184–188.

Griffin, P., and Locke, L. (1986). This is not Palo Alto. *Journal of Physical Education, Recreation and Dance*. 57(4), 38–41.

Griffin, P., and Placek, J. (1983). *Fair play in the gym: Race and sex equity in physical education*. Amherst, MA.: University of Massachusetts.

Grossman, P., Wilson, S., and Shulman, L. (1989). Subject matter knowledge for teaching. In M. Reynolds, ed., *Knowledge base for the beginning teacher*. New York: Pergamon Press.

Hall, R.V. (1970). *Managing behavior*. Meriam, KS: H & H Enterprises.

Halverson, P. (1987). The effects of peer-tutoring on sport skill analytic ability. Unpublished doctoral dissertation, The Ohio State University, Columbus.

Hamilton, K. (1974). The effects of a competency-based format on the behavior of student-teachers and high school pupils. Unpublished doctoral dissertation, The Ohio State University, Columbus.

Hayman, J., and Moskowitz, G. (1975). Behavior patterns and training needs of first-year teachers in inner-city schools. *Journal of Classroom Interaction*. 10.

Hellison, D. (1973a). Humanism in physical education. Paper presented at the Northwest Conference on Secondary Physical Education. Portland, OR. November.

Hellison, D. (1973b). *Humanistic physical education*. Englewood Cliffs, NJ: Prentice-Hall.

Hoffman, S. (1977). Skill analysis as a teaching competency. In R. Stadulis, ed., *Research and practice in physical education*. Champaign, IL: Human Kinetics.

Hollaway, S. (1988). Concepts of ability and effort in Japan and the U.S. *Review of Educational Research*. 58(3), 327–346.

Holt, J. (1964). *How children fail*. New York: Pittman.

Housner, L. (1990). Selecting master teachers: Evidence from process-product research. *Journal of Teaching in Physical Education*. 9(3), 201–226.

Howe. B., and Jackson, J. (1985). *Teaching effectiveness research*. Victoria, BC: University of Victoria.

Huber, J. (1973). The effects of a token economy program on appropriate behavior and motor task performance of educable mentally retarded children in adapted physical education. Unpublished doctoral dissertation, The Ohio State University, Columbus.

Hughley, C. (1973). Modification of teacher behaviors in physical education. Unpublished doctoral dissertation, The Ohio State University, Columbus.

Hutslar, S. (1977). The effects of training cooperating teachers in applied behavior analysis on student teacher behavior in physical education. Unpublished doctoral disseration, The Ohio State University, Columbus.

Jackson, P. (1968). *Life in classrooms*. New York: Holt, Rinehart, & Winston.

Jackson, P. (1980). The way teaching is. In K. Ryan and J. Cooper (Eds.), *Kaleidoscope: Readings in education*. Boston: Houghton Mifflin.

Jansma, P., French, R., and Horvak, W. (1984). Behavioral engineering in physical education. *Journal of Physical Education, Recreation and Dance*. 55(6), 80–81.

Jensen, E. (1988). *Super-teaching*. Del Mar, CA: Turning Point.

Jewett, A., and Bain, L. (1985). *The curriculum process in physical education*. Dubuque, IA: Wm. C. Brown.

Johnson, D. (1981). *Reaching out: Interpersonal effectiveness and self-actualization*. 2nd Ed. Englewood Cliffs, NJ: Prentice-Hall.

Johnston, J., and Pennypacker, H. (1981). *Strategies and tactics of human behavioral research*. Hillsdale, NJ: L. Erlbaum Associates.

Jones, D. (1989). Analysis of task structures in elementary physical education classes. Unpublished doctoral dissertation, The Ohio State University, Columbus.

Jones, D., Tannehill, D., O'Sullivan, M., and Stroot, S. (1989). The fifth dimension: Extending the physical education program. *Journal of Teaching in Physical Education*. 8(3), 223–226.

Kagan, S. (1990). The structural approach to cooperative learning. *Educational Leadership*. 47(4), 12–16.

Kalectaca, M. (1974). Competencies for teachers of culturally different children. In W. Hunter, ed., *Multicultural education*. Washington, D.C.: American Association for Colleges of Teacher Education.

Kent, I., and Nicholls, W. (1972). *I amness: The discovery of self beyond ego*. Indianapolis: Bobbs-Merrill.

Kleibard, H. (1973). The question in teacher education. In D. McCarty (Ed.), *New perspectives in teacher education*. San Francisco: Jossey-Bass.

Kneer, M., and Grebner, F. (1983). Teamed for excellence. *Journal of Physical Education, Recreation and Dance*. 54(7), 20.

Kniffen, M. (1985). The effects of individualized video tape instruction on the ability of undergraduate physical education majors to analyze selected sport skills. Unpublished doctoral dissertation, The Ohio State University, Columbus.

Kounin, J. (1970). *Discipline and group management in classrooms*. New York: Holt, Rinehart and Winston.

Kozol, J. (1972). Free schools fail because they don't teach. *Psychology Today.* 5, 30.

Lambdin, D. (1981). The minus system: A behavior management technique. Unpublished paper, St. Andrew's School, Austin, TX.

Lambdin, D. (1986). Winning battles, losing the war. *Journal of Physical Education, Recreation and Dance.* 57(4), 34–37.

Lawless, S. (1984). The effects of volleyball game modifications on children's opportunity to respond and academic learning time. Unpublished doctoral dissertation, The Ohio State University.

Leonard, G. (1968). *Education and ecstasy.* New York: Delacorte Press.

Locke, L. (1973). Teacher education: One minute to midnight. In *Preparing the elementary specialist.* Washington D.C.: American Association for Health, Physical Education and Recreation.

Locke, L. (1975). The ecology of the gymnasium: What the tourists never see. *Proceedings of Southern Association for Physical Education of College Women.* (ERIC Document Reproduction Service No. ED 104823).

Locke, L. (1977). Research on teaching physical education: New hope for a dismal science. *Quest.* 28, 2–16.

Locke, L. (1979). Learning from teaching. In J. Jackson, ed., *Theory into practice.* University of Victoria Physical Education Series. Victoria, British Columbia: University of Victoria.

Locke, L. (1982). Research on teaching physical activity: A modest celebration. In M. Howell & J. Saunders, eds., *Proceedings of the Commonwealth and International Conference on Sport, Physical Education, Recreation and Dance.* Brisbane, Australia: Department of Human Movement Studies.

Locke, L., and Griffin, P. (1986). Introduction. *Journal of Physical Education, Recreation and Dance.* 57(4), 32–33.

Locke, L., and Massengale, J. (1978). Role conflict in teachers/coaches. *Research Quarterly.* 49, 162–174.

Locke, L., Siedentop, D., and Mand, C. (1981). The preparation of physical education teachers: A subject-matter-centered model. In *Undergraduate physical education programs: Issues and approaches.* Washington, D.C.: American Association for Health, Physical Education, Recreation and Dance.

Locke, L. (1986). Analysis and discussion: What can we do? *Journal of Physical Education, Recreation, and Dance.* 57(4), 60–63.

Lortie, D. (1975). *Schoolteacher: A sociological study.* Chicago: University of Chicago Press.

Luke, M. (1989). Research on class management and organization: Review with implications for current practice. *Quest.* 41, 55–67.

Lund, J. (1990). The effects of accountability on response rates in physical education. Unpublished doctoral dissertation, The Ohio State University, Columbus.

McDaniel, T. (1979). The teacher's ten commandments: School law in the classroom. *Phi Delta Kappan.* 60, 703–708.

McKenzie, T. (1976). Development and evaluation of a behaviorally-based teacher center for physical education. Unpublished doctoral dissertation, The Ohio State University, Columbus.

McKenzie, T., and Rushall, B. (1973). Effects of various reinforcing contingencies on improvement in a competitive swimming environment. Unpublished paper, Department of Physical Education, Dalhousie University.

McLeish, J. (1981). Effective teaching in physical education. Unpublished paper, Department of Physical Education, University of Victoria, British Columbia.

McLeish, J. (1985). An overall view. In B. Howe & J. Jackson, eds., *Teaching effectiveness research*. Victoria, BC: University of Victoria.

Madsen, C., and Madsen, C. (1972). *Parents, children, discipline: A positive approach*. Boston: Allyn & Bacon.

Mager, R. (1962). *Preparing instructional objectives*. Belmont, CA: Fearon Publishers.

Mager, R. (1973). A universal objective. *Improving Human Performance: A Research Quarterly*. 3, 181–190.

Mancuso, J. (1983). Model of excellence. *Journal of Physical Education, Recreation and Dance*. 54(7), 24–25.

Marks, M. (1988). Development of a system for the observation of task structures in physical education. Unpublished doctoral dissertation, The Ohio State University, Columbus.

Marks, M. (1988). A ticket out the door. *Strategies*. 1(2), 17, 27.

Massengale, J. (1981). Role conflict and the occupational milieu of the teacher/coach: Some real working world perspectives. In V. Crafts, (Ed.), *1980 National Association of Physical Education in Higher Education Proceedings*. Champaign, IL: Human Kinetics.

McDonald, F., and Elias, P. (1983). *The transition into teaching: The problems of beginning teachers and how to solve them*. Berkeley, CA: Educational Testing Service.

Medley, D. (1977). *Teacher competence and teacher effectiveness*. Washington, D.C.: American Association of Colleges of Teacher Education.

Medley, D. (1979). The effectiveness of teachers. In P. Peterson and H. Walberg, eds., *Research on teaching: Concepts, findings and applications*. Berkeley, CA: McCutchan.

Metzler, M. (1979). The measurement of academic learning time in physical education. Unpublished doctoral dissertation, The Ohio State University, Columbus.

Metzler, M. (1989). A review of research on time in sport pedagogy. *Journal of Teaching in Physical Education*. 8(2), 87–103.

Moore, G. (1977). Descriptive behavior analysis in a resident school camp. Unpublished doctoral dissertation, The Ohio State University, Columbus.

Morris, J. (1968). Diary of a beginning teacher. *National Association of Secondary School Principals Bulletin*. October, 6–22.

Mosher, R., and Purpel, D. (1972). *Supervision: The reluctant profession*. Boston: Houghton Mifflin.

Mosston, M. (1966). *Teaching physical education*. Columbus, OH: Merrill.

Mosston, M. (1981). *Teaching physical education*. 2nd Ed. Columbus, OH: Merrill.

Mosston, M., and Ashworth, S. (1986). *Teaching physical education*. Columbus, OH: Merrill.

Myrick, R. (1969). Growth groups: Implications for teachers and counselors. *Elementary School Guidance and Counseling.* 4, 35–42.

NEA Reporter (1980), January.

Novak, M. (1976). *The joy of sports.* New York: Basic Books.

Oliver, B. (1978). The relationship of teacher and student presage and process criteria to student achievement in physical education. Unpublished doctoral dissertation, Stanford University, Palo Alto.

Olsen, P. (1974). Graduate education and new jobs in education. *Theory Into Practice.* 13, 151–158.

Ormond, T. (1988). An analysis of teaching and coaching behavior in invasion game activities. Unpublished doctoral dissertation, The Ohio State University, Columbus.

Osgood, E., and others (1957). *The measurement of meaning.* Urbana: University of Illinois Press.

O'Sullivan, M. (1989). Failing gym is like failing lunch or recess: Two beginning teachers' struggle for legitimacy. *Journal of Teaching in Physical Education.* 8(3), 227–242.

O'Sullivan, M., Stroot, S., and Tannehill, D. (1989). Elementary physical education specialists: A commitment to student learning. *Journal of Teaching in Physical Education.* 8(3), 261–265.

Parker, M. (1984). The effects of game modifications on the nature and extent of skill involvement in volleyball and softball. Unpublished doctoral dissertation, The Ohio State University, Columbus.

Patterson, A. (1980). Professional malpractice: Small cloud, but growing bigger. *Phi Delta Kappan.* 62, 193–196.

Phillips, A., and Carlisle, C. (1983). A comparison of physical education teachers categorized as most and least effective. *Journal of Teaching in Physical Education.* 2(3), 62–76.

Pieron, M. (1980). From interaction analysis to research on teaching effectiveness: An overview of studies from the University of Liege. Unpublished paper, Department of Physical Education, The Ohio State University, Columbus.

Pieron, M. (1981). Research on teacher change: Effectiveness of teaching a psychomotor task in a microteaching setting. Paper delivered at the American Association for Health, Physical Education, Recreation and Dance Convention. Boston, April.

Pieron, M. (1983). Teacher and pupil behavior and the interaction process in P.E. classes. In R. Telema, et. al., eds., Research in school physical education. Jyvaskyla, Finland: The Foundation for Promotion of Physical Culture and Health.

Pieron, M., and Cheffers, J. (1982). *Studying the teaching in physical education.* Liege, Belgium: Association internationale des Ecoles Superieures d'Education Physique.

Placek, J. (1983). Conceptions of success in teaching: Busy, happy and good? In T. Templin and J. Olson, eds., *Teaching in physical education.* Champaign, IL: Human Kinetics.

Popham, W., and Baker, E. (1970). *Systematic instruction.* Englewood Cliffs, NJ: Prentice-Hall.

Postman, N., and Weingartner, C. (1969). *Teaching as a subversive activity.* New York: Delacorte Press.

Powell, L. (1969). *Communication and learning.* New York: American Elsevier.

Premack, D. (1963). Rate differential in monkey manipulation. *Journal of the Experimental Analysis of Behavior.* 6, 81–89.

Premack, D., and others (1964). Reinforcement of drinking by running: Effect of fixed ratio and reinforcement time. *Journal of the Experimental Analysis of Behavior.* 5, 91–96.

Quarterman, J. (1977). A descriptive analysis of physical education teaching in the elementary school. Unpublished doctoral dissertation, The Ohio State University, Columbus.

Randall, L., and Imwold, C. (1989). The effect of an intervention on academic learning time provided by preservice physical education teachers. *Journal of Teaching in Physical Education.* 8(4), 271–279.

Rate, R. (1980). A descriptive analysis of academic learning time and coaching behavior in interscholastic athletic practices. Unpublished doctoral dissertation, The Ohio State University, Columbus.

Raths, L., Harmin, M., and Simon, S. (1966). *Values and teaching.* Columbus, OH: Merrill.

Rife, F. (1974). Modification of student teacher behavior and its effect upon pupil behavior. Unpublished doctoral dissertation, The Ohio State University, Columbus.

Rink, J. (1979). Development of an instrument of the observation of content development in physical education. Unpublished doctoral dissertation, The Ohio State University, Columbus.

Rink, J. (1985). *Teaching for learning in physical education.* St. Louis: C.V. Mosby.

Rog, J. (1986). Everyone seems satisfied. *Journal of Physical Education, Recreation and Dance.* 57(4), 54–56.

Rogers, C. (1969). *Freedom to learn.* Columbus, OH: Merrill.

Rogers, J. (1974). On introducing contingency management. *National Society for Programmed Instruction Newsletter.* April, 13.

Rolider, A. (1979). The effects of enthusiasm training on the subsequent behavior of physical education teachers. Unpublished doctoral dissertation, The Ohio State University, Columbus.

Rolider, A., Siedentop, D., and Van Houten, R. (1984). Effects of enthusiasm training on subsequent teacher enthusiasm. *Journal of Teaching in Physical Education.* 3(2).

Rosenholtz, S. (1987). Workplace conditions of teacher quality and commitment: Implications for the design of teacher induction programs. In G. Griffin and S. Millies, eds., *The first year of teaching: Background papers and a proposal.* Chicago: University of Illinois at Chicago.

Rosenshine, B. (1970). Evaluation of classroom instruction. *Review of Educational Research.* 40, 279–300.

Rosenshine, B. (1979). Content, time, and direct instruction. In P. Peterson and H. Walberg, eds., *Research on teaching: Concepts, findings, and implications.* Berkeley, CA: McCutchan.

Rosenshine, B., and Stevens, R. (1986). Teaching functions. In M. Wittrock (Ed.), *Handbook of research on teaching.* New York: Macmillan.

Rushall, B., and Siedentop, D. (1972). *The development and control of behavior in sport and physical education.* Philadelphia: Lea & Febiger.

Ryan, K. (1970). *Don't smile until Christmas.* Chicago: University of Chicago Press.

Ryan, K., and Cooper, J. (1972). *Those who can, teach.* Boston: Houghton Mifflin.

Schwager, S. (1986). Battling boredom at mid-career. *Journal of Physical Education, Recreation and Dance.* 57(4), 42–43.

Segrave, J. (1981). Role preferences among prospective physical education teacher/coaches. In V. Crafts, ed., *National Association of Physical Education in Higher Education Proceedings.* Champaign, IL: Human Kinetics.

Sherman, M. (1979). Teacher planning: A study of expert and novice gymnastics teachers. Paper presented at the Pennsylvania State Health, Physical Education and Recreation Association Meetings. Philadelphia.

Siedentop, D. (1972). Behavior analysis and teacher training. *Quest.* 19, 26–32.

Siedentop, D. (1980). Physical education: Introductory analysis. 3rd Ed. Dubuque, IA: Wm. C. Brown.

Siedentop, D. (1981). The Ohio State supervision research program: Summary report. *Journal of Teaching in Physical Education.* Spring, 30–38.

Siedentop, D. (1983). Research on teaching in physical education. In T. Templin and J. Olson, eds., *Teaching in physical education.* Champaign, IL: Human Kinetics.

Siedentop, D. (1983). *Developing teaching skills in physical education.* 2nd Ed. Mountain View, CA: Mayfield.

Siedentop, D. (1986). The modification of teacher behavior. In M. Pieron and G. Graham, eds., *Sport pedagogy.* Champaign, IL: Human Kinetics.

Siedentop, D. (1987). High school physical education: Still an endangered species. *Journal of Health, Physical Education, Recreation and Dance.* 58(2).

Siedentop, D., ed., (1989). The effective elementary specialist study. *Journal of Teaching in Physical Education.* 8(3). Monograph.

Siedentop, D. (1990). *Introduction to physical education, sport and fitness.* Mountain View, CA: Mayfield.

Siedentop, D., and Eldar, E. (1989). Expertise, experience, and effectiveness. *Journal of Teaching in Physical Education.* 8(3), 254–260.

Siedentop, D., Herkowitz, J., and Rink, J. (1983). *Physical education for elementary children.* Englewood Cliffs, NJ: Prentice-Hall.

Siedentop, D., Mand, C., and Taggart, A. (1986). *Physical education: Teaching and curriculum strategies for grades 5–12.* Mountain View, CA: Mayfield.

Siedentop, D., and Olson, J. (1978). The validity of teacher behavior observation systems in physical education. In L. Gedvilas, ed., *Proceedings of the National College Physical Education Association for Men.*

Siedentop, D., and Rife, F. (1978). Developing a learning environment for badminton. *Ohio High School Athlete.* 33, 17–19.

Siedentop, D., Rife, F., and Boehm, J. (1974). Modifying the mangerial efficiency of student teachers in physical education. Unpublished paper. School of Health, Physical Education and Recreation, The Ohio State University, Columbus.

Siedentop, D., Tousignant, M., and Parker, M. (1982). *Academic learning time—physical education coding manual.* Columbus, OH: School of Health, Physical Education and Recreation.

Silberman, C. (1970). *Crisis in the classroom.* New York: Random House.

Simon, S., Howe, L., and Kirchenbaum, H. (1972). *Values clarification.* New York: Hart.

Silverman, S. (1985). Relationship of engagement and practice trials to student achievement. *Journal of Teaching in Physical Education.* 5, 13–21.

Singer, R., and Dick, W. (1974). *Teaching physical education: A systems approach.* Boston: Houghton Mifflin.

Slavin, R. (1980). Cooperative learning. *Review of Educational Research.* 50, 317–343.

Slavin, R. (1988). Cooperative learning and student achievement. *Educational Leadership.* 45(2), 31–33.

Slavin, R. (1990). Research on cooperative learning: Consensus and controversy. *Educational Leadership.* 47(4), 52–55.

Smith, B. (1983). Closing: Teacher education in transition. In D. Smith, ed., *Essential knowledge for beginning educators.* Washington, DC: American Association of Colleges for Teacher Education.

Smith, L., and Geoffrey, W. (1969). *The complexities of an urban classroom.* New York: Holt, Rinehart and Winston.

Soar, R., and Soar, R. (1979). Emotional climate and management. In P. Peterson and H. Walberg, eds., *Research on teaching: Concepts, findings, and implications.* Berkeley, CA: McCutchan.

Son, C-T. (1989). Descriptive analysis of task congruence in Korean middle school physical education classes. Unpublished doctoral dissertation, The Ohio State University, Columbus.

Stallings, J. (1976). How instructional processes relate to child outcomes in a national study of follow through. *Journal of Teacher Education.* 27, 43–47.

Stallings, J. (1980). Allocated academic learning time revisited, or beyond time on task. *Educational Researcher.* 9, 11–16.

Stallings, J., and Kaskowitz, D. (1974). *Follow through classroom observation evaluation, 1972–73.* Menlo Park, CA: Stanford Research Institute.

Stephens, T. (1978). *Social skills in the classroom.* Columbus, OH: Cedars Press.

Stewart, M. (1980). Teaching behavior of physical education teachers in the natural environment. *College Student Journal.* 14, 76–82.

Stroot, S., and Bumgarner, S. (1989). Fitness assessment—putting computers to work. *Journal of Physical Education, Recreation and Dance.* 60(6), 44–49.

Stroot, S., and Morton, P. (1989). Blueprints for learning. *Journal of Teaching in Physical Education.* 8(3), 213–222.

Sulzer, B., and Mayer, G. *Behavior modification procedures for school personnel.* Hinsdale, IL: Dryden Press.

Taggart, A. (1989). The systematic development of teaching skills: A sequence of planned pedagogical experiences. *Journal of Teaching in Physical Education.* 8(1), 73–86.

Taylor, J., and Chiogioji, E. (1987). Implications of educational reform on high school programs. *Journal of Physical Education, Recreation and Dance.* 58(2), 22–23.

Templin, T. (1981). Teacher/coach role conflict and the high school principal. In V. Crafts, ed., *National Association for Physical Education in Higher Education Proceedings.* Champaign, IL: Human Kinetics.

Templin, T. (1983). Introduction. *Journal of Physical Education, Recreation and Dance.* 54(7), 15.

Tinning, R., and Siedentop, D. (1985). The characteristics of tasks and accountability in student teaching. *Journal of Teaching in Physical Education.* 4(4).

Tousignant, M. (1981). A qualitative analysis of task structures in required physical education. Unpublished doctoral dissertation, The Ohio State University, Columbus.

Tousignant, M. (1983). PSI in PE—it works! *Journal of Physical Education, Recreation and Dance.* 54(7), 33–34.

Tousignant, M., Brunelle, J., and Morency, L. (1986). Smooth routines and happy actors. *Journal of Physical Education, Recreation, and Dance.* 57(4), 50–53.

Tousignant, M., and Siedentop, D. (1983). The analysis of task structures in physical education. *Journal of Teaching in Physical Education.* 3(1).

Tumin, M. (1977). Schools as social organization. In R. Corwin and R. Edlefelt, eds., *Perspectives on organizations: The school as a social organization.* Washington, D.C.: American Association of Colleges of Teacher Education.

Tyler, R. (1950). *Basic principles of curriculum and instruction.* Chicago: University of Chicago Press.

Wang, M., and Palincsar, P., (1989). Teaching students to assume an active role in their learning. In M. Reynolds, ed., *Knowledge base for beginning teachers.* Washington, DC: American Association of Colleges for Teacher Education.

Weinstein, G., and Fantini, M. (1971). *Toward humanistic education: A curriculum of affect.* New York: Praeger.

Westcott, W. (1977). Effects of teacher modeling on the subsequent behavior of students. Unpublished doctoral dissertation, The Ohio State University, Columbus.

Whitehurst, G. (1972). Academic responses and attitudes engendered by a programmed course in child development. *Journal of Applied Behavior Analysis.* 5, 282–292.

Wilkinson, S. (1986). Effects of a visual discrimination training program on the acquisition and maintenance of physical education students' volleyball skill analytic ability. Unpublished doctoral dissertation, The Ohio State University, Columbus.

Williams, R., and Anandam, K. (1973). *Cooperative classroom management.* Columbus, OH: Merrill.

Woods, S., and Dodds, P. (1983). Using equity for professional self-renewal. *Journal of Physical Education, Recreation and Dance.* 54(7), 32, 36.

Wurzer, D., and McKenzie, T. (1987). Constructive alternatives to punishment. *Strategies.* 1(1), 7–9.

338

Wynn, C. (1974). Teacher competencies for cultural diversity. In W. Hunter, ed., *Multicultural education*. Washington, D.C.: American Association for Colleges of Teacher Education.

Young, R. (1973). The effects of various reinforcing contingencies on a second-grade physical education class. Unpublished doctoral dissertation, The Ohio State University.

Zakrajsek, D., and Carnes, L. (1986). Individualizing physical education. 2nd Ed. Champaign, IL: Human Kinetics.

Index